Le Corbusier

Le Corbusier

H. Allen Brooks, Editor

Essays by
Rayner Banham
Tim Benton
H. Allen Brooks
Alan Colquhoun
Charles Correa
Norma Evenson
Kenneth Frampton
Danièle Pauly
Vincent Scully
Peter Serenyi
Jerzy Soltan
Manfredo Tafuri
Stanislaus von Moos
André Wogenscky
Iannis Xenakis

Princeton University Press
Princeton, New Jersey

Published by Princeton University Press,
41 William Street, Princeton, New Jersey 08540
In the United Kingdom: Princeton University Press, Guildford,
Surrey

A hardcover edition of this book, under the title *Le Corbusier: The
Garland Essays*, is simultaneously published by Garland Publishing,
New York and London. All of these essays originally appeared in
1982-85 in the 32 volumes of *The Le Corbusier Archive* (a catalogue of
the Le Corbusier drawing collection at the Fondation Le Corbusier,
Paris), published by Garland Publishing and the Fondation
Le Corbusier.

Library of Congress Cataloging-in-Publication Data

Le Corbusier.

  "Originally appeared in 1982–85 in the 32 volumes of The Le
Corbusier archive (a catalogue of the Le Corbusier drawing
collection at the Fondation Le Corbusier, Paris)"—T.p. verso.
  Originally published: New York : Garland, 1987.
  Includes index.
  1. Le Corbusier, 1887–1965—Criticism and
interpretation.   2. Architecture—France.   3. Architecture,
Modern—20th century—France.   I. Brooks, H. Allen (Harold
Allen), 1925–   II. Banham, Reyner.   III. Le Corbusier,
1887–1965. Le Corbusier archive.
[NA1053.J4L37   1987]   720'.92'4   87-45513
ISBN 0-691-00278-9 (pbk.)

3rd printing, 1989

Printed in the United States of America.

Contents

Foreword — H. Allen Brooks — vii

Working with Le Corbusier — Jerzy Soltan — 1

The Significance of Le Corbusier — Alan Colquhoun — 17

Le Corbusier's Formative Years at La Chaux-de-Fonds — H. Allen Brooks — 27

Le Corbusier, 1922–1965 — Vincent Scully — 47

Le Corbusier's Designs for the League of Nations, the Centrosoyus, and the Palace of the Soviets, 1926–1931 — Kenneth Frampton — 57

Villa Savoye and the Architects' Practice — Tim Benton — 83

La Maison des hommes and *La Misère des villes*: Le Corbusier and the Architecture of Mass Housing — Reyner Banham — 107

The Unité d'Habitation, at Marseille — André Wogenscky — 117

The Chapel of Ronchamp as an Example of Le Corbusier's Creative Process — Danièle Pauly — 127

The Monastery of La Tourette — Iannis Xenakis — 143

Timeless but of its Time: Le Corbusier's Architecture in India — Peter Serenyi — 163

Chandigarh: The View from Benares — Charles Correa — 197

"Machine et mémoire": The City in the Work of Le Corbusier — Manfredo Tafuri — 203

Urbanism and Transcultural Exchanges, 1910–1935: A Survey — Stanislaus von Moos — 219

Yesterday's City of Tomorrow Today — Norma Evenson — 241

Biographies of Contributors

Index

Foreword

by H. Allen Brooks

When I first came to Le Corbusier studies a dozen years ago, it was because my career as architectural historian was largely devoted to Frank Lloyd Wright and his contemporaries and I felt it was time for a change, a change that was highly motivated and yet contrived. And Le Corbusier was the only natural choice. Why? For one thing, he was the "enemy," the one architect whom a Wright admirer must denigrate, just as a Corbu enthusiast was expected to knock Wright. But more importantly, I was compelled by instinctive reasons, of which I shall list three, the first being that, as a historian, I find it infinitely more challenging, exciting, and rewarding to cope with great minds rather than secondary or tertiary ones, especially when those minds are still in their formative stage. And even a Wright fan acknowledges that the other great mind applied to architecture during the twentieth century was that of Le Corbusier. But how could I accept the "cardboard architecture" (Wright's phrase) of Le Corbusier's so-called International Style designs of the 1920s and 1930s and simultaneoulsy remain loyal to Wright? Such a step, I found, was intially unnecessary because during his first thirty-three years even Le Corbusier himself looked upon an international style as anathema since his own energies were being focused entirely upon creating a regional style that took its inspiration from native vegetation, local landscape, and the geological character of mother earth—especially its surface stratifications of sedimentary rocks. Indeed, had Le Corbusier lived in the American Midwest, and been a generation younger, is it not conceivable that he—not Wright—would have invented the prairie house!

Yet the mere mention of this youthful affinity provides a bridge between these men, and traversing this bridge is an easy matter if one momentarily forgets about Le Corbusier after the age of thirty-three (i.e., after 1920) and concentrates on those rich formative years that underlay virtually every act of his later career, though not always in the most obvious ways. These were the years of Charles-Edouard Jeanneret, the name I should be using because not until the autumn of 1920, at the behest of his then mentor and close friend, Amédée Ozenfant, did they coin the pen name Le Corbusier with which Jeanneret signed his articles on architecture, reserving his real name for what he considered his more important occupation as

painter. I say "coined" because when Jeanneret and Ozenfant launched their periodical *L'Esprit Nouveau* in 1920 they were almost the sole contributors, a fact obscured by their assuming a variety of pseudonyms under which to write on different topics—including reviews of their own books, paintings, and buildings. Very convenient! And as Ozenfant selected his mother's name, he advised Jeanneret to do the same, but as Madame Jeanneret was a Perret and her son had apprenticed under the Parisian architect Auguste Perret, this would never do. But further along the maternal line Jeanneret recalled the portrait of Lecorbesier that hung over his mother's piano in his childhood home at La Chaux-de-Fonds (painted in 1841 by Victor Darjou, the picture is now in the collection of the Musée des Beaux-Arts of that Swiss town). Ozenfant proposed changing the middle "e" to "u" and giving the name a nobler ring by splitting it in two—thus Le Corbusier. This, for Jeanneret, probably had the romanticism of recalling his childhood mentor L'Eplattenier, and ultimately the "u" provided for his nickname Corbu, which is a play on the French word for raven (*corbeau*); like so many Frenchmen Jeanneret was a great admirer of Edgar Allan Poe. To close friends he signed his letters "Corbu" or with the sketch of a raven as the one shown here:

(I must add that the British annoy me with their false familiarity, their name dropping, by insisting on calling him "Corb."*)

---

*In the office he was simply called Monsieur or Monsieur Le Corbusier, but behind his back he was referred to as Corbu. His family and childhood friends called him Edouard. Wright was addressed as Mr. Wright, behind his back was spoken of as Mr. Wright, and even today the tradition persists of calling him Mr. Wright—thus in lectures I often hear myself saying Mr. Wright rather than Frank Lloyd Wright or, heaven forbid, Wright. So imagine my consternation when, after launching one day with Walter Gropius, we went to his office where his staff addressed him, to his face, as "Grop"!

So it was not Le Corbusier but rather pre-1920 Jeanneret who provided me with the bridge to cross from Wright to Le Corbusier because on the opposite embankment I saw the same indigenous, spontaneous values that turned both architects toward nature and led them to reading Viollet-le-Duc and Victor Hugo. Both were the product of an age, yet Jeanneret, younger by twenty years, was not the product of *his* age but rather of an earlier one that, by pure chance, corresponded more closely to the generation of Wright. Therefore in the early twentieth century, while Wright was designing houses that recaptured the horizontal silhouette of the prairies and incorporated stylized sumac, hawthorn, or other regional plant life in his art glass, Jeanneret was designing houses with the silhouette of spruce or fir trees and, like Wright, was using stylized nature forms for his ornament—including the patterns for his window mullions. Yet in 1929 when Le Corbusier assembled volume one of his so-called *Oeuvre complète,* he willfully excluded all of this built work from the first sixteen years of his architectural practice in order to convey the impression that he had begun his career (in 1920), as a precocious designer who was very much up to date. Nothing could have been further from the truth!

It was this romantic, nature-orientated affinity that drew me instinctively across the bridge, which proved not wide, and provided the second reason that compelled me to select pre-Le Corbusier as the logical complement to my studies on Frank Lloyd Wright. Meanwhile the third reason (having unwisely, perhaps, committed myself to listing three) entails all the potentially wrong (or were they right) reasons for choosing Jeanneret—whether it be my fondness for downhill skiing, the desire to work in a language not my own (and preferably French), or finding myself actually obliged to live in Europe. Well now, what could be more perfect than selecting someone from that mountainous country of Switzerland who spoke French and whose major architectural archives were in Paris? Thus my third criterion was as easily fulfilled as were number 1 (great mind) and number 2 (a romantic, a lover of nature).

With the bridge between Wright and Jeanneret so easily crossed the question remained of whether I could traverse the gap from Jeanneret to Le Corbusier. Yet here

again the master helped because any study of Jeanneret reveals quite clearly how late-Corbu (after World War II) became absorbed with recollections of his youth, references that add layers of (often private) symbolism to his work. Not only did superficial symbols such as trees reappear, but also many hitherto unidentified connotations such as those deriving from the Jura farmhouse (where he resided in 1910 and again in 1912), references that gave form to his projected church at Firminy and, earlier, the assembly chamber at Chandigarh—as discussed in my essay that follows. Likewise, Le Corbusier's pilgrimage chapel at Ronchamp, undeniably his most popular building, was conceived and designed as a response to the surrounding mountains as well as to its dramatic hilltop site—evocations that originated with his childhood training and have nothing to do with his more cerebral excursions related to the International Style of the 1920s. Also his youthful discovery (in 1911) of the Villa Adriana at Tivoli provided the idea for the periscope-like light towers at Ronchamp, while his visit to the Chartreuse d'Ema at the age of nineteen found enduring expression when he was in his sixties and seventies in a series of *unité d'habitation* beginning with that at Marseilles, completed in 1952.

Once this bridgehead into the territory of late-Corbu was well established, the passage to his middle years (those often lumped with the International Style) was only a question of closing the gap of about a dozen years, and this could be done by filling in from either end. This proved far easier than I expected because I had always admired the Villa Savoye at Poissy (1928–30)—in my opinion, the greatest architectural work created in Europe during the twentieth century, and perhaps since the beginning of the Industrial Revolution. Rather high praise (though you will note my exclusion of North America from that phrase). I am greatly moved by the Villa Savoye—not as emotionally or instinctively or immediately as by Ronchamp, which is more popular in its appeal, but more profoundly moved at Poissy, even though Ronchamp is probably a more perfect and flawless realization of everything that Le Corbusier wanted to say at that particularly poignant moment in time. But Poissy is a supreme synthesis, a summation; it is a classic moment rather than the pioneer.* It has tremendous depth and richness resulting from its endless overlays of meaning, so finely interwoven into a finished fabric. It satisfies not only the emotions but the intellect as well. It speaks to many issues; it is the quintessence of an ideal. And this search for an ideal unites its architect with his youth since Jeanneret was obsessed with the notion of discovering, of isolating, a universal idea for architecture that he could then perfect and champion as his goal. His letters, especially from Paris where he studied during 1908 and 1909, were tormented by this need, which eluded him for so many years to come. Thus, the Villa Savoye was as much his "objet type" as the briar pipe; it stood for perfection, an expression that celebrated the act and imagery of our machine age—not always literally but more importantly (for him) as an object type. So if the twenties, and perhaps the early thirties, were a more cerebral, puristic, carthusian phase for the architect, its roots nevertheless lay deep within the intellect of the younger Jeanneret, while its more emotive flowering awaited his final twenty years (he died in 1965). Thus, using the analogy of the tree, I had become acquainted with its roots, its rationally structured trunk, its branches, and, near the end of its growing season, the flowering of this marvellous thing—this product of a brilliantly creative mind.

* * *

When requested by Garland Publishing to commission a series of essays for their planned thirty-two volume *The Le Corbusier Archive* with its 32,000 drawings of architecture, urbanism, and furniture from the archives of

---

*Today it is hard to think of Ronchamp as a pivotal pioneer, but, when being built in the early 1950s, it was a lively topic among those of us in graduate school. Perhaps it was only a work of large-scale sculpture, or a monument, or something as yet undefined? Thus it was with great relief, and some satisfaction, that the following September one of our group returned from France to report that, in his opinion, Ronchamp was architecture. This account may seem ridiculous, or something worse, but be assured that in 1954 it was a burning issue. Remember, we were being taught by the generation of Nikolaus Pevsner, who had laid down the dictum that a bicycle shed could not be architecture; at best a bicycle shed was a building, or maybe nothing but a structure. (Oh, John Ruskin, your legacy rests heavily upon us.)

the Fondation Le Corbusier in Paris (the largest architectural publication ever undertaken), I proposed that, instead of a team of architectural historians each writing about one of the major works represented, we seek greater diversity among both authors and type of topic assigned. I must have been thinking, to use an architectural analogy, of an axonometric projection wherein one sees various faces simultaneously rather than viewing only one thing at a time. I wanted to contrast articles that were broad against those that were narrow and deep, with obvious overlaps serving to stimulate the reader's mind. I sought to juxtapose different views rather than avoid them.

Equally essential were articles discussing the man, his personality, work habits, and creative process. Therefore, the first, and particularly perceptive, article is by Jerzy Soltan, who worked with Le Corbusier during four crucial years from 1945 to 1949.* Others approach our subject from different angles, including Iannis Xenakis—now internationally known as a composer and music theorist—who spent twelve years with Le Corbusier and collaborated closely with him in creating the La Tourette monastery, about which he writes, as well as being largely responsible for the Phillips Pavilion at the Brussels World's Fair.

Historians also examine Le Corbusier's creative process, most notably Danièle Pauly, who, using the chapel at Ronchamp as her theme, records the on-going synthesis by which Le Corbusier combines a variety of real and remembered images to achieve his final scheme. Meanwhile that classic gem, the Villa Savoye, is scrutinized by Tim Benton, who isolates no less than five successive variations as the design evolves—and also charts the making of the drawings, the letting of contracts, the rapport with the client, and relevant problems. Indeed, most authors speak of Le Corbusier's habits of design, even though their emphasis may be directed elsewhere.

As for architecture and urbanism, six distinct articles serve as overviews. Alan Colquhoun writes on the significance of Le Corbusier as an architect, and Manfredo Tafuri discusses his urbanism. His architectural career is then chronologically divided between myself, treating his for-

---

*A similar essay concerning the 1920s was sought from José Luis Sert, but despite our efforts, which included a taped interview, we were too late.

mative years in Switzerland, and Vincent Scully, discussing his mature work after his arrival in France. For urbanism, the initial twenty-five years (up to World War II) are analyzed by Stanislaus von Moos, with the last quarter century surveyed by Norma Evenson, thereby bringing two different viewpoints into play.

A broad subject was undertaken by Reyner Banham, who, as a person fond of megastructures, writes on the architecture of mass housing. One of these housing units, the *Unité d'habitation* at Marseille, is then treated in depth by André Wogenscky who collaborated with Le Corbusier on the scheme. Kenneth Frampton discusses three palatial public structures, the League of Nations, Centrosoyus, and Palace of the Soviets, all designed between 1926 and 1929. And finally, two essays concern the same topic: Le Corbusier's work in India. One is written by Peter Serenyi, an American architectural historian, and the other by Charles Correa, an architect from India. The subject may be the same, but the articles are quite different.

And should the reader note the absence of essays about Le Corbusier as writer, painter, or sculptor, it is simply because this is a collected work drawn from *The Le Corbusier Archive* (Garland Publishing, New York, and Fondation Le Corbusier, Paris, 1982–1985). However, this does not imply that an anthology did not suggest itself at a very early stage.

Finally, I wish to express thanks to the Fondation Le Corbusier and its staff on behalf of all those authors, including myself, whose research was enriched, and perhaps even made possible, by their cooperation and amiable assistance. And we are all indebted to Garland Publishing for their vision, courage, and persistence in bringing this monumental Le Corbusier series into existence. Also, in conclusion, let me express my gratitude to the many scholars whose time, wisdom, and skills went into preparing this panoply of essays that are being published, significantly, to coincide with the centennial of Le Corbusier's birth in 1887.

Working with Le Corbusier
*by Jerzy Soltan**

August 1, 1945—the first day of my work with Le Corbusier. Around nine in the morning, I was at his atelier, 35, rue de Sèvres, in Paris. Physically, the atelier exhibited a strange charm and, indeed, was the antithesis of "modernism." From the outside, from the little patch of greenery—the Square Boucicault and the rue de Sèvres—you confronted an old, quiet, classicist façade. You entered the building through a little gate, part of a large *porte-cochère*, and passed into a tiny courtyard. Here you were under the eyes of an imposing female concierge. She examined you warily. From the courtyard you turned left and got the full taste of the premises: a huge, white gallery-corridor some thirty yards long, five yards wide, with a long row of classicist bay windows on your right leading to a cloister garden. All of a sudden you realized that you were in a Jesuit monastery. The bay windows opened onto a sunny courtyard. The brilliant light filtered through old sycamore trees. A mosaic of leaf shadows danced on the floor around your feet. In the courtyard you noticed one or two black-cassocked figures, breviaries in hand, quietly enjoying a monastic promenade. The sun's rays were full of dusty particles. The building was old, dirty, smelly, and broken down. It would later be totally razed, but when I entered it for the first time it was very much *there*, full of an odd sort of attraction. The ground-floor galleria led to a staircase whose darkness seemed particularly intense after the sunniness that preceded it. Off the second landing was a door in total darkness. The door led to the upper-level equivalent of the ground-floor gallery: the atelier!

Eighty to ninety feet long and ten to fifteen feet wide, the atelier was in fact a section of a long, white, dead-end corridor. A row of large

windows was on one side, and a blank wall faced them. This wall separated the atelier from the neighboring Saint Ignatius Church. Sometimes, on particularly quiet days, or in the evenings after work, or on the weekends, a Bach fugue or a Gregorian chant trickled from the church into the atelier. On this summer day, the atelier was not only full of sun, the sound of birds, and the rustling of leaves, it was also full of bric-a-brac. Old drafting tables, broken stools and chairs, creaky easels, broken and half-broken architectural models in various scales, rolls of drawings, drafting utensils—all this competed for space in the second, deeper half of the atelier-corridor. And, of course, covering everything was a thick layer of dust. Dust had been gathering here for six years, since the beginning of the war and the decay of the atelier into a *débarras*. It was awakening at this time to its new, postwar life. The forward part of the atelier was more orderly. Along the outer wall and perpendicular to it were a few drafting tables, some stools and chairs. Drawings were pinned up on the "church wall"; facing the windows, between the tables and the wall, a large iron stove, installed ad hoc, dominated the space. And in front of the stove, wearing indescribably dirty, formerly white drafting overalls, reigned Gerald Hanning, Corbu's only collaborator at that time.

I soon discovered that Hanning, with his so very Anglo-Saxon name, was French. We quickly struck up a close friendship. Now that I had joined him, we would have two people to move around, depending on whom Corbu would assign to what. Since each project had its own microspace, Hanning changed tables as he turned to each of them. At the entranceway, to the left, was the boss's table.

Le Corbusier's working hours were implacably regular. During my four years at the atelier, he worked at the rue de Sèvres from two in the afternoon to around seven. The hour of 2:00 P.M., I soon learned, was holy. If you were a minute late you risked a reprimand. At first Corbu arrived

*Parts of this essay might be known to those who attended talks and lectures I gave on subjects related to my work with Le Corbusier. I am particularly grateful to Margaret Rapp and Kevin Rackstraw for helping me to put together these reminiscences.

either by subway (a convenient, direct metro line connected his Michel-Ange-Molitor station with the atelier's Sèvres-Babylone) or by taxi. Later on he started driving his old pistachio-green Simca Fiat convertible. In his last years it would be the taxi again. The process of returning home revealed quite a lot about Le Corbusier's character. If the work went well, if he enjoyed his own sketching and was sure of what he intended to do, then he forgot about the hour and might be home late for dinner. But if things did not go too well, if he felt uncertain of his ideas and unhappy with his drawings, then Corbu became jittery. He would fumble with his wristwatch—a small, oddly feminine contraption, far too small for his big paw—and finally say, grudgingly, "C'est difficile, l'architecture," toss the pencil or charcoal stub on the drawing, and slink out, as if ashamed to abandon the project and me—and us—in a predicament.

During these early August days, I learned quite a bit about Le Corbusier's daily routine. His schedule was rigidly organized. I remember how touched I was by his Boy Scout earnestness: at 6 A.M., gymnastics and . . . painting, a kind of fine arts calisthenics; at 8 A.M., breakfast. Then Le Corbusier entered into probably the most creative part of his day. He worked on the architectural and urbanistic sketches to be transmitted to us in the afternoon. Outlines of his written work would also be formulated then, along with some larger parts of the writings. Spiritually nourished by the preceding hours of physical and visual gymnastics, the hours of painting, he would use the main morning time for his most inspired conceptualization. A marvelous phenomenon indeed, this creative routine, implemented with his native Swiss regularity, harnessing and channeling what is most elusive. Corbu himself acknowledged the importance of this regimen. "If the generations to come," he wrote, "attach any importance to my work as an architect, it is to these unknown labors that one has to attribute its deeper meaning." It is wrong to assume, I believe, as some have sug-

gested, that Le Corbusier was devoting this time to the conceptualization of shapes to be applied directly in his architecture; rather, it was for him a period of concentration during which his imagination, catalyzed by the activity of painting, could probe most deeply into his subconscious. It was probably then that Le Corbusier was producing his remarkably sensitive poetic metaphors and associations.

It was not long after I settled into my work routine that I received one of my most intense Corbusierian shocks. To appreciate its intensity, one has to remember my own background. From a provincial school of architecture, I had brought with me to Paris the "form-follows-function" and *neue Sachlichkeit* spirit. In my earlier milieu, discussions of aesthetics were simply missing; visual concerns were smuggled in as afterthoughts, if they appeared at all. Such considerations were not becoming to a serious, socially minded architect. Imagine my amazement, then, when during an argument with Corbu about the final permutations of the St.-Dié project, he turned to me and said, "Mais mon cher Soltan, il faut que ce soit beau." This remark, of course, destroyed my argument. I was demolished, demolished but also delighted: Le Corbusier had offered me, openly, aboveboard, a marvelous gift that for years I had been eyeing secretly, from a distance. "Il faut que ce soit beau"—it has to be beautiful. To have the guts not only to speak of visual quality but to put one's thought so bluntly!

Hanning left the atelier and did not return. The short-lived trio was reduced again to a duo. It was Le Corbusier and me alone. The financial situation did not improve. The projects were not backed up by any solid commissions, and as a result, Le Corbusier could not pay me. Eventually my military commitment ended (I was not formally demobilized after World War II and six years of P.O.W. camps until this time) and with it military board and lodging. I had to live. Corbu agreed that I should moonlight in the morning and work for him in the afternoon. Through Hanning I obtained some work, first with a group of young former collaborators of Corbu's (Bossu, Dupré, Miquel, and Senvat) and second with Pierre Jeanneret, so that I found myself a member of two duos: in the morning with Pierre Jeanneret, in the afternoon with Corbu.

Most of the people who worked with Corbu had a love-hate relationship with him. A number of factors worked to create this ambivalent response. First, I already knew Le Corbusier well enough to realize that he was not easy to get along with. He was quick to anger and could be quite nasty. Second, there were political objections to him. After all, he did go to Vichy to sniff out the Pétain regime. Nothing came of it, but for those who want to see the worst, the fact remains. These same people forget that some twenty years earlier, Corbu had worked in the Soviet Union backed by the Trotsky group, the more en-lightened, artistically receptive milieu in the Russian Revolution. When Stalin and his obscurantists came to power, Le Corbusier's building chances in the Soviet Union evaporated. Neither could Corbu's enemies guess that five years later he would undertake his fruitful relationship with the Roman Catholic church through the artistically active French branch of the Dominican order. It is in fact owing to this order that Le Corbusier got the chance to realize some of his most meaningful work: the chapel at Ronchamp, the monastic building complex of Notre Dame de la Tourette, the unfinished chapel at Firminy. Politically, nonetheless, Corbu represents a confusing, contradictory picture and one easily subject to different interpretations according to the bias of the observer. To some, his backing by enlightened Marxists and condemnation by Stalinists indicate a praiseworthy sort of radicalism. To others, his distance from the French Communist party, to which several of his close friends like Fernand Léger and Picasso adhered, was proof of his disloyalty. Again, some would see in his dealings with the Vichy regime evidence of fascist sympathies, while others would emphasize his quick retreat from that group. And finally, Le

Corbusier's work for the Dominican order might appear daring and progressive to some (the order was unorthodox enough to have had difficulties with the Vatican) and a retreat into clericalism to others.

My own contact with Corbu led me always to think of him as a man full of boyish eagerness to try everything to win a commission, a tempting piece of work, an exciting project. Never mind the dangers, never mind the not-yet-healed wounds from the previous skirmish. As long as a tempta-tion was there, Le Corbusier would jump at it. For those who are not able to accept the depth of his youthful eagerness to land good work, Corbu will always remain a political mystery. His artistic complexity was so evident that corresponding simplicity on other levels (political, for instance) seems to me to have been almost inevitable.

During my very first days with Corbu, I realized that while I was, of course, expected to give the projects as much of myself as I could, each project was really his own—his own flesh and blood. My experience in Poland, working as a student for mature, locally famous architects, had led me to believe that I was hired to give the project if not its total quality, then at least its unique coloration. I often suspected that the project meant more to me than to my boss, that, in fact, the boss did not "live" the work in full. In Le Corbusier's case, one never had any doubt that he was willing to give it his whole self. Some time later, when the atelier was in full swing, I asked him what would be the optimum number of projects he felt he could handle simultaneously, on different levels of advancement; what number would make him the happiest? Corbu, perplexed, hesitated for a while and then shot back, "Five." Indeed, is it possible to have more if one has to hold them totally?

Yes, Corbu's work was *his*. It was, so to speak, physiologically his. But at the same time, he never spoke about the processes related to the production of his work in the first person. He would never say "I." It was always "we." Other architects, whose contribution to the birth of a building is often not much more than hiring the right team and drinking the right cocktail to secure the commission, would sprinkle the conversation with "I's": "I did it, I imagine, I feel, I. . . ." It sometimes seems that the number of "I's" is in inverse proportion to the boss's input to the work, inverse to his creative potency. In Corbu's case, the "we" becomes, then, quite proper. The project was his. Applying this inverse logic, he would say "we did it, we imagine, we'll do it this way." Perhaps too, the plural represents a kind of residue of the old *Esprit Nouveau* times, when he wrote under several names to make the publication more convincing. A crowd of participants is more than a **Charles-Edouard Jeanneret, an Amédée Ozenfant. We**: Jeanneret, Le Corbusier, Saugnier. . . . Sometimes the "we" became a royal *pluralis maiestatis*. Le Corbusier would jot down a new variant of a solution. A few minutes later he would pick the sketch up again and say, "Well, here is something we drew as a possible counter-proposal."

When someone literally lives his work, when his very existence constitutes a creative process, the strain of that process can sometimes be a curse. Le Corbusier himself called this phenomenon *les angoisses de la création*—the pains of creation. I quickly discovered just how intense those pains could be, not only for the author, but also for his entourage, myself included.

The projects in the atelier were preceded by serious and conscientious research. Conceptualization, of course, went on simultaneously. A half-lucid, half-unconscious "feedback" and "feed-forward" process operated in Corbu's mind. (I learned then about the investigatory method Le Corbusier wanted applied: from the general to the particular and from the particular to the general. I will write more about this method later.) He immersed himself deeper and deeper into the project. Each afternoon he brought from home new ideas, new sketches, new notes. They were not easy to decipher. Corbu

had the ability to communicate clearly what he really felt had to be done, but he also had his own sense of how much information to give, where to stop. The sketches at some point became fuzzy, a sign that they represented more his digging into the subconscious, his guessing, than a finished proposal. He would then pass them on to me—to us—sometimes with a mischievous smile. The role of the team was then to interpret, clarify, and present the concept for his scrutiny, in a precise graphic form, sometimes as a model. The more intuitive his thoughts, the more difficult it became to decipher his notes. I first learned to read them with the help of Hanning. Later I had to do it by myself in the empty atelier. Later still, when the team grew, it was the whole group who put heads together in consultation, led by the most experienced job captains, experts in "Corbu reading."

As time went on, Corbu's notes became more and more complex, his evaluation of our interpretations more sharp and intolerant. Every day at 2:00, just before his appearance, a cloud of panic hovered over the atelier. And then the day would come when the door opened and one felt that Corbu was a different man: He zooms directly to the table of the job captain responsible for the project, keeping his hat and coat on. He is in a hurry. Awkwardly, he pulls a crumbled piece of paper from his pocket. He puts it on the table and says, "This time I believe we've got it." He is smiling. I give a sigh of relief. Maybe the world is not so bad after all, and I am not such a complete idiot. Corbu leaves me with his latest product. He leaves me to absorb it. Later on he will approach my table again, but instead of starting another discussion of the same project, he will tackle a completely different subject. "Soltan, what about a little repast today? We received a small gift from the country and my wife's rabbit in wine sauce is really quite good." This invitation became the ultimate sign of peace, as well as approval and thanks for the last few days' work. It was also an apology. Corbu was aware of his weaknesses, the intemperance of his behavior. He could not overcome it, but he tried hard to counterbalance it. For me the dinner was not merely a social pleasure. Corbu guessed, as many years later he frankly admitted, that the moonlighting did not represent a basis for an adequate budget. In fact, during this period I was often simply hungry. Food was scarce in France in the summer of 1945; all of it was very expensive, and most of it was tightly rationed.

During the years with Corbu, I experienced several periods of these pains related to the conceptualization of the incoming projects. Indeed, what struck me as particularly interesting was the permanence of this anguish. One would have expected the intensity of pain to decrease, perhaps even disappear, with age and experience. But the truth of the matter is that instead of diminishing, it tended to grow. Perhaps this growth had to do with the growing sense of responsibility, of expectation of permanent excellence, and of fear that the previous success was the last one, that this magnificent and mysterious ability to synthesize—to create—might be exhausted, might even die. It is also clear that the pains accompanying the birth of a concept are in direct proportion to the concept's boldness and novelty. The more daring and authentically inspired the aim, the more talent involved in conceiving and carrying an idea through to completion, the more one pays spiritually for it. Conceiving mediocrities does not require creative mental agonies—life becomes smooth and even.

To catch the ineffable, one has to use sensitive hunting techniques. My first particularly complex problem was the town center of St.-Dié. Corbu brought some sketches from home. He wanted to pursue his peculiar pictorial thinking in the atelier. He sat down at my table and fumbled for some drawing tool. I helped him to an array of pencils and pens. He rejected them all with signs of disgust. How could I suggest he use such inappropriate instruments to perform such a sensitive operation? "Haven't you a piece of charcoal?" he asked. No, I did not. In my own limited architectural career, in the rare moments when the boss would sit at the table and try to convey some ideas pictorially, a fat pencil or a pen would suffice. Thus I was baffled. Charcoal belongs in a painter's studio, for sketching an old-fashioned still life or nude, not in a modern architectural workshop where no-nonsense things had to be traced in a *sachlich* atmosphere. I remember how, in my past, the less the bosses knew about what they wanted to do, the fatter the pencil would be, the more aggressive the ink, the more permanent the nonimage. One line would follow and cover the other, strengthening the brutality of the unknown—strong, full, sure lines. The surer the lines, the less content there was behind them. One would be tempted to hypothesize that the shaky line of the charcoal and the fluent line of a fat crayon or magic marker represent two different worlds. One delves into the deepest areas of consciousness and the subconscious in search of inspiration. The other attempts to hide its emptiness behind a plethora of bold and assertive lines. These lines reveal an instinctive hope that the boldness will, when applied long enough, be converted miraculously into ideas.

Now, all of a sudden, Corbu wanted a piece of charcoal. I found a forgotten stub in a drawer. He started sketching with a deliberately shaky hand. He stopped for fractions of a second. He went on. Meanwhile he succeeded in erasing half of what he began with. The charcoal stub was ridiculously small in his big fingers. He stopped again. He returned with a light, jittery line to the spots that had already been drawn and erased. The new line was almost the same—almost. He barely looked at the drawing. His eyes were "turned inward," attending to his subconscious. Finally, he stopped. He looked this way and that at the drawing. He pondered it, and then he said, "Maybe it's worth retaining?" He pulled out his own pen, an old Parker 51, and traced with a slow movement on top of the charcoal the final (for the time being) version of the concept. Then he looked at the fancy utensils on the table: automatic pens, mechanical pencils, those brand new tools the magic markers, all the drawing gadgets he had been fascinated by. He fumbled among them and said, "Il ne faut pas immortalizer des âneries" (They are no good! One should not immortalize stupidity.).

Another example of the "hunting for excellence" technique was Corbu's use of model building as an integral part of the design process. Presenting architectural ideas through a model is, of course, an age-old visual communication technique. However, architects normally use models to communicate things already conceived and even drawn. Used in this way, the model becomes merely an additional way of presentation. Obviously, a spatial presentation of an object conceived for space may in some cases reveal features not noticeable in the mostly orthogonal projection of a technical drawing. Perspective isometric or axonometric drawings might be more revealing in some respects; they tend, however, to neglect or distort some important features of the object (e.g., proportions). An obvious mistake in a project revealed by the model might be corrected, time permitting. Yet it sometimes happens that the model reveals an error inherent in the very principle of the concept—or, in fact, a lack of concept. Correcting is then of no value. The project should be started anew. And then again and again it might go wrong if the process of checking through the model occurs too late. Architects do not normally build models as an integral part of the process of conceptualization. But this approach does more than spare mistakes and time by eliminating negative features. It also introduces completely new possibilities, increases the scope of the results. In my architectural work before joining Le Corbusier, I participated in, or witnessed, many visual disasters caused by the late introduction of a model into the design process. Likewise, in my "after-Corbu" time, I watched how the "matchbox" buildings were expected to be ipso

facto improved and enriched by introducing, for instance, large empty volumes. Thus any void, any double, triple, or quadruple aperture between floors became synonymous, for many, with excellence, whatever purpose, size, shape, or relationship it might represent. Any void, any hole, began to be glorified as INEFFABLE SPACE. Timely use of a model may indeed change meaningless emptiness into positive expression of spatial relationships and may help greatly in rational connection of function. At the rue de Sèvres, the model did not have to be precise or particularly elegant to fulfill its purpose. On the contrary, a "licked-out" model might be rejected as confusing; it pleases the eye not through the quality of the principle it represents but as an object, slick and smooth.

What charcoal represents on the plane of a drawing, plasticine represents in volume. Little bricks of this fat clay are not only easily cut but are easily malleable. I watched them under Corbu's fingers. I saw how the charcoal sketches began to appear as interpretations of the clumsy, topsy-turvy clay toys illustrating the burgeoning idea of, perhaps, the city center of St.-Dié or the first proposal of the housing development of La Rochelle. The charcoal followed the spatial study in clay. The charcoal sketch was translated once again into the language of plasticine and then went back on paper. And so it went until the black ink of the fountain pen fixed the project for a while.

When Corbu accepted the study of the Currutchet house in La Plata, the job captain of the project was a close friend, Roger Aujame. The La Plata-Aujame team's "territory" in the atelier was adjacent to mine. Thus I could follow the development of events there. The project from the outset became a typical model-leading case. The lot was small and tight. The plan logically had to rely on a vertical organization. The other planning trump cards were terraces and *brise-soleils* (sun breakers). Distributing spaces (open and enclosed) on the numerous levels, connecting them with ramps and staircases, and covering them with different types of roofs, ceilings, and flying slabs became the main themes of the spatial game. The relations between solids and voids, orthogonal and slanting, were very complex indeed. To develop these relationships on paper using standard projection techniques was impossible, particularly if "developing" means more than connecting in the physical sense of the word—making the respective areas accessible.

"Il faut que ce soit beau." After all, the plan was conceived in this particular sophisticated way in order to give occasion for developing sophisticated design as well. No amount of spatial imagination can grasp the complexity of some relationships if it is not helped in some new way. Even less can real visual quality be infused into these relationships. This "new" way amounts simply to giving the model, and not the drawing, the leading role in the process. The role of the drawing is thus limited to annotating the model.

Some analysts attribute the success of these very spatial projects of Corbu's simply to his talent. They are, I think, both wrong and right— wrong if they assume that the program in its total complexity was "manipulated" in the traditional way by an extraordinary spatial imagination, but right if they accept that his talent also encompassed the ability to devise techniques of investigation and control that allow the imagination to operate on a higher, perhaps new level. It seems to me not only possible but useful to separate these two abilities. They are obviously connected, but I submit that a "regular"—normal— spatial imagination could assimilate the investigatory technique "drawing follows model" and hence considerably improve the understanding and further the quality of the proposed space. At least one could expect that most of the blatant, disarming naïveté and blunders would be eliminated. Conversely, one could argue that a traditional analysis of Corbu's buildings, conceived in the manner mentioned above, yields little. Indeed, a normally prescribed, long series of plans

or sections of the Currutchet house or the chapel in Ronchamp, based on the usual projection, taken even in the smallest of intervals, and executed with painstaking devotion, results in a number of drawings, handsome in themselves perhaps but meaningless as far as real comprehension of the space involved. Yet it is this type of investigation that one could see performed in the most renowned schools of architecture in the world in the period when Corbu was particularly in vogue. Parenthetically, it is logical that this kind of misunderstanding became part of the subsequent disenchantment with Le Corbusier and eventually, in many cases, an angry rejection of his work.

The following saying of Corbu's strikes me as fitting here—a good antidote to a large dose of "thinking form": "Pour bien dessiner il faut du talent. Pour faire un beau programme il faut du génie" (To design well, you need talent. To plan well, you need genius.). Many students of Le Corbusier who know him mainly through his form seem unaware of this motto. For them, the notion of planning is probably understood as a dry list of required square footages, functions to be accommodated, prescribed dimensions, and so forth. In this perspective, the "precooked" plan is presented to the architect as a must. Indeed, this way of understanding the notion of planning is very far from what Corbu intended.

I worked with Gerald Hanning on the project of the *unité du grandeur conforme* (unit of the proper size). It was a theoretical project preceding the project of the Marseille unit. At the time we studied it, nobody had any idea whether it would ever be erected—much less erected in Marseille. The whole plan here was proposed by the architect, starting with the optimum size, number of inhabitants, and hence types of apartments: their spatial principle, the principle of their grouping. To each of the planning items, Corbu introduced his own peculiar attitude in its manifold aspects. He strove to convey the reality and prose of life as well as its charm and poetry.

The holy Corbusierian principles of modern architecture would be kept: free plan, independent construction, free ground floor, free elevations, and open roof. But then these principles in turn expressed a variety of others. Thus the freeing of the ground represented economic and socio-political attitudes of Corbu's. The terrain would be the property of the community. The socialization of the terrain would lead, of course, to many new planning possibilities, circulation solutions, and so on. The next step was the visual expression of this common ownership of the city terrain. The type of construction allowed the building to be raised from the soil so it barely touched the ground. But then the free ground floor also represented the poetic and purely visual longing to express the "new space," the "continuum of space," a relatively recent notion introduced to modern language by science and visually tackled already by Cubism. Raised above the ground, on its independent construction, the building ceased to be a spatial obstacle, particularly as it was raised on a powerful base slab, "the artificial ground" (*le sol artificiel*). It floated in the air. Indeed, there was a continuous air flow below and around it. Around also means above, on top of it. The roof, now something more than mere protection from snow or rain, had to open up for more active purposes. Everything connected with view belongs there: sun, space, greenery, the sky and its clouds, the landscape with its treetops and mountaintops, as well as its man-made domes, towers, and spires. But these "essential joys" (*joies essentielles*) belong to everyone. They are collective property. They are also good catalysts for social life. The activities on the top should therefore be community activities. A gym could perhaps be constructed, with a track around the roof slab. Next, a kindergarten—bright with its brilliant colors—basking in the sun.

But then what would happen between the base and top? What would be revealed outside by the facades? At the foot of the building and on its top, community; in between, privacy—the individual framed by social life. What is individual should logically be formulated by the individual user. To what extent can this be done? How far does technology allow the individual family (using perhaps some combinatorial analysis) to create a small, private world around itself? Not much seems to be possible in this respect, particularly given the conditions in 1945 (just as in Corbu's earlier projects that were not built at all). Yet it is enough to have a look at the perspective views of two housing units traced by Hanning and then, as always, studied in detail and "filled in" by Corbu to see that the individual housing cells are all different. (See *Oeuvre complète, 1938–1946* [Zurich: Girsberger, 1946], p. 172). The overall rigor was secured by the sun breakers, the organization of which remained in the hands of the master builder, the architect of the "vertical city." Later on, when the theoretical study became the Marseille building, even this small attempt to individualize the cells proved unrealistic and was dropped. The perspective sketches became, therefore, the only real evidence of the underlying idea.

The allocation of space to services has always been a debatable point. Should it not be on the ground floor? Or at least on the second floor, if the ground level has to be completely free? The whole building traffic has to pass through the lowest level. Everybody would then notice the services and drop in when passing by. The logic of this seems undeniable. On the other hand, if the building is big enough, it might deserve not only "feet" and a "hat" but to be given a "heart," a center where the inhabitants would converge. To converge is more than to "drop in when passing by." It requires more of a mental and even, for some inhabitants, physical effort. It becomes an activity in itself and not just a by-product of entering the building. It does not merely strengthen the entrance, which exists independently; it creates a completely new occasion for the enhancement of life. And, after all, is it not the good planner's task to identify new values in life? Of course, such an undertaking is always a risk. An improperly conceived element can wither and become a painful liability, if not a disaster. A planning hazard is involved here. No one, however, can accuse Corbu of shrinking from risk. There is also the visual factor. The service area is in itself a tempting architectural theme. Properly expressed and located, it could enrich the general appearance of the building. Finally, a clearly outlined heart somewhere in the central area could help the inhabitants identify the position of their individual dwellings on the face of this mountain. It is easier to recognize a site in relation to a defined center than merely somewhere between the base and the top of the tower.

The planning of a housing unit for a few hundred apartments represents an exceptionally rich problem. Let me compare it with the Currutchet house in La Plata, Argentina. Infusing excitement into the planning of a medium-sized house for a surgeon, on a tight downtown lot—an infilling—allowed less room for the imagination. Yet the very ordinariness of the subject represented the main challenge. The smallness of the lot meant piling the necessary spaces up. Piling up meant that vertical connections became important. The work of a doctor meant strong connections with the outside world—the patients—which led to problems of circulation again. All these considerations belong to the domain of logic, the prosaic. In the case of the La Plata house, the poetic dimension lay in raising the physical connectibility of the respective function to the level of a continuum of spaces. To achieve this, open volumes were woven into the fabric, terraces, and wells/shafts. Open volumes meant a lot of "outer surfaces," a situation somewhat similar to that of Poissy. But here we were in the *brise-soleil* period. Thus these devices were profusely used to protect apertures and terraces. In this way a banality was converted into a plan for a "spatial bibelot." "Il y a suffisamment d'éléments ici pour faire une architecture," Corbu said (There are enough

elements here to make an architecture). A particularly sophisticated design method was to be used to put into space this theoretical set of requirements. A planning paradigm, rational and poetic but verbally describable, had to be given visual form.

In the early stages of my work at the rue de Sèvres, I learned that here too a project had to be preceded by data gathering and processing, a research study. It was during these days that I first heard the words "from general to particular and from particular to general." I do not remember when and how Corbu used this formulation of the research strategy for the first time. In itself the principle of considering any project both in a larger context and accepting the impact of even small details was not new to me; all architectural offices accepted that. What struck me as new was the stress on the simultaneity of the two efforts. Yet it was so perfectly logical! To allow one of the two poles, the general or the particular, to take the leading role amounts to accepting a minor role for the second. The complete simultaneity of these studies is, of course, physically impossible. Realistically speaking, it is enough to have the two attitudes interwoven. This interweaving requires a considerable amount of discipline. It is so tempting when embarked on one of the two directions to pursue one at the expense of the other to its ultimate resolution.

The atelier was quite well prepared to deal with some of the introductory studies. Indeed, often enough Corbu referred us to his and Pierre Jeanneret's collected works. "Go and check this in the Girsberger . . . ," he would say. (Girsberger was the Swiss publisher of these books.) Thus, using the already acquired experience catalogued in an impeccably organized way, Le Corbusier was assuring his work's continuity, saving time and money.

When I first arrived at the atelier, I discovered that among the studies in progress, an important role was assigned to the new system of measures baptized Le Modulor—the Golden Module. The project reveals a great deal about the duality of its author's personality. Conceived to unify the world's technology, it was intended to add a certain humanistic quality that technology lacked. On one side, it used mathematics in an attempt to operate on the objective, quantifiable level; on the other, it attested to romantic, lyrical longings to "capture beauty."

At this time, I was Corbu's only assistant and I was at the rue de Sèvres only in the afternoon. All work had to be done in these few hours. The Modulor's turn was usually after the other projects had received their daily attention. The sun was setting. It was getting late. Bach's or Handel's music penetrated the atelier from the adjacent church. A perfect mood was created for this type of project. Corbu was not strong in mathematics, but he was very much under its spell. He started the Modulor time usually with some remarks related to his work with Hanning and his collaboration with Elisa Maillard, a mathematician who helped him during the first stages of the study. But soon "the objective pole" was abandoned, and Corbu delved with delight into the mythical aspects of the golden section, Pythagoras, the Fibonacci series. The role of the enlightened outsider played by Maillard and her mathematics was taken over here by Matila Ghyka, the Greek scholar and aficionado of the golden mean, whose writings about it are an interesting mixture of objective information and poetic fuzziness. It was clear that Ghyka took particular delight in this fuzziness.

To work with Corbu on that subject vividly illuminated the role of intuition in human creativity. Sometimes his sentences were impeccably clear and purposeful. At other times, he fell into something that might appear to be gibberish, only to become purposeful again. In no architectural or urban design projects did I notice this same level of objective and poetic intensity. This intensity is illustrated by many of Corbu's drawings, but the best visual symbol of the Modulor, better than the popular silhouette of the

human figure with the raised hand, is a seemingly insignificant drawing (Le Modulor [Paris: l'Architecture d'Aujourd'hui, 1950], p. 100). There, after an infinitely long, precise, and technical presentation of the combinatorial possibilities the Modulor panels could offer, Corbu balked at this objectivity, thumbed his nose at the reader, and drew a little willfully naïve flower as the summation of this technological display. In one stroke he placed what was serious in this study in proper perspective.

Time went on. The situation of the atelier improved slowly. Soon things became stable enough for Corbu to risk accepting more help with his work. This help materialized in the persons of Roger Aujame and André Wogenscky. Both men were French, both at odds with the Ecole de Beaux Arts and interested in Le Corbusier. A third important personality dropped in every now and again, the structural engineer Vladimir Bodiansky. I soon learned that he was of Russian extraction and by profession an aircraft designer. Far older than we were, he could do some work with Le Corbusier.

Our monastic atelier protected us from the intemperance of the outer world, news about the war included. Eventually, however, some information penetrated even the thick walls of this fortress. We learned, for instance, about the supposed sensational design of the Japanese submarines. We also learned that they were tailored to the measure of seamen different in size from Europeans. I am reminded of the first words of greeting uttered by Corbu at our initial encounter when he scolded me for being too tall. I therefore half-seriously, half-facetiously proposed that we compute a new series of measurements for the Modulor based on the dimensions of a man 155 or 160 cm. tall instead of the 175 cm. we were working on then. This proposal led to new discussions on the subject of how universal the measurements, and hence the whole system, could be. All of this occurred on the eve of Corbu's first postwar trip to the United States. He was going there as consultant to the French government. The problem: design of the seat of the United Nations in New York, a great international task that would mean several trips over the ocean for Corbu and would end in architectural war.

At the atelier, the project of the high-rise housing unit began to pass from theory to reality. André Wogenscky took command of it. I was assigned to the urban design section of the office. At this time that meant La Rochelle and St.-Dié. I was also in charge of the Modulor. Corbu left for the United States highly excited over what would happen in New York. We expected that he would be absent a long time. But suddenly, a couple of days later, the door opened and Corbu entered with a small suitcase. He was obviously coming directly from the airport. Keeping his coat and hat on, he zoomed to the Modulor table. The short sojourn to the United States revealed to him a blunder in the Modulor reasoning. The Americans were tall and the United States intensely industrialized; one had to recognize these facts. The Anglo-Saxon measures—the foot, the inch—are far more human than the metric system's meter, an arbitrary segment of the equator's length, or the centimeter, an arbitrary part of the meter related to it only by decimal order. A six-foot-tall man should be the starting point of our anthropometric considerations. Corbu was enchanted by this new development, and he left me with the new computations. Soon he was on his way back to New York.

The atelier settled down to work. A few new people joined us. Wogenscky tried to introduce some real order. Visible proof of his efforts was the physical change in the organization of space. First, all the bric-a-brac filling the rear part of the atelier was cleaned up and classified (real treasures in drawings, models, books, and magazines could be found there). The nobility of the atelier's proportions became even clearer. Then the drafting tables were moved from the window side to the wall side of the corridor. In this way a long series of quasi cubicles was formed by the tables abutted on the dead wall and perpendicular to it. A long

table was placed along the window wall. The space, we discovered, was sufficiently wide not only to provide room for adequate circulation but also to allow people to sit and work at the table. The whole setup proved far more roomy than the old one. Contact with the windows was more direct, and through them we could see the courtyard with its superb trees. We could then sense the monastic mood of the building even more deeply. The entire atelier was finally repainted white, and Corbu, during one of his visits from New York, decided to create a large mural on the rear "final" wall of the corridor. Indeed, this wall played a unique role in the space and begged for special attention.

The decision to realize the Marseille housing unit, combined with the commission to design the Duval factory in St.-Dié, set the office off on a new track. A wave of new people entered the atelier. Bodiansky would lead the "technology department." A group of Greeks completed the new staff: Candilis (architecture), Hadjidakis (engineering), Provelenghios (architecture), and Xenakis (engineering).

In the meantime, Corbu lost his New York war and returned to Paris for good. We first heard about events there in little bits and pieces. It was difficult to get a general picture. But then, all of a sudden, he decided to organize a press conference in the atelier. It was the only press conference that took place at the rue de Sèvres in my four years there; Le Corbusier tended to keep the atelier off limits. But in the United Nations case he was so angry that he wanted to use as many means as possible to communicate his feelings. The conference was organized rather informally. We, the Corbu team, sat at our working tables. The guests walked around, looked at the work in progress, and chatted with some of us. Then they were invited to an area close to the entrance that had been cleared in preparation for the main meeting. Here Le Corbusier offered his report of the events. I will try to repeat it here from my notes.

After the decision that the site of the newly founded United Nations would be located in New York on a plot of land overlooking the East River, the members of the United Nations embarked on a series of discussions about what the building itself should look like. The delegations of the member countries invited their most prominent architects, Le Corbusier among them, to serve as advisors. Thus an architectural superteam backed up the diplomats and politicians at the conference table, a team encompassing the architectural elite of the period. Simultaneously a technical committee was created to carry out the task. But what was the task? In Corbu's mind it was the conceptualization of the plan of the building and then the creation of a proper design proposal.

Difficulties emerged at the first meetings. With the participation of so many individuals holding their own architectural banners aloft, there was no hope of reaching a peaceful agreement. A professional competition among the advisors was decided upon. The technical committee remained outside this melee among the great ones. When the competition was announced, Corbu asked that Bodiansky, the engineer, also be invited. The request was granted. Bodiansky joined Le Corbusier in New York.

Le Corbusier won the competition though Oscar Niemeyer, representing Brazil, submitted a project somewhat similar to Corbu's. They decided to join forces for the further development and execution of the buildings. There was no doubt in Corbu's mind that he had "hooked" a superb job. But then the technical committee, created to carry out the demands of the United Nations, emerged as another factor! The council had, as a result of the competition, produced a project. Now the technical committee took over its implementation. But whose project was it really? Le Corbusier's? The council's? Herein lay the dilemma. In terms of its architectural creator, there was no doubt that the project was Corbu's. But administratively, legally, it belonged to the United Nations. The fact that the technical committee was headed by an

architect of considerable renown in the United States (Wallace Harrison, who, on top of everything else, happened to have some family contacts with the donors of the valuable plot of land the buildings would be built upon, the Rockefellers) did not help matters. Whatever the explanation, the project was, as Corbu put it, "pinched" from him and passed along to Harrison. Thus Le Corbusier claimed that for the second time in his life he was cheated out of work by an international organization. In 1928, it was the League of Nations in Geneva. Now it was the United Nations in New York. In the first case, his project was fraudulently discarded; in the second, it was accepted and then given to another architect. Which was worse? To have one's work discarded or to see it destroyed by an architect incapable of handling it as the author himself could have?

Corbu adopted various tactics for dealing with his customers. The case of La Rochelle-Pallice, for example, represented an approach very different from that toward the United Nations.

I took over the project from Gerald Hanning and worked on it with Corbu as a sort of job captain. When it came time to contact the client in La Rochelle, we had André Wogenscky do it. Later on I began commuting there myself. Never in my time did Corbu take the trouble to go there in person. At the time for the final presentation, we expected Corbu to go to La Rochelle personally and do the presentation himself or at least to honor the client with his presence. But Le Corbusier decided not to go. The task of introducing the project to the mayor and the city council went to me. I was not eager to do it at all. Granted, I knew Le Corbusier's philosophy. I also knew the project well, and I was known to quite a few city officials; but I was not French, and my spoken French revealed that I was not a native. I was recognizably *un métèque*—a bloody foreigner. Corbu himself was a naturalized Swiss (French Swiss, indeed, but still Swiss).

The meeting took place in the city hall, a beautiful old *hôtel particulier* converted into offices.

I did my job as well as I could. Then the mayor took the floor: "Sir, what you propose might perhaps be possible in the country of your master (*Monsieur votre patron*). It might perhaps be possible in your own country—incidentally, I do not happen to know where you are from. But it is not possible in La Rochelle. I thank you very kindly for your presentation." Period. I personally suspected that Le Corbusier was quite aware of the danger involved and, guessing what the result of the meeting would be, decided to spare himself a few unpleasant moments. He accepted the defeat with no comment.

I want, however, to finish the city of Richelieu's story on a more cheerful note. One day, at the very beginning of my participation in the La Rochelle study, Corbu left me with some sketches and then disappeared for an extended weekend. Left alone, I put my whole inexperienced sensibility into the interpretation of his ideas. A few days later, Le Corbusier returned. As usual he went from project to project, from table to table. He finally reached the La Rochelle table with the rendering of his last concept. He leaned on the table, looked carefully at the drawing, and then exploded: "Et qu'est-ce que c'est ce Tchaikovsky-la?" (And what is this Tchaikovsky here?). In this way I learned at the same time that he was not fond of Tchaikovsky and that he did not appreciate my so very sensitive rendering of his concept. He snatched a piece of tracing paper, slammed it down on top of the Tchaikovsky study, grabbed a charcoal stub, and started sketching. He searched for the basic principles, no jitters, no fiddling about, no swooning in subtleties. Corbu could not have expressed his opinion more tersely. The Tchaikovsky phrase will remain with me forever.

At the rue de Sèvres, the intensity of the work grew. More and more help was needed. Everybody had to work full time now, with payment or without. The unsalaried personnel were still plentiful. These were the *stagiaires*: young architects who wanted to work for Corbu and were willing to do it for nothing. They were either equipped with a grant or scholarship from their respective countries or were wealthy enough to be there without remuneration. These collaborators often caused problems. Some of them joined the atelier in full cognizance of what it represented. Some came simply because they had heard vaguely about Corbu and believed that his name, though controversial, would do no harm appearing on their curriculum vitae. Still others came simply because they wanted to stay in Paris and our office might be helpful in extending a visa. The last group was the most dangerous. They were of course advised that they were expected to do serious work. Room in the atelier was scarce; each station had to produce. The newcomers listened, accepted the conditions, and after a few days of work, began to cultivate absenteeism. Then came the unpleasant moment of firing, a task often assigned to me, since with my ability to manage several languages I could convey the news to the delinquent in his or her native language, which somehow sweetened the pill. In this way, I became the atelier's bouncer.

For Corbu himself, the unpaid labor force represented yet another problem related to his personality and character. He was very careful about money. He was also very concerned with the atelier's productivity and with his own economy of time and effort, not for financial reasons but simply because he was so full of ideas, he personally wanted to do so much, that he dreaded the waste of his own time. Long discussions of projects were wasteful and to be avoided, but with a large number of collaborators it was not easy. Thus Corbu tried to reduce the number of discussants by dealing only with job captains. He expected this to increase the productivity of the lower ranks—they were never to be disturbed. The work should continue uninterrupted. His own presence at the drafting table should not be considered a pretext to stop, to listen, to watch. He wanted to limit his own time involvement to brief verifications and instructions given only to the chiefs. But every now and again a discussion between him and a job captain developed. It was unavoidable. Heads at the neighboring tables then started to turn, eavesdropping began, peeping Toms started gathering around, counting on Le Corbusier's myopia. Soon enough he would erupt with a sermon about the difficulty of running a large office, financial pressures, feelings of responsibility that should be shared by the whole team.

As far as the devotion to work and its quality go, he was infinitely demanding. "Il faut coucher avec l'architecture," he said—you must take architecture to bed. It was his way of saying that it takes time and love to deal with architecture. But financial pressures really did exist, not so much, I believe, because Corbu himself was badly paid by his clients as because with all his thriftiness he was lavish in spending money on work: on research, on renderings, and on presentations. Often, however, Corbu could be generous and thoughtful to his collaborators in a most charming way.

It was the very end of December 1946. My wife had just had a baby. At this time we moved from the room the Wogensckys were graciously lending us on the rue de Tolbiac to a studio loaned by a relative on the boulevard St.-Germain. A strange situation developed. Here we were like church mice, underfed and without money, residing in one of the most luxurious urban settings in the world. We were one block from the Chambre des Députés and the Seine with a good view of the place de la Concorde. My wife had just been driven, with the little one, from the Maternité Baudelocque to our new home. It was New Year's Eve. Limousines swished along the boulevard St.-Germain to and from the Concorde. Evening dress, white and black ties, glimmered as they passed. We had hardly any food at home. The doorbell rang. It was the house superintendent with a huge parcel. "A gentleman has just left it for you." We opened the package. It was full of holiday goodies along with a magnum of champagne and a large rooster—a folklore symbol

from the south of France—made of papier-mâché and polychromed in resplendent colors. A small card read, "From Yvonne and Corbu." A little checking with the superintendent established the identity of the bearer. Le Corbusier had brought the parcel himself.

The dinner parties at Corbu's to which I was invited were always small, a maximum of two to three guests. Madame did the cooking herself and did it very well indeed. A certain amount of tippling usually took place. The favorite drink was, of course, pastis—a drink of the Mediterranean region known also as absinthe. Among the regular guests during this period with whom I became acquainted were the Franco-Romanian architect Jean Badovici, the poet Pierre Gueguen, and, of course, from the atelier, Roger Aujame. Corbu knew the Parisian artistic world well enough but seemed to shun social life. I often felt that the obsession about hoarding his time for artistic and intellectual production was growing. The smallest distraction was anathema to him.

On the other hand, he helped me in meeting people outside the atelier group and his domestic regulars. In my free time—Saturday afternoons (Saturday mornings we still worked regularly), Sundays, and holidays, sometimes even on workdays in the evening—I did some visual dabbling myself. Every now and then I showed what I did to Le Corbusier. He was always appreciative and encouraging; he once grunted something about how little of this type of involvement existed among contemporary architects and how one could see the consequences of that in their work. But he seldom came out with real criticism. "Ah, you should show this to Léger," he would say, "and that to Brancusi, he would be pleased." Then, lo and behold, he started arranging appointments for me with these generally inaccessible friends of his. He even checked on the results of these appointments. "And how did it go with Fernand? And what did Brancusi say?"

Le Corbusier held an infinitely high opinion of Picasso. One evening, after dinner in his studio,

Corbu showed me his last personal work. A discussion developed. The name of Picasso popped up; I was somehow comparing his role in the contemporary visual world and contemporary culture with Le Corbusier's, and Corbu interrupted: "Mais mon cher Soltan, Picasso c'est un génie et moi . . ." I left for home that night with particularly warm feelings toward my host.

Sometime later, on the occasion of another evening at Corbu's home and after the guests dispersed, Mme. Le Corbusier grabbed my sleeve and pulled me away to a corner. "Mais dites donc, Soltan, Corbu c'est un grand bonhomme, n'est-ce pas?" She felt uncertain and was, in fact, full of doubt. I tried to convince her as well as I could that her Corbu was really "quite a guy"!

Le Corbusier was not lavish in quoting the great of the world, whether living or dead. Among the latter, however, a man he deeply admired was the Renaissance painter Piero della Francesca. In our talks his name came up several times, particularly in relation to the different systems of regulating lines and hence to the Modulor. I tried to squeeze from Corbu as much as I could about his opinions of his own former architectural bosses. He did not seem to have been enchanted with them; thus he was less communicative than usual. One day we were discussing the *pilotis*, the columns that supported the Marseille building. It was a complex problem, as they had not only to support the whole structure but also to serve as shafts for all the utilities, water and sewer pipes, and so on. Corbu made a most unorthodox and unexpected proposal. I protested: "But M. Le Cor-busier, it is impossible to do that." Corbu shot back: "Mon cher Soltan, Peter Behrens disait toujours," and then changed his voice to imitate Behrens: "In Architektur ist alles möglich," and he banged the table with his fist. In this way I learned that Corbu's German was excellent, that he kept alive his memories of the Behrens times, and that, sometimes, he did not exclude the possibility of raping (a little) the virtue of architectural chastity.

And as for his contemporaries . . .

It was evening, after work. The atelier was empty. Under a meager light, Le Corbusier perused a new publication on contemporary, ultramodern architecture. Behind him stood two of his main acolytes of the period, André Wogenscky and myself. The book (I wish I could remember precisely what it was) encompassed the most important modernistic works from all over the world. Corbu thumbed slowly through the pages. He grunted. With his grunts he expressed more and more clearly his dissatisfaction. Finally he exploded: "C'est moche, ça!" (It's ugly, this stuff!). And then Wogenscky, in his implacable, puritan loyalty to the modern: "Oui, Monsieur Le Corbusier, mais ce sont des frères." Le Corbusier listened, remained frozen for a moment, then banged the book shut. "Oui, vous avez raison." Then he stood up and left. I remained alone in the dark atelier that evening to ponder this scene. I was quite pleased with this condemnation of what Corbu condemned; this type of architecture that somehow—I then did not know how—came to be called the "International Style" with Corbu even considered a leading force in it. I find it ironic that I joined Corbu precisely because in my mind he was not part of it!

The Modulor study moved forward quickly after Corbu settled on the six-foot-tall human specimen on which it would be based. The last version of computations was done, and I soon traced the first Modulor tape, which we copied and distributed in the atelier. Corbu cheerfully carried one copy of the tape in his pocket. Everybody in the atelier started using it. And then Modulor clashes began to occur. Le Corbusier would ask somebody in relation to a project, "How did you get to this proposal?" "The Modulor suggested it," ran the answer. Corbu would find the solution wrong and change it. The number of similar cases grew. The Modulor argument reappeared more and more frequently. Corbu's reactions became more and more hostile. Finally, one day he became furious. He ordered the use of both the tape and the numbers reaching beyond the tape stopped. They prevented their users from clear thinking and feeling. They easily became a sort of panacea for all architectural illnesses, a substitute for logic and imagination. Yes, the Modulor could be used, but rather as a "corrector" of ideas, as a means to reach for perfection but not as an initiator of ideas among those incapable of conceiving them.

Sometime in autumn 1948, I decided that the time had come for me to think about leaving Corbu. The timing was not good. New things were brewing in the atelier. The Dominicans Couturier and Regamey were appearing on the horizon. It might mean some work for Corbu. This work materialized later in the form of the chapel of Ronchamp, the monastery at Eveux, eventually even the church at Firminy. Gautham Sarabhai came from India to visit the atelier. The result of this visit was Corbu's involvement in projects and realizations of buildings in Ahmedabad. People capable of working with Corbu were in demand. At this moment Roger Aujame was brought over from Marseille to lead the team of the difficult La Plata-Currutchet project.

The financial situation of the atelier, however, changed little. Aside from occasional moonlighting, I did short periods of full-time work with other architects. To help me out financially, Corbu threw some writing my way. Consequently, I became acquainted with publishers interested in him and his ideas—and in new ideas in general. I observed that Corbu did the same with some of his other close collaborators. The decision that I would leave the atelier was made in the little Modulor cube (7′5″) office at the rue de Sèvres. The gist of the decision as spelled out by Corbu: "It is in the nature of life that things change." After four years with him, it was time for me to bring

something new into my life. "Best of luck, mon cher Soltan." As always, when the matter was serious, I was deeply moved by Corbu's directness, simplicity, and warmth. The last day of July 1949, I left the atelier exactly four years after I had entered it.

I saw Corbu for the last time in 1965, on the eve of his departure from Paris for his customary August vacation. By that time, his wife had already passed away. I visited him at the atelier. The "sacred" rhythm of his day had by then changed considerably. Indeed, now it was reversed. Corbu spent the mornings at the rue de Sèvres and was too tired in the afternoons to move around much. But one felt that he did not want to admit any major changes in his life. He knew, and everyone around him knew, that his heart was in bad shape.

From the atelier, we took a taxi to his home, at rue Nungesser-et-Coli. We had lunch there. Corbu offered me a drink. The sun was resplendent on the terraces. All sorts of plants were in bloom. Far away, Mont Valerian was vibrating in the summer heat; nearby, bees and flies buzzed around their heads. What will you have? Something light. Perhaps a Dubonnet. And you? Corbu poured himself a double pastis, hardly taking any water. It is a deadly beverage, and I protested mildly. Corbu dismissed my grumbling. He was smiling but serious. As long as he was alive he would not allow himself to be pampered. As long as you live, live with gusto! After luncheon, however, he weakened visibly. Yes, he thought he would lie down. A Mediterranean siesta—nothing more. Kindly, but firmly, he saw me off.

A few weeks later, I learned about his death at Cap Martin-Roquebrune.

The Significance of Le Corbusier
by Alan Colquhoun

Le Corbusier, more than any other architect of the modern movement, insisted that architecture was the product of the individual creative intelligence. The order it created was ideal, not pragmatic. If he said, "The house is a machine for living in," it was not to annex architecture to a branch of empirical science, but to use the machine as a model for a work of art whose form and structure were determined by laws internal to itself. The laws which applied to technology were different from those which applied to architecture, the first being directed to the solution of practical problems, the second to the creation of states of mind. In both cases, however, the desired results could only be obtained by understanding the laws which controlled their production. From this point of view Le Corbusier's famous statement can be interpreted as a metaphor for an aesthetic theory which underlay avant-garde art in general, and which had been anticipated in Konrad Fiedler's concept of the "opacity" of the work of art.[1] Le Corbusier and Ozenfant reformulated this theory in their discussion of Cubism: "In true Cubism there is something organic which passes from the interior to the exterior. Cubism was the first to want to make the picture an object, and not a species of panorama as in old painting. . . ."[2] But the analogy made by Le Corbusier between a building and a machine was more than a poetic metaphor; it was based on the assumption of an ontological identity between science and art. For the first time—so we can reconstruct the implicit argument—technology and architecture, reality and its representation, could be seen as converging. Technology, freed from the domination of brute and intractable matter by the application of scientific laws, was approaching the condition of immateriality. Its products no longer demonstrated the conflict between matter and spirit, as in the Renaissance; they adumbrated the dissolution of matter *into* spirit. Architecture, as an art, no longer had the task of creating meaning by means of signs attached to the surfaces of buildings. The "meaning" of architecture was now immanent in the pure forms which the new technology made possible. Like a *poesis* in which words are identical with the ideas which they represent, architecture

had no more need of the mediating role of conventional and arbitrary signs; it would become its own sign. In this fundamental belief of "functional" architecture we see both a reflection of modernist dogma in general and a special ingredient, connecting this dogma to progress and technology, and bringing to the forefront redemptive and eschatological themes which were merely recessive in the other arts. Architecture was to be not only the symbol but also the instrument of a new society. Henry Provensal, a writer who strongly influenced the young Jeanneret, put the matter thus: "Science, which begins by enfeebling sentiment, ends by strengthening it."[3]

But if this idea of the fusion of art and technology was at the basis of modern movement theory, in the case of Le Corbusier it was combined with a concept of architecture derived from an older tradition—that of classicism. According to this view, architectural value could only be measured against an absolute and timeless standard. The test of technology was not only that it released new energies but that it made possible a return to the fundamental and ahistorical principles of architecture, as exemplified in the great "classical" periods—calm periods in which the means available were exactly equal to the ends desired.

The theory of architecture put forward in Le Corbusier's articles in *L'Esprit Nouveau* in the early 1920s was, in fact, an attempt to fuse two contradictory points of view—one stemming from the tradition of seventeenth-century classical thought, and the other from German idealist historicism. According to the first, architectural value rests on eternal principles and natural law, and the various technical modifications to which it is historically subject are seen as irrelevant to its essence. According to the second, architectural value is relative to its position in history, and does not depend on any principles which can be established a priori. In this case technology must appear as one of the essential parts of architecture, since no architectural value can be established independently of its empirical application at a particular time and place. Whereas the first qualifies the value of the exemplum with a belief in the universal power of reason, the second discards the exemplum and replaces it with immanent values that emerge from the historical reality in which they are embedded. The incipient relativism of the second point of view was an apparently intractable problem to German historicist thought. It was countered, as Friedrich Meinecke pointed out, either by setting up a particular historical period as the paradigm of the "organic" society, or by "the flight into the future," which reinstated the ideal as the inevitable goal of human progress, and invoked Hegel's notion of the "cunning of reason" in history.[4]

It was this version of historicist idealism which inspired the modern movement in architecture, and it was this view which Le Corbusier attempted to reconcile with the older idealism of the classical tradition. In the *Esprit Nouveau* articles there is an unresolved conflict between the two points of view—a conflict in which the architect and engineer play varying roles. While the works of the engineer reflect the underlying mathematical order of the universe, the engineer is also seen as representing the blind forces of history, and as working toward the solution of practical problems. His works constitute the highest collective achievement of mankind, and lead toward the rational organization of society. On the other hand, it is precisely the fact that the engineer is not consciously concerned with values, and is free from ideology (in himself he is a man of "mediocre destiny"[5]), that makes it impossible for him to replace the artist-architect, whose task is to satisfy a longing for images of the ideal. It is thus that Le Corbusier justifies the role of the artist-architect in an industrial society and establishes architecture as simultaneously a work of technology and a work of art. Although the architect and the engineer employ different means and have different intentions, they are both working to the same historical ends; architecture cannot ignore technology, as it did in the nineteenth century. We therefore find in Le Corbusier a double assertion. On the one hand, he invokes historical destiny and demands a total commitment to technology, and ultimately, to the techno-

cratic state. On the other, he clings to the idea of the architect as creative subject who transforms technology into art, material production into ideology. In the final analysis the *Kunstwollen*—to use Riegl's term—is seen as coinciding with the will to form of the individual artist. But in this dialectic the engineer and the architect are not simply juxtaposed; they interact. The architect, whose task is to create an image of perfection, can only do this through the prism of a "reality" whose realm is that of engineering. It is in this way that Le Corbusier adjusts both classicism and historicism, the idea of perennial beauty and that of technological progress, so that they interact, while retaining a certain dialectical independence. At the same time, by an apparent act of submission, the architect comes to dominate the engineer, and the world of material reality is swallowed up by an aesthetic intention.

Assessments of the value of Le Corbusier's architecture inevitably tend to oscillate between the two poles he himself set up, depending on whether attention is focused on his technocratic utopianism or on his buildings and projects as part of an avant-garde, yet autonomous, architectural tradition. It is possible—and legitimate—to see his architecture, as one sees twentieth-century avant-garde painting, music, and literature, as the product of a relationship between the creative subject on the one hand and an objective world on the other, an objective world consisting both of an internalized artistic tradition and of external reality. This relationship is not based on any a priori definition of the ideal or on any confining notion of artistic form. To reject his work because it is thus predicated on creative freedom and because its reference to the tradition is oblique and reductive would be tantamount to rejecting the entire tradition of modernism. If, on the contrary, we accept the viewpoint of modernism, the part technology plays in the works of Le Corbusier appears as a means to artistic freedom, to the opening up of new worlds of aesthetic meaning. Its relation to social utopia is then "weak" in the sense applicable to other avant-garde art forms. This explains the continued value placed on Le Corbusier's architectural aesthetic—a valuation which often exists alongside a total rejection of his view of a society dominated by technology, and the quasi-fascist politics that this view entailed. Yet understandable—and even inevitable—as this double critical standard may be, it runs the risk of reducing the work of Le Corbusier to a species of "chamber music," and of concentrating on individual works whose systematic relation with each other and whose social and political content can be conveniently ignored. But we should be missing the essential quality of Le Corbusier's work if we ignored the fact that each individual project was not only an object in its own right, but a fragment of a greater whole, taking its place in an entire system. Nor was this system "artistic" in a narrow formalistic sense: it was based on a reinterpretation of the historical relationship between architecture and the social realm. However much our judgment of Le Corbusier's work tends toward this critical compartmentalization, his work must first be seen as a whole, since its overall assumptions shed light on its smallest parts.

The dichotomy between engineering and architecture set forth in *L'Esprit Nouveau* is symptomatic of a dialectical tendency which runs through all Le Corbusier's theory and practice, where a number of oppositions are either stated or implied: Order/Disorder; Platonic Harmony/Contingency; Mind/Organism; Form/Structure; Symmetry/Asymmetry. Though given a new urgency by the need to absorb the spirit of historicist idealism and accommodate the disruptive forces of technology, this dialectic belongs essentially to an eighteenth-century tradition. It is totally absent in the theory and practice of the Dutch and German architects of the modern movement. (It is not by chance that Le Corbusier quoted Laugier in support of his ideas about urban planning.)

The relation between this recurring dialectic and the formal principles of his architecture can be seen most clearly if we compare the principles set out in the early chapters of *Towards a New Architecture* (*Vers une architecture*, collected from the articles in *L'Esprit Nouveau*) and his houses of the 1920s. The classicism inherent in Le Corbusier's conception of architecture is immediately apparent in his definition of the three parameters of design— Volume, Surface, Plan. It is volume that establishes the primary experience of geometrical solids seen in light. It is, however, the surface bounding the volume which, properly speaking, constitutes architecture, since the surface must contain openings referring to the practical organization of the building. There is thus a direct transition from pure geometrical form to the functional characteristics of the form, which bypasses the traditional role of structure and its symbolic representation. The structure, in Le Corbusier's system, is a concealed skeleton which simply provides a hidden and implicit order. The surface must be "patterned" but in such a way as to preserve the unitary quality of the volume, and without the order provided by a classical structural module. The pure cube and the regular grid provide a discipline within which the size, position, and degree of penetration of the voids can be determined by improvisation, following the suggestions of the plan. The plan itself is free of structural constraint; but this does not mean that it does not possess its own inherent order. In discussing the plan of the House of the Tragic Poet in Pompeii, Le Corbusier says: "Everything is on an axis, but it would be difficult to apply a true line anywhere. The axis is in the intention, and the display afforded by the axis extends to the humbler things which it treats most skilfully (the corridors, the main passages, etc.) by optical illusions. . . . You then note clever distortions of the axis which give intensity to the volumes. . . ."[6] It is clear from this that Le Corbusier's conception of the plan is itself dialectical; there is a natural order and symmetry which is modified by the pressures of convenience and use.

In all these prescriptions there is a common dialectical theme. Freedom and improvisation, or technical determinism, are not presented as absolutes, as they are respectively in expressionist or *sachlich* architecture. They are seen as only taking on meaning within an ordered and ideal framework, and in relation to a field—whether this field is seen to be established by the rational grid or the Platonic volume. Le Corbusier's formal syntax is therefore grounded on principles similar to those developed by Gestalt psychology, and involves the establishment of the same controlled spatial field as exists in Cubist painting. Painting and architecture each transform a putative "reality" into a virtual world whose reality is both phenomenal and tautological. In the houses at Garches and Poissy there is a constant ambiguity due to the fact that the cube of the building is simultaneously established and denied, creating an aesthetic tension which the mind is always trying to resolve.

The analogy between Le Corbusier's houses and his own Purist painting is much more literal and figural than the analogy with Cubism as a whole. In both cases a "Platonic" regular frame defines a field in relation to which a number of objects are arranged—bottles, glasses, pipes in the paintings; staircases, bathrooms, passages, closets in the houses. Both objects and spaces usually take the form of hollow containers whose curved convex surfaces project into, and interlock with, the neutral field. In considering this figural system, formal analysis must give way to an analysis of content and meaning. The arrangement of architectural volumes could have a direct analogy with only one kind of painting: *still-life*. Not only are the objects of a still-life susceptible to a high degree of abstraction without losing recognizability

(an essential property of Cubism which distinguishes it from abstract painting); they also have a certain range of connotations which relates them to the contents of a house. As Meyer Shapiro has pointed out,[7] the elements of a still-life belong to a class of intimate, domestic, bourgeois objects whose meaning is derived, in the first instance, from their dependence on human action and purpose. Moreover, the objects of a still-life do not have a fixed spatial relationship to each other (unlike, say, the parts of a machine, or the protagonists in an allegorical scene). They can be arranged at will, and therefore stand for the notion of the freedom of the artist. The freedom of arrangement of the objects given by technology which Le Corbusier insisted on is analogous to this, and relates him to a nineteenth-century tradition which relieved the artist of responsibility for public statements and made him master of a private domain of sensibility. Allowing for the necessary transposition of scale, the solid volumes in Le Corbusier's "Purist" houses correspond to the objects in his paintings both in their flexibility of arrangement and their functions and connotations. In the traditional *hôtel particulier*, of which the Corbusian houses are a kind of inversion, these humble and intimate spaces were concealed in the *poché* space between the principal rooms. In Le Corbusier's houses (in which there are no longer any domestic secrets), they become the main elements of plastic organization. Interacting with the spatial field, and flooded with a neutral and uniform light, they suggest a domestic life of informal but purposeful, bracing activity, and of continuous aesthetic stimulation.

In his articles in *L'Esprit Nouveau*, and in his houses of the 1920s, Le Corbusier may be said to have laid the foundations of his architectural aesthetic and to have projected a new style of private life. As in the case of a number of other architects of the modern movement, the private bourgeois residence was the experimental laboratory in which many of the basic ideas of a new architecture were developed. In recent years critical attention has tended to focus on this phase of formal exploration, but, if we look on Le Corbusier's influence within a larger time scale, we see that this was not always the case. In the period immediately after the Second World War, when the objective conditions of reconstruction and of welfare-state capitalism seemed momentarily to confirm Le Corbusier's conception of the architectural types of a new social order, his larger public buildings were the primary object of attention. Among these it is necessary to make a distinction between individual public buildings, designed as self-contained entities and appearing to establish a comprehensive typological repertoire, and mass housing and urbanism. In the 1920s Le Corbusier's researches into the repeatable private dwelling (the "cell" from which the whole of architecture should grow) and the city went hand-in-hand, underlining the extent to which "the housing problem" was seen as coextensive with the problem of the modern city. If we exclude the office buildings which formed the commercial core of the city, public buildings played no greater part in his urban plans than they did in the much less comprehensive plans of Hilbersheimer, Gropius, or May. Yet in the 1920s and early 1930s Le Corbusier designed a number of public buildings to be injected in an existing urban fabric—buildings whose relation to his ideal city plans remained entirely unexplained.[8] Among the most significant of these projects were the Salvation Army Hostel and the Swiss Pavilion in Paris; the League of Nations building in Geneva; the Rentenanstalt office building in Zurich; the Centrosoyus and Palace of the Soviets in Moscow. At least part of the fascination that these projects held for architects and schools of architecture in the 1940s and 1950s lay in the fact that they offered entirely new solutions to characteristically modern problems, while at the same time they could be assimilated to the compositional principles of the Ecole des beaux arts. Their novelty lay in their

exploitation of the freedom provided by modern construction, and in their asymmetry and flexibility of articulation. But these new elements, which radically reinterpreted the traditional formal syntax of architecture, were subjected to a more or less traditional compositional procedure, and this seemed to give "architecture" a new lease of life and to justify Le Corbusier's claim that the perennial values of architecture (its "deep structure," to use modern linguistic terminology) were compatible with the acceptance of the most radical technical and formal innovations. A striking feature of these projects was their physical detachment from their immediate environment, but this quality was not likely to appear strange to architects who were familiar with Beaux Arts projects of the turn of the century or their epigones in schools of architecture throughout the world. Such projects were frequently characterized by programmatic complexity and public symbolism and were designed for imaginary sites with no context. They established a sort of raison d'etre for the "architect-as-composer," operating on a tabula rasa where the nineteenth-century equation Function : Form could be clearly asserted. Although most of these projects by Le Corbusier, unlike the Beaux Arts projects, were, in fact, adapted to severe site constraints (and owed much of their brilliance to this fact), they were nonetheless thought of as complete entities, as *Gestalten*, breaking the continuity of the urban tissue (Salvation Army Hostel, Centrosoyus, Rentenanstalt) or placed as objects in a weakly defined field (Swiss Pavilion, League of Nations, Palace of the Soviets).

If there is a single predominant characteristic of these projects, it is that of logical articulation and elementarization, and in this they depart from the paradigm of the cube established in Le Corbusier's "4 house types." They exhibit an extreme suppleness and freedom of relationship, rejecting the massive, courtyard *partis* of traditional public buildings; but they exhibit, at the same time, a control of the phenomenal field set up by the buildings themselves. The characteristic elements are narrow slabs and centroidal volumes, linked by a system of "universal joints" (in extreme cases, like that of the Palace of the Soviets, allowing for wide compositional transformations). The supple and active nature of these compositions is clearly linked to the notion of the machine, with its articulated parts—a feature still found in those paradigmatic machines of the 1920s, automobiles, airplanes, and ships— and, as in such machines, the separate parts tend to have their own symmetrical and figural independence. Unlike other articulated projects by contemporary architects, however (e.g., Hannes Meyer's design for the League of Nations building), Le Corbusier's compositions create boundaries and establish a spatial and plastic order by means of frontalized planes and axial movement. The principal masses are conceived of as traditional and dominant *corps de logis* with connected outbuildings. (The development designs for the Salvation Army Hostel show that Le Corbusier was thinking throughout in terms of quite traditional *corps de logis* and *avant-corps.*[9]) But the outbuildings now take on the character of "organs" similar in conception to the solid convex volumes within the cube of the house. In the houses these "organs" are generally contained within the hollowed-out cube and only occasionally penetrate its surface. In the Salvation Army Hostel they form elements of a controlled procession (*and* a process of control) before penetration of the slab, whereas in the houses they are events marking a *promenade architecturale* within and through the cubic volume. The Palace of the Soviets (which is exceptional in Le Corbusier's work in its constructivist quality) consists entirely of such "organs" linked by *passerelles* and ramps, and is experienced as a picturesque ensemble against the larger "field" of the city—as in the Campo Santo at Pisa. A further feature of many of these projects is the interpenetration of volumes, a kind

of "simultaneity" made possible by raising the main volume on piloti, and constituting a version of the "free plan" which allows the ground floor (reception, concierge, public rooms) to be developed on a different axis from that of the main floors, with their regular cellular subdivisions. As much as the houses of the 1920s, these projects conform systematically to the "5 points"—piloti, roof terrace, free plan, free façade, and *fenêtre en longeur*—and exploit them in a number of ways.

However strong the influence of Le Corbusier's public buildings of the 1920s and early 1930s may have been on architects of the immediate postwar period, his own postwar work shows a significant change in direction. The most striking evidence of this is the change from crystalline forms and precise detailing deriving from the use of smooth rendered surfaces and steel and glass curtain walls, from which all suggestion of material substance has been abstracted, to the use of massive sculptural forms, tactile surfaces, and the crude detailing associated with the use of raw concrete, brick, and wood. Although the immediate cause of this change was no doubt the shortage of steel in the postwar period in Europe, it also seems to have been the result of a change in attitude which was already manifest in his work in the 1930s. This can be inferred, not only from the introduction, in his paintings of the 1930s, of "objects of poetic reaction"—organic *objets trouvés* and the human figure—but also from the use, in his buildings, of local materials—particularly in a series of houses he designed for rural settings (the Errazuriz house in Chile, the de Mandrot house at Le Pradet, and the house at Mathes.)

Le Corbusier's loss of faith in the application of industrial techniques to architecture dates from considerably before the war, and seems to have been the result of his own failure to interest either the government or industrial management in the mass production of housing. It should be mentioned here that Le Corbusier's conception of standardization and rationalization had been significantly different from that of the German architects of the modern movement, as exemplified in the housing program undertaken in Frankfurt under the direction of Ernst May. Whereas for May and his collaborators the problem was to arrive at the miminum apartment by the standardization of dwellings as a series of fixed types, for Le Corbusier the problem was to standardize only certain elements with highly specific functions, falling under the category of "equipment," and leave the architect free to arrange these elements according to artistic principles and within an envelope which need not be fixed a priori. This entailed a sort of architect's "patent" on the entire design, and subjected the pragmatic process of rationalization to decisions on the part of the artist-architect, subsuming (as in his theory) the presumed rationality of the production process to an all-embracing artistic will. It is only in the light of Le Corbusier's notion of a dominant spiritual ideal which would give direction to the industrial process (carried out by the man of "mediocre destiny") that we can explain how it was possible for him to abandon, in the 1930s, an internationalist rationalism, imbued with Platonic meaning, for a renewed belief in the primacy of "the heart" over "the head," and a return to concepts in many ways similar to the vitalistic and regionalist ideas of his youth in La Chaux-de-Fonds. The change is clearly seen in his letter to Karel Teige of 1929, in which he refutes the deterministic ideas of the *neue Sachlichkeit* architects of the political left.[10] (A close reading of *Vers une architecture*, however, shows that this change was perhaps more one of emphasis than of substance.) The shift in view must also be seen in relation to the new political climate in Europe in which, under the influence of the economic depression, the internationalist optimism of the postwar years gave way to nationalist sentiment and authoritarian systems of government. In the early 1930s there was a general reaction against the avant-garde, especially in Russia and Germany where it had established a foothold in government-sponsored projects, and a return to tradition, whether classical or vernacular. Both Le Corbusier's connection with French syndicalism (which in its belief in direct action and its concept of cultural renewal had close analogies with fascism) and his interest in the development of regional and peripheral cultures date from this period. Not only did he turn his attention to urban projects for Rio de Janiero and Algiers, but, in these projects, he abandoned the geometrical approach of his earlier city plans in favor of an "organic" and "geographical" urbanism in which giant linear megastructures followed the natural contours of a primordial nature, and which were set in relation to the horizon of mountains and sea (a theme renewed later in his design for the Capitol of Chandigarh). In Algiers this new concept of urban form was expressive of a romantic notion according to which North African and French traditions could be integrated—to create a new Mediterranean culture—reminiscent of the Pan-Germanism of the National Socialists, and implying a partition of the world into regions of "natural" culture. The city is still seen as the visual analogue of a technological organization, but it now becomes an extension of nature, and is experienced as a "distant" panorama, either from the vantage point of the individual dwelling or, in a more idealized form, from the air.[11]

"Reconstruction," under the aegis of the postwar welfare state, provided Le Corbusier for the first time with a symbolic and practical role which no longer depended on utopian projection or authoritarian global intervention. Nevertheless his postwar work continued to develop many of the themes of the 1930s and 1940s. In this work there is a new stress on the isolated building as a unique monument set in nature—no longer the artificially "natural" nature of the early city plans, but a nature already humanized by cultivation and containing evidence of a vernacular building tradition. There is an attempt—at Cap Martin,

Ronchamp, La Tourette, and the buildings at Chandigarh and Ahmedabad in India—to draw ideas from a generalized "Mediterranian" tradition, from ancient or mythological typologies, or simply from the genius loci. The pure stereometric forms of a rationalized and Platonized technology give way to a greater lyricism—to sloping surfaces, catalan vaults and free plastic modelling. The concrete frame now becomes a kind of *charpenterie* suggesting those machines reproduced in the Encyclopedia of which Roland Barthes says, "The wood which constitutes them keeps them subservient to a certain notion of *play*; these machines are (to us) like big toys."[12] Whereas Le Corbusier's interest in proportional systems had, in the 1920s, taken the form of an a posteriori checking of regular surfaces, after the war it became, with the "modulor," a numerical scale which could give Platonic validity to the smallest details and the most irregular and "romantic" forms. The attempt was to show (against all empirical evidence) that mass production and standardization were compatible with the greatest artistic freedom, and, as such, it was merely an extension of the philosophy propounded in the 1920s. At the same time there is an increased interest in the mathematical regularity underlying organic forms, referring back to his studies of nature under the tutelage of L'Eplattenier at La Chaux-de-Fonds, and to the Neoplatonism and symbolism of the 1890s.

The most characteristic postwar development was the almost universal adoption of the *brise-soleil*, which became the signature of Le Corbusier's late style, as piloti had been of his early work. The *brise-soleil* was a means of counteracting the vulnerability of the fully glazed façade to heat gain without having to return to the traditional hole-in-wall solid façade. In a manner wholly characteristic of Le Corbusier's dialectical logic, the ideal transparency of the external wall was not abandoned; its effects were counteracted by the addition of a new element. But the *brise-soleil* was

more than a technical device; it introduced a new architectural element in the form of a thick, permeable wall, whose depth and subdivisions gave the façade the modeling and aedicular expression which had been lost with the suppression of the window and the pilaster. It must therefore be seen as a step toward the recovery of the architectural tradition. It also made it possible to transform the slab or the tower, as at Algiers or in the Chandigarh Secretariat, into a monumental form whose surface could be manipulated to create a hierarchy of scales, proportional both to the human being and to the building as a whole.

The *brise-soleil* thus contributed to the monumental isolation of the individual building. Even in the area of housing, the development of the *unités d'habitation* led to the monumentalization of a type that had previously been seen as part of a continuum, or as the shimmering backdrop to vegetation. The increased interest of Le Corbusier in the linear city is indicative, not only of a continuation of the regionalist philosophy exhibited in the plans for Rio de Janiero and Algiers, but also of the postulation of an "invisible" infrastructure—now little more than the mental hypostasization of the existing exchange routes of industrial capitalism—which allows for the piecemeal and ad hoc development of individual monumental buildings. If the *unités* show a continued preoccupation with the prewar theme of mass housing, they nonetheless reflect a more pragmatic approach to the establishment and dissemination of modern architecture, in which the grip of economic rationalization has been relaxed in favor of a more "culturalist" view of architecture. The rationalization of collective living seems, more than ever, to have as its objective the creation of oneiric and symbolic objects and to stress the polarity to which urbanism has now been reduced—private life : nature.

The tendency toward monumentalization in Le Corbusier's later work accentuates the conflict between architecture as a symbolic form and architecture as the expression of a collectivized society. The greater the effort to "humanize" the unit of mass housing or of bureaucratic slab, the more problematic becomes the equation between architecture and technology. We are forced to detach our experience of the building as an aesthetic object from our idea of the economic and industrial nexus of which it is a part.

The sense of unreality that this engenders is reinforced by the contradiction between architecture considered as the transformation and subversion of the tradition, and architecture as a common, "popular" practice based on technical norms. The adoption of norms was bound to lead to the formation of habits and conventions and to deny the demystifying and desacralizing task that avant-garde architecture had set itself. This process of familiarization has indeed taken place over a large area of contemporary architectural production.

The ideological and subversive role that Le Corbusier gave to architecture has itself been subverted by the "natural" development of capitalism and its recuperation of the avant-garde. We must therefore see Le Corbusier's architecture as historical phenomenon and disengage it from its original ideological context. Its subversiveness is part of its self-contained aesthetic and remains a constantly renewable experience, after the vision of a totally renewed society, of which it was originally a part, has receded from view. Le Corbusier's architecture belongs to a "tradition of the new" which has now taken its place in our critical canon.

The split in our responses to the work of Le Corbusier no doubt owes something to the contradiction, apparent to the modern sensibility, between the alienation of modern life and the mythical power of art—a contradiction which Le Corbusier was well aware of and wanted to resolve by the uniting of architecture and engineering. Le Corbusier's monumental studies of Rio de Janiero, Algiers, and Chandigarh (where a newly founded

"liberal" state could offer him the same opportunities that a declining empire had offered Lutyens forty years earlier) have something of the romantic and tragic grandeur of eighteenth-century neoclassical fantasies, and evoke the dreamlike image of a technological world transformed into pure form. But the purely architectural qualities of these unrealized or only partially successful projects of national symbolism are in most respects as great as they are in those other late works— Ronchamp, La Tourette— whose programs no longer confront the problem of power, but rather retreat into a quietistic world where, as in the early houses, art and social existence are no longer in conflict.

Our ambivalence toward Le Corbusier reflects his own ambivalence toward the modern world, and is the result of the uncertainties of our age. On the one hand, his concept of technocracy and his view of architecture as the means of moral and social regeneration seem seriously flawed. On the other, the plastic subtlety and metaphorical power of his buildings—their originality and certainty of touch—cannot be denied. And yet his indisputable greatness as an architect can hardly be dissociated from the grandeur of his vision and the ruthless single-mindedness with which he pursued it. If in so many ways Le Corbusier was deluded, his delusion was that of the philosopher-architect for whom architecture, precisely because of the connection which it implies between the ideal and the real, was the expression of the profoundest truths. He occupies one of those rare moments in history when it seems that the vision of the artist and the man of passion converges with a collective myth.

NOTES

1. See Philippe Junod, *Transparence et Opacité* (Lausanne: L'Age d'homme, 1976).
2. A. Ozenfant and C.-E. Jeanneret, *La Peinture moderne* (Paris: Crès, 1927).

3. Quoted by Paul Turner in *The Education of Le Corbusier* (New York: Garland Publishing, 1977), p. 18.
4. Friedrich Meinecke, *Historicism: The Rise of a New Historical Outlook* (London: Routledge and Kegan Paul, 1972).
5. Le Corbusier, *Urbanisme* (Paris: Crès, 1925).
6. Le Corbusier, *Towards a New Architecture*, trans. F. Etchells (New York: Holt, Rinehart and Winston, 1960), pp. 175–6.
7. Meyer Shapiro, "The Apples of Cezanne," in Shapiro, *Modern Art, 19th and 20th Centuries* (New York: George Braziller, 1978).
8. It is true that Le Corbusier shows two of these buildings (the Salvation Army Hostel and the Centrosoyus) extended as part of a continuous urban tissue, similar in form to the *à redent* housing of the Ville radieuse. But since they are smaller in scale and more differentiated than these, they have a purely analogous relationship to them. Moreover, their status as public buildings would seem to be compromised as soon as they are seen as part of a continuum.
9. See Brian Brace Taylor, *La Cité de Refuge di Le Corbusier 1929–33* (Rome: Officina Edizione, 1979).
10. Le Corbusier, "In Defense of Architecture," trans. George Baird et al., *Oppositions* 4 (October 1974): 93–108.
11. For a comprehensive study of Le Corbusier's various projects for Algiers, see Mary McCleod, "Le Corbusier and Algiers," *Oppositions* 19/20 (1980).
12. Roland Barthes, "The Plates of the Encyclopedia," in Barthes, *New Critical Essays* (New York: Hill and Wang, 1980).

Le Corbusier's Formative Years at La Chaux-de-Fonds[1]
by H. Allen Brooks

Those who read Le Corbusier's *Oeuvre complète* are often unaware that the first sixteen years of executed work are excluded from the text. Only an impression remains—of a young designer who needed no lengthy training in his youth. We sense that, fresh from art school and continental travels, he arrived in Paris, where, after participating in the Salon d'automne of 1922, he obtained his first commissions—the Ozenfant studio and villa at Vaucresson. Yet, in truth, he had already practiced architecture for many years and was anything but a budding youth; at thirty-five he was more nearly approaching middle age.

Since 1905 his prodigious energy had been directed toward architecture and the related arts. Throughout long years he assimilated much that added up to artistic maturity. But our sketchy knowledge of this period can impede our understanding of the true depth and richness that is to be found in much of his later work. To cite a single example: the Assembly Chamber at Chandigarh. The form, we are assured by all writers, depends upon evaporating or cooling towers, its symbolism a celebration of modern technology. Yet in what way does this symbolize the democratic process? Should we accept as fact, as this interpretation suggests, that Le Corbusier's architecture is devoid of all but mechanistic meaning? Why should it not symbolize loyalty, fraternity, cooperation, and those other values we might associate with a democratic or family circle, its members congregated around a friendly fireside hearth? And this is precisely the interpretation I wish to suggest, a hypothesis open to ridicule by anyone unaware of the highly original form—so overlaid with symbolism—of the chimney in a Jura farmhouse. Such farmhouses Le Corbusier photographed and painted in his youth, and during later years he resided in these chimney chambers (Figures 1–4). His almost mystical attachment to these tall, truncated, windowless, roof-piercing rooms is more than clear, and their symbolism as a democratic gathering place undeniably appropriate. Certainly,

cooling towers were also on the architect's mind, contributing the near-parabolic upward curve, but their scalding interiors were more appropriate to Dante's inferno than to Chandigarh—or the church at Firminy. Thus, lacking knowledge of Le Corbusier's youth, observers have interpreted these works at a mechanistic level, when in fact their symbolism is far more spiritual.

A fondness for ambiguity, the presence of multiple interpretations, is a characteristic basic to Le Corbusier's personality. An equivalent of ambiguity in philosophical terms is dualism, which sees the world as consisting of both spiritual and material things. We must recognize these traits in Le Corbusier if we wish to understand the man. Yet it is often difficult to see how he managed to reconcile contradictory tendencies without worrying about their inherent conflicts. Perhaps it is for this reason that he did not develop a true system of architectural thought. But despite such ambiguities, a single constant remained uppermost in his mind: idealism (using the term in its nineteenth-century philosophical sense), wherein intellect, not materialistic or pragmatic concerns, remained the dominant mode.

From the above it can be inferred that Le Corbusier's approach to design was essentially intellectual, although it was occasionally modified by willful spontaneity. The former tendency, being related to idealism, favored classical characteristics such as symmetry, clarity, order, and linearity, while the latter frequently resulted in the most unexpected and seemingly irrational happenings. In this way tremendous vitality, as well as diverse layers of meaning, was interjected into his work, and perhaps this explains why some people are so strongly attracted to his designs while others view them with displeasure.

The title of one of his books, *Creation Is a Patient Search*, says much about his approach to design. All of his work, in whatever medium, was interrelated and part of a lifelong search for visually rewarding, symbolically relevant form. Yet, this title fails to convey his intense sense of mission, one that embraced not only the belief in a creative elite—certain persons with the rare power of pure invention—but, more specifically, one that saw himself as an individual destined, in some uncertain way, to serve as a prophet for his fellowman.

The beginnings of these personal traits are all observable in his earliest years, long before the pseudonym "Le Corbusier" was concocted at the age of thirty-three. Christened Charles Edouard Jeanneret, and known familiarly by his middle name, he was born in 1887 at the Swiss watchmaking center of La Chaux-de-Fonds, located high (1,000 meters) in the Jura mountains, whose pastoral appearance belies the harshness of the climate. Regionalism dominated much of his thinking as a youth. His mother's ancestors (including a Lecorbesier, whose name the boy would later modify and adopt) were members of the petite bourgeoisie, and her income as a piano teacher was essential to the family budget. The Jeannerets, by contrast, were artisans concerned with watchmaking or, more precisely, the decoration of watches. Floral designs executed in colored enamel on watch faces was the grandfather's specialty; watch faces of unblemished white enamel were the father's forte, and engraved designs on metal watchcases was the intended profession of the son. Mass production, standardized parts, and the assembly line were largely unknown (or at least still a novelty) in this home industry of, often, one to five employees. Competition was severe, recessions frequent, and the future (for both the product and the atelier system of production) was nothing short of dismal. Yet in April 1902, at fourteen years and six months of age, Edouard was enrolled in the applied art school (Ecole d'art) to be trained as a watchcase engraver.

Providence, it is said, intervenes in strange ways; two different, unpredictable factors ultimately freed the boy from the family trade. The first was fragile eyesight that, after three years, precluded continuance of the visually exacting work of engraving; the second was a strong-willed teacher

and mentor, Charles L'Eplattenier, who decided that Jeanneret would become an architect. Both school and family accepted this verdict, and in June 1905, in his eighteenth year, Edouard launched full time into the study of architecture at the same school.

The Ecole d'art, however, was not a school of architecture. It offered no courses in structures, materials, mathematics, physics, or engineering. Thus Jeanneret's studies underwent relatively little change: from design and the application of ornament to watchcases, he changed to design and the application of ornament to buildings. Drafting was substituted for engraving. He studied under the same instructors, most notably L'Eplattenier, who was professor of *dessin et composition décorative*. In the best Ruskinian tradition, only the aspects of a building that were "added" and "unnecessary to construction" sincerely interested L'Eplattenier and his pupil. This left an indelible mark on the boy. And, in spite of what historians of the functionalist persuasion have urged upon us these past fifty years, Le Corbusier was the product of his training: it was, except as expressed in his rhetoric, only the visible aspects of architecture, and not practical systems of construction or the natural (as opposed to symbolic) expression of materials, that truly interested him. For a man whose reputation was made through the use of ferro-concrete, it is amazing how little (if anything) he contributed to its development—*except* at the aesthetic (decorative) level, and there his contribution was very great.

More must be said of L'Eplattenier and his teaching. He believed that all truly original historical styles had been derived from nature; that the simplified essence, not visual reality, was what we must distill from nature's forms; and, finally, that the ultimate objective of a truly creative mind must be the development or invention of a symbolically appropriate *regional* style, one based on the dominant characteristics of a specific geographic and cultural region. For the Jura, identified with the Suisse romande, he saw the *sapin* (spruce or fir tree) as the most typical natural form, along with the stratified limestone of the Jurassic rock. Such ideas were not new; they owe much to Owen Jones (*The Grammar of Ornament*) as well as to Ruskin, Morris, and others. Yet L'Eplattenier's call for a purely local style, one based on the natural forms of the particular region, was uncommon, and the application of these ideas to architecture he largely left to Jeanneret. It is one thing to adapt, say, the spruce tree to ornament, but quite another to transmute it into a building form. And unlike other concurrent movements, such as the Prairie School in the American Middle West, the objective was less that of appropriateness *to* a region than that of an appropriate symbolic decorative form derived *from* the region.

Jeanneret's preoccupations with this problem dominate his earliest architectural designs. Steep, gently curving roofs recall the *sapin's* silhouette; however, these forms were excessively expensive to construct. For practical reasons Jeanneret reduced certain natural elements to their basic geometric shapes: the simplified spruce tree became an equilateral triangle, while stratified bedrock was regularized as a corbel (Figures 6, 7).

L'Eplattenier firmly believed in the value of practical experience, and especially the enthusiasm it engendered for learning. He tirelessly sought realistic commissions for his students, and by 1910 had become so successful that he and his students intended to build, with the moneys they had earned, a building of their own. Already by 1905 he had begun this process (by arranging for two students, Jeanneret and Léon Perrin, to submit projects to a building committee that had already commissioned an architect), and before the year was out he persuaded one of the art school's directors, Louis Fallet, to let Jeanneret design his house. Of course, Jeanneret knew nothing about construction, a problem that L'Eplattenier resolved by asking an architect friend, René Chapallaz, to serve in this capacity, merely paying a fee to Jeanneret for the façade and interior designs. This expedient did little to improve Jeanneret's knowledge of construction

except to demonstrate that the flowing, plastic shapes he liked were impractical to build.

The modest house for Louis Fallet (which, nevertheless, took fifteen months to construct) is not unusual for the period, except for the emphasis given the cross-gables and the profusion of (relatively quiet) ornament adorning nearly all of the exterior surfaces (Figures 5, 6). The *sapin* is the basis for this ornament, whether recognizable in sihouette or reduced to such simple geometric shapes as the triangle (thus the gables probably symbolize trees). Even the window mullions represent denuded tree branches, while the iron railings of the balcony create a picture (in outline) of trees silhouetted against billowing cumulus clouds. Masonry corbels recall stratified rock, and the metal door handles are carefully sculpted lizards. The vocabulary of interior ornament is somewhat similar and occasionally suggests indebtedness to Owen Jones in various, if not always formal, ways. The two-story, pine-paneled central hall (the word "hall" is used, thus suggesting an English origin for this idea) is the only unusual feature of an interior otherwise rather small and almost cramped. Along the back of the house a one-story lean-to shelters the watchmaker's atelier. The sgraffito of the exterior, as well as much of the interior detail, was executed by Jeanneret and his schoolmates.

With such ornamental profusion, one would expect the design to lack unity and coherence. The remarkable thing is that it does not. And when compared to most of Chapallaz's other work of the period, the Villa Fallet is clearly a superior design. Credit, therefore, should go to Jeanneret for the success of his creation; at the same time we should recognize that he received advice and critiques from various quarters during the many months he devoted to producing this design.

Jeanneret's intellectual development assumed new dimensions at this time with his introduction to serious reading. This did much to shape his thinking while simultaneously serving to confirm his own, still not completely formed, ideas—germinal ideas that initially attracted him to certain books. Indeed, it is amazing how important the written word became for him, as Paul V. Turner has justly demonstrated.[2]

Other than monographs on artists, Jeanneret must have read his first theoretical book—Henry Provensal's *L'Art de demain*—while employed on the Villa Fallet. Although much of the text is extraneous, a close reading (especially of those sections bracketed by Jeanneret) reveals many traits later identified with Le Corbusier as well as various beliefs that he ultimately embraced. These include elements of Hegelian idealism, since Provensal called for unity between spiritual and material things, between art and science, while emphasizing the dominance of intellectual over emotional values. Provensal accepted the notion that there are universal principles that govern quality in art and expounded the elitist position that few individuals possess the power of original invention.

Thoughts concerning superior or special beings received encouragement from such other sources as Edouard Schuré's *Les Grands Initiés* (L'Eplattenier's unusual choice as a going-away present in September 1907), his *Sanctuaires d' orient*, Nietzsche's *Ainsi parlait Zarathoustra*, and Ernest Renan's *Vie de Jésus*, all apparently read between 1907 and 1909. This is a rather unexpected group of readings for someone embarking upon the study of architecture, but from the marginal markings (especially in the latter two) it is apparent that Jeanneret was seeking not knowledge so much as guidance. He sometimes sought parallels between himself and various prophets, including Jesus, and similarly sought appropriate modes of behavior identified with savior-figures—traits that he already possessed or might adopt. Struggle, sacrifice, solitude, the lonely search for perfection, power of mind over matter were all notions that he underscored in the volumes or otherwise noted, thus making it evident why he chose such reading.

On September 3, 1907, with the Fallets belatedly installed in their new home, Jeanneret left for Italy, and so begins "phase two" of his architectural education. This phase, like a university program, lasted four years, yet never included any formal schooling. It consisted, rather, of summer travels and winter layovers in larger cities (Vienna, Paris, Berlin) while sketching in museums or apprenticing with local architects (Perret, Behrens). The itinerary included Italy, Vienna, France, Germany, the Balkans, Turkey, and Greece before Jeanneret returned home via Italy for Christmas in 1911, after which he undertook to practice his profession.

He embarked on his travels with his Baedeker at hand, H. Taine's *Voyage en Italie* (2 vols., Paris, 1907) approvingly read at every stop, and Ruskin's *Les Matins à Florence* (Paris, 1906). He and his school chum Léon Perrin visited some sixteen towns and cities in northern Italy over a nine-week period. His long, jocular letters are brimming with information and enthusiasm and, when combined with his many extant sketches and drawings, give us a vivid impression of what he saw and how he chose to view it. The major surprise is how rarely he discusses and sketches architecture—a fact that as late as 1911 his father was to remark upon with some concern. Clearly, Jeanneret was still a decorator at heart, and when he spent six hours sitting opposite Or San Michele one day, it was not the building that he sketched, nor the Donatello sculpture, but rather the marble-encrusted niche. Giotto, Gozzoli, and Angelico were apparently his favorite "decorative painters" (his phraseology), a preference which closely conforms to the taste of the times, and Michelangelo's works in the Medici Chapel were his favorite sculptures. On the rare occasion when architecture was sketched (inevitably late-medieval, not Renaissance), a full-front or perspective study was carefully done, always including details as well as notes. Color fascinated Jeanneret. It was not until his final day in Florence that he visited Brunelleschi's dome, and even then he saved part of that day to revisit his favorite Gozzoli frescoes.

One architectural experience, however, compensated for the lack of all the others. This was his visit to the Carthusian monastery, or certosa, in the Ema valley near Galluzzo, some three miles southwest of Florence. Ruskin particularly recommended it, and Jeanneret saw it soon after his arrival. It was perhaps the most important architectural experience he ever had. It was the one building he wanted to—and did—revisit at the conclusion of his four-year trip. And throughout his life, in various writings, he restated the fact that the "chartreuse d'Ema" was the basis of much of his later work, including the Immeubles-villas (1922), L'Esprit Nouveau Pavilion (1925), and the various unités. To his parents he wrote (Sept. 14, 1907), "J'y suis allé hier à la Chartreuse . . . j'y ai trouvé la solution de la maison ouvrière type unique. Seulement le paysage sera difficile à retrouver. Oh ces moines, quels veinards." ("I visited the Chartreuse here yesterday . . . there I found the answer for individual workers' housing. But the landscape will be hard to duplicate. Oh those monks, what lucky fellows.")

From Italy, with its art of the past, the youths proceeded to Vienna, where L'Eplattenier had directed that they study the modern movement. Jeanneret also needed training in method and technique, particularly since he had two new houses to design that winter. Characteristically, however, the travelers arrived ill prepared, convinced only (from reading art journals) that Vienna was the place to be. They had no friends, no contacts, no addresses, and little command of the German language. To make matters worse, Jeanneret took an almost immediate dislike to the architecture he had come to study; the designs of Wagner, Hoffmann, Olbrich, and others he deprecated as sanitary buildings comparable only to bathrooms or Dutch kitchens. He made relatively little effort to see them and no real effort to meet with their designers. He lamented that the photographer's skill had deceived him. Nor did he respond to the heavy baroque so characteristic of many Viennese buildings; medieval design was

more to his liking. He also regretted (with some satisfaction) that November was too late to register for any formal schooling. And as contemporary art was of so little interest, he rarely attended exhibitions—although he did frequent museums. His few extant Viennese drawings contain no examples of Secession art and architecture, only medieval interiors and furnishings. He took drawing lessons from Karl Stemolak, the sculptor with whom Léon Perrin was studying; this, he said, helped him to learn to see. And while riding the tram, he read the books of Edouard Schuré.

The one thing that struck him favorably in Vienna was the music (both his mother and brother were muscians). Strauss and Weingartner were then conducting, and at the opera Bizet (he also read *Carmen* in the streetcar) and Puccini received his special praise. He found Wagner difficult to enjoy completely. During one exceptional week he managed to attend four operas and one concert.

Most of his time, however, was spent designing houses for the brothers-in-law Albert Stotzer and Jules Jaquemet. These were to be built north of L'Eplattenier's home, itself not far from the Villa Fallet. Both clients were teachers with a restricted budget, and each house was to contain a rental unit. Again Jeanneret acted in partnership with Chapallaz, but the design was Jeanneret's own. This time, however, he had no one nearby with whom to consult. He found designing a painful and laborious process and railed against L'Eplattenier's dictum that he must become an architect. Three months were spent designing the nearly identical houses, and regularly Jeanneret sent home prints, drawings, and even models for critiques and commentary. These designs passed through the same simplification process we saw at the Villa Fallet; curved roofs gave way to gambrel roofs, and extensive decoration was reduced to almost nothing. The designs for both houses were a synthesis of specific sources: notably, L'Eplattenier's own house of 1902, certain features from eighteenth-century

Jura farmhouses, and contemporary details traceable to non-Secession sources. The finished buildings are a credit to the young designer, largely because of their pleasant proportions and the absence of too much minute detail (Figures 7–10).

Finishing these designs kept Jeanneret in Vienna far longer than he intended. He and Perrin planned to visit Paris, but L'Eplattenier had directed them to Dresden. Thus they avoided both mentor and parents by not returning home. On March 15 they left Vienna for Paris, passing via Munich, where Chapallaz joined them to discuss the Stotzer and Jaquemet plans. They then traveled together to Nuremberg, a city that enchanted Jeanneret. He loved the medieval fortifications, old houses, and Gothic furniture exhibited in museums, and of all of these he made extensive sketches.

(We should observe that there is no evidence to prove, or even strongly suggest, that Jeanneret ever worked for Josef Hoffmann. The exaggerated claim of those biographers who say he spent five, or in one case six, months in Hoffmann's office is so unrealistic as to be absurd—especially since his Vienna stay lasted only four months and five days.)

Paris posed no linguistic problems, but, as in Vienna, they arrived completely unprepared. Jeanneret lacked ideas on the subject of employment, and missed the exams for admittance into school. Three months were lost while seeking appropriate work; however, the final choice—the Perret Brothers—proved entirely satisfactory. Jeanneret desperately needed knowledge of construction—how a building was put together. The Perrets were specialists in structural engineering; they often executed structure on buildings designed by others, just as Chapallaz had had to do for Jeanneret. Along with their knowledge of ferro-concrete, they emphasized standardization and industrialization of building components, all of which eventually proved important to Jeanneret's future. Jeanneret enjoyed a warm friendship (ruptured in the twenties) with Auguste Perret, who offered much advice on matters

of education. The job was ideally tailored to his needs: Jeanneret worked mornings only, with afternoons free to study in museums. His fascination with the decorative arts continued, yet under the Perrets he soon learned that there was something more to architecture.

His taste remained conservative. The garage Ponthieu of 1907, which represented the Perret Brothers' most recent work, is logically said to illustrate the level of Jeanneret's interests. Yet this assumption seems quite wrong. Only for buildings dating from before 1903 did he demonstrate (by making drawings, etc.) an active interest. Not until years later would he praise the garage Ponthieu.

At heart he was still a medievalist. Weeks were spent crawling over Notre Dame and filling notebooks and large sheets with beautiful detail drawings. His apartment, first at rue des Ecoles and later at quai St. Michel, overlooked the cathedral, which was obviously his favorite building. Rather than praising Perrets' work, he waxed enthusiastic about 124, rue Réaumur, perhaps because he saw in this metal structure the modern equivalent of the Gothic rib. Museums sponged up his time: the Musée de Cluny, the Louvre, the Musée Ethnographique, where he ceaselessly sketched and demonstrated a growing concern for non-European cultures and their decorative arts. Paintings (if we exclude medieval tapestry) he did not copy.

His reading became more diverse: Baudelaire, Flaubert, Rousseau, but also Nietzsche (*Ainsi parlait Zarathoustra*) and Renan (*Vie de Jésus*). He carefully outlined Corroyer's *Style roman* and bought (at Perret's urging) Viollet-le-Duc's ten-volume *Dictionnaire*. Jeanneret developed the habit of burying himself in libraries.

Except for day trips, he did not travel much. Early in the summer of 1908 he visited Rouen and Le Havre and the following spring spent some days in London with L'Eplattenier. His first trip home was for Christmas 1908, and in May 1909, his parents visited Paris. Finally, in November 1909, he left Perret after sixteen months of part-time service, terminated his affairs in France, and returned home for the winter, intending to go to Germany in the spring. He had reached the midpoint in his four-year program of travel and apprenticeships.

Before arriving home, he announced his intention to live in an old Jura farmhouse and, after passing the holidays with his parents, moved into a primitive barn-house on the slopes of Mont Cornu some distance from the town (Figure 3). For three months he braved the rigors and solitude of winter warmed only by a chimney hearth—the spatial concept he would later re-create at Chandigarh and Firminy (Figure 4).

L'Eplattenier continued to gain in popularity among both students and community, and Jeanneret was immediately swept into these affairs. Any misgivings he had about his teacher's failure to introduce him to building tectonics were soon forgotten. Work had been obtained by the master for his followers: the decoration of the vast hall of the new post office, the interior and exterior of the new crematorium, and the entrance hall of the Hirsch pavilion at the observatory in Neuchâtel. Soon organized as the Ateliers d' art réuni, the group talked of building proper quarters, and for this Jeanneret proposed a preliminary design. Based on cubes and a pyramid, its spatial concept was a first manifestation of his visit to the chartreuse at Ema, what with its separate studios, each with a garden, arranged around a central space. The abstract, cubistic massing had no precedent in his earlier designs nor close sequel in the future, yet it recalls the geometry he praised a decade later in his essay, "The Lesson of Rome."

L'Eplattenier, at this time, gave a lecture on the design of cities, and his new interest he soon communicated to his pupil. For several months Jeanneret devoted himself to researching and writing a book "La Construction des villes," much of the manuscript being completed by October. Camillo Sitte's *Der Städtebau* (1889) was his guide, providing the fundamental theme as well as the general layout. Le Corbusier's *Urbanisme*, published in 1925, is in many

respects a purging of the author's soul; its opening tirade against donkey paths a private condemnation of his still unpublished book.[3]

In early April Jeanneret set off for southern Germany, analyzing streets, squares, and plazas wherever he went and researching in Munich libraries. His spirits were high, and now he was more aggressive. Impressed by the work of Theodor Fischer, he met the man and found him warm and friendly. Had work been available, he would happily have entered into his employ. L'Eplattenier, meanwhile, obtained a grant that would enable his protégé to write about the decorative arts in Germany. This provided not only the means to travel but also the entrée for meeting people and visiting schools and factories. Surreptitiously, it also funded "La Construction des villes."

In June Jeanneret attended the Werkbund Congress in Berlin, where he met, among others, Hermann Muthesius. While there, he attended the Allgemeine Städtebau exhibition and the Ton-Kalk-Cement exhibition. He concluded that in addition to Peter Behrens he would like to work for Bruno Paul and the planner Hermann Jansen—another admirer of Sitte's. Language remained a problem, but he was studying it as much as four hours every day.

From the moment of his arrival in Germany we are aware of one outstanding fact—Jeanneret had undergone a radical change in taste. He abandoned his nineteenth-century viewpoint about medieval art and accepted contemporary ideas about chaste classicism. Only in urban matters did he remain within the medieval fold, though this too was to change by 1915. Being (at last) in tune with the times, he responded favorably to the work of Fischer, Behrens, and Paul—while painting, sketching, and buying postcards of Sans Souci, the Nymphenburg Palace, and the Odeonsplatz in Munich rather than Germany's Gothic structures that had so charmed him in 1908. He also discovered white and became so enchanted by it that he vowed he would install lime pits in all his houses so that the owners could whitewash them every year. What caused his conversion is not immediately clear. No single event or person was apparently responsible, only the prolonged exposure to the classicism of France.

In midsummer he returned to La Chaux-de-Fonds to prepare for the dedication of L'Eplattenier's sculpture, Monument of the Republic. Once these tumultuous ceremonies were finished, he went back to Germany to resume research while awaiting word from Behrens about possible employment. On November 1 he began five months of full-time employ in the latter's office, but he found Behrens too autocratic and tyrannical. Nor did he like his overly polite, well-dressed office mates. In sum, the whole Berlin experience he found objectionable and usually avoided mentioning it in later life. Yet it profoundly influenced him. Behrens' interest (unlike Perret's) was the flesh and not the bones of structure, which caught Jeanneret by surprise. His first work was on the A.E.G. Elektra Boathouse, and this and other Behrens buildings influenced his later designs. So too did the German preoccupation with regulating lines, as used in Behrens' office and best known through the writings of August Thiersch. Here lay the seeds for Le Corbusier's *tracés régulateurs* and still later for his modulor.

While in Berlin (actually Neu-Babelsberg), he read A. Cingria-Vaneyre's *Les Entretiens de la Villa du Rovet* (Geneva, 1908), a book that clarified for him his future. At one and the same time it vindicated his earlier ideas on Jura regionalism and justified his new-found interest in classicism—a truly remarkable union. The book's theme was the need to create an artistic identity for the Suisse romande, a region that in spirit was not northern but rather Mediterranean. Cingria compared the landscape of Greece and Constantinople to the Suisse romande and recommended a calm, simplified classicism of strong geometric character as the design type most appropriate to the mountainous region.

On April 1, a date that he had long awaited, Jeanneret left Behrens and embarked on seven weeks

of intensive research and travel relevant to his *Etude sur le mouvement d'art décoratif en Allemagne* (published the following year). Then in May he and Auguste Klipstein departed on their relatively well-known journey chronicled in *Voyage d'orient* (published posthumously), which took them via Vienna through the Balkans (where Jeanneret was captivated by popular art and shipped many earthenware pots back home) to Constantinople, which fulfilled his highest expectations. There he sketched, painted, and photographed all that he saw. The geometry and clarity of the mosques fascinated him, as did the wooden architecture that lined the streets. Seven weeks were spent in Constantinople, more than was allotted for the whole of Greece.

The next stop was Mt. Athos (where Jeanneret was deathly ill) and then on to Athens, where Jeanneret became enraptured with the acropolis. He treated it with sacred reverence yet left us few drawings or photographs to verify this fact (the same was true for Ema). Germany helped prepare his classical eye, yet nowhere had he experienced such magnificent light as in Greece. He visited museums, sketching Mycenaean jewelry and full-size sculpture. Surprisingly little travel, however, was undertaken in Greece, and an intended trip to Jerusalem and Egypt was soon renounced—perhaps partly because an endless bout with diarrhea left both travelers in a rather unstable state.

Instead they went to Italy, entering at Brindisi, visited Naples and Pompeii, and spent a couple of weeks in Rome, where antiquity, not the Renaissance or baroque, absorbed their time. Their six-month trip was drawing to a close; for Jeanneret it was the end of four years (and two months) of self-directed education. At twenty-four (he celebrated his birthday in Naples) he must launch into his profession. One last thing remained to be done—a visit to the chartreuse in the Ema valley near Florence en route home.

L'Eplattenier had already provided for Jeanneret's future. On January 1, 1912 he would become professor of architecture in a Nouvelle Section of the Ecole d' art where L'Eplattenier was director. Thus each step in Jeanneret's development, away from engraving and toward becoming architect, urbanist, author, and teacher, had been tenderly guided by L'Eplattenier, without whom, it is safe to say, we would never have had a Le Corbusier.

Once back at La Chaux-de-Fonds, Jeanneret again rented an old farmhouse outside of town, though this time he shared it with some former schoolmates. Most were involved in the Ateliers d'art réunis with Léon Perrin as president and Jeanneret the very active secretary.

Two good commissions came his way in 1912, the first since 1908 and the first to be executed without the aid of Chapallaz. One was for his parents, the other for Georges Favre-Jacot, a well-off industrialist who founded the Zenith watch company in the nearby commune of Le Locle (Figures 12–18). Both designs indicate Jeanneret's acceptance of current German architecture (they would have looked at ease in Berlin) while also manifesting eighteenth-century qualities of design. Both are stuccoed white. The Jeanneret-Perret house is the more Behrens-like, yet each shows an assimilation of ideas that is quite remarkable; no single source is evident. The open T-shaped room arrangement within the Jeanneret-Perret house is entirely unexpected and lends a spaciousness that is much more American than European in character.

Jeanneret had gotten off to a flying start—two important houses and a teaching post within the first few months of private practice. Yet his good fortune was not to last. Four years passed before he designed another house, and within two years he left the Ecole d'art. L'Eplattenier's Nouvelle Section was just too susceptible to attack—by politicians who accused it of not serving local industry, and by "old-section" teachers, who felt threatened as they saw an overly popular colleague's empire grow. Jeanneret fought throughout the early months of 1914 to preserve the Nouvelle Section, but in the end both he and L'Eplattenier resigned rather than see their objectives thwarted.

Although Jeanneret built no houses for four years, he was certainly not inactive. He designed all kinds of things; but, except for a few room remodelings and a great deal of furniture, nothing was actually built. He enjoyed designing interior decoration and enthusiastically bought (on commission, usually in Paris) fabrics, furnishings, paintings, and so forth for his clients.

The list of larger unbuilt works is long: in 1913 a five-story combination retail store and factory (for Ditisheim), that perhaps shows an awareness of the Chicago School; and then in 1914 a 120-unit cité-jardin subdivision for Arnold Beck, for which Hellerau and Hampstead served as models; a country house for Felix Klipstein, which may have antecedents in farm houses of the Dordogne region of west-central France; a competition entry for the Hôtel de Ville at Le Locle (the design is lost); and the well-known Dom-ino project, which was an ideal (though technically impractical) structural solution for mass-produced housing. The last, initially worked out with the aid of Max Dubois, absorbed much time for several years, first in perfecting the structural design, then in planning appropriate room layouts for low-cost housing, and finally in creating a series of exteriors. Ultimately, it was the Dom-ino idea (freeing exterior and interior walls from structural constraint) rather than the (uneconomical) constructive solution that attracted Jeanneret to this scheme.

Meanwhile the First World War was raging, but as a Swiss national Jeanneret was relatively free to travel; in addition, his eyesight exempted him from service. In 1915 (again with the collaboration of Dubois) he submitted a competition design for the Pont Butin over the Rhône near Geneva, and during the summer spent three intensive months at the Bibliothèque nationale in Paris re-researching his book "La Construction des villes." He was convinced that publication would establish his reputation among those responsible for postwar reconstruction, but his newly found enthusiasm for eighteenth-century planning ideals (Patte particularly) meant that the whole project had to be rethought and rewritten. It is these new ideas that would resurface first in *L'Esprit Nouveau* and then in *Urbanisme* during the 1920s.

For Jeanneret 1916 was the climactic, and final, year at La Chaux-de-Fonds. His long-nurtured plan for moving to Paris was soon to materialize; before doing so, he executed the two most important commissions of his early career. One was La Scala cinema, a work that he undertook under somewhat dubious, perhaps unethical, circumstances, since René Chapallaz was the chosen architect whom Jeanneret managed to supersede. In the end he used Chapallaz's plan and structural system for his own; only the elevations were entirely redesigned. These are fascinating, however, because of the many layers of interpretation that may be read into their highly original forms. The synthesis, which can never be fully comprehended, ranges with amazing breadth. It probably includes such diverse sources as the Italian sixteenth century (della Porta's Villa Aldobrandini at Frascati and perhaps certain works by Palladio), Bern's fifteenth-century Town Hall, Louis Sullivan's bank at Owatonna (of which he had seen dramatic photos in 1914), and maybe some afterthoughts of Mackintosh, all brought together with a truly eighteenth-century sensibility about form. The façade, alas, was resurfaced after a fire about 1970, and the rear elevation has gained some unwanted baggage (Figures 19–20).

The villa for Anatole Schwob was designed at exactly the same time as the cinema, during the summer months of 1916. It began modestly enough but rapidly became pretentious as the client's enthusiasm grew. This additive process is clearly incorporated in the design. The first plan was a perfect square with two semicircular apses at either side; it was two stories tall (FLC31.827).[4] Against this was later impacted a more linear, closed, three-story "addition" fronting on the street and terminated by a totally different cornice (Figures 21–24). Finally Schwob asked that the kitchen be elevated from the basement, and Jeanneret obliged by adding it along the garden wall.

Thus he never redesigned as the program grew, he just kept adding on. The range of ideas synthesized in this work is quite remarkable, and although they parallel those of La Scala, one should also compare them to Jeanneret's own earlier work (Villa Jeanneret-Perret and a project he did while with Auguste Perret) as well as the Suisse romande farmhouse. (Yet contrary to what others have written, I find no influence by Frank Lloyd Wright.) The evocative blank square of the north façade was discussed by Colin Rowe, who rightly saw Italian Mannerist sources coming into play,[5] yet it is possible, even probable, that when it was first proposed, Jeanneret intended some kind of (mosaic) decoration. Later, however, he would be content that it was bare.

The interior, which until recently was intact, boasts a two-story living room set against a south wall of glass, with halls, corridors, and windows furnishing an overview from the floor above. It is a noble space that provides areas of retreat (Figure 24).

Jeanneret was fired, rehired, and sued before the work was done. Schwob complained of gross cost overruns (which his expansive ideas should have led him to expect) plus irregularities (kickbacks to the architect). Thus the building was never finished as designed. Ornament not already executed was omitted, and less costly materials were substituted in the finished work. Schwob also accused Jeanneret of negligence caused by prolonged absences in Paris. Against this charge Jeanneret defended himself by providing a tribunal with many detailed, often full-scale, dated drawings of his continuing design work on the Villa Schwob; as a result, these drawings have survived (FLC30.085–30.116). Years later the matter was settled out of court, with Schwob paying Jeanneret his agreed-upon commission.

Why did Jeanneret leave La Chaux-de-Fonds for Paris is a question often asked. The real question should be, why did he stay so long at home? With his ambition, dedication, and proven ability, why did he remain year after year in an economically depressed town of under 40,000 inhabitants? The magnetism of L'Eplattenier and Cingria had long since weakened. Yet it was not until Max Dubois (a Swiss childhood friend now installed in Paris) could provide him with an office, a secretary, a telephone, a job, and temporary quarters in which to live that Jeanneret was willing to risk the move. But once these were assured, he left with alacrity.

1. This brief account is based on a full-length study of Charles-Edouard Jeanneret's formative years (1887–1920) that the author is currently writing.
2. Paul V. Turner, *The Education of Le Corbusier* (New York: Garland Publishing, 1977).
3. For an analysis of the manuscript and accompanying illustrative material, see H. Allen Brooks, "Jeanneret and Sitte: Le Corbusier's Earliest Ideas on Urban Design," in Helen Searing, ed., *In Search of Modern Architecture: A Tribute to Henry Russell Hitchcock* (Cambridge, Mass.: MIT Press, 1982).
4. FLC indicates the Fondation Le Corbusier rubber stamp number. These numbers were added to the drawings ca. 1973.
5. Colin Rowe, *The Mathematics of the Ideal Villa and Other Essays (Cambridge, Mass.: MIT Press, 1976), pp. 30–57.*

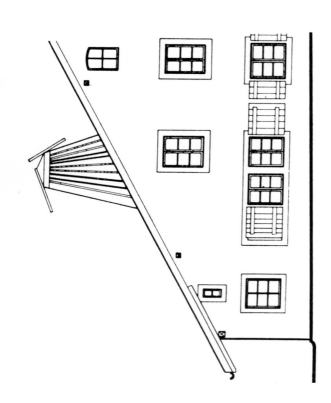

Figure 1. Chimney (of squared timbers) in Jura farmhouse. Shown with roof and siding removed. Grand-Cachot-de-Vent, Val-de-Travers, 16th to 18th century.

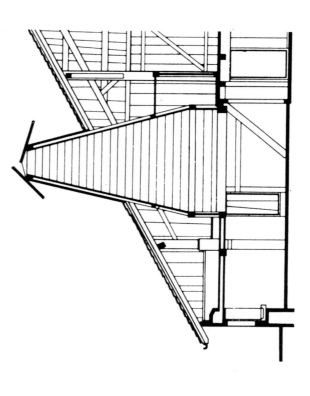

Figure 2. Chimney (section and elevation) of Jura farmhouse (Jean Courvoisier, *Les Monuments d'art et d'histoire du Canton de Neuchâtel*, Vol. III, Basel, 1968, p. 121).

Figure 3. Farmhouse, Mont Cornu, where Jeanneret wintered January– April, 1910. Note chimney with sloping cover that may be tilted open to emit smoke and admit light (photo © H.A. Brooks).

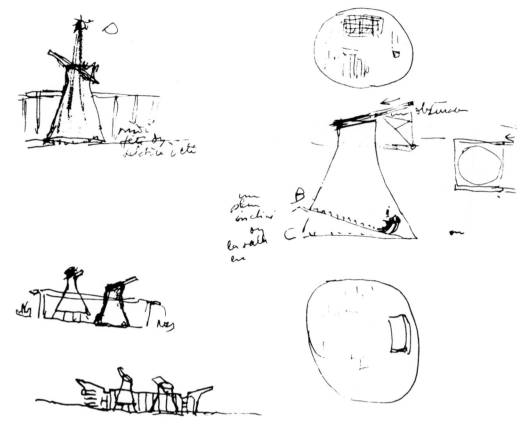

Figure 4. Le Corbusier, preliminary studies for Assembly Chamber, Chandigarh, dated 1954 (Le Corbusier, *Creation is a Patient Search*, N.Y. Praeger, 1960, p. 210).

Figure 5. Villa Fallet, La Chaux-de-Fonds, 1906–07 (photo © H.A. Brooks).

Figure 6. Villa Fallet, detail of metal, wood, masonry, and sgraffito ornament (photo © H.A. Brooks).

Figure 7. Villa Stotzer, preliminary project, December 1907 or January 1908, pencil and watercolor on tracing paper (private collection).

Figure 8. Villa Stotzer, La Chaux-de-Fonds, 1908. Photograph circa 1909 (private collection).

Figure 9. Villa Jaquemet, preliminary project, dated February 10, 1908, pencil and charcoal (?) on tracing paper (private collection).

Figure 10. Villa Jaquemet, La Chaux-de-Fonds, 1908 (photo © H.A. Brooks).

Figure 12. Villa Jeanneret-Perret, La Chaux-de-Fonds, 1912 (photo circa 1916).

Figure 11. Ch. E. Jeanneret at La Chaux-de-Fonds, circa 1912.

Figure 14. Villa Jeanneret-Perret. Living room looking toward dining room. Desk (left) fireplace (right) and ceiling lamp designed by Jeanneret who also chose the wallpaper (photo circa 1915–16).

Figure 13. Villa Jeanneret-Perret, La Chaux-de-Fonds, 1912 (photo circa 1916).

Figure 16. Villa Favre-Jacot. Detail of east facade (photo © H.A. Brooks).

Figure 15. Villa Favre-Jacot, Le Locle, 1912. Entrance (East) facade (photo © H. A. Brooks).

Figure 17. Villa Favre-Jacot, Le Locle, 1912. Garden (West) facade (photo © H.A. Brooks).

43

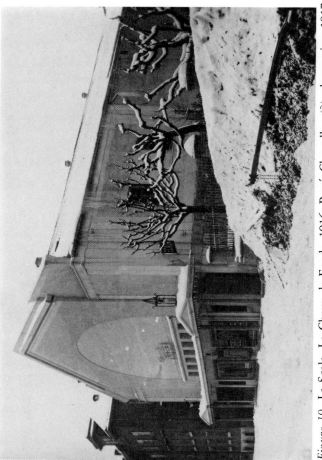

Figure 18. Villa Favre-Jacot, South side. Photo presumably by Ch. E. Jeanneret, circa 1914–16, with Albert Jeanneret on terrace.

Figure 19. La Scala, La Chaux-de-Fonds, 1916. René Chapallaz (?) photo, circa 1917.

Figure 21. Villa Schwob, construction photo.

Figure 20. La Scala, La Chaux-de-Fonds, 1916. Photo, courtesy of Etienne Chavanne, circa 1960.

44

Figure 23. Villa Schwob, La Chaux-de-Fonds, 1916 South (garden) facade (photo © H.A. Brooks).

Figure 22. Villa Schwob, La Chaux-de-Fonds, 1916. North (entrance) facade (photo © H.A. Brooks).

Figure 24. Villa Schwob. Living Room. Photo taken 1920 or 1921 (collection Le Corbusier, Paris).

Le Corbusier, 1922–1965
by Vincent Scully

This is a daunting moment to be asked to write a critical assessment of Le Corbusier's mature work. The research of so many talented scholars at the Fondation Le Corbusier and elsewhere over the past decade has turned up such a richness of new and highly specific information about Le Corbusier that an older critic like myself, who has not directly participated in that research, cannot help but fear that his historical perspective, not to mention his critical instincts, may well be contradicted at any moment by newly discovered and unexpected facts. At the same time, the universal questioning of the principles and forms of modern architecture now taking place—in which this writer has been involved for some twenty years—also forces us to look at Le Corbusier's work in several new lights. One cannot write about it now quite as one could in 1961. His urbanism, for example, cannot help but be judged as faulty in conception and highly destructive in practice, especially as we have seen it more or less universally carried out in American redevelopment and the French "New Towns," not to mention at Chandigarh itself, at Brasilia, and elsewhere.

This major and inescapable fact, touching architecture's primary reason for being, which is to shape the human environment as a whole, tends to cast a shadow over other considerations and even over our view of Le Corbusier's individual buildings themselves. And even these, which are so much more lively and varied than his urbanistic framework, now invite questions that many of us would not have posed two decades ago. Does, for example, the elimination of almost all directly associational and most purely plastic detail that his buildings of the twenties shared with those of De Stijl, Gropius, Mies, and so many others constitute in fact a serious reduction rather than a liberation of architecture's vocabulary? Does the so-called Modern Movement, or rather that specific part of modern architecture that Hitchcock and Johnson called the International Style, represent, despite the many acknowledged masterpieces that it produced, a

temporary and, as seen at this moment in time, almost inconceivable aberration in the general development of architectural tradition and of modern architecture as a whole? Does not such reductiveness, if it should indeed be regarded as that, represent a romantic primitivism that is hard to square with the complex urbanistic traditions that have in fact formed modern cities and, indeed, all types of contemporary buildings? Logically, at least, that reductiveness cannot be regarded as having much to do with the various technocratic arguments with which Le Corbusier, like his contemporaries, so often defended his forms. Here, though, Le Corbusier's view was from first to last markedly different from that of his Northern European colleagues. It was always visual, never emotionally reductive, as theirs often was. For him, architecture was a "play of forms under the light," an art to "touch my heart." The question that must be asked, therefore, is what was the character of that vision, and of that emotion, and of the forms they brought into being?

Physiological answers to such questions are as inadequate as psychoanalytical ones. The brain is total in its grasp of phenomena, of their purely visual no less than of their technical sides. It is always arranging matter, taming the intractable. Its conceptual structures direct how we see, and its intentions guide our hands, which, as Le Corbusier always insisted, are also its teachers. One cannot reduce the workings of that complex organism to the promptings of one condition or to the exploitation of, or reaction to, one peculiarity. Yet we cannot help but be especially interested in Le Corbusier's way of seeing in view of the fact that his mature style of the twenties, different in fundamental visual ways from everything he had done before, began with the loss of sight in his left eye. That loss was exactly contemporary with his first painting in oil, the famous white cube, *La Cheminée*, of 1918, and, according to Le Corbusier, was caused by his nighttime work on the large sketch for it. Referring to himself in the third person, as he so often rather disquietingly tended to do, he later wrote: "L-C lost the use of his left eye when doing this drawing at night: separation of the retina."[1]

While eye specialists will tell us that the retina cannot be separated in quite this way and though Le Corbusier had suffered from eye trouble since childhood, still the fact remains that his retina did separate at this time, while he was working on his "cube." It left him permanently blind in that eye, since no surgical procedure to deal with that condition was developed until the 1920s, and the operation must be done at once. Le Corbusier therefore operated with monocular vision throughout the rest of his life. A person in that state will never think about it and will function perfectly normally until all at once a staircase will flatten out before him or he will reach for something handed to him suddenly and miss it by a foot. Instantly, he will think the stairs back into perspective or adjust his hand. In other words, like all of us, he thinks in three dimensions but must keep thinking, even if unconsciously, all the time. This can enormously sharpen his faculty of seeing and heighten his excitement in it; he lives inside the drama of a world opening and closing around him. He "sees" all planes as flat with linear edges, but he "thinks" them into depth and rounded contours.[2] His hand helps him, too, as it tests the plasticity of objects. Le Corbusier's Purism, which insists on graspable shapes with definite edges, as well as his passionate outburst at Vassar against Caravaggio's chiaroscuro, ought to be recalled here. Similarly, his very preoccupation with painting, beginning, so he tells us, with La Cheminée, of which he says, "This first picture is a key to an understanding of his approach to plastic art: mass in space: space," now becomes wholly comprehensible. "Mass" and "space" were what he had to find visual equivalents for, to make himself see them. And thereafter, so he tells us, he painted every single morning of his life, beginning each day by mastering its visual phenomena, out of which most of the supremely pictorial shapes of his

architecture, beginning with its governing cube, were to come into being.

One might object that flat planes and linear edges, for example, had already begun to characterize the early phases of the International Style before Le Corbusier's first works of that kind appeared. One thinks especially of Rietveld and van Doesburg, whose isometrics of 1920 are strikingly monocular, flipping back and forth as they do between two and three dimensions. There is no doubt that the vision was already being shaped by other people—and for various reasons, preoccupation with the flat plane of a canvas probably foremost among them—but it was Le Corbusier, in 1922, who suddenly exploited that new vision architecturally and endowed it with the special dramatic aura that was to enable it to dominate the architectural world. The interior of his Ozenfant house literally explodes into space; all the old details of the great European tradition, which had qualified edges and modified changes of plane, are burned away in the whiteness of the light. All planes are as thin as paper, all frames are as taut as lines. High up in space, one plane curves alone, modeling the white light. Whatever the mechanism by which the architect was seeing, he was clearly doing so with an excitement about flatness, thinness, light, and an elimination of detail that had never before been so passionately felt by any architect. He was exploiting his own way of seeing with a fierce and liberating joy. According to that way, the space could not go flowing out on the horizontal, as Mies' space of the twenties was soon to do. It needed a clearly conceptual frame of reference close by on all sides: hence the hollow vertical cube, against which all advances and recessions in depth can be judged, can be "ranged." The cube of air also serves another of the determinants of Le Corbusier's design: its Platonism, which had been much in evidence in Ozenfant as well. That side of classicism, which is at once late antique, medieval, and Renaissance, was joined in Le Corbusier by his love for Greek temples, in which he had read the hardness, linearity, and heroic activism that also characterize the Ozenfant interior. All the materials of his earlier maturity were thus gathered together in this house for an artist, glorifying the romantic creator and setting him free as the self-appointed shaper of the modern world. It was the ideal program for Le Corbusier to begin with, far more so than his house at Vaucresson of about the same time.

The Maison La Roche, of 1923, was in the same vein. Late in life Le Corbusier was to call it his "house of thunder." In it the visual excitement became daring and vertiginous. The edges of the planes in the great hall dance forward and back within their defining volume; the long wall of the gallery curves; the ramp dives down; the ceiling of the top floor of the hall bends our heads, as if we had optically misjudged its position. We are not quite sure where anything is; we walk with the alertness of hunters through a strange and challenging environment, beset by Le Corbusier's thunderous forms. It is perfect that the Fondation Le Corbusier is housed here.

To be sure, there are many other lines of approach to Le Corbusier's work of this period. From a more largely schematic point of view, we might start with his Ideal City of 1922, that same fateful year when he laid out for the first time the overwhelming Neoplatonic vision that was eventually to shape so many of the new cities of the twentieth century and to destroy too many of the old. Like a futurist, he hailed the automobile and the airplane and heroized the capitalist "manager." In these enthusiasms he echoed the proto-Fascist aesthetics of the period, as his general air of athleticism also did. But the major outlines of his plan, with its radiating avenues, is right in the French classical tradition, stemming from Versailles and here especially recalling L'Enfant's Washington. Three building types are proposed for it, and they progressively attack the density of its fabric. The first is a traditional quadrangular housing type, which still respects the street. The second is a long linear building à redents, which resembles the fencelike château of Versailles itself, defining not a street but a vast garden. Finally, cruciform skyscrapers tower in superblocks of jardins anglais and wholly destroy all previous kinds of urban definition.

To begin with, Le Corbusier designed only the first type, proposing immeubles-villas on a wildly luxurious scale. It was not realistic housing, like the quadrangles of Amsterdam or Vienna of the same period; it remained "ideal," visionary, divorced from serious social concerns but reflecting a tenacious middle-class belief in the reform of society through art. Its apartment unit became the basic weapon of Le Corbusier's assault upon the architectural world, the vehicle of his visual propaganda. From it he built his Pavillon de l'Esprit Nouveau of 1925 and extracted his Citrohan house type, recalling the Aegean megaron in form, which he refined from 1922 onward and built at Stuttgart in 1927. By that time he had it standing on its pilotis legs, so that the whole body of the building became taut, thin, light, and energetic. It was very Greek in a triple sense, suggesting at once a hero's house, a Platonic form, and a sculptural body. Inside, here as in the Pavillon, Le Corbusier's springy staircases bounded up through the high spaces. It was after all the liberation of life that he wished to embody in his machine à habiter— and a peculiarly youthful life at that. The settings do not suggest the raising of families, despite Le Corbusier's numerous references to the "family hearth." Wright's domestic interiors of the early twentieth century really do make us think of the heavily interwoven "family romances" of Freud, with which they share a sense of dominant parental authority most of all, but Le Corbusier's suggest liberation from authority and freedom of choice, like that of the anti-Oedipe schizophrenic mode that was later to be proposed by Deleuze and Guattari. We are not intended to relax under the comforting direction of continuous horizontal planes; we climb up, we come out on the roof, we look out, at least in theory, over Paris. Le Corbusier's strange and epoch-making linear drawings, traced over drafted originals (the line wavers at the edges of perception), beautifully convey the intended effect of advance and recession within high volumes of space. Even the smallest spaces are torn apart by shamelessly exaggerated perspectives and the dramatized inter-action of unusual shapes. "Ce n'est pas très pratique, mais c'est original," said a friend to Cook about his house at Boulogne-sur-Seine, where the great living room is all challenge and tumult, from which one ascends to the roof garden, overlooking the Bois. It is adult play, not least in the Stein Villa at Garches, where we are led to an entrance façade as thin as something only drawn, not constructed. It is pure *disegno*, where an aesthetic at once optical in method and Neoplatonic in implication has accomplished what none of the endless generations of European architects seeking the Ideal had previously been able to do: it has abolished mass, modeling, and contour, has indeed conquered matter and achieved the status of pure Idea. Behind that magic screen every kind of spatial wonder lies waiting to deploy, because the Dom-ino system of *pilotis* and slab has liberated the plan, too, from structural matter. Other aspects of Le Corbusier's classicism, whether Palladian or Greek, now seem much less significant than this Neoplatonic de-materialization, which might be seen as the very climax of Renaissance theory and which was clearly the essence of Le Corbusier's art of the twenties and of the International Style as a whole once he had put his stamp upon it.

These unimaginably original syntheses of eye and mind culminated of course in the Villa Savoye, which is the most optically complex and the most perfectly Neoplatonic of all the houses. It is as labyrinthine as a brain; the experience is literally "cerebral," contained as it is within a thin shell lifted above the ground. That shell creates a pure environ-ment devoid of mass, a purely Neoplatonic drawing of square and circle, like those of the Renaissance "Man of Perfect Proportions" that the inhabiting human body stretches to fill. It is led to do so by

movement through spaces that are partly enclosed and partly open, penetrated by the diagonal of the ramp but always enframed. One is inside a wholly realized hollow object, the image of a world. Standing on its legs, the building is a kind of creature too, but much less so than the Citrohan type, because it is not directional. Rich in ambiguities, it seems at times tethered rather than supported by its columns, lifting above the grass, offering us a panorama of passage over the land. It is also the richest in ship imagery of all of Le Corbusier's buildings of this period. How wonderful, too, that a work of such complex and wholly gratuitous art could be seen as the result of a systematic process of design, involving the famous "Five Points" of *pilotis, toit jardin, plan libre, façade libre, fenêtre à échelle humaine (en longueur)*. By the late twenties Le Corbusier was describing those points as the necessary criteria, the sine qua non, of the new architecture. Having done so, he instantly discarded them.

By 1930 he was already building the de Mandrot house with its bearing walls of rough masonry, and in the immediately succeeding years he proposed or built several other houses of a similar preindustrial solidity and peasant cast—one of them for Chile and brazenly ripped off by Antonin Raymond in Japan. ("Les grands esprits se rencontrent," was Le Corbusier's comment.) Academics of my genera-tion can vividly remember students of the late 1940s condemning Le Corbusier for what they regarded as this total betrayal of the machine age and the machine aesthetic, indeed of everything in which he had professed to believe before. Their mistake, encouraged of course by his own polemic, lay in regarding him as primarily a conceptual artist and a prescriptive prophet. He was those things in part, and often pretended to be them wholly, but he was in fact an instinctive artist before everything else.[3] And he was an artist of a special kind: not primarily an architect in the traditional way, who knew about how to build and to get along with preexisting buildings and with the complexity of urban conditions, but an artist, architect by choice, who was driven to seek out the beginnings of things. His ultimate concern was with the essence of illusion, with fantasy, myth, and disguise. Hence the machine aesthetic, though enormously liberating for a while, was clearly a reductive one. It was finally not enough for him, indeed could not be. He had to explore, go deeper, out of which a profoundly heroic primitivism was eventually to arise. Even his preoccupation with total planning was an aberration of his will to make everything his own individual art. By the early thirties it led him toward the "Four Routes" of his linear city, radiating across Eurasia and culminating in godlike gestures like the highway megastructures for Algiers and South America. Looking at them today one feels once again the wild thrill of a wholly arbitrary but magnificent vision at landscape scale. Precisely because of all this Le Corbusier was destructive of the real urban environment, which was infinitely more complex than he was willing to face or, indeed, competent to control.

His loyalty, unswervingly given, was to his own vision, his primal search. It might of course be argued that he was in some sense forced inward during the thirties, first by his loss of large public commissions such as the League of Nations of 1927 and the Palace of the Soviets of 1931 and secondly by the general rise of antimodern totalitarianism in Europe. Whatever the case, once cut off from the big world, he was somehow directed, like so many other modern men in a similar situation, toward primitive experience. Surrealism played a part in it; his de Beistegui roof garden of 1931, with its fireplace and its grass, was a wholly surreal environment. Surrealism and the primitive lent some of their flavor to his own apartment at the Porte Molitor: rough party wall, camp chairs challenging *sièges à grand confort* in lively conversations, curving stairs with masklike chair backs up above. There he mounted an exhibition of what he described as "art *called* primitive," in which he showed a cast of the *Athenian Calf Bearer* barbarously polychromed. This conjunction of archaic

Greek sculpture with primitive feeling was to be central to many of his later, heroically conceived forms. In 1925 he wholly reversed the Five Points and thrust a weekend house underground, with heavy concrete vaults and grass on the roof. A blown-up photograph of one of the Ionian *korai* from the Acropolis of Athens floated in its skylight, looking more Oriental than ever and indeed suggesting the Khmer sculpture that Malraux was dramatizing during this time in his romantically savage novel *La Voie royale*. France *outre-mer*, colonial France tied to Africa and Asia by links of affection and violence, France that regards itself as having a special flair for such things: all that is suggested in this elegant cavern, this ironic grotto half underground. One says ironic because there remains a kind of intelligent distance, especially apparent in the furniture, a marvelously active collection of the popular, the primitive, the high tech, and the *en serie*. During these same years the work of Frank Lloyd Wright was also exhibiting an exotic and consciously primitive character, in this case a profoundly Amerindian one. Wright seems very straight and serious with such forms. With Le Corbusier there is more comment and a marvelous pictorialization. A sense of ironic play still persists, and everything is still linear and taut.

Directly after World War II, however, the tone changed. The war was a disillusioning period for Le Corbusier. His revered "managers" had turned out badly; his Villa Savoye was brutalized and used as a barn. Perhaps in part for that reason he became a "Brutalist" himself. His Maisons Jaoul picked up the theme of the weekend house and endowed it with a truly awesome mass. As if in some sorrowful anger the thin factory sash and the stuccoed walls of the earlier work are ruthlessly cast aside. The machine-age materials and images, upon which Le Corbusier had once so insisted, are buried under an avalanche of brick and concrete. The effect of weight is as exaggerated as that of lightness was before. It is as if Le Corbusier is *inventing* mass, perhaps to convince himself that it can really exist. Americans may be reminded of some of Frank Furness's dramatically compressive masses, equally primitive in their power though suggestive of the archaic machinery of their time. In the Maisons Jaoul enormously scaled concrete lintels are carried on thick bearing walls of brick but are so hefty themselves that they can span voids and still carry further masonry stories. The interior space is rigidly controlled by the span of the Catalan vaults between the lintels, thus setting up long dark tunnels that, though sometimes opened to a second story, are totally different from the high, bright interiors of the twenties. One is now in a cavernous darkness lit by isolated shafts of light. The theme of "liberation" is entirely given up; the aim now seems to be permanence, solidity, and some emotional connection with chthonic forces.

No reversal could be more complete or, so it appears at this moment in time, more tragic. That difficult word can be used here in a double sense. The environment created by the Maisons Jaoul does seem to possess the dark mythic grandeur of the ancient tragic mode, but the houses also have consequences that may be described as tragic insofar as the Brutalism and the late modernism they triggered did indeed turn out to be the ultimate destruction of the old urban fabric through their exaggeratedly anticontextual and aggressive design. It is true, as we have noted, that Le Corbusier's urbanism had always been destructive of the traditional city, but until the Brutalist, late modern period, that urbanism had remained theoretical, largely unrealized. Only now in the Brutalist decades of the fifties and sixties did the overall urbanistic scheme begin to take hold. But leaving that aside and thinking only in terms of the relationship of new buildings to old ones in existing cities, it seems obvious that the Ozenfant house, for example, got along very well with the other houses on its little street. Even with its original saw-toothed roof, it was basically a simple block enclosed by flat walls, just as they were, and if it employed a different system of surface decoration, that hardly mattered very much in any basic contextual sense. It was still the urban tradition of the house block, which at once kept the architectural order of the city and could be decorated as one liked, so creating a certain variety within the larger order. All that continued to hold pretty well even through the period of the Gothic Revival, which did in fact represent what turned out to be a minor assault upon it. But with the Brutalist followers of the Maisons Jaoul all that changed; true barbarians invaded the town. Their scale tended to become so great, their *béton brut* so uncouth, their massing so structurally exhibitionist and assertive that there could be little question of the new buildings getting along with the old. The civility of the town was violated. At the time, thinking of the Neoplatonic thinness of the twenties, I described Brutalism as a reinvestment of European architecture with its traditional physicality. Now I think that judgment was dead wrong; the new physicality was not traditional, but primitivistic. The thin, planar, weightless forms of the twenties were not in themselves destructive of the urban tradition at all, so long as they remained, as they could have done, only one of many substyles within its palazzo-block mode. But the Brutalism initiated by Le Corbusier in the Maisons Jaoul would have none of that. It was a true declaration of hatred for the laws of the city (perhaps, as has been suggested, for bourgeois society as a whole), certainly for all contextual groupings across the generations and indeed for everything invented before it. Now buildings really began to stand on their heads and reinvent the wheel and blow things apart. Only now did modern architecture truly begin to destroy the town.[4]

Yet how complex it all is, and how it pulls at our instincts, because the Maisons Jaoul are magnificent as well, sculptural presences somber and splendid, freighted with ancient signals, heavily masked. They are brutal, but they are also heroic, mythic antagonists not only of the soft life of the town but of Nature as well. In that direction, though with some interesting exceptions, almost all of Le Corbusier's architecture now moved. The mighty *unité* at Marseille took his earlier apartment blocks, especially his Swiss Pavilion of 1932, and transformed them into a unified sculptural figure, manipulating *pilotis* and *brise-soleils* so that it became a muscular giant standing on its legs. Its muscularity strongly suggests that of the Temple of Hera II at Paestum, which Le Corbusier had published several times and which he regarded as an Archaic building. Hence the archaically aggressive figure in the Modulor of 1948 set the sculptural shape of the trend. The rough concrete, too, played an essential part. With it other aspects of the eye-mind relationship come again into play. The experience is now markedly tactile. The mind knows through the hand's modeling of matter. It escapes from optical illusion into a physical "reality" like that of primitive sculpture. This is exactly the opposite of the method and effects of the twenties except for the mighty fact that, because of his years of mornings painting in the studio, where he had been working with such shapes ever since the twenties themselves, Le Corbusier was always able to endow the primitivistic forms with a distinctly optical wit. They move through and past each other in unexpected combinations. They are "pictorialized" and "ironicized," even while they are lumbering like prehistoric monsters into our world. Because of this and because of their powerful abstraction, their images remain multiple. The *unité* is a giant, a temple, an aircraft carrier. Its *pilotis* are the legs of a colossus, a bomber's tires; the shapes on its roof are maritime, a medieval city, a dirigible's hangar. The roof is a mountaintop itself. The schematic organization of the building as a whole is amazing enough, with its interlocking apartment units, double-height living areas charged with rudely modeled peasant furniture by Charlotte Perriand, and long slots of bedrooms from which each occupant, *insonorisé* from the neighbors, looks out at only the largest of Mediterranean realities, the mountains and the sea. Theoretically there should have been a fleet of *unités* maneuvering in the plain. Where is the old city now, when citizens inhabit not urban quadrangles, evoking palaces as, say, in the Social-Democratic housing of

the twenties in Vienna, or even neutral slabs suggesting a well-behaved proletariat allowed a look at the grass, as in the *Siedlungen* of Berlin from the same period, but a kind of ship, touching chords of identification not with civilization but with teams, crews, war bands, cults. It is exhilarating; one feels the pull toward it and the destructiveness in it, the impatience and the violence. There is a splendid photograph of the *unité* at Nantes that best captures the feeling. The giant, harsh, savagely painted vessel plunges into, wipes out, the town.

We are in the realm of basic Mediterranean religion and myth, not of the Enlightenment, as if once the machine aesthetic was given up, everything in between having been contemptuously abandoned, only the primordial could remain. At Marseille a concrete play mountain on the roof echoes the shapes of the mountains on the horizon. So at Sainte-Baume Le Corbusier had hoped to build a pilgrimage center for one of the three Marys within and under a sacred mountain with a lifting peak like a prow. Frustrated in these hopes, he built the prow into the pilgrimage church of Notre-Dame-du-Haut at Ronchamp, which was another sanctuary of the goddess on a mountaintop. It hardly seems necessary to try to talk here about all the things that Ronchamp is: a bell ringing in what Le Corbusier called its *acoustique paysagiste*, an airplane taking off out of Hadrian's villa and the sanctuaries of Sardinia, the cavern under the airfoil, wrapped in earth, piercing the sky, the mass collapsing, rising. The images are innumerable and overlapping. In the end it would seem once again to be the decades of painting that made it possible for Le Corbusier to model such eccentric and active shapes as architects had hardly imagined before. There is nothing like them, not only in their asymmetry but also and especially in their lack of dominance by any of the systems—spatial, structural—whereby even the most apparently fantastic of architects, such as Gaudi, had consistently ordered their forms. It is pure gesture, the space as well as the mass, modeled by the painter's/sculptor's hand. One is reminded of the action painting and the abstract expressionism of the same decade, especially that of Franz Kline. Like such painting, Le Corbusier's buildings are experienced in primarily physical, empathetic terms, and whatever associations they may suggest remain shifting and cloudy. They are no less powerful for that. In the end, at Ronchamp it is, I think, the bell we most experience, as its movement swings from the hooded presence to the left of the doorway and rushes around the rear of the building in one great curve to burst outward on the end toward the exterior altar, its pulpit swinging in it like a clapper before the curved sounding board of the wall behind it, the whole splitting as with one great booming note at the lifted prow.

Firminy is less than this but still more personal, an elemental goddess-cone. La Tourette is again a drama of hill and horizon. It lifts off the slope; its cloister does not touch the earth but is raised with a couple of tormented shapes at ambiguous levels above the ground. Much has been rightly made of Le Corbusier's debt to the Cistercian monastery of Le Thoronet for some of these forms, but the differences are striking, too. There is no rest at La Tourette, only an uncompromising hardness, modified by light. Even more than Ronchamp it seems the very essence of religion and of monasticism is particular—not ethics or good intentions or a vague reverence, but terror, discipline, passion, devotion, and sorrow. The stern high box of the church, like the crudest shaping of rough matter into the least inflected of shapes, is burst apart beside the high altar by piercing shafts from the "cannons of light," detonating the multiple altars with fierce reds and blues. Outside, the monks' cells, almost exactly like the bedrooms in the *unité* at Marseille, are lifted to the horizon like one massive concrete beam. We sense that this, in contrast to the artist's house with which he began, is now Le Corbusier's ideal program: ascetic and majestic, personal and communal in a single, basic sense, stressing in the end a tragic and very Hellenic relationship between men and the natural world.

What can we say of Chandigarh at this moment in time? It is in many ways such an awful city, such a demonstration of how not to build a new city, especially in a searing climate. It has at the same time so much nobility and grandeur, and such brutal workmanship, which is ascribed, rather slanderously, to untrained local labor but which arises in truth out of the most European of hungers for a lost primitive state. It is in every way the projection of European attitudes, myths, and problems upon a non-European culture and environment. Kahn's Dacca lies in partial ruin not so far away; it is another western dream of timeless order, there of the circle and the square once more. But Chandigarh, like Le Corbusier's other late works, has passed beyond the Platonism of his youth. Now its Titanic gestures (one cannot call them Olympian) deploy before the greatest mountains of all, far greater and more terrible than those of Greece. Can those Hellenic gestures sustain themselves in such a place, far away from the Aegean homeland, farther than Alexander's soldiers were on the Indus plain? In the first photographs of the High Court at Chandigarh a sentry stood at attention before the piers. Empathetically we identified with them and him and recognized the human act of law that makes the city, raised, like that embodied in the Temple of Athena at Paestum, before the mountain's face.

Then Le Corbusier himself blew it all apart with his wonderful, powerfully visual irony: the piers were painted various heavy reds, blues, and greens. The Indians took over and erected a Lally-columned shelter all across the face of the monumental *brise-soleil* and replaced the soldier with pots of straggly flowers. ("Venturi's mother's geraniums," a student called them almost fifteen years ago.) The image is in fact a telling one in view of what has happened between the early sixties and today. The heroic, primitivistic image Le Corbusier's late work embodied has fallen into disrepute. The civil virtues of cities and of the long-standing classical and vernacular traditions that have made cities now seem much more germane to architecture and to human life as a whole than do a few tragic gestures, however archetypal and grand. We would not give those gestures up, but neither would we permit them to destroy the town. Even those architects and critics, not a few, who remain obsessed with Le Corbusier tend universally to reject his late work in favor of his light, bright, fundamentally more civil buildings and projects of the twenties.

It is also true, as John White has pointed out, that Le Corbusier showed several flashes of a very different sensibility in his late years, different alike from those that directed his early and most of his late work. It was a sensibility toward skeletal construction in steel, which he had never really exploited before. His Roq et Rob structural scheme was one example, his Heidi Weber Pavilion in Zurich another. Even his Carpenter Center at Harvard departed from the *béton brut* that his followers were religiously exploiting in Cambridge. It is a light box (and ballon) of smooth concrete, and though it breaks up the urban order right enough, it does so in a disarmingly charming manner.

It is clear that Le Corbusier would have continued to change. How can he then be assessed? There was never an architect like him, never one really so free, like some strange amateur. In that he was also a prodigious destroyer, an anti-Christ burning the world. Nor was there ever after Imhotep another architect so influential—it is not too soon to say, so immortal—who was so responsible for changing the environment as a whole and having it built up around his own cosmic schemes. Certainly there was never one, not even Michelangelo, who after all worked within the classical tradition, who

was so anarchically personal, indeed so "divinely" creative, in his work. At the same time he persistently called for routinely applicable, objective standards. He was the most modern of men, a complex structure not yet wholly understood, therefore seeming contradictory to us, hard to pin down. In the end he seems to contend only with the angels, in the ageless contests of myth, and his death in the Mediterranean was of that kind.

Notes

1. Le Corbusier, *Creation is a Patient Search* (New York: Praeger, 1960), p. 55. So far as I know, Le Corbusier never published this fact anywhere else, and Francesco Passanti tells me that it is never mentioned in his correspondence.
2. Those for whom monocular vision can be corrected by a contact lens, as Le Corbusier's could not be (and, as it happens, this writer's—who claims no other kinship with Le Corbusier—can be), can testify to the enormous, sometimes dizzying changes in perception that result, especially in terms of spatial interval and the chiaroscuro of contours.
3. Why not, after all, give up the so-called machine aesthetic, no less arbitrary than any other, unless its stripping of architectural form had some essential human meaning: as an image of social leveling, for example, perhaps even as one vehicle of social revolution? But Le Corbusier did not see it that way. "Architecture *or* Revolution" was his motto. Many architects and critics of the former persuasion remain intransigent to this day. They "see" politically—"morally," they might say, incorrectly—not aesthetically; Le Corbusier was the reverse.
4. The work of Mies and his followers may be taken as the great exception to this development of the fifties and sixties. In its reductiveness, however, it at least tended toward a similar end.

Le Corbusier's Designs for the League of Nations, the Centrosoyus, and the Palace of the Soviets, 1926–1931
by Kenneth Frampton

The three palatial public structures designed by Le Corbusier and Pierre Jeanneret between 1926 and 1931 are effectively the apotheosis of their first career, coming as they do at the end of an ecstatically enthusiastic period during which they still subscribed to the manifest destiny of the machine age. And yet, while these works seem to have been conceived as large mechanisms, they were, nonetheless, just as decidedly organized and inflected by monumental systems of order and control deriving directly from the French rational classical tradition. This literal dichotomy between an engineer's aesthetic and architecture, to coin the duality about which Le Corbusier's *Vers une architecture* of 1923 had been structured, was first given an overtly mechanical-classical formulation in the Le Corbusier and Pierre Jeanneret entry for the Société des Nations (SdN) competition on which they started to work in April 1926.

Société des Nations (League of Nations), Geneva, First Project on the Mon Repos Site, 1926–1927.

It is obvious that the vast program for the SdN complex compelled Le Corbusier to think out his Purist architectural format at a new scale, and in so doing, he tackled for the first time the problem of evolving an appropriate modern form for the accommodation of a representative structure. The culture of Purism, as elaborated by this time, hardly embraced the issue of monumentality within its purview. Thus, in March 1926, the brief for the Société des Nations was enough to overwhelm a young and ambitious architect, not only because of the spectacular beauty of the lakefront site—the parkscape bordering Lac Léman outside Geneva— but also because of the utopian and international scope of the organization and the enormous scale of the program. The basic accommodation required was as follows: a 2,500-seat auditorium, together with foyers and ancillary suites for the general secretary, and for the press, together with the usual telephone and telegraph services and six large commission rooms; a secretariat block comprising fourteen separate bureaucratic sections belonging to the Société; a council chamber; an additional six or seven commission rooms; and a library. The building had to be laid out on a 66,406-square-meter site, bordered on the west by the Geneva-Lausanne road and on the east by Lake Geneva (Lac Léman) itself.

While the general axial, classical structure of Le Corbusier's Société des Nations is fairly well known from the published drawings, the subtle way in which a sense of ordinance and propriety was achieved, together with the specificity of certain references, is perhaps not so immediately evident. And yet, for those who were privileged to examine the drawings closely (above all, one must assume, the jurors themselves), Le Corbusier's SdN drawings are inscribed with intertextual references which not only insist on a neoclassical reading, but also make pointed asides as to the specific roots of Le Corbusier's architectural culture. One assumes that H.P. Berlage, John Burnet, Josef Hoffmann, Victor Horta, Charles Lemaresquier, Karl Moser, and Ivar Tengbom, to mention the most worldly members of the jury, could hardly have missed the intention of the two protagonists caricatured under the section of the peristyle to the Assembly Hall; for the seated figure with his high-heeled boots and boater is patently August Perret, while the standing silhouette with homburg and walking stick is Le Corbusier himself (Figure 1). The ironic inference is clear enough; the old and the new representatives of rational classicism are here, for a moment, situated side by side on the threshold of a new era. A reference of an equally cryptic nature, and one which has only become evident through the publication of this archive material, is the sculptural group over the general secretary's suite at the apex of the Assembly Hall, facing over the lake. Four figures are depicted on the high pedestal above this presidential pavilion (Figure 2), and these are as follows: a lion on the left, a horse and a man standing together in the center, and on the right, a crow. The strange iconography of this sculptural group requires some explanation. The central figures are apparently derived from the Dioscuri, transposed by Behrens (after Schinkel's Altes Museum) into a symbol for the German State and used by him on top of his St. Petersburg Embassy of 1912 and again in the Festhalle erected for the Werkbund Exhibition of 1914. Le Corbusier's free interpretation of this icon is not without certain implications, for the horse, instead of being restrained by a man, is now running free—surely a sign of Dionysian energy—while the remaining male figure, instead of being rigidly frontalized, as in Behrens' version, adopts a graceful assymetrical posture, evocative of Apollonian calm. The attendant beasts left and right comment at a more intimate level on the generic meaning of the inner dialectical pair, for the lion seemingly stands for Jeanneret, while the crow, poised as if on the verge of flight, is clearly meant to signify as the image of a pun, the "crow-like" one, that is, the volatile personality of Le Corbusier himself. Le Corbusier's awareness of being technically dependent upon the expertise of his more technocratic cousin is confirmed by the compensatory statement which he made late in life: "I am the sea and he is the mountain and as everyone knows these two can never meet."[1]

Aside from these idiosyncratic, yet significant references, rational classicism is present as a legacy in Le Corbusier's SdN Assembly Hall in ways which are more overt (Figure 5 and 23.183*): first of all in the Palladian structuring of the assembly head building about an ABABA rhythm, then in the provision of a peristyle, labeled as such, and finally in the elaborate hierarchical sequence of entry comprising a *scala regia* followed by a *pas perdus*. This sequence continues under the belly of the auditorium itself as a *promenade architecturale*

*Ed. Note—Reference to drawings identified by a five-digit number such as 23.183 in the text of this essay refer to the Fondation Le Corbusier number of the particular drawing. The drawings alluded to by the FLC numbers are found in Volumes III, IV, and IX of *The Le Corbusier Archive* Series published by Garland Publishing, Inc. (New York and London, 1982).

(Figure 3) and is perhaps comparable to that long corridor which, with more sinister intent, is featured in Albert Speer's New State Chancellery of 1937. In this instance, however, the long and impressive promenade terminates in the general secretary's suite facing out over the lake (23.288).

Rational classicism is evident in the proposed cladding of the polished granite veneer, in the paving and intercolumnation of the principal lobbies (Figure 5, 23.183, and 23.1179)—surely indebted to Perret's Théâtre des Champs Elysées foyer of 1912 (Figure 4)—and even in the organization of the Secretariat library which seems to make an explicit reference to Henri Labrouste's Bibliothèque Nationale, above all in the organization of the reading room and in the placement of the bookstack to the rear (23.190, 23.253). Classicism is also evident in the studies for the placement of sculptural enrichment, in the low relief sculptures shown under the *porte cochère* fronting the Assembly Hall (see 23.194 versus 23.246 [Figure 10]). Apart from this, Julien Gaudet's classical "elementarism" is directly utilized by Le Corbusier as a compositional method in the alternative layout which he was to append to the main site plan bearing the caption: "An alternative proposal employing the same compositional elements."[2]

Neoclassical again, or in any event within the architectural tradition of the Enlightenment, was the dramatic proposal made for illuminating the assembly chamber. This large volume was dialectically conceived as being lit through translucent glazed surfaces, on which the light would play in more or less the same way, irrespective of whether the source was natural or artificial. It is characteristic that Le Corbusier referred to this manner of illumination as though it were some kind of patent device or technological breakthrough, comparable to the ducted air-conditioning system which he adopted for the main chamber. Adjacent to his diagrams illustrating the system of *chauffage par le procédé d'aération ponctuelle*, he provided a parallel plate, demonstrating the precepts of *éclairage étincelant*—sparkling light—which showed how the assembly hall would be illuminated throughout the day by diffused light, coming through three top lanterns and through translucent double-glazed curtain walls, flanking the auditorium (23.178). It may be claimed that through this arrangement, he was able to combine classical Enlightenment symbolism with modern technology. Thus while permanently and evenly illuminated during the day, the hall would literally glow with light at night, thereby symbolically suggesting the wisdom and diligence with which the nocturnal deliberations of the SdN would assure security to the world at large. A notion of transcendental technology is also implicit in those plates which compare *les salles de format favorable à l'acoustique* to more traditional circular or semi-circular shapes classified as *anti-acoustique* (23.216). The care with which the acoustics of the hall were worked out in consultation with Gustave Lyon is indicated in 23.187 and again in 23.216, where the adopted scheme bears the caption: "All the reflected sound waves are parallel to the walls, there are no secondary reflexions."

The transcendence of modern technique is also evident in the steel framing to the main hall where the primary longitudinal trusses take their roller bearing support off two sets of twin reinforced-concrete pylons (Palladian format) which are also used to bracket the main elevator shafts. This hierarchical structural order is complemented by the integration of these trusses with the transverse frames and with the lantern roof lighting as sketched out in drawing 23.262 and finally incorporated into the actual framing layout developed by the Zurich engineers Terner and Chopard in January 1927 (Figure 6). It is interesting to note how this framing was simplified by the architects for the final presentation, the number of bracing members being reduced (Figure 1) and the curtain wall being greatly simplified (23.170). The Terner and Chopard design also makes Le

Corbusier's debt to Behrens' AEG Turbine Factory of 1910 explicit, above all in the exposed hinged joints flanking the outer perimeter of the hall, where each truss takes its hinged bearing off a stubb concrete column.

It is convenient to mention at this juncture Le Corbusier's habit of transposing a given typological solution to another context, whereby a kind of internal code is established, displacing the attributes of one situation to another. Thus, the twin reinforced-concrete pylons of the SdN Assembly Hall reappear as the intermediate attached *piloti* to the Pavillon Suisse of 1932, thereby bestowing upon a fragmentary *redent* slab, drawn from the typology of La Ville Radieuse the connotation of being a "monumental" front, comparable to the frontal presence such a form as this first had in the SdN building! This apparent "transposition" is also supported by the partially radial configuration given to the plan of the foyer situated to the rear of the Pavillon Suisse. Are we justified in seeing this ancillary block as though it were the vestigial remains of the SdN auditorium?

The "machinism" which permeates Le Corbusier's SdN proposal makes itself most manifest in the complex circulation system adopted for the Assembly Hall. That this system was privately conceived as some kind of biological metaphor is dramatically indicated in the sketch plan of the hall depicting three superimposed levels (Figure 7). This drawing includes a brief sketch of an aorta conceived as a kind of Klein bottle or bivalve where the public passes through one half and the journalists through the other. This scissors stair system which alternatively delivers its users to the A or B floors (clearly annotated as A and B in the large section of the hall shown on Figure 1) is first sketched out in two alternative forms on drawing 23.263, the journalists and visitors entering into the A section of the stair and the general public entering into the B. The transverse section drafted out in Figure 4 shows how the B floors only give access to public galleries while the A floors feed the two-story committee rooms, *les salles des grandes commissions*. The overall system for classifying the users of the hall is first shown clearly in the plan 23.237, which also gives indications as to the separate system of service access and shows the twin elevators serving the main body of the hall.

Machinism of a more mechanical order is evident in the fenestration to the Secretariat, which is fitted throughout with sliding steel sashes, that is, the *fenêtre en longeur* which Le Corbusier had characterized in his Five Points of a New Architecture of 1926 as the typical mechanical element of the house. The Secretariat fenestration complements this mechanism with a sliding, lightweight tubular steel cleaning cradle—the so-called *passerelle bicyclette*—which was designed to be suspended from the reinforced-concrete cornice running around the top of the curtain wall façade. This cornice was also envisaged as having roller shutters fitted to its underside, while a comparable inner slot afforded a pelment for the curtains on the line of the internal sill below. It is typical of Le Corbusier's technological romanticism that this integrated façade, complete with built-in radiators, should be accorded a certain metaphorical status in his account of the SdN debacle published under the title *Une Maison—un palais* in 1928. "I have one master," he wrote. "It is the past"; and elsewhere in this book, opposite an axonometric of the Villa Garches which he regarded as a prototype for his Palais des Nations, he wrote, ". . . we are strengthened by the past because the past has proven to us that under conditions of clarity and lasting equilibrium, the house becomes typified, and that when the type is pure, it possesses an architectural potential . . . ; it is able to elevate itself to the dignity of a Palace."[3] Conversely, he referred to his Palais des Nations as "the administration house of the nations; it is an organism, a mechanism of precise ends. It is a machine for living in."[4] Elsewhere in *Une Maison—un palais*, under the elevation of his SdN Secretariat block, he displayed a diagram of the

garden façade at Garches, drawn to the same scale and accompanied by the caption: "The disposition of the windows is the same as those on the Villa Garches."[5]

This transposition of a house into a palace and vice-versa is a key notion underlying Le Corbusier's output and the elaborate metaphorical substance of his entire endeavor is incomprehensible if we do not understand that it is grounded in this fundamental notion of a transposable hierarchy. The house/palace syndrome is conceived by Le Corbusier as the archetypal double. On this dialectical base, compounded of both classicism and utopian socialism, he established his metaphorical fulcrum: a Purist mythology derived in part from the antique and in part from the technology of the nineteenth century. To this end he combined, in his book *Précisions* of 1930, a sequence of telling images: A. J. Gabriel's Palais de la Concorde, an ocean-going liner, the SdN Secretariat block, and his own version of what he thought of as an American skyscraper. Not only was the house now transposed into the palace, but the liner, in its turn, was read as a classical structure, thus permitting the SdN Secretariat to be seen as a transcendental integration of the two. This particular identification of the baroque palace with the ocean liner may well have its origins in the utopian socialist theories of Victor Considerant, particularly his *Considerations sociales sur l'architectonique* of 1834.

Despite this assumption of classical attributes, the early sketches for the Assembly Hall indicate the difficulty Le Corbusier experienced in bringing himself to project a totally monumental façade, evident, for example, in Figures 8 and 9 (the latter dated November 16, 1926, and sheet 23.402. As these drawings make clear, Le Corbusier had first thought of handling the principal elevation in much the same way as he had treated the entry façade of the Villa Garches; that is to say, he considered relieving the sobriety of a basically symmetrical Palladian *parti* with asymmetrical secondary elements. Similar asymmetrical inflections are evident in the placement of massed flags in early sketches for the SdN as shown in Figure 10. Once again, as sheet 23.402 indicates, the twin monumental stair to the foyer was originally placed on the exterior, in a manner not dissimilar to the projecting garden stair at Garches.

Le Corbusier regarded his SdN site layout as a *conception paysagiste* (23.249), a phrase evoking both English picturesque and German romantic classicism, and this hybrid intent seems to be confirmed by his use of both the *allée classique* and the *bosquet anglais*. However, the principles according to which the building and its landscape would have been integrated into the existing site went well beyond the scope of the nineteenth-century eclectic landscape tradition, for as Colin Rowe and Robert Slutzky have pointed out, Le Corbusier's SdN project introduces a series of parallel longitudinal planes and spatial slots running perpendicular to the main east-west axial approach. A visitor approaching via the *cour d'honneur* would have had to pass through a series of guillotine planes which, either built or planted, granite or green, would have had the effect of deflecting the eye to lateral views of the lake and its attendant foliage. The center of axial vision would alternately compress frontally and expand diagonally, thereby creating a perceptual ambiguity as to the size and scale of the spatial slots suspended in front of the Assembly Hall.[6]

Centrosoyus—Central Union of Consumer Co-operatives, Moscow, 1928–1929

The Soviet Central Union of Consumer Co-operatives expanded very rapidly under the auspices of the New Economic Policy of the Soviet Union and in January 1928, it organized, in conjunction with the Society of Civil Engineers, an initial competition for new premises on an 11,000-square-meter site bordered by the old radial axis of Myasnitskaya Prospect—renamed Kirov Street in 1935—and cut by two new routes, the new Myasnitskaya Prospect and a boulevard linking the

old and the new streets (cf. plans 15.684-15.692 and perspectives 16.114, 15.689, 16.246). Out of the 32 competitors who entered the initial competition, B.M. Velikovsky and V.M. Vionov received the first prize. Two further competitions were staged for the same project on exactly the same site; the first of these was an international competition involving a number of foreign competitors, including Max Taut and Sir John Burnet as well as Le Corbusier, and the second, with predominantly Russian competitors, was staged in October 1928.

It is somewhat paradoxical that Le Corbusier was to emerge as the winner from this, the third and last competition, traveling to Moscow in early October and presenting his second project there on October 22. As Jean Louis Cohen has informed us in his essay, "Cette Mystique: l'URSS":

On October 27th, the majority of the Soviet participants in the third competition declared that it was indispensable for the future of the new architecture to entrust full control to Le Corbusier and Pierre Jeanneret, and this was done on the 30th. (During this period, Le Corbusier had been running around town: he held a conference presided over by Lunacharsky at the Polytechnic Museum; Alexander Vesnin presented him with 150 architectural projects drafted by his students; he met with Ginzburg, Eisenstein, Meyerhold, etc.) In this address, the competition participants pointed out that "the conservative traditions continue to remain in command," therefore, "Le Corbusier's project will be a clear and effective representation of the architectural ideas of today."[7]

In his four successive schemes for the Centrosoyus (the first dating from October 1928, and the last finished in Paris in January 1929 and accepted by the Soviet authorities in the following March, see 15.879), Le Corbusier was able to re-use some of the typological components which he had first developed in his design for the Société des Nations, although it has to be admitted that in this transposition a number of modifications took place, above all, the initial appearance of the typical Radiant City slab block, first built out in the Pavillon Suisse of 1932. In fact, it is possible to claim that the *parti* adopted for the Centrosoyus anticipated in certain aspects the layout of the Pavillon Suisse—namely the frontal slab with the primary public element to the rear (see sketch layouts 15.923). That Le Corbusier tried out many *redent* variations is evident from Figure 12. The initial scheme seems to have been worked out in a very naive way. Early preliminary sketches show that he even considered a tower (16.238, 16.222, and 16.223) and quite different means of access. For example, elliptical ramps are shown inside on drawing 16.066.

The evolution of the Centrosoyus passed through four separate stages of which the first was a series of sketches in which Le Corbusier evolved the Centrosoyus in the forms of a perimeter block (Figure 13, 16.238, 16.222, 16.223, and 16.239). One of these early drawings (Figure 14) also shows the Centrosoyus complex surrounded by other ministries, projected in *redent* formation on the adjacent sites. The second stage and the first definitive *parti* (see sketches 16.246 and 15.671) was published in Le Corbusier's *Oeuvre complète 1910-29* and in *L'Architecture Vivante* (see drawings 15.879 and 15.687). In this version the assembly hall is oriented on a northeast/southwest axis with the frontal seven-story slab blocks ranging exactly parallel to the new "boulevard" and to the Myasnitskaya Prospect respectively. This composition has a schematic quality absent from the penultimate project which was also published in *L'Oeuvre complète 1910–29*. In this third and almost final version the assembly hall has been rotated ninety degrees so that it aligns on a northwest/southeast axis, while the layout of the frontal blocks has been orthogonally rearranged. The result is that only the slab along Myasnitskaya Prospect is now parallel to the street frontage. The other principal block facing the new boulevard is no longer parallel with its frontage (15.692, 15.684, 16.052, 15.917, and 15.918). It appears that in the fourth and final version an alignment with the street frontages was insisted upon by the Soviet authorities

(16.113, 15.836, 15.871, and 16.114). This much is hinted at in drawing number 15.932 dated March 1929, in which Le Corbusier distinguishes between *notre project décembre* and *leur project mars 1929.*

In the earliest Centrosoyus scheme, the main elements of Le Corbusier's initial SdN scheme are reproposed for the Moscow situation. Like pieces of the Cubist collage, the original SdN Secretariat wing is apparently dismembered and redistributed about the perimeter of the Myasnitskaya site, while an assembly hall of reduced size is reconstituted in the center of the block. This is particularly evident in the boulevard elevation of the first scheme where the SdN elevation is replicated, including projecting balconies at either end (Figure 15). These balconies are eliminated in the later schemes. Le Corbusier also made an equally classical, i.e., axial, use of sculpture in the Centrosoyus, as in the axial placement of Soviet industrial and agricultural symbols in the boulevard facade (see 15.707, 16.689, 23.194, and 23.246). In the second scheme for Centrosoyus the whole complex is elevated above the ground on *piloti*, creating an extensive and freely planned foyer underneath. This move, consistent with the precepts of the Five Points, is seminal since it introduces a more fluid concept of circulation into Le Corbusier's general repetoire; above all, in this case, it brings about an elaborate sequence of ramps which are initially combined together to provide alternative summer and winter routes to the 1,000-seat auditorium, elevated at the first floor. As this extremely elaborate provision would indicate, Le Corbusier became obsessed with circulation at this time, a fixation which assumed for him the status of a biological metaphor. Of his final project for the Centrosoyus, in which, ironically enough, the circulation had been simplified, he wrote:

It is obligatory to classify this vast crowd entering and leaving at the same time. It is necessary to make a kind of forum for such occasions; for people whose overshoes and furs will be covered

with snow in winter, one must provide well-organized check rooms and systems of circulation. . . . A system of pilotis almost entirely covers the ground. These raise the offices into the air which do not begin until the first floor. Underneath one is able to circulate freely in the open or in a forum of enormous size served by two principal entrances. Within this forum are to be found elevators, paternosters (continuous elevators arranged in a chain), and immense helicoidal ramps which, replacing stairs, allow for rapid movement. It has been appropriate to set up such a classification in a building which knows two moments; the first, a period of disorderly flux on a vast horizontal ground plane like a lake, the second a period of stable, immobile work, sheltered from noise and comings and goings, the offices where each one is in his place and controllable . . . Circulation is a word that I used incessantly in Moscow, in order to explain myself, to the point that several delegates from the various Soviets ended up getting nervous about it . . . I stuck to my position . . . Architecture is circulation. If you weigh this point, you will find that it condemns academic methods and consecrates the principle of the pilotis.[8]

The circulation of the fourth and definitive Centrosoyus project is, in fact, extraordinarily ingenious and elegant. It consists fundamentally of two separate sequences. The first of these is a pair of free-standing helicoidal ramps which, together with the elevators, serve the office accommodation; the second is an elaborately ramped *promenade architecturale* linking the two separate entrances, situated on the old and new Myasnitskaya streets, respectively. The point of this bipartite system was to provide independent access to the auditorium from both the city and the Centrosoyus foyer. The Centrosoyus is thus the occasion for a totally new concept of interior space in Le Corbusier's work; that is to say, for the invention of the warped floor plane as a distributory surface extending through a forest of *piloti*. This lake-like space, which departs radically

from any Beaux Arts concept of distribution, re-emerges as a tour de force in the free-flowing *plans inclinés* of Le Corbusier's Palais des Soviets of 1931.

In the Centrosoyus Le Corbusier paid greater attention to the elevations flanking the principal streets at the expense of the other façades which, while they are developed in elevation, are left unconsidered from a three-dimensional or plastic point of view. It seems as if the main street facades were thought of as the only representative fronts worthy of elaboration. That the same mythically "aeronautical" detailing was also proposed for the Centrosoyus, as in, say, the Villa Garches and the SdN project, is borne out by use of *tube d'avion* as an elliptical section for the balustrading of the Centrosoyus (16.156).

**Société des Nations,
Second Project, Parc de l'Ariana
Site, 1929.**
The exact conditions under which Le Corbusier and Pierre Jeanneret came to work on a second project for the SdN in February 1929 remains shrouded in mystery (23.278). The official selection of a new site seems to have provoked Le Corbusier into making one last effort to gain the commission by producing an alternative proposal for the site, which he submitted in April 1929. Although this initiative was ill-received, Le Corbusier used the occasion to lodge a formal complaint, pointing out that their first project had been plagiarized by the academic architects who had been selected to work on the final building: Messrs Nenot, Vago, Lefevbre, and Broggi. Le Corbusier constructed comparative analyses of the individual Beaux Arts schemes submitted by each of these competitors, in order to prove that these men had infringed the budget restrictions of the original competition conditions (23.204, 23.218). This was to be of little avail, however, for the Nenot design was officially approved by the SdN in June 1929.

The main interest of this second proposal resides in the light it throws on Le Corbusier's working method, for here once again, as in the Centrosoyus, he adopted an elementarist approach to recombining the components of his original SdN entry (23.296, 23.278). Taking a similar tack as in their Centrosoyus design, Le Corbusier and Pierre Jeanneret rendered the Secretariat as a loosely connected sequence of *redent* slabs (23.265, 23.269). Against these linear *redent* formations, they placed helicoidal ramp forms taken directly from the Centrosoyus, and these elements were to remain in the final version of the second project, where the Secretariat block is finally resolved as a U-shaped complex (23.201, 23.202, 23.306). The Secretariat court shown at the position A, on drawing 23.202, is thus served by a vehicular access which passes in and out of the court, through bridged entrances, the movement taking the form of a continuous system of one-way circulation (23.272, 23.328, 23.329). Behind this court was situated the forecourt to the Assembly Hall (B on 23.202). The Assembly Hall is virtually identical to that used in the original SdN scheme except for straightening out the *pavillon du président*. In an early sketch for the Ariana site, the Secretariat and the Assembly Hall face each other to form a single *cour d'honneur*. Other variations include the initial integration of the library with the Secretariat (23.275, 23.269). The library was soon to be detached, however, and thereafter located parallel to the Assembly Hall, to the southeast of the existing *allée* (23.278). In this position it was also partially aligned with the Musée de l'Ariana on the opposite side of the *allée*.

The design of this free-standing library form is of particular interest, for it introduces a new type into the Corbusian repertoire (23.306). Organized about a top-lit book stack and foyer, an elongated version of this plan was subsequently adopted for the library in the Cité mondiale, designed in the same year for the philanthropist Paul Otlet, on a site situated to the northwest of the Ariana Park. As far as detailed expression is concerned, provisional sketches indicate that the main façade of the library would have been based on the entry elevation to the Villa Garches (23.306).

The Parc de L'Ariana site was situated inland to the west of the Geneva-Lausanne road. Thus, where the layout of the first project had been determined largely by the configuration of a lakeside site, the second was predicated upon the notion of running a main axis parallel to an existing line of trees, entitled in the proposal the *avenue de la bibliothèque* (23.202). Thereafter, as in the first SdN proposal, the *parti* came to be structured about a series of layered planes cutting up the lateral space between the front elevation of the Assembly Hall and the rear of the Secretariat complex (23.329).

Palace of the Soviets Competition, Moscow, 1931.

After the abortive Palace of Labor competition staged in 1923, the competition for the Palace of the Soviets started in earnest with two interrelated contests: the first, an international trial run, staged in June 1931 and limited to invited participants—a competition in which the foreign architects included Le Corbusier, Perret, Gropius, Mendelsohn, Poelzig, Brazini, Lamb, and Urban—and second, an open international competition which was publicly announced on July 18, 1931, with a closing date set for October 30. This second competition, which was, in fact, extended for an extra month, generated 160 entries, of which 24 were by foreign architects. It is characteristic of the context and the revolutionary spirit of the time that 112 additional proposals were also received from non-professionals.

The Palace Construction Council, chaired by no less a figure than V.M. Molotov himself, selected a number of individual Soviet architects and architectural teams to "work out a plan for the Palace in order to define what further designing was required and to make the competition requirements more precise." Individual entries were duly received from such distinguished members of the Soviet avant-garde as Konstantin Melnikov, N.

Ladowsky, and Moisei Ginzburg (who submitted a scheme in collaboration with G. Hassenpflug), while group submissions were made by most of the established Russian architectural factions, such as ASNOVA, ARU, SASS, and the recently formed political groups such as VOPRA.

None of these entries, however, irrespective of whether they were Russian or foreign, finally met the hypersensitive standards of the Palace Construction Council, on whose board sat such Party luminaries as Kaganovich and Marshall Voroshilov, the then Commissar for Defense. As far as the Bolshevik establishment was concerned, almost all the entries could be faulted for either excessive formalism or excessive functionalism. Alternatively they were simply deemed as lacking in sufficiently accessible references of a suitably socialist and historical character. Thus the evidently divided Palace Construction Council rebuked the ARU entry for exceeding the site boundary, with the following rather naive but nonetheless caustic commentary: ". . . if it was the comrades' intention to point out the inadequacy of the proposed site, there was no need to design a whole project at all."

These and other such damning judgments were handed down as part of the Resolution of the Palace Construction Council, which, issued on February 28, 1932, announced three premiated awards, one to an unknown American, Hector Hamilton, and two others, which were the invited schemes submitted by Ivan Zholtovsky and Boris Iofan. The initially commissioned foreign architects were all unplaced, although some received special mentions. Likewise, the representatives of the Soviet architectural avant-garde largely failed to win the approval of the Council. Not even the premiated designs of Hamilton and Iofan escaped stricture, with the result that a veil of critical censorship was drawn over the entire affair. In retrospect this may be regarded as anticipating the Central Committee Resolution of April 23, 1932, which called upon all the arts to support Soviet power and in so doing paved the way for the

universal adoption of the so-called socialist realist style some five years later.

Like many of the competitors, Le Corbusier was quick to realize that the program for the Palace of the Soviets was of megastructural proportions. It was this which he had in mind when he wrote retrospectively in *Prélude* in March 1932:

Bolshevism means everything at its biggest. The biggest proposition. The biggest undertaking. The maximum. Going to the root of the question. Seeing the question through to the end. Envisioning the whole. Breadth.[9]

The scope of the initial program required no less than two separate large auditoria—the one seating 15,000, the other seating 6,500—plus four separate smaller auditoria arranged in pairs, the first pair accommodating 500 and the second 200 people. The two larger halls were to have been served by a large amount of ancillary accommodation. The whole brief divided operationally into three groups whose specific accommodation broke down as follows: Group A, comprising a 16,500-seat auditorium together with a restaurant, stage ancillaries, and a certain amount of bureaucratic space given over to diplomats, press, etc. (27.593, 27.477); Group B, consisting of a 6,500-seat hall with a similar range of ancillaries, plus an exhibition hall, two large reading rooms, each with a capacity of 200, and a library capable of holding 500,000 volumes (27.722, 27.490); Group C, consisting of the twin 500- and 200-seat halls plus additional restaurant space, etc. (27.676). The total area proposed for this entire accommodation was 38,810 square meters.[10]

This program made it clear that the whole palace should be capable, when used to its capacity, of accommodating the mass pageantry of the Soviet State; that is to say, it should form a fitting setting for a whole series of events ranging from spontaneous public manifestations to the circus-like performances of V. Meyerhold's "bio-mechanical stage," or it should be able to accommodate such tattoo-like spectacles as Nikolai Evreinov's "theatricalization of everyday life!" Le Corbusier was obviously very aware of these demands when he described his project in the following terms:

The program called for an immense complex of halls, offices, libraries, restaurants, etc; massive productions with a stage capable of accommodating 1,500 actors and a considerable amount of scenery. The annexes of such a hall are quite extensive; first, the cloakrooms (it snows in Moscow!) and the vestibules, all sorts of lounges and restaurants. These last named elements were called "The Forum" by the authors; a very exact network of circulation permitting the various categories of spectators access to their respective locations; ambassadors, foreign press, Soviet press. Extensive accommodation for actors.

In addition there had to be a way for parades coming from the outside to cross stage and then to go out after making an appearance.[11]

That large-scale manifestations were given the utmost priority in the design of Le Corbusier's Palais des Soviets is borne out by the elaborate system of "mass circulation" (27.272), and by the visionary May Day perspective rendering, included as part of the final presentation (27.249).

Le Corbusier's *parti* took the strategy of the "continuously inclined plane," implicit in the extensive foyers and ramps of the Centrosoyus, to its ultimate conclusion, the primary aim being to facilitate uninterrupted mass movement in three different areas: on the ground-level concourse between the two large halls and their ancillaries, on the elevated open-air agora with its capacity for accommodating mass demonstrations of up to 50,000 people, and in the partially elevated *plans inclinés* or foyers of the large auditoria, rising upwards over basement parking to terminate in switch-back ramps giving access to the auditoria *parterres* above. At only one point in this whole complex, namely, at the entrance to the 6,500-seat Salle B, were the pedestrians permitted to approach a building, at grade level, under normal conditions. Thereafter the "warped" foyer ascended

toward a datum, which was about a story's height below the lowest level of the raked 6,500-seat auditorium. From this threshold, ramps doubled back into the vomitories above. Two mezzanine restaurants were to have been suspended between these large *plans inclinés*, one for public (+ 15.00) and one for delegates (+ 19.00). Access to these restaurants was to be via the same switch-back ramps mentioned above, which were rhetorically expressed as glazed "tubes" on the exterior flanks of the small hall (Figure 16 and 27.242). Beneath an interior perspective showing this circulation system Le Corbusier wrote:

. . . veritable "classification machines"; the various classes of visitors, while mutually seeing each other, follow these precise routes which lead them automatically to their destination. (The routes, inclined planes, constitute a kind of routes de montagnes.)[12]

A similar switch-back system was developed for the 16,500-seat hall, otherwise known as Salle A, where pedestrians entered from the center of the site through a complex filter of coat-checking counters (27.251). Alternatively, they could gain direct access from the basement (which provided for automobile circulation and storage) via various elevator/stair cores, arranged around the perimeter of the large hall (27.272, 27.243). Once again, Le Corbusier developed the notion of the building as a "classificatory device," only now, as in the Meyer/Wittwer design for the Société des Nations of 1927, the process of classification was to be largely effected through the combined interaction of automobile movement and restricted elevator access. The archive is replete with sketches examining different ways for combining vehicular flow with the isolation of various classes of users (Figures 17 and 18 and 27.839 and 27.787). Again, a mezzanine restaurant for delegates plus a kitchen, etc. was to be inserted between *les deux plans inclinés* of the foyer and the raked shell of the auditorium. The effort expended in trying to resolve all this complex movement through a series of sloping floor planes and coordinated ramp landings, together with the provision of food service to the suspended restaurants, is shown in a sequence of study sketches—including Figure 19 (dated November 24, 1931), and drawings 27.233, 27.784, and 27.791.

One of the most ingenious parts of the whole composition is the heterogeneous mixture of accommodation which would have literally encased the stage, fly-tower, and scenery dock of the 6,500-seat auditorium. This galleried complex was integrated with the 500- and 200-seat twin auditoria which made up the bulk of the Group C accommodation. Level by level, this ancillary accommodation of the 6,500-seat hall seems to have been organized as follows. The lower level (+ 19.00) would have accommodated the stage, the scenery dock, changing rooms, and the grade-level library entrance and elevator/stair core, all of which had direct corridor access to the twin auditoria to the rear. The next two levels (+ 23.00 and + 27.00) were largely devoted to the library, the card catalogue, a collection of various reading rooms, offices, and a small lecture space. The subsequent floor (+ 31.00) was given over entirely to exhibition purposes. It was also the point at which an elevated two-story slab of offices projected out from the auditorium "bustle" to link the fly-tower to the acoustical shell behind the open-air tribune (27.249). The remaining floors, asymetrically added to the mass, were devoted to further reading rooms and book stacks.

This archive material testifies to the effort expended in designing this extraordinary machine, above all, the tremendous energy involved in attempting to manipulate *les plans inclinés* so as to coincide with the level of the suspended restaurants and the vomitories to the elevated auditoria. The 6,500-seat hall clearly presented as many difficulties in this respect as the larger volume, even if its actual section was derived directly from the auditorium of the Centrosoyus. Among the numerous study sketches devoted to

resolving the multiple systems of access to this particular hall, sheets numbered 27.603, 27.879, 27.401 (Figure 17), 27.557, and 27.493 give an indication of the range of difficulties encountered.

The other critical problem was the invention of a structural system which would be appropriate to both the colossal mass and the irregular roof sections of the larger auditoria. As late as November 1, Le Corbusier remained uncertain as to how to render the roof structure of these outsized volumes. This section (27.583) also reveals that he had yet to arrive at the absolutely spinal organization of the composition: witness the eight variations published in *L'Architecture Vivante* (Fall and Winter 1932), p. 30, entitled *les diverses étapes du project*, of which the last is dated 22 November.

The unstructured elevation of the largest auditorium, as seen from the elevated podium/plaza, already shows the compositional problems imposed by such a large mass (Figure 20) and at the same time indicates the possibility of using an exposed suspension structure as a way of breaking down its scale. To engage in structural expressionism, at such a colossal scale, was, of course, to break decisively with the *classical* principle of integrating the structure with the auditorium roof, which was indeed the policy adhered to in the SdN entry and the Centrosoyus. The intent here, however, as evidenced in the earliest sketches (27.497, 27.381), was to create an enormous sky-sign construction capable of playing a role comparable to that assumed by the Eiffel Tower in Paris (see left-hand sketches on Figure 21).

The hyperbolic arch solution finally adopted also relates to Le Corbusier's Purist habit of transposing a plan configuration into a section and vice versa, so that the arch trajectory reflects almost directly the hyperbolic plan of the auditorium. We have to assume that the decision to use such a rhetorical structure—namely, the cable suspension of eight radial steel girders from a parabolic concrete arch, together with the secondary cable suspension of an auditorium shell from the girders themselves—was, at least in part, motivated by designing for a "constructivist" culture. One senses that after the international debacle over the monumentality of his Cité mondiale, Le Corbusier was determined to prove himself to be more constructivist than the constructivists themselves. On the other hand, as the partially oblique elevation of this structure would indicate (27.245), the arch was also intended to function as a surrogate "dome" and as such to respond both formally and symbolically, not only to the other subordinate dome or crown-like element of the small hall, but above all, to the towers and spires of the Kremlin (27.247). The monumental iconic power of this invention has been confirmed by history; it has been appropriated by other designers since, above all by Adalberto Libera in his project for a gateway-arch to the entrance of the EUR' 42 site in Rome and in Eero Saarinen's final realization of the idea in the Gateway to the West, erected at St. Louis in 1967.

An appropriate system of structural suspension for the smaller hall was no less easy to devise, as the drawings 27.582 (Figure 22), 27.596, 27.849, and 27.870 readily display. Once again the initial impulse was to adopt a steel framing system similar to that used in the SdN Assembly Hall, complete with roller joints which take their bearing from pylons located to either side of the proscenium arch (27.418). As it is, this structure was never fully worked out, no provision being made for the flytower structure to receive the load of the six radial girders spanning the depth of the hall.

As one would expect, great effort was also invested in evolving the most effective acoustical shells for each of the auditoria, as is shown by the profile developed for the 6,500-seat hall by Gustave Lyon on November 17 (Figure 23), and by all the subsequent efforts at refining and integrating this profile with the exterior mass of the hall and its

suspended roof system (see drawings 27.382, 27.380, 27.379, 27.285, and 27.286). Equal care was expended on the 16,500-seat hall, which naturally posed greater problems from the point of view of acoustics. The more or less insuperable problem of projecting the human voice in a volume which was over 100 meters deep was met in this way:

The voice of the actors and the figures on the stage is separated from the audience by an 11-meter-wide 'abîme' (note the Wagnerian term). All the sound from the stage is collected at a height of 30 meters by a microphone (above the stage) which then relays the sound to a loudspeaker situated at a mathematically determined position in front of the stage. This source projects the sound waves on the acoustical shell of the ceiling, which distributes the sound evenly throughout the auditorium (with a loss of no more than 10% in the last row).[13]

It is interesting to note that the difficulty of arriving at an appropriate solution for the hall of such unprecedented dimensions caused Gustave Lyon to collaborate with two scientific specialists, namely, a certain Morin of the Ecole polytechnique and a Dr. Marty from the Ecole normale (see drawing 27.239 for the details of the acoustical system adopted).

As in the SdN and the Centrosoyus, Le Corbusier employed the elementarist method of French rational classical composition in resolving the final mass and axial order of the Palais des Soviets. This accounts for the eight variant layouts, ostensibly arrived at between October 6 and November 22, 1931, and for other variations shown on some of the sheets in the archive (Figure 24, 27.937). (The above dates, incidentally, raise an unsolved historical problem—given that Le Corbusier worked for three months on the second competition, the nature of his first submission at the end of June remains a mystery.) These variations often implied not only different modes of urban composition, but also different approaches to the problem of site access; thus the variation shown on Figure 24 quite clearly presupposes that the bulk of the mass movement would come from the banks of the Moscow River. An equally elemental approach was also taken toward the integration of the so-called Group C with the stage, fly-tower, and ancillary accommodation located to the rear of the small auditorium (see drawings 27.341-27.343, etc.).

Needless to say, as in their Société des Nations and Centrosoyus, Le Corbusier and Pierre Jeanneret attempted to equip their Palais des Soviets project with an overall plenum air-conditioning system which was intended to distribute the conditioned air in the continuous interspace separating the outer and inner membranes of the major auditoria. This, their so called *respiration exacte*, was never made successfully operative either in the Centrosoyus or in the Armeé du Salut headquarters, built in Paris in 1933, although whether this failure was due to fundamental misconceptions or to the backwardness of technology at the time has yet to be established. In any event, it is another example of the biological myth which was to be integral to Le Corbusier's conception of the machine: the idea of a transcendent technology whose most refined application would manifest itself in organic form. A comparable organization is also implicit in the double-layered (concrete and plaster) shell roofs to the respective auditoria and in the warped planes that permeate the entire body of the building. This much is also hinted at in the concept of the circulation itself, where the apparent "absence" of the mass user is compensated for by the various ramps which announce its future presence. This seems to be linked to the metaphorical significance which Le Corbusier ascribes to the concept of a *régime fluvial* where the mass is conceived as flowing in much the same way as water up and down the 10-meter-wide ramps serving the public podium.

Although many factors undoubtedly contributed

to Le Corbusier's growing disillusion with the manifest destiny of the machine age, none could have had such an impact on his morale as the total rejection of his Palace of the Soviets at the hands of the Russian authorities. This refusal, comparable to the rebuff he had suffered in the SdN competition, was all the more bitter, given the encourgement he had just received from the Soviet State, through the commissioning of the Centrosoyuz, the largest structure he was to build until the completion of the *Unité d'Habitation* at Marseille in 1952. As a man committed to the idea of progress and to a broadly conceived notion of the Enlightenment, he simply could not comprehend the Soviet decision. Whether he was a bourgeois architect or not seemed to him to be an irrelevant issue. What was at stake, as far as he was concerned, as the letter that he sent to Anatole Lunacharsky on May 13, 1932, makes clear, was whether or not the Soviets would continue to advance under the symbolic sign of a rising machinist culture.

The Russian dismissal of the work as inappropriately industrial seems to be insensitive when one observes the delicacy with which the project was finally rendered. Once again, as in this Société des Nations design, he was to treat the continuous glazing and the stone veneer (in this instance, Caucasian tuffa 45 centimeters thick) as though they were generically the same material. Thus the "machinism" of the exposed suspension construction was deliberately mediated by the classical symmetry of the overall composition, by numerous peristylar episodes, effected by the *piloti* and by the equally classical syntax of the skin revetment, be it stone or glass, that is to say, by the general horizontal coursing capped by string courses, etc. And while the relation of the complex to the existing urban fabric of Moscow is possibly the most questionable aspect of the scheme, when looked at in retrospect, the palace, despite its evident constructivism, was also patently hierarchic and monumental, cradling within its body "a space of public appearance" which was hardly less classical and political in its overall appointment than the Athenian agora.

NOTES

1. See *Aujourd'hui, art et architecture* 51 (November 1965):110. Special number dedicated to Le Corbusier. Cited in a reportage by Jacqueline Vauthier-Jeanneret and Christian Hunziker.

   Such a dualistic formulation is typical of Le Corbusier, and the whole of his life and work is shot through with this Manichean vision which almost certainly derives, in the last analysis, from his Cathare background. The imagery of the Dioscuri is patently dualistic, for in numerous versions of the Greek myth the twin "brothers" are opposite and complementary. As the offspring of Zeus, Pollux is immortal, while the other, Castor, was originally destined to age and die. The former is associated with the sun, the latter with the moon. They were often represented in ancient Greece as cavaliers, the former being pugilistic, the latter being a horse trainer. As P.V. Turner points out in his thesis *The Education of Le Corbusier* (New York: Garland Publishing, 1977), C.E. Jeanneret would have first become familiar with Greek mythology at the age of sixteen when he was given Maxime Collignon's *Mythologie figurée de la Grèce* (1912). While this work mentions the Dioscuri, it does not comment at length on their attributes. However, it does mention that they were often depicted as two men standing side by side and leading their respective charges by their bridles.

   An account of C.E. Jeanneret's adoption of his pseudonym in October 1920 is given by Amadée Ozenfant in his *Mémoires 1886–1962* (Paris: Seghers, 1968), wherein he informs us that Jeanneret's cousin had been named Lecorbésier, which was then modified to Le Corbusier. As for the crow metaphor, this appears to have been derived from the figure known in the middle ages as *Corbusier*, who was assigned by the church to kill crows that happened to perch on the spires of churches, thereby preventing them from befouling the cross. The fact that the *corbeau*, or the raven, is the alchemical symbol of change from material to spiritual, from black to white, etc., only returns us to the dualism in which Le Corbusier shrouded his persona. I am indebted to Beatriz Colomina for her help with this material.

2. Le Corbusier, *Une Maison—un palais* (Paris: Crès, 1928), pp. 96–97.

3. Le Corbusier, *Une Maison—un palais*, p. 68.

4. Le Corbusier, *Une Maison—un palais*, p. 78. The mechanized nature of the facade to the SdN is alluded to on p. 103, in a text which reads: "La 'passerelle-bicyclette' de netoyage des fenetres (ossature de beton, fenetres coulissantes, caisson exterieur des volets roulants) est une situation technique pure. Elle apporte une solution esthetique pure."

5. Le Corbusier, *Une Maison—un palais*, p. 103.

6. See Colin Rowe and Robert Slutzky, "Transparency: Literal and Phenomenal," *Perspecta* 8 (1963): 45–54.

7. J.L. Cohen, "Cette Mystique: l'URSS," *Architecture, Mouvement et Continuité* 49 (September 1979): 75. A slightly different and expanded version of the same article was published in English; see *Oppositions* 23 (Winter 1981):88.

8. Le Corbusier, *Précisions sur l'état présent de l'architecture et de l'urbanisme* (Paris: Crès, 1930), pp. 46, 48.

9. Le Corbusier, "Bolche ou la notion du grand," *Prélude* (March 1932); later in *La Ville radieuse* (Paris: Editions de l'Architecture d'Aujourd'hui, 1935), p. 182.

10. See *L'Architecture Vivante* (Autumn/Winter 1932):2–14, 17–30.

11. Le Corbusier, *L'Oeuvre complète 1929–34*, 5th ed. (Zurich: Les Editions d'Architecture, 1952), pp. 123–124.

12. *L'Architecture Vivante* (Autumn/Winter 1932):26.

13. See *L'Architecture Vivante* (Autumn/Winter 1932):10.

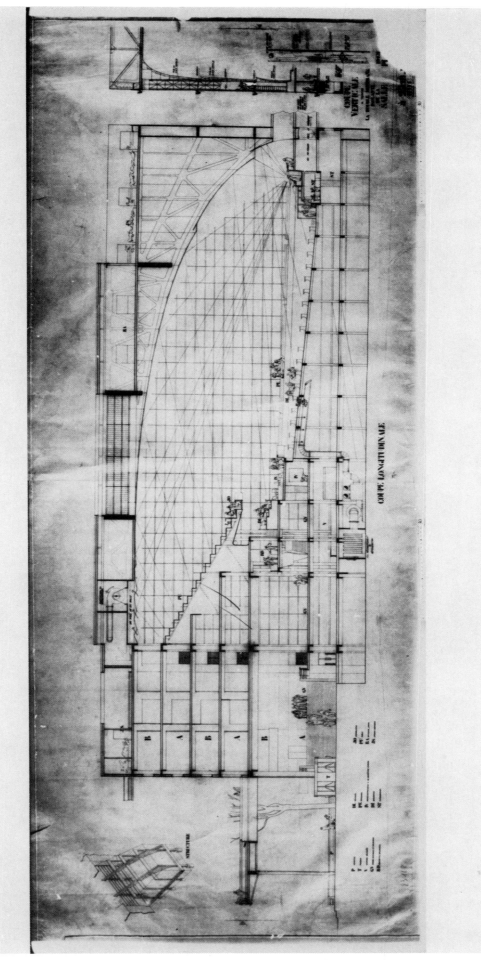

Figure 1. Palais de la Societe des Nations, Geneva, Switzerland (1927). Cross-section of great hall (Fondation Le Corbusier #23.168).

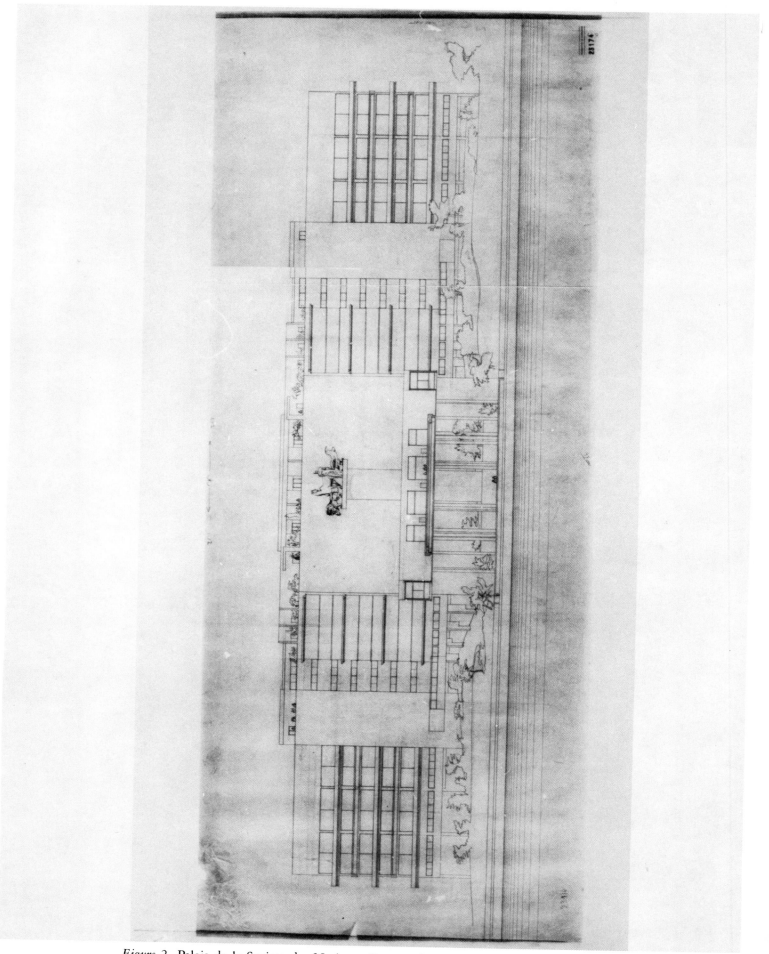

Figure 2. Palais de la Societe des Nations, Geneva, Switzerland (1927). Elevation, principle facade; outlines; equestrian statue (Fondation Le Corbusier #23.174).

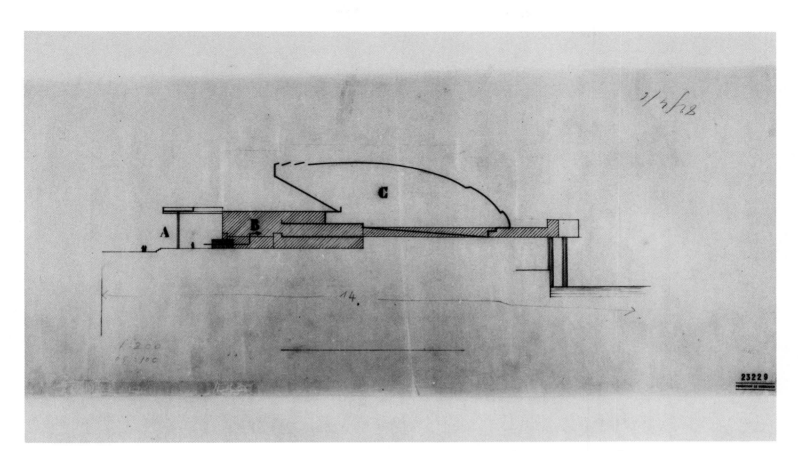

Figure 3. Palais de la Societe des Nations, Geneva, Switzerland (1927). Section of a room and auditorium with outline (Fondation Le Corbusier #23.229).

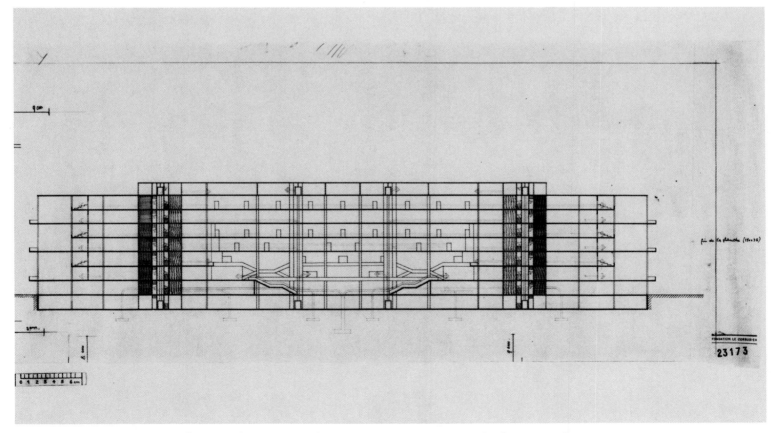

Figure 4. Palais de la Societe des Nations, Geneva, Switzerland (1927). Elevation/section (Fondation Le Corbusier #23.173).

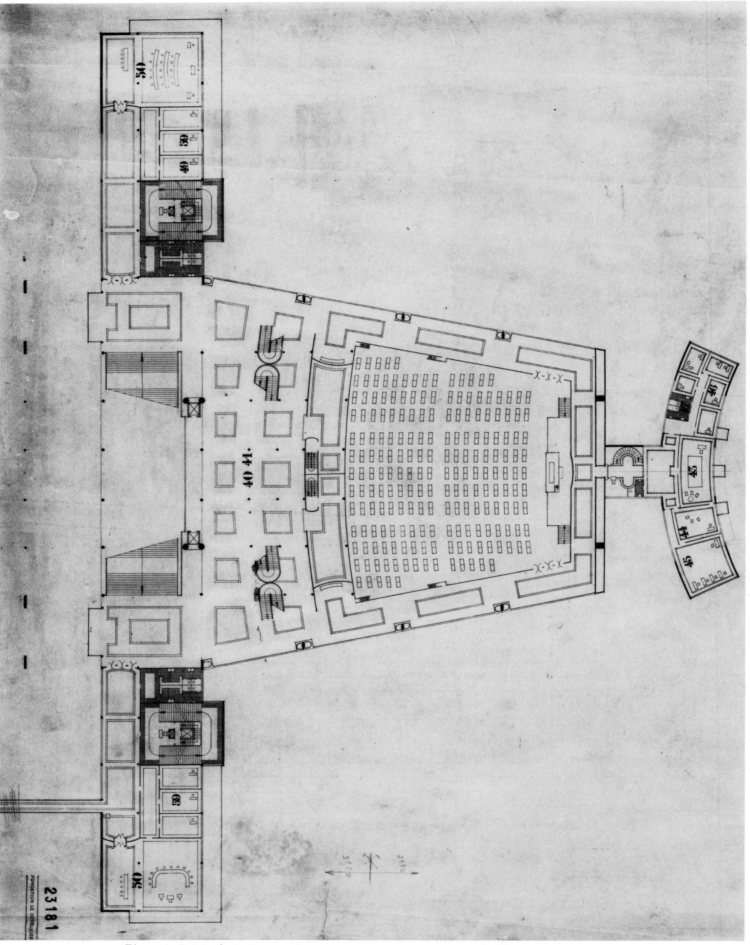

Figure 5. Palais de la Societe des Nations, Geneva, Switzerland (1927). Main room, ground floor (Fondation Le Corbusier #23.181).

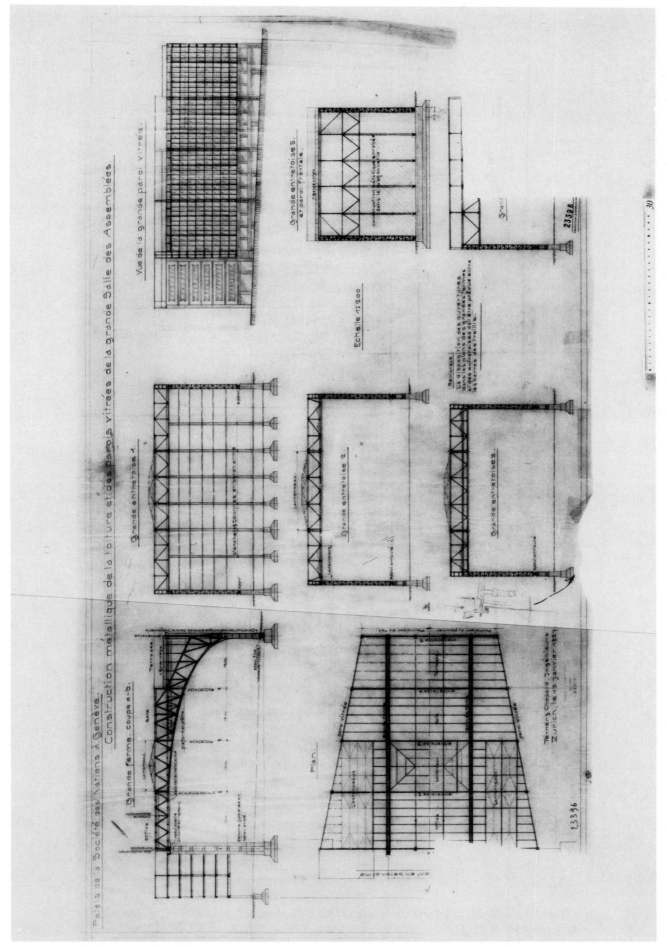

Figure 6. Palais de la Societe des Nations, Geneva, Switzerland (1927). All-metal construction of the roof and glass walls of the great hall of assemblies (Fondation

75

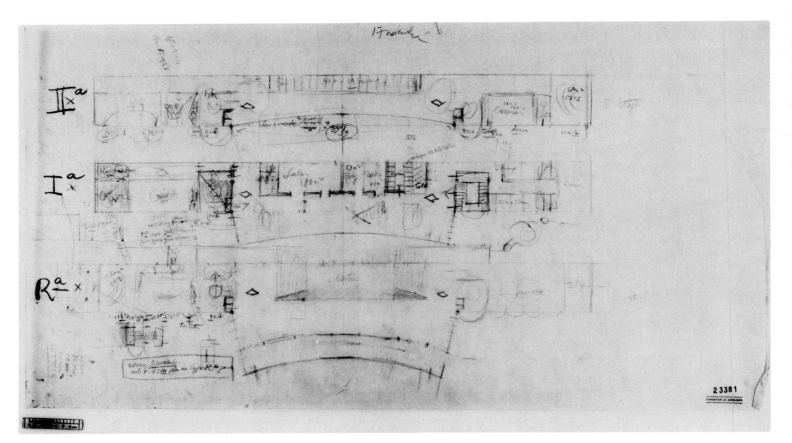

Figure 7. Palais de la Societe des Nations, Geneva, Switzerland (1927) (Fondation Le Corbusier #23.381).

Figure 8. Palais de la Societe des Nations, Geneva, Switzerland (1927) (Fondation Le Corbusier #23.227).

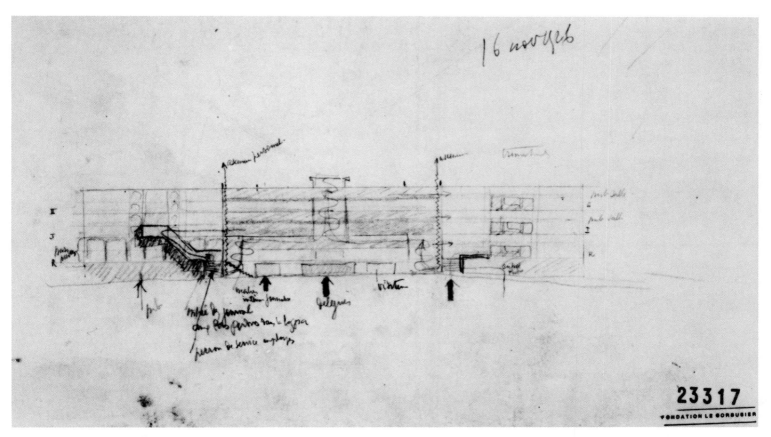

Figure 9. Palais de la Societe des Nations, Geneva, Switzerland (1927). Cross-section of the facade (Fondation Le Corbusier #23.317).

Figure 10. Palais de la Societe des Nations, Geneva, Switzerland (1927). Facade (Fondation Le Corbusier #23.246).

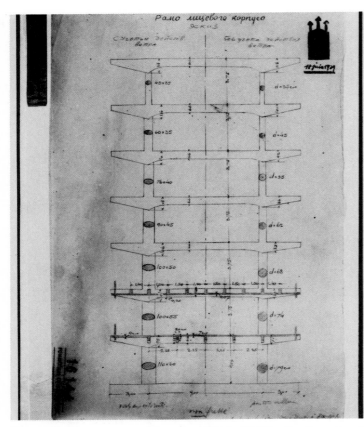

Figure 11. Centrosoyus, Moscow, USSR (1927). Outline sketch of the skeleton of the facade (title in Russian) and schematic section of the skeleton of the building (Fondation Le Corbusier #16.144).

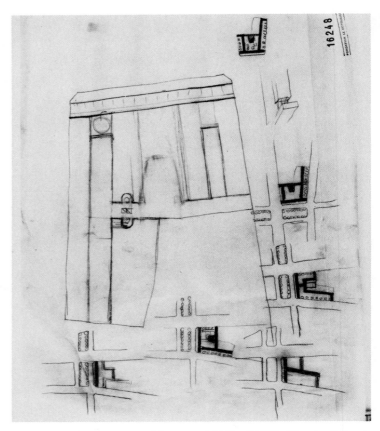

Figure 12. Centrosoyus, Moscow, USSR (1927). The building's foundations (Fondation Le Corbusier #16.248).

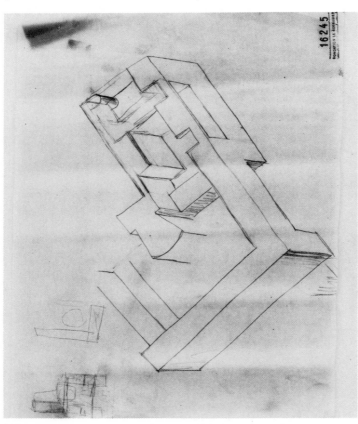

Figure 13. Centrosoyus, Moscow, USSR (1927). Axonometric projection of the building (Fondation Le Corbusier #16.245).

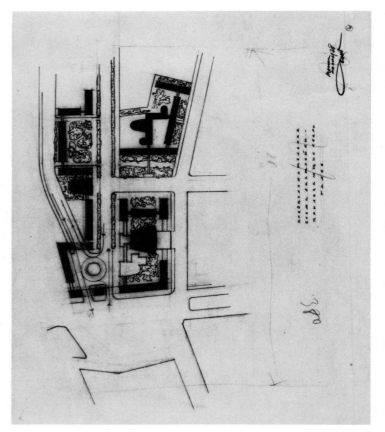

Figure 14. Centrosoyus, Moscow, USSR (1927). Plan of building's foundations (Fondation Le Corbusier #16.111).

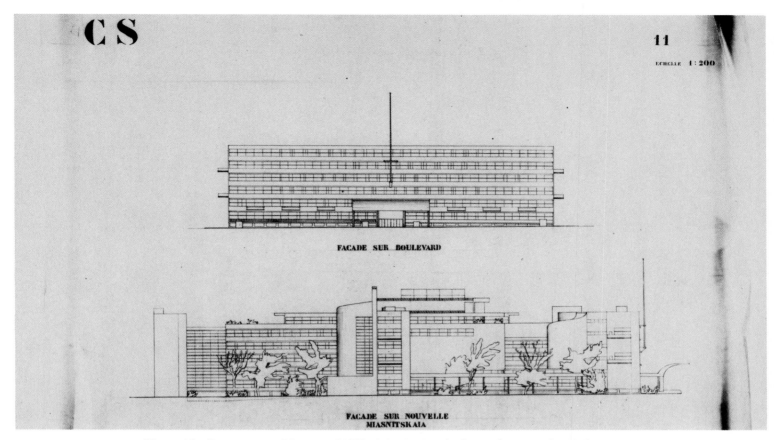

Figure 15. Centrosoyus, Moscow, USSR (1927). Facade facing boulevard and facade on Nouvelle Miasnitskaia (Fondation Le Corbusier #15.685).

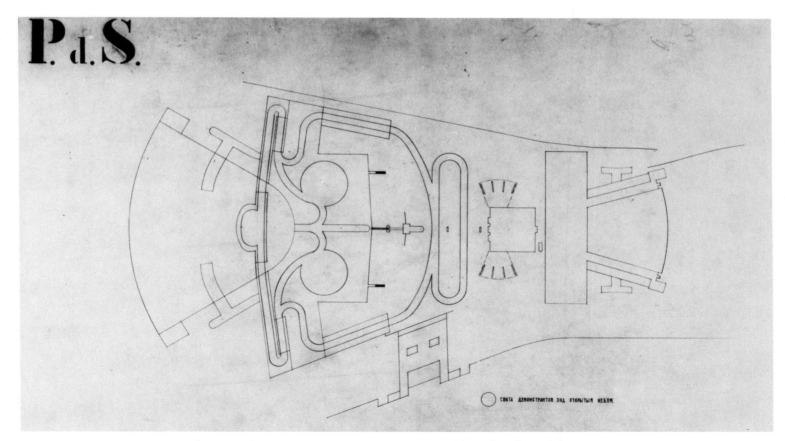

Figure 16. Palais des Soviets, Moscow, USSR (1930). Plan of entire palace (Fondation Le Corbusier #27.266).

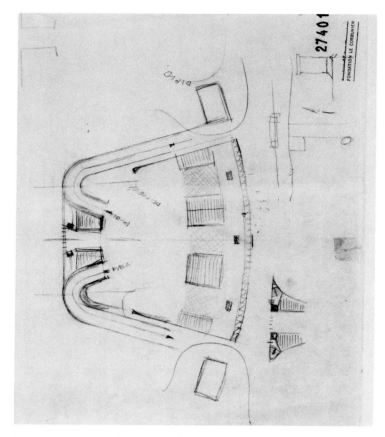

Figure 17. Palais des Soviets, Moscow, USSR (1930). Plan of the approach with captions (Fondation Le Corbusier #27.401).

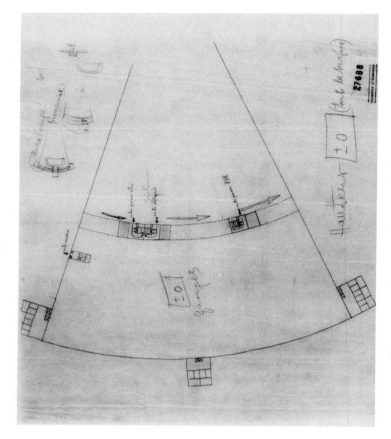

Figure 18. Palais des Soviets, Moscow, USSR (1930). Plan of one level (Fondation Le Corbusier #27.688).

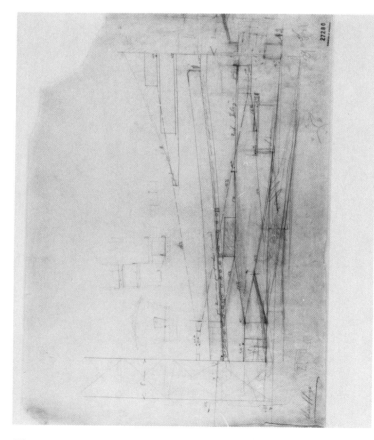

Figure 19. Palais des Soviets, Moscow, USSR (1930) (Fondation Le Corbusier #27.280).

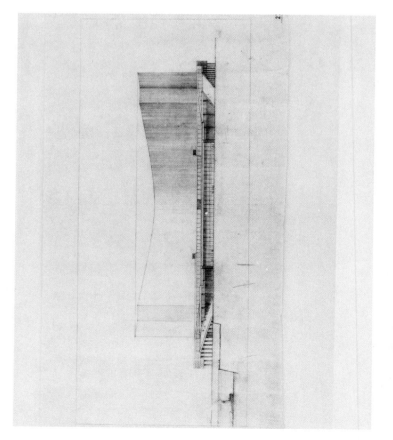

Figure 20. Palais des Soviets, Moscow, USSR (1930). Elevation of facade (Fondation Le Corbusier #27.933).

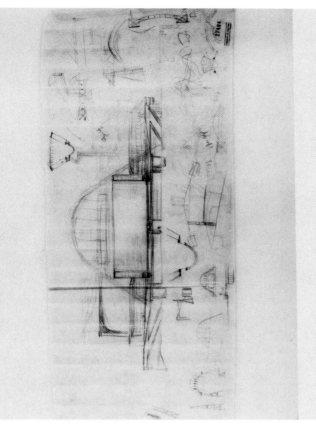

Figure 21. Palais des Soviets, Moscow, USSR (1930). Facade study (Fondation Le Corbusier #27.494).

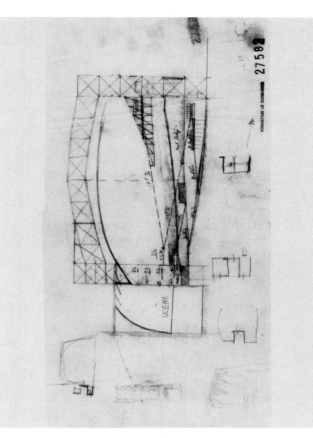

Figure 22. Palais des Soviets, Moscow, USSR (1930). Section of a room (Fondation Le Corbusier #27.582).

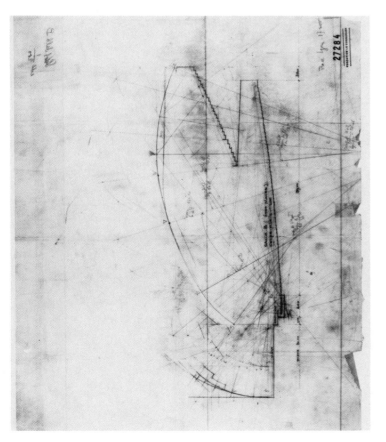

Figure 23. Palais des Soviets, Moscow, USSR (1930). Room B, 6,000 seats (Fondation Le Corbusier #27.284).

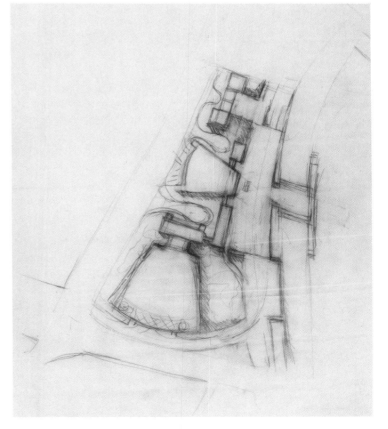

Figure 24. Palais des Soviets, Moscow, USSR (1930). Study sketch of the entire plan (Fondation Le Corbusier #27.560).

Villa Savoye and the Architects' Practice
by Tim Benton

L'Idée architecturale est un phénomène péremptoirement individuel, inalienable. Il est bien de pousser l'idée jusqu'à L'état de pureté.[1]

So extraordinary and almost otherworldly is the Villa Savoye in its appearance that it might seem hard to justify a reading of it that stresses the typical, the classic, or the standard. And yet, in many ways, the Villa Savoye can be shown to have resulted, at least in its general form, from a natural and spontaneous expression of the vocabulary, ideas, and methodology of the work of the previous five years. But it is also essential to stress the uniqueness of the building and its particular moment in the changing attitudes of its architects.

In a lecture on October 11, 1929, in Buenos Aires, Le Corbusier himself drew attention to the place of the Villa Savoye as a culmination of a set of houses extending from the Maison La Roche-Jeanneret in 1923 via the Villas Stein and Baizeau. A drawing, included both in the Buenos Aires lecture and in the first volume of the *Oeuvre complète* (Figure 1),[2] is designed to demonstrate the synthesis achieved in the Villa Savoye:

> The fourth type [the Villa Savoye] has the external purity of form of the second [the Villa Stein]; in the interiors, it combines the advantages and qualities of the first and third [La Roche and Baizeau]. A pure type, very generous, full of resources, too.[3]

In the lecture, he finished with a tour of the house, using two sheets of drawings to illustrate his analysis (Figures 2, 3). He noted:

> The house is a box in the air, pierced all around, without interruption, by a long window. No more hesitations about playing architectural games with space and mass. The box is in the middle of the prairies, dominating the orchard.

> From the interior of the vestibule, a gentle ramp leads up, almost without noticing it, to the first floor where the life of the owner is deployed: reception, bedrooms, etc. Taking their views and light from the regular perimeter of the box, these different rooms adjoin each other radially from a suspended garden which is there like a distributor of light appropriated from the sun. It is onto the suspended garden that the sliding walls of glass of the salon and several other rooms are opened in all freedom; thus the sun enters everywhere, to the very heart of the house.

> From the suspended garden, the ramp becomes external and leads to the roof and the solarium.

> The latter is also linked by three turns of a spiral staircase to the cellar dug into the earth below the *pilotis*. This spiral, pure vertical organ, is inserted freely into the horizontal composition.[4]

He then went on to suggest that the house could be transplanted to Biarritz or even to the Argentinian pampas. A sketch (Figure 3) showed a treelike formation of drives linking 20 standard Villa Savoye houses in the middle of the countryside, without spoiling it:

> The inhabitants, who will have come here because this countryside was beautiful with its country life, will contemplate it, preserved intact, from the height of their suspended garden or from the four sides of the long window. Their domestic life will be inserted into a Virgilian dream.

> I hope that you will not blame me for having deployed before your eyes this example of *taking liberties*. They have been taken because they have been acquired, seized from the living source of the stuff of modern life. Poetry, lyricism, produced by technology.[4]

It is worth extracting this passage in extenso because it not only sets the scene for an understanding of the design but also introduces the subtle balance between the ideal and the practical in Le Corbusier's ideas. Part of the description is specific to the site, but each feature of the house rests on standard solutions, "certainties" acquired in Le Corbusier's 1920s practice, confirmed by the slogans in his writing. To cite only some from *Précisions*:

> Architecture is circulation[5]
> Architecture (more exactly, the house) consists of illuminated floors[6]
> Free plan, free façade[7]
> I compose with light[8]

And, as Figure 3 demonstrates, Le Corbusier saw no irony in treating the Villa Savoye as a prototype standard housing cell.

Compared with the earlier texts of the 1920s, the Buenos Aires lectures employ a relaxed and almost ecstatic vocabulary that betrays a moment of extreme confidence in the development of Le Corbusier's ideas. The repeated stress on freedom, on the body, on nature, on individuality and will, the relative lack of obsessive concern with the details of structure, materials, and cost are remarkable.

Within a month of returning from South America, Le Corbusier was to embark on one of the last of his great houses, the Villa de Mandrot.[9] Here there was to be a dramatic shift in priorities, away from the hermetic purity of the box on stilts, the pure prism, the complete enclosure, the machine materials. Rough stone and plywood facings, an organic embedding in the split-level site, an extrusion of functions, and, above all, a collaboration with a local Italian-born mason, Aimonetti, produced a building that, formally at least, seems to belong to a different world.

In trying to show how the Villa Savoye, at least in the first designs published in the *Oeuvre complète 1910–1929*, emerged naturally from the imagery and dogmas of the 1920s, we will have to distinguish between the accumulated repertoire of forms in the earlier work and the arrival at certain received truths that carried a special status in his ideas. For example,

we might list features like the ramp (already on show in the La Roche house), or the steel spiral staircase and the mushroom-shaped toilet extrusion on the first and second floors (both incorporated in the Stein house), or any number of details such as the fireplaces, the concrete "tablettes," the partition walls incorporating built-in cupboards and wash basins on both sides, and so on. These, if you like, belong to the category "tricks of the trade" and are described as such in his lectures.

But behind these devices lie the more universal discoveries, the flat roof and roof garden, the terrace as an extension of the living area, the ideological association of vehicular circulation with the ground-floor plan, the *pilotis* as an expression not only of modern structure and a Platonic device to lift living away from the soil but also of the revolution in urban life that would follow from lifting whole cities off the plane of commercial and personal transportation. These are emblematic devices carrying "proofs" at several levels at once. For example, the search for a standard window must be read on numerous levels (Figure 4).[10] The *fenêtre en longueur* served first as an expression of concrete structure; just as the medieval masons had a type of window related to stone pier and rib construction, so there were different windows in the Renaissance and the nineteenth century that, when "honest," related to the nature of wall construction. But the *fenêtre en longueur* was also an interior solution, the most efficient way to distribute light. And it was a storage solution; underneath the long windows, whether in a house, or the secretariat of the League of Nations, or the Centrosoyus building, built-in cupboards allowed for storage and concealed distribution channels for services. Finally, it was a technical solution: Le Corbusier and Pierre Jeanneret repeatedly tried to patent their sliding window, in different forms, in France and Switzerland. Furthermore, by 1928, the long window was one of two "façade solutions" (the other being the *pan de verre* for larger buildings). The Villa Savoye showed that it had reached the status of a cliché, that is, a solution imposed on a problem by instinctive choice, overriding minor difficulties. Only this can explain the extension of the long southwest window across the empty first-floor terrace, and we have the evidence of the project of November 26, 1928 (Fondation Le Corbusier [FLC] 19.428), to show that Le Corbusier himself recognized some ironies in its deployment.

There are other features of the project published in *Oeuvre complète 1910–1929* that can be shown to have derived directly from the search for "ideal" solutions. For example, the dimensions 5, 2.5, and 1.25 meters inform the layout of the grid of *pilotis* and several other elements. And these dimensions are typical of the early design stages of other 1920s projects. Second, the functions of living on the first floor have been rigorously "classified," in true Cartesian style: for each façade, a type of activity. To the northwest, with the beautiful view, a full-length salon; to the southwest, a sun-trap terrace; to the southeast, the bedrooms for his son and guests; to the northeast, the services. Third, Le Corbusier pursued his search for an ideal expression of circulation unifying car and man, city and country, more comprehensively than in any other project since the League of Nations drawings. The villa is linked to the Savoye town apartment at 105, rue de Courcelles, by a 30-kilometer car drive, and this link is manifestly expressed in the plan. Furthermore, the scale of the house derives not only from Vitruvian man, but from what one must call the Vitruvian automobile: the ground-floor dimensions match the turning circle of a large car. Car circulation and human circulation meet in the hall. It will be no surprise to find a sketch (Figure 10), discussed below, that makes this identity of ramp and car circulation complete. Finally, we can perceive in the play of forms on the roof more than an expression of functions (solarium, bedroom, and associated rooms). They can also be read autonomously in Purist terms as an expression of the aesthetic certainties of the Phileban solids.

In the completed building, these "type" solutions are less visible or absent (Figures 14, 15). In the later stages of the design, the pressure of practical solutions introduced a more pragmatic

and picturesque sequence of visual sensations which can be referred to the Corbusian notion of the *promenade architecturale*. The development from the Platonic to the phenomenological during the design process is itself characteristic of Le Corbusier's 1920s work.

A tension between the ideal and the pragmatic runs through all Le Corbusier's work and theory. Many of the 1920s houses were designed for relatively hard-up clients with difficult requirements and awkward urban sites that allowed for only one or two visible façades. The struggle to adapt the overarching dogmas of his theory to these problematic circumstances lends much of the interest and some of the content of his work. The Villa Savoye appeared to offer an "ideal" brief: design a perfect house in a perfect site for a perfect, or at least uncomplaining, client. The obvious parallel with the Villa Rotanda of Palladio is supported by an intriguing marginal sketch on a sheet of details datable to December 1928 (Figure 5). In both cases, the "ideal" villa can be defined as a four-façade house on a hill and stands in relation to the other work of both architects in comparable ways. To put it another way, the Villa Savoye was an unconstrained response to the dogmas of the Five Points.[11] The sketches illustrating these in the Buenos Aires lectures provide a schema for the Villa Savoye more naturally than for any other house (Figure 6).

To support this analysis, it is important to recognize that key features of the Villa Savoye design can be shown to have emerged from the early stages of designing another house "with a view," the Villa Baizeau in Tunis. The Baizeau site was a narrow one, a crucial constraint on the whole design. The "natural plan," as Le Corbusier emphasized in *Une Maison—un palais*, was square.[12] But the first two projects for the Villa Baizeau also represented the problem of bringing cars across the front of the façade to offload passengers into the entrance hall before turning into a garage.[13] The sketches for the smaller second scheme even look superficially like the Villa Savoye.[14] This was in March 1928, and on one of the elevation drawings for this second scheme can be seen a selection of perspective sketches that are so strikingly like the Villa Savoye that they must be accounted for (Figures 7, 8).[15] My argument is not that there is any material connection between the two commissions at this stage, since there is no evidence that the architect had even met the Savoyes until six months later. Rather, these sketches represent doodles fantasizing on the potential of the Baizeau scheme released from the constraints of site. The hovering first-floor living area, with its long window and extravagant sculptural extrusion on the roof, are, it seems to me, purely an instinctive extrapolation of the Corbusian language, responding to the cliff-top site and the notion of free circulation at ground level.

Superimposed over part of another drawing for the Baizeau scheme (FLC 8.507), this time datable to around August 30, there is a square plan with garaging for three cars and a bullnosed vestibule (like the Maison Cook) adjoining what must be a ramp (Figure 9).[16] This time, I believe that the Savoye scheme was in his mind, since the dimensions would seem to be consistent.

Two sheets of sketchbook that appear to have been drawn during the adaptation of the Villa Meyer drawings for the Villa Ocampo (in September 1928) give a more explicit sign of the origins of the Villa Savoye (Figures 10, 11).[17] This time, the association with the Poissy site is much stronger. We see the trees, the domed site, the oblique angle of the boundary wall, the access from the southeast, and, most significant of all, an indication of an orientation on the angle ("S" on the plan), all of which describe the Poissy site precisely.

What makes these drawings almost unique in the 1920s corpus is their vagueness and ambiguity. Le Corbusier is responding here to ideas at a high level of abstraction. They include scribbled outlines indicating little more than an L-shaped or Z-shaped configuration responding to the opposed pull of sun and view.[18] But they also include worked-out plans, section and site plans of a house whose most extraordinary feature is an access drive from the southeast that rises on *pilotis* to first-floor level and

passes an L-shaped *porte-cochère* projecting from the first-floor plan before descending through the plan to ground level to a garage to the left and an exit drive to the right. So abstract and impractical is this idea that it involves running the cars through the corner supports of the building, indicated by two arrows on the plan.

And yet, the first-floor plan includes the essential features of the Villa Savoye today: salon to the northwest, terrace to the southwest, services to the northeast, and some kind of accommodation on the remaining side. The service staircase, as in the developed first project, runs parallel to the ramp. Another plan is more ambiguous about the cars, apparently relying on the fall of the land to allow pedestrian access to the first floor up a short ramp.

My contention, therefore, is that prefiguring ideas for the Villa Savoye can be found among the drawings for other schemes in 1928 and that these ideas emerged from a level of idealist abstraction based on a synthesis of the earlier work.

It is my view that, almost unique among the 1920s houses, the Villa Savoye is a "free" design—an example, indeed, of "taking liberties."[19]

Before looking in any detail at the design history of the house, I would like to make some observations about reading architectural plans as evidence and about my own methodological assumptions. William Curtis, whose book on the Carpenter Center has set standards in the analysis of Corbusian drawings, wrote recently:[20] "Unfortunately, the evidence of Le Corbusier's sketches for the Villa Savoye is incomplete, patchy, and not firmly dated."[21] Having studied several buildings of this period, all with different kinds of lacunae in the evidence, I now feel confident that this is not accurate.[22] True, few of the 316 drawings for the villa and the lodge are dated, but only a handful cannot, I believe, be placed with accuracy (within a few days) into the order of things.

My own procedure has been to divide the drawings into five "projects" for the main villa and one for the lodge (projects A–E and project L), each one subdivided into variants but fixed in relation to specific dated drawings. Thus, project A can be dated to the period leading up to October 10, 1928), project B to November 5–7, 1928, project C to November 7–26, 1928, project D to December 1928–February 1929, project E to February 1929 onward. The dated drawings for the lodge extend from April 27, 1929, to February 24, 1930.[23]

An object lesson in the pitfalls awaiting the historian who assembles drawings according to a plausible "development" toward the finished design can be drawn from a study of a set of pencil numbers added to the corners of the key plans for the building. These arrange an "order" that might seem logical but one that is contradicted by a weight of evidence and that cannot possibly be sustained. The first 25 pencil numbers refer to the drawings of the middle and end of November (project C); the next group are from the first project of October (project A), followed by drawings datable to November 6–7 (project B).

There is no doubt about the main stages of the design and the causes for rejecting or modifying them. During September, the scheme eventually published in the *Oeuvre complète, 1910–1929*[24] was developed through a number of minor variants, to be presented to the client between October 6 and 14, 1928. That this project was taken seriously by the architects is shown by the number of detailed drawings, more even than for the design as built, and by a complete set of tenders and costings that were assembled during late October and early November.[25] Why was this project not built?

Here we must enter into a discussion of the client and of the economics of the enterprise. In many cases of Le Corbusier's domestic architecture, and the still-running saga of the Villa Baizeau was a case in point, the reasons for abandoning one design and starting again can be documented in terms of a straightforward conflict with the client's intention. For the Villa Savoye, we have two versions of the client's brief, a list of requirements by Madame Savoye herself and a sheet of notes of a meeting by Pierre Jeanneret. We also have a list of comments by Madame Savoye on the drawings of the October

scheme.[26] Although there are several points in which Le Corbusier's design does little justice to Madame Savoye's original stipulations, she herself makes no mention of them. Instead, her remarks are mostly concerned with details of electric power points, the separation of the wine cellar from the fruit store, and so on.[27] On one matter that might have been substantive, her request that her bedroom should be oriented to the east, no effect can be seen in the intermediary designs of November, although the December project does indeed shift her bedroom accordingly. But if Madame Savoye was not the cause of the abandonment of the first project, where must we look for an explanation? Fortunately, the answer is straightforward and characteristic in kind of all Le Corbusier's houses.

The tenders for the first project came in at the beginning of November, and on the fifth of November Pierre Jeanneret began to total up the estimates. However he worked it out, and with whatever marginal cuts to individual tenders, the result came out at about 785,060 francs, and that was including a mere guess for the lodge and nothing for architect's fees.[28] That this sum was very much more than the Savoye family had intended to pay for a summer cottage is not a matter of guesswork. When, in December, Pierre Jeanneret wrote with the costings of what he called his third project, he was specific about the cuts that had been effected in response to the client's wishes.[29]

If there is one factor that unites every domestic design by Le Corbusier and Pierre Jeanneret that I have studied, it is that the first projects are always too expensive and always need trimming down. It was the case, for example, with the La Roche house, the Stein house, and the Baizeau house. But the remedy, in each case, was relatively obvious. La Roche lost the ground floor under the gallery, the Steins lost the service wing that had projected on one side, and for the second design for Lucien Baizeau, Le Corbusier simply chopped a bay off the length of the house. The Villa Savoye, however, was a different matter. The first project was not only based on the canonic 5-by-5-meter grid, it was also founded on the dimension of the turning circle of a large car and the space required to bring a gently sloping ramp up through the house without dividing the plan in two. To reduce the area of the Villa Savoye by one bay in each direction, the obvious solution, would have rendered both features of the planned space inoperative. But Le Corbusier and Pierre Jeanneret embarked on a series of designs (Project B) that, while retaining the basis of the first- and second-floor plans, dismantled virtually every other feature of the design that renders it formally recognizable and intellectually unique.[30] The ramp, the U-shaped ground-floor plan with its free-flowing concept of circulation, the *fenêtre en longuer*, the image of the *boîte en l'air*, the whole horizontality and naturalness of the project were sacrificed. What emerged by November 26 was (Project C) an extraordinary play of volumes and spaces, incorporating a brutal juxtaposition of vertical staircase mass (with a *pan de verre* window) and horizontal planes.[31]

This was a short-lived episode in the design. What I have called Project B, including the designs of November 6 and 7 and associated drawings, includes only 14 drawings, exclusively in plan, but it does incorporate calculations of areas from which an estimate of cost can be made (ca. 350,583 francs).[32] The next project went somewhat further. In 37 drawings, for a preliminary idea and two variants, we find sections and elevations as well as plans and another set of calculations of areas that would have given a crude building cost of ca. 464,269 francs.[33] This project was submitted to the client on November 26 in four sheets incorporating plans, elevations, and sections, but there is no record of the client's response to it or of the reasons for abandoning the scheme. It is fair to assume, however, that Le Corbusier had little enthusiasm for this extraordinary departure and that as soon as he and Pierre Jeanneret had thought through the original problem, that of reducing the cost of the first project, the solution quickly presented itself.

Three main ingredients were needed. First, instead of relying on the tender for the first project

by his regular builder Summer (originally 482,000 francs, but reduced by negotiation to 433,000 francs),[34] Le Corbusier turned to a verbal estimate by C. Cormier of 350,000 francs, noted on a page of sums dated November 5, 1928,[35] and proceeded to calculate as follows:

Cormier (1 Project)	350,000	
Suppression top storey	58,000	
	292,000	
Reduction 10% area	29,000	
	263,000	
The rest	150,000	
	413,000	
Lodge	30,000	
(Total)	443,000	
	44,000	(architect's honoraria)
(Grand Total)	487,000[36]	

On the basis of this ad hoc estimation, which turned out to be just over half the actual cost of completing the building, Le Corbusier presented a set of drawings to M. Savoye on December 21.[37]

This was essentially the first project, reduced from a 5-meter grid to 4.75 meters (giving an area of roughly 19.00 by 21.50 instead of 20.00 by 22.50) and with the master bedroom squeezed into the first-floor plan, leaving only a staircase housing and solarium on the top floor.

Two points must be made about this exercise. First, there can be little doubt that Le Corbusier and Pierre Jeanneret practiced a conscious deception on their client as to the actual cost. When the tenders for the new scheme came in, in February 1929, the total presented to M. Savoye amounted to 558,690 francs.[38] In this total, no estimate is included for the entrance gate and driveway (ca. 20,000 francs) or for landscape gardening and planting (ca. 48,000 francs), nor was a proper tender for the lodge obtained (it was not even designed at this stage). At several points where tradesmen had submitted alternative estimates using cheaper materials, these had been adopted, although there can be no doubt that Le Corbusier always intended to use the more expensive versions. For example, Le Corbusier was so adamant about the use of plate glass for his windows that he had risked a major row with the client of the Cook house over this issue. And yet the February costings included ordinary glass and the use of distemper for internal walls and plaster render for the external walls (both changed in the course of execution for the much more expensive use of oil paint and special "jurassite" exterior finish and the use of Cimentol paint).[39] Furthermore, a month after the contracts to builder and tradesmen had been issued, the design was changed quite substantially, in a set of drawings that are sufficiently different to warrant the nomination of Project E.[40] The staircase was rotated and made open all round; there were substantial changes (two sets, in fact) to the apartment for the chauffeur on the ground floor; expensive alterations to the height dimensions of the ground floor involved the addition of 9 centimeters to the height of windows, which had already been manufactured; and repeated alterations to the plumbing and central heating conduits allowed the builder to put in for extras amounting to nearly double the contracted estimate.[41] The result was a building history more than usually fraught with wrangles over cost and depredations to the structure due to post hoc piercing of the brittle partition walls and floor slabs. A similar story can be told of the Villa Stein: again contracts were issued on plans that were not in their final form. We must conclude that Le Corbusier and Pierre Jeanneret had great difficulty completing the design process except under the urgent pressure of building activity in progress. Building work was already under way in April 1929, when the final set of plans was produced, and the production of drawings extended until June, by which time construction had reached the first floor.[42]

What use are we to make of this information? Building houses is a notoriously messy business, and there may well be architects who regularly experience the order of difficulties and stresses that seem to accompany all Le Corbusier's undertakings. But there is no doubt that Le Corbusier had a peculiar horror of the practicalities of building,

although he left all the routine supervision and designing work to Pierre Jeanneret and the assistants. Indeed, in 1934 he felt able to say:

> I must admit that I am not au fait with this [a complaint about the central heating], which was a matter between Mme. Savoye and my associate Pierre Jeanneret. . . . Never having followed this affair, it is difficult for me to offer an exact opinion. . . .[43]

Le Corbusier's direct involvement with clients or tradesmen was restricted to the more forceful begging letters or threats, and his intervention in the design process was as much by scribbled comments and marginal sketches as by full-scale drafting. Again, however, I feel that in the case of the Villa Savoye, the main explanation for this is that, having worked out the main ideas at a very early stage, he had little interest in seeing the design through all of its ramifications. He was involved in the drawings for the abortive November projects and for the first sketches for the December scheme, but the bulk of the elaboration of the final version was by Pierre Jeanneret and the assistants, of whom the most consistent contributor was Albert Frey.[44] In Le Corbusier's dualistic dialectic between ideal and practical, his own impact was invariably formal and generalizing, adding breadth and depth to solutions and contributing the curved, flowing forms to Pierre Jeanneret's more patient elaboration of planning spaces.

But Le Corbusier also worked on dense, detailed drawings in which major decisions were taken and worked through. The sheet FLC 19.583, drawn to a scale of 1:100, embodies the essential features of the first project and is in Le Corbusier's hand. A similar sheet, FLC 19.634, probably by Pierre Jeanneret, must have been drawn shortly after, incorporating some minor modifications and a first-floor plan at a larger scale of 1:50. Although it is possible that Le Corbusier made some preliminary sketches for 19.583 which have been lost, the evidence of other projects would not support it, as he declared: "Now that I have appealed to your *spirit of truth*, I would like to give you architectural students the *hatred of drawings*. Architecture is created in the head."[45]

There are some drawings of the site that may precede this one, and a curiously anomalous group of sections and perspectives that do not correspond exactly to any of the variants for the first project, but I assume that the latter must be explained by simple deviations among the assistants and a failure to read Le Corbusier's dense sketches on FLC 19.583 with sufficient accuracy. This key drawing incorporates a number of minor features that were altered before the definitive set of drawings for the first project was elaborated: square *pilotis*, a *fenêtre en longueur* instead of a full-height window to the hall, a three-quarter-height window to the salon on the terrace side, the characteristic addition of a spiral staircase from the second-floor terrace to the roof, and so forth. None of these changes represents a fundamental shift in the design concept. The 48 drawings of the final version of the first project include several sections, elevations, and plans at a scale of 1:20, mostly intended to provide information for the 14 interior details, elevations, and axonometrics at this scale. The inked presentation plans, sections, and elevations were invariably at a scale of 1:50. It is symbolic of the priorities in the design that the first of the stencil-numbered presentation drawings, FLC 19.412 (LC 1096), should have been for the first-floor plan and that, as in most of his schemes, this should be labeled *rez-de-chaussée*, the real ground floor being labeled *soubassement*.

When we come to the decisive departure from the idea of the first project, around November 5, 1928, my judgment is that the first drawings are also of the first-floor plan. Three drawings (FLC 25.036, 25.043, and 25.039, among the Baizeau drawings) indicate a plan not dissimilar to that of the first project for the Villa Savoye, but on a grid of 3 by 5 meters (17.50 by 15.00) and without the ramp. There follows a set of loosely drawn charcoal drawings of all three plans (FLC 19.659, 19.699, 19.698) in which the disastrous consequences for the ground-floor plan are first encountered and in which

a partial remedy is sought by extending the cantilever to the sides (southwest and northeast) in order to add as much breadth to the salon as possible, so that room can be made for the kitchen and pantry. Another set, dated November 6, 1928, is then worked up from these charcoal sketches (FLC 19.660, 19.645, 19.636) probably by Pierre Jeanneret, followed by the November 7 variant (FLC 19.663, 19.662, 19.714, 19.523, 19.661) in which the cantilever is returned to the northwest and southeast façades. What emerges from studying the development of these sketches is that the residual curvature of the ground-floor plan and the awkward arrangement of arrival and departure of cars become untenable. On the first floor, the plan becomes increasingly clearly divided into three slices, with the central portion given over to the staircase block. It is this theme, that of a dominant staircase mass, that led to the next solution.

A single drawing, FLC 19.700, with four plans on it, builds on the motif of a circular staircase rising through the house, scattering the organs of each floor plan on either side. The explosion of the ground-floor plan is indicated clearly. At this point, the clear articulation into a grid of 5-meter bays loses clarity, and the next scheme abandons the regular grid almost completely.

Project C can be divided into two variants by some minor adjustments, such as the direction of the staircase (clockwise, then counterclockwise), some details of fenestration, and the provision of balconies on the roof of the second-floor rooms. Thirty-seven drawings, including FLC 19.700, were devoted to this scheme. Three points could be made about it. The *pan de verre* facing the staircase block was very much in Le Corbusier's mind, with the League of Nations scheme behind him and the Centrosoyus still in play. Furthermore, the great window, facing southwest, produced a spectacular effect on the almost windowless northeast side, now the façade you would see on arrival by car. Light striking down through the open staircase hall would have brilliantly illuminated the ground-floor hall window facing northeast, in what would otherwise have been a dark, blocklike silhouette. Second, as already mentioned, the presentation of the *pan de verre* on the southwest façade involved the opening out of the window over the terrace, always a rather controversial idea. It was this single factor, as much as the projection of the back wall of the garage onto the plane of the southwest façade, that led Le Corbusier to close off the two "wings" of the first-floor plan on that side. Third, the exploded ground-floor plan allowed Le Corbusier to "classify" the organs of the circulation and service bedrooms with even more clarity than in the first project. The chauffeur's family and the two maids were given separate *existenz-minimum* cells that are so close in design to Maison Minimum or indeed the lodge plans that they could be mistaken for each other (see FLC 20.753).

In all these things we can see Le Corbusier's mind working to gather what he can from the wreckage of his scheme and associate it to his general principles. Above all, the space created for the staircase on the first-floor plan led to the solution that resolved the problem of the first project. If the salon, kitchen, and pantry could be accommodated on the northwest front, why not move the son's and guest bedrooms around and fit in the master bedroom on the southeast, where Madame Savoye had explicitly wanted it? Furthermore, the thematic introduction of a contrast of vertical with horizontal was not lost. Although the December scheme involved the deployment of a service staircase that would have had little formal impact on the interior, being enclosed by a wall, the April emendation revealed the "pure vertical organ" that may have made nonsense of the function of a staircase intended to move servants discreetly from bedroom and ironing room to kitchen but one that adds enormously to the drama of the entrance hall. Another dramatic discovery in December was the "rhetorical" window facing the end of the ramp on the top floor, which survived as a reminder of the placing of the master bedroom in the first project.

The development of the presentation drawings for the December 17 scheme shows every sign of

being rushed through with unseemly haste. It is difficult to be certain which drawings preceded the stencil-numbered set and which were prepared between December 1928 and February 1929, when the tenders for the new project were called in. Few major modifications are involved, apart from a reduction in size of the cellar. It is clear that no real thought was given to the main lines of the design until some time between February 21 and March 9, 1929, when the basement plan FLC 19.436 (LC 2089) was produced in which the staircase has been reoriented to its final direction. But the set of final plans did not emerge until April 12, by which time a second important decision had been taken, to remove the chauffeur's apartment from the ground-floor plan and place it, with that of the gardener, in a double lodge. Other changes differentiate the March drawings from those of April: modifications to Madame Savoye's bathroom, the arrangement of corridors to the son's room and guest room, the placing of the service doors in the setbacks on the southeast side, and so on.

The history of the design of the lodge is intriguing for two reasons. First, it is quite clear that Le Corbusier conceived of the lodge in terms of the plans he had made in 1928 for the Maisons Loucheur, semidetached houses to be dry-assembled using steel structure and zinc-lined walls. The first designs for the lodge postdate the final version of the plans for the main villa of April 12, 1929, and were for a double house, to include both the chauffeur and the gardener.[46] Second, this decision, which would have involved a lodge costing 76,300 francs instead of the 30,000 estimated in February, depended on the decision to remove the chauffeur's apartment from the ground floor of the villa to make room for an additional suite for guests.[47] This guest apartment was actually constructed and had to be adapted back for use by the chauffeur after June with a new wall and additional plumbing, when the lodge proved too expensive.[48] The small single lodge was designed during June, passing through three variants to the final scheme of July 7. The cost is difficult to disentangle from the accounts, but it was around

50,000 francs (including a contract of 32,000 francs for the builder).[49]

The lodge is an emblematic building, forming a visual and conceptual bridge between the forms of the Villa Savoye, with its demonstration *fenêtre en longueur* hovering over *pilotis*, and the mass-housing prototypes that, since the Dom-ino and Citrohan schemes, had included numerous variations of the Maison Minimum.

At this point we must ask what real effects the circuitous design history of the building had on the Villa Savoye as we see it. First, we can point to the forms that must be read in terms of an accretion and transference of meaning. The bellied curve of the master bedroom in the first project becomes an empty shell, a solarium (Figure 12). The window, which originally lit the bedroom, now serves as a rhetorical gesture, the culmination of the *promenade architecturale*. In many of Le Corbusier's designs, master bedrooms have the curving walls and expansive form connoting both luxury and an anthropomorphic reference. But these forms also worked, in the Villa Savoye, at a purely formal level, as a sensuous response to the purity of the prism below. We saw this in the sketches for an unparticularized building (FLC 24.983). It is typical of Le Corbusier that he tried to put this sensual, fleshy feel back into the master bedroom with the elaborate "swimming-pool" bathroom fittings and concrete "chaise longue" posture slab. The long false window screening the terrace on the southwest side is made more paradoxical by the aerofoil shape of the *pilotis* (Figure 13). A similar detail appears in the *pilotis* of the ramp (Figure 15). We have noted the significance of the free-standing spiral staircase (Figure 14). Most of the losses in clarity, the complex variations in grid, the complications of the classification of façades into distinct living functions, the tangle of corridors and toilets on the first floor, have little overriding impact. The basic imagery is almost identical, so much so that plans for the first project are frequently reproduced accompanying the photographs of the completed buildings.[50] And yet much of the impact of the ramp today depends on

the contrast with the open vertical staircase (Figure 15), a juxtaposition only added in the final stages of the design.

Sadly, the painting scheme for the house has not survived in the documents, apart from some mention of burnt umber, grey, and black for some of the concrete fitments and blue for the salon walls.[51] An interesting reference is provided by Celio the painter, who charged extra for repainting the ground-floor external walls "red, then after new instructions green."[52] A sheet showing the painting scheme for the lodge confirmed the use of dark green for the ground-floor walls, dark grey for the sides, and "pale English green, No. 2" for the main wall on the first floor, facing the entrance (Figure 16).[53] Clearly, lodge and villa shared the rooted colors of vegetation, the colors of the prairie and the orchard, and this idea overcame the more usual use of russet or red for the shaded lower portions of Le Corbusier's domestic buildings (for example, those at the Weissenhof-Siedlung). Finishes in the villa generally were upgraded substantially during construction, as has been mentioned. The first project would have used rubber flooring not only for the ramp but for the bedrooms as well, but Madame Savoye insisted on parquet for the latter. Much money was spent on the exotic turquoise mosaic surfacing of the bath and surround for Madame Savoye's in *graiblanc*.[54] The light fittings included a trough with 28 light bulbs (15 watts each) running along the joint between wall and ceiling in the master bedroom, and a glass tube with 40 light bulbs (25 watts) was designed and introduced spanning the salon.[55] Most of these, along with the windows, were replaced in the 1960s, after damage sustained during and after the war. A surprisingly large bill, contested by the client, was submitted by Le Corbusier's favorite landscape gardener.[56]

Le Corbusier was sensitive about the technical quality of his buildings, but the material history of the Villa Savoye is a sorry one. The total cost, not counting various direct payments by the clients that are not recorded in the Le Corbusier archives, was around 815,000 francs, but the story does not end there. Right up until 1937 the house was providing a catalogue of disastrous technical failings. The first of a litany of pathetic letters from Madame Savoye is dated March 24, 1930;[57] the terrace, garage, and cellar were flooded, rain was coming in through the boudoir window, the noise of the rain on the skylight over Madame's bathroom was "infernal and would stop us sleeping," and so on. On April 30, four months after the builder had claimed that his work was substantially finished, work on the plumbing, central heating, and wiring channels was causing severe problems. Cormier included a sketch showing one of the partition walls completely cracked from top to bottom, after the attentions of the electrician. The central heating engineers, by bending their pipes between a *piloti* and the down-pipe in the garage, had pried the latter loose at the top, causing more flooding on the terrace above.[58] The installation of the electric cooking apparatus in June 1930 was held up, causing extra expense, due to the lack of sufficiently powerful wiring.[59] Although Le Corbusier wrote claiming his final account of honoraria on September 6, 1930,[60] repairs and finishing continued throughout the winter, and it is not certain that the house was permanently inhabited before the spring of 1931 (painting was still in progress in July), although in a letter of July 13, 1931, Le Corbusier claimed that the house had been lived in for a year. On December 19, 1931, Cormier reported that there were 4–5 centimeters of water in the cellar after a rainstorm due to the siting of a land drain just by the southeast wall (needed due to the lack of mains drainage for the servants' rooms).[61] In April 1934, water was still penetrating into the cellar, the central heating system was proving inadequate, requiring a more powerful boiler, the walls were producing saltpeter deposits, and humidity was still a problem. On September 7, 1936 Madame wrote again:

> It's raining in the hall, it's raining in the ramp, and the wall of the garage is absolutely soaked. What's more, it's still raining in my bathroom, which floods every time it rains.[62]

Furthermore, the lodge was uninhabitable because of condensation and humidity, and these problems recurred in September 1937. As Madame Savoye tartly remarked: "Nevertheless, there always seems to be someone in your office to send me visitors, if not to reply to my letters."[63] On October 11, 1937 she wrote:

> After numerous demands, you have finally accepted that this house which you built in 1929 is uninhabitable. Your ten-year responsibility is at stake and I have no need to foot the bill. Please render it habitable immediately. I sincerely hope that I will not have to take recourse to legal action.[64]

After agreeing to the measures to be taken, Le Corbusier concluded that correspondence with a letter to M. Savoye:

> Anyway, I would like to convince you confidently that we will do our best to satisfy you and that you must consider us as the *friends of your house*. Furthermore, I would like to remain your friend too; our relations having always been trustworthy. I am and will always remain the friend of my clients.[65]

And on an earlier occasion, on June 28, 1931, with parts of the house still unfinished, he had written to thank Madame for dinner:

> You should place on the table of the hall downstairs a book pompously labeled "Golden Book," and each of your visitors should inscribe their name and address. You'll see how many fine autographs you will collect. This is what La Roche does in Auteuil, and his Golden Book has become a veritable international directory. Having said that, let me thank you once again, yourself and M. Savoye, for all the pleasure and real joy it has given me to find your house so perfectly inhabited. It's not that usual.

One final word. Perhaps the two planters in the entrance hall would gain by being sown with vivacious, abundant, high, unruly plants.[66]

Art, for Le Corbusier, transcends reality.

Notes

Abbreviations used in the Notes for reference to drawings and documents:

FLC: Fondation Le Corbusier rubber stamp numbers, added to the drawings ca. 1973.

LC: The stenciled numbers placed on presentation drawings by the atelier and logged in a "Black Book," usually with a precise date and increasingly, after 1929, with the name of the draftsman.

Doc.: Pencil numbers used to identify the individual sheets of documents in the boxes of archive material at the Fondation Le Corbusier. These numbers may become redundant as a result of a rationalization of the archive.

1. Le Corbusier, *Précisions sur un état présent de l'architecture et de l'urbanisme* (Paris: Vincent, Fréal, 1930; 1960 edition), p. 134.
2. Published in *Précisions*, p. 134.
3. *Précisions*, pp. 135–136.
4. *Précisions*, pp. 136–138.
5. *Précisions*, pp. 136–138.
6. *Précisions*, p. 48.
7. *Précisions*, p. 42.
8. *Précisions*, p. 132.
9. See Bruno Reichlin, "La Ville de Mandrot à le Pradet (Var) 1929–32," in *Le Corbusier: La Ricerca paziente* (Lugano: 1980). One drawing for this project includes a copy of the Villa Savoye on a neighboring site (FLC 22.309).
10. *Précisions*, p. 54ff.
11. Seven points are listed in "The Plan of the Modern House": "free plan, free façade, independent skeleton, long windows or *pans de verre, pilotis*, roof garden, and the interior equipped with *casiers* and stripped of furniture," *Précisions*, p. 123.
12. Le Corbusier, *Une Maison-un palais* (Paris: Crès, 1929), p. 7.
13. Tim Benton, "La Matita del Cliente," *Rassegna* 3 (1980): 17–24. The five main stages of the design of the Villa Baizeau in Tunis are recounted in this article.
14. See FLC 24.985. The dates for the five main stages of the Baizeau design are as follows: Project A—February 16–24,

1928; Project B—March 9; Project C—end of June; Project D—1st variant, August 30; 2nd variant, September 18; Project E—various variants extending from November 1928 to May 1929.
15. FLC 24.983, south elevation, Villa Baizeau, Project B. Of 13 distinguishable marginal sketches on this drawing, only 2 relate specifically to the Baizeau project.
16. At the scale used for the Baizeau plans on this sheet, the square plan would measure ca. 22.5 by 23.25 meters.
17. Five drawings for the Ocampo project were completed on September 18, 1928. Only a few other drawings record this scheme, which was a routine reworking of the Villa Meyer project. Of the three sketchbook pages pasted onto the sheet FLC 31.044 (0.21 by 0.27 each), one is clearly for Ocampo, while the other two deal with the Poissy site.
18. A sheet of drawings matching these can also be found among the archives for the Planeix house (Planeix, doc. 2).
19. See also the introduction to the house in the *Oeuvre complète, 1929–1934* (Zurich: Girsberger, 1957), p. 24.
20. Edward F. Sekler and William Curtis, *Le Corbusier at Work: The Genesis of the Carpenter Center for the Visual Arts*, Cambridge, Mass.: Harvard University Press, 1978.
21. William Curtis, *Modern Architecture since 1900* (New York: Phaidon, 1982), p. 192. See also his Unit for the Open University course A305, History of Architecture and Design 1890–1939 (Unit 17) (1975). My own work on the drawings for the Villa Savoye began in connection with a radiovision program for this course (RV17), which included a fold-out sheet of the main stages of the design. (This sheet was inadvertently included among the Le Corbusier drawings in the Fondation at the numbering stage [FLC 19.479]).
22. Tim Benton, "Le Corbusier's *Propos Architectural*," *Le Corbusier: La Ricerca paziente*, pp. 23–44. I was able to set out the design stages of the Villas La Roche, Stein, Baizeau, and Savoye in the Lugano exhibition, 1980. See also my "Drawings and Clients: Le Corbusier's Atelier Methodology in the 1920s," *AA Files* 3 (1983):
23. Fixed points for dating these projects are given by the stencil numbers on presentation drawings and some dates added to the drawings themselves. For Project A; they are LC 1096–2008 (October 10, 1928) and LC 2011 (October 14). For Project B, five drawings are dated in pencil: FLC 19.635 and 19.636 (November 6, 1928), 19.662, 19.714, 19.661 (November 7, 1928). Project C has a presentation set—LC 2030–2033 (November 26–27, 1928)—as does Project D—LC 2054–2058 (December 17, 1928), LC 2090 (February 9, 1929). Project E includes LC 2089 (February 21, 1929), LC 2104–2105 (April 12, 1929), and onward. Several other drawings fitting into this scheme are dated on the drawings. To group the variants within the

"projects," I have used the documents in the FLC as well as a logical analysis of the progression of ideas. For dated lodge drawings, see notes 46 and 49.

24. *Oeuvre complète, 1910–1929* (Zurich: Girsberger, 1960), pp. 186–188.

25. I count 77 drawings for the variants of Project A, not including the "prefiguring" drawings (such as FLC 8.507, 24.983 and 31.044) or two drawings (FLC 25.044 and 8.522), which may relate to the Savoye scheme. By contrast, the Project E schemes (February 1929 onward) number only 51 drawings, excluding the lodge.

26. FLC doc. 285 (Madame Savoye's two-page brief), FLC doc. 767 (Pierre Jeanneret's note), FLC doc. 762 (Madame Savoye's comments on drawings with LC numbers 1096–1099). None of these are dated.

27. For example, she wanted in the salon "indirect lighting and lamps over the dining table . . . this room should not be strictly rectangular, but include comfortable corners." Other references are to separate lodgings for the gardener and chauffeur (the latter to be housed over the garage) and an approving reference to the kitchen of the Villa Church at Ville d'Avray.

28. FLC docs. 120, 590 (both dated November 5, 1928) and docs. 145, 144, 239. Totals above 785,000 francs reflect errors in addition; those below fail to incorporate some of the subtotals.

29. FLC docs. 596 and 119 (copy), dated December 21, 1928: "We include the blueprints for the third study of your house at Poissy. We have carried out the reductions which we think will allow us to reach the proposed price."

30. Under Project B, I include FLC 25.036, 25.043, 25.039 (first variant); 19.659, 19.699, 19.698 (second variant); 19.660, 19.635, 19.636 (third variant); 19.663, 19.662, 19.714, 19.523, 19.661 (fourth variant).

31. For the starkest contrast, compare the perspectives from the west for Project A (FLC 19.424, LC 2007, October 10, 1928) with that for Project C (FLC 19.702, ca. November 26, 1928).

32. FLC 19.523 (the torn fragment from FLC 19.714) includes calculations comparing Project B with the "other project" (Project A). The latter is costed at 725,000 francs (sic; correct total is 726,750), based on a crude method of multiplying different categories of floor area by different factors. My estimate for Project B duplicates these procedures.

33. In Project C, I include 38 drawings, of which FLC 28.740 and 25.037 have been filed under Baizeau and 20.753 under Maisons Minimum. FLC 19.710 includes the calculations of areas on which my cost estimate is based.

34. FLC docs. 146 (October 26, 1928) and 54 (October 31, 1928).

35. FLC doc. 120.

36. FLC doc. 760 (undated, in Pierre Jeanneret's hand).

37. In Project D, the first variants include FLC 19.709, 19.701, 19.558, 19.560, 19.559, 19.555, 19.557, 19.712, 19.708, 19.561, 19.556, 19.568, 19.711, 19.528. The remaining 67 drawings that correspond closely with the scheme sent to the client on December 21 include the set LC 2054–2058 (dated December 17, 1928) but also a number of drawings that include modifications carried out in the process of supplying details to the tradesmen and builder for their tenders during January and February 1929. At least two of these drawings, LC 2090–2091 (March 9, 1929), overlap with the first drawings for Project E.

38. FLC doc. 593 (February 15, 1929).

39. For example, FLC docs. 757–758 (Cormier's tender of February 7, 1929) specifically offered an alternative exterior treatment *en ciment pierre grésé* that would have involved a supplement of 22,000 francs. Cormier also included alternative estimates for more expensive floor tiles and a cavity wall treatment of the partition wall between master and son's bedrooms. All three were ignored in the calculations of cost by Pierre Jeanneret, but all were rapidly adopted (FLC doc. 678–679, April 18, 1929). Similarly, the painter and glazier Celio offered plate glass as an alternative to cheap glass for the windows at the price of 9,000 francs, and Pierre Jeanneret noted that this sum had been "agreed," although, once again, it was left out of the calculations for submitting to the client (FLC doc. 325–330, February 7, 1929).

40. FLC 19.436, LC 2089 (dated February 21, 1929), indicates a basement plan with the staircase orientation changed. It seems that work on the new scheme was going on during March, but no drawings were sent to the client or builder until the final set, which date from April 12, 1929, onward (e.g., FLC 19.439, LC 2104).

41. Cormier's detailed accounts, including extras, were submitted in five *mémoires* and summarized in a letter of December 29, 1930 (FLC doc. 886–887). Cormier's total bill came to 414,884.60 (compared to the original contract of 276,000 based on the tender of February 7 and the contract of March 5, 1929 [FLC doc. 759]). For the ensuing haggle, see FLC docs. 259–263, 871–878.

42. FLC doc. 713–714 and 680. On April 20, 1929, Cormier was already able to charge 38,925 francs for work on foundations and the cellar. By the time the last details were being drawn (e.g., FLC 19.469, LC 2172, June 19, 1929), Cormier's bills had reached 156,200 francs (FLC doc. 708–711, June 24, 1929) for work on the first and second stories.

43. FLC doc. 307, August 2, 1934.

44. His name appears frequently in the "Black Book," which logged the LC number drawings. In a letter to the author, he wrote (August 28, 1976): "Yes, I was in the atelier, rue de Sèvres during the period you mention, from September 1928 to July 1929. . . . Looking thru the *Oeuvre complète* . . . Verlag Girsberger, 1930, I remember working on some of the plans pages 190 and 191. I also worked on detail sections of walls, floors and parapets that I do not find published. In connection with the Villa Savoye, I drew the typical details on page 174 of the above publication for use on this and other jobs for DOORS, WINDOWS, CABINETS, AND ROOFS. . . . Le Corbusier normally concentrated on the design part of the projects, coming to the atelier more in the late afternoon, evening or night."

45. *Précisions*, p. 230.

46. For the double lodge, there are 22 drawings, including FLC 18.273. Apart from two rather tentative drawings, FLC 19.720 and 19.612, all relate very directly to the dated drawings: FLC 19.610 (April 27, 1929), 19.449, (LC 2124, May 6, 1929), 19.450 (LC 2125, May 7, 1929), 19.457, (LC 2160, June 5, 1929), 18.273 (June 9, 1929). There is no evidence for any serious design for the lodge at an earlier date, confirmed by the lack of tenders by the builder, but some apparently early site plans (FLC 19.544, 19.545, 19.718, 23.276) do include some indications of a lodge.

47. FLC doc. 131 includes rough calculations by Pierre Jeanneret for a "large lodge" (76,300 francs) compared to a "medium lodge" (64,000 francs). The former sum included one estimate that can be dated to May 17, 1929 (FLC doc. 251–252).

48. FLC doc. 893–895, Cormier's letter, August 3, 1929.

49. For the single lodge there are only nine drawings, including FLC 18.312 (filed under Loi Loucheur) and 8.681 (filed under Guiette). The dated drawings are FLC 19.470 and 19.471 (LC 2189, July 7, 1929). In addition, there are details of the dog kennel and siting, mostly from January and February 1930.

50. E.g., *Oeuvre complète, 1929–1934*, p. 25, where the wrong section is illustrated, a mistake that has been faithfully copied in countless later publications.

51. FLC doc. 279–284, Celio's bill, July 10, 1931.

52. FLC doc. 317–320, Celio, December, 1930.

53. FLC doc. 124, sketch by Pierre Jeanneret dated May 27, 1930.

54. See Cormier's sketch, FLC doc. 134 (January 8, 1930).

55. Perfecla's bill, FLC doc. 277 (March 24, 1930).

56. FLC docs. 628 and 638 (March 31, 1930), doc. 640 (May 13, 1930) and docs. 639 and 637 (May 31, 1930) included Crépin's list of plants and layout of planting. A letter by Le Corbusier to Crépin (FLC doc. 265, July 17, 1930) appeals to the latter's loyalty, claiming that Le Corbusier had insisted to Madame Savoye that Crépin should be chosen for the job. Crépin was also the gardener for the Stein house and had a reputation as an artistic landscape artist. Site drawings by Pierre Jeanneret in January 1930 (e.g., FLC 19.539, LC 2282) show a deviation from the rectilinear arrangement of drives with flanking flower beds, introducing a proposed picturesque treatment of curving drives and informal beds of plants.

57. FLC doc. 764.

58. FLC docs. 776–777.

59. FLC docs. 139–140 (July 17, 1930).

60. FLC doc. 768.

61. FLC docs. 220–223.

62. FLC doc. 313. See also FLC doc. 8 (July 17, 1930), a letter from Louis Notté, an expert called in by the Savoyes to advise on the central heating, who recommended a larger boiler.

63. FLC doc. 34 (September 7, 1937).

64. FLC doc. 712.

65. FLC doc. 581 (October 31, 1937).

66. FLC doc. 599.

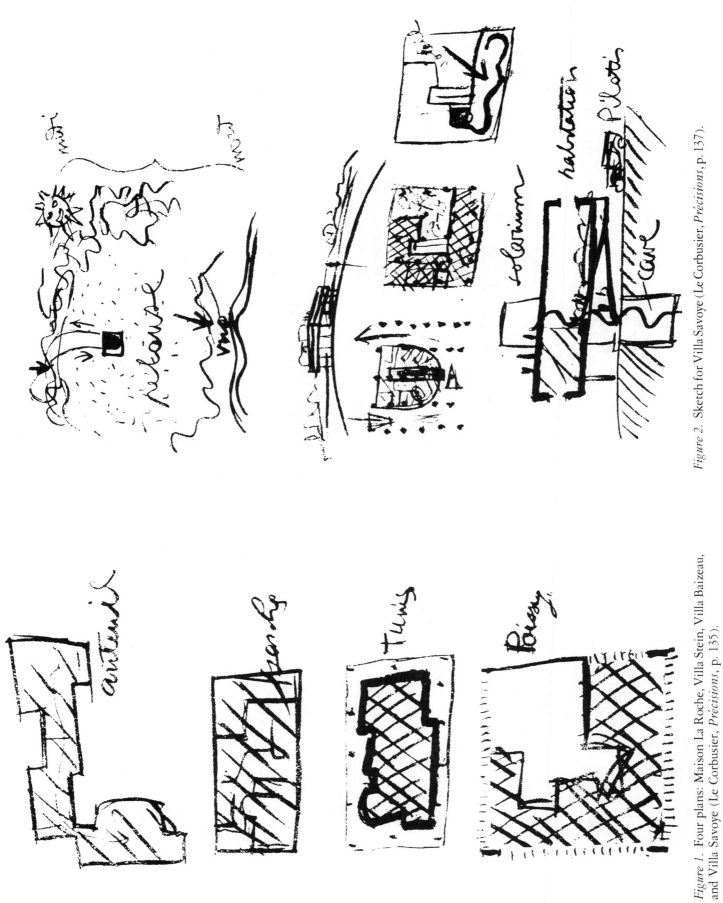

Figure 2. Sketch for Villa Savoye (Le Corbusier, *Précisions*, p. 137).

Figure 1. Four plans: Maison La Roche, Villa Stein, Villa Baizeau, and Villa Savoye (Le Corbusier, *Précisions*, p. 135).

Figure 4. Studies for the window (Le Corbusier, *Précisions*, p. 55).

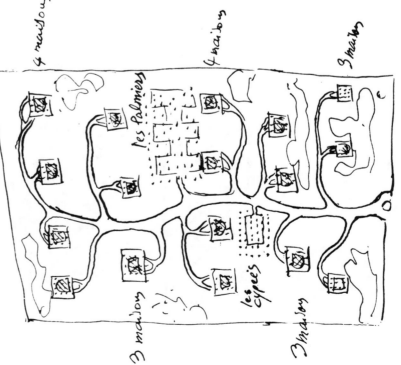

Figure 3. Sketch of Villa Savoye as a standard cell (Le Corbusier, *Précisions*, p. 139).

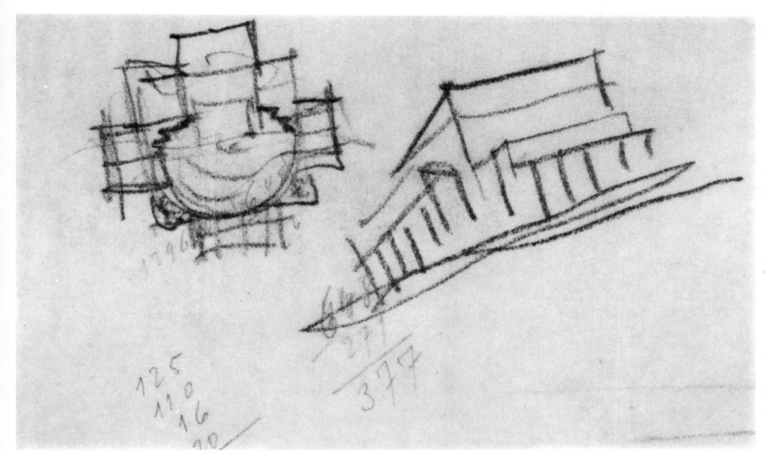

Figure 5. Detail of marginal sketches, December 1928 (Fondation Le Corbusier #19.505).

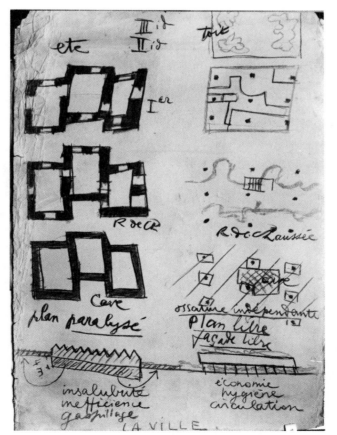

Figure 6. Sketch made to illustrate Buenos Aires lecture, October 1929 (Fondation Le Corbusier).

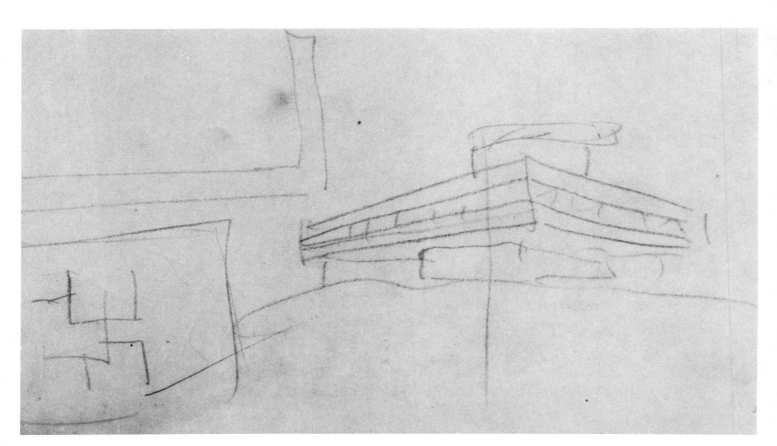

Figure 7. Detail of marginal sketch for Villa Baizeau (Fondation Le Corbusier #24.983).

Figure 8. Detail of marginal sketch for Villa Baizeau (Fondation Le Corbusier #24.983).

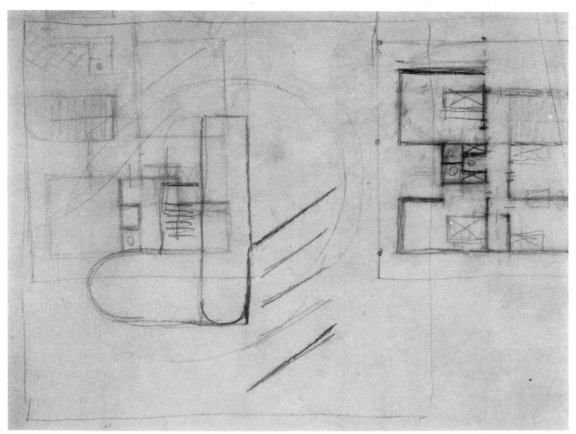

Figure 9. Detail of plan superimposed on plan for Villa Baizeau (Fondation Le Corbusier #8.507).

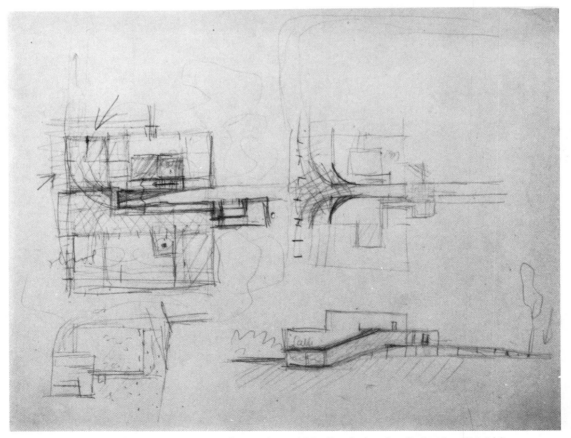

Figure 10. Detail of sketchbook page, September 1928 (Fondation Le Corbusier #31.044).

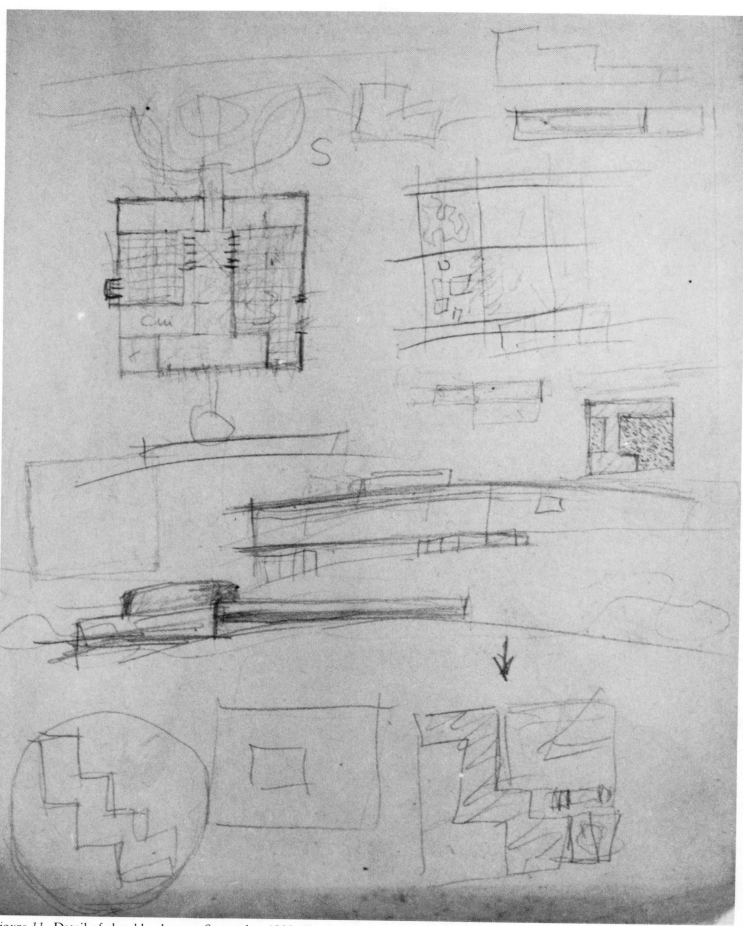

Figure 11. Detail of sketchbook page, September 1928 (Fondation Le Corbusier #31.044).

Figure 12. Villa Savoye, view from the northwest. Photograph courtesy of Tim Benton.

Figure 13. Villa Savoye, view from the west. Photograph courtesy of Tim Benton.

Figure 15. Villa Savoye: ramp. Photograph courtesy of Tim Benton.

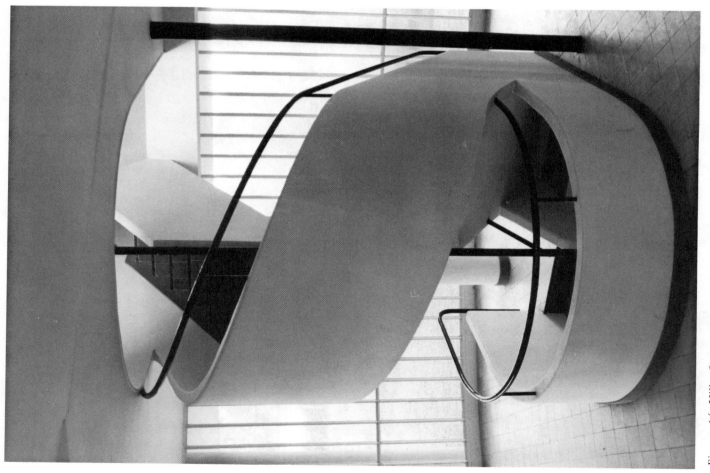

Figure 14. Villa Savoye: spiral staircase, in hall. Photograph courtesy of Tim Benton.

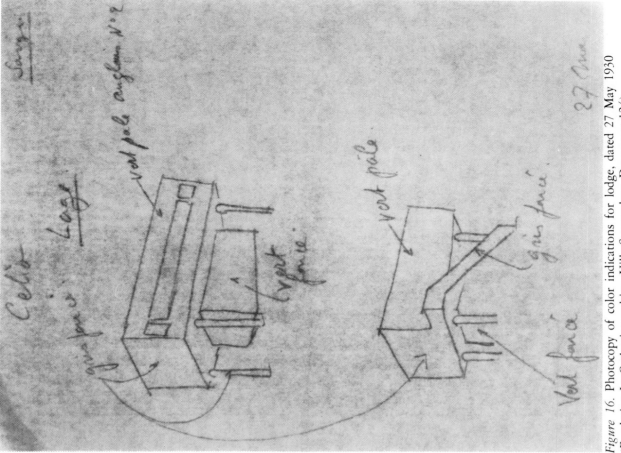

Figure 16. Photocopy of color indications for lodge, dated 27 May 1930 (Fondation Le Corbusier archive, Villa Savoye box, Document 124).

La Maison des hommes and La Misère des villes: Le Corbusier and the Architecture of Mass Housing
by Reyner Banham

By 1926 Le Corbusier had become enough of a public figure—at least in the little world of architecture—to be interviewed about his views on the future of housing for the magazine *La Construction Moderne*. Just how he had arrived at this modest eminence with so little built that could normally be classified as "housing" other than the Frugès scheme at Pessac must be a confused and confusing story, but the very confusions and contradictions of his career and published ideas may have helped, not hindered, his rise to prominence.

Indeed, as seems clear from the enthusiastic response of Henri Frugès to what he *supposed* to be Le Corbusier's views on housing,[1] the very diversity of miscellaneous proposals and concepts already advanced in Corbu's publications by 1925 pretty well guaranteed him a sympathetic audience, because they contained something for everybody and touched off resonances across the whole gamut of progressive opinion. The legendary persona of Le Corbusier that emerged from the far less interesting Swiss citizen Charles Edouard Jeanneret was assembled from parts as disparate as those of a Dada collage—and with equally provoking effect.

Le Corbusier's most obvious appeal seems to have been to the continuing Futurist sensibilities of those who had "learned the lesson of the Machine" during the War and saw in his proposals for mass-produced housing a rational extension of what had already been achieved by industrial manufacturing. They looked for analogous reductions in consumer costs to solve "the housing problem" by making new houses affordable for all classes of society.

Although the concept of *les maisons en série* was always offered as a purely technical proposal in itself, its political overtones and possible political consequences were never ignored by Corbu nor by his admirers. The very phase "the housing problem" was political in origin and application, since the dislocations and destructions of the War had sharpened the political impact of any decisions, large or small, affecting the housing stock of all European nations. Yet here was Le Corbusier—*cet inconnu*—claiming to possess a political panacea:

Architecture or Revolution
Revolution can be avoided

(the famous closing phrase of *Vers une architecture*).

The conviction such slogans carried, however, depended on more than just a proposal that houses be mass produced, whatever the politics of that technical proposal. That margin of conviction seems to have come, somehow, from the almost accidental juxtaposition (but not integration) in the Corbu collage persona of two political concepts of housing that, though both radical, are also in most ways radically opposed to one another.

These two concepts, or radical traditions, can be characterized as the monumental-revolutionary and the cottage-cooperative. The first has its roots mainly (but not exclusively, by the time Corbu absorbed it) in the *phalanstère* of Charles Fourier, that early nineteenth-century "Versailles for the People" within whose palatial format citizens would cultivate their individuality and mobility (and thus, paradoxically, their interchangeability) while the traditional structures of the biological family and the bourgeois state withered around them. As von Moos has pointed out,[2] the form of the *rue à redents* used for urban housing in all of Corbu's city-planning exercises of the twenties looks remarkably like Victor Considérant's well-known design for a phalanstery of 1840, multiplied end-to-end all over the city area. And wrapped up within this monumental housing package there tends to come—with varying degrees of political assertiveness, according to Corbu's mood and the climate of the hour—some version of the idea of the liberation of the members of the biological family from one another and from the tyranny of the bourgeois domestic routine by the provision of communal services within the block.

In all the variants of this package, from the central recreation spaces and communal service crew of the *immeuble-villas* of 1922 to the crèche and communal laundry and rooftop social areas of the *unité* at Marseille, one will also find echoes of other post-Fourier concepts of communal and

socialist living. In all of these—and they range
from the Soviet projects of Nikolaev, Ginzburg,
and the like at one extreme[3] to the modest
proposals for the revival of the medieval traditions
of collegiate life implied in Wells Coates's Isokon
apartments in London at the other—monumental
concentration of living space into a single block
gives the human and economic warrant for the
provision of services that would be unthinkable if
spread over large areas of low-density, single-family
dwellings.

In many of Le Corbusier's most brilliant mass-
dwelling projects such communal servicing is
predicated upon the forceful liberation of the
inhabitants from the bourgeois biological family—
the Swiss and Brazilian students in their respective
university hostels in Paris, the monks of La
Tourette and—most cruelly—the *pauvre gens de
Paris,* for whom the two Salvation Army buildings
and the *asile flottante* were conceived. Indeed, as
the plan of the Cité de Refuge all too clearly
shows, even those poor down-and-outs who were
still pair-bonded in residual versions of the
traditional family were rigorously segregated, men
at one end of the block, women at the other, by
separate but equal staircases with an inviolate party
wall between. Only the unavoidable biological bond
between infant and nursing mother was left
unbroken in this Taylorized pursuit of the calculus
of charity, but this rare concession to unreformed
humanity was banished to the rooftop, where it
could not spoil the symmetry of the system below.

In opposition to this monumental and radical
tradition born of a nineteenth-century view (with
roots in the revolutions of the eighteenth) that
saw society as composed of free and mobile
individuals without claims on or obligations to one
another stood another revolutionary tradition
that sought rather to encourage the mutual
dependencies of the nuclear family as a counterbalance to the exploitive corruption of the free
and mobile individual by capitalism. In this
tradition, to which Le Corbusier was also heir, each
family would have its own house, its own land,

and a stake in the means of production via
cooperative ownership of agricultural and industrial
resources. The appeal of this tradition to the kind
of progressive industrialist who so often figures as
a patron of Corbu's architecture, from Frugès
onward, was that it also gave the citizen a
compelling stake in the maintenance of the social
status quo, since his prosperity as a cooperative
shareholder or profit-sharing employee depended
on never disrupting the flow of production or the
marketing of goods.

This may seem a harsh judgment on the
Garden City movement, which Ebenezer Howard
had launched with such excellent humanitarian
intentions at the beginning of the nineties, but
once the Garden City concept had been diluted into
the Garden Suburb format by welfare-conscious
employers like Krupp and the lessons of George
Pullman's model city south of Chicago had been
absorbed, the architecture of the low-density
Garden City did, indeed, begin to look like one of
the ways in which revolution could be avoided.

It should be remembered that in the world in
which Le Corbusier grew up and acquired his
education as an architect the Garden City in all its
ramifications (including the *Ciudad Lineál* of the
Spanish urbanist Soria y Mata) was the ruling
idea-in-good-currency in progressive urban design
and that all his housing projects and patentable
construction systems from Monol and Dom-ino
down to Pessac and beyond had been conceived
within its categories and social assumptions. At the
time that *La Construction Moderne* interviewed
him for his views on housing he would have been
known—but for two design concepts—almost
exclusively as an architect of tame cottages for
tamed workers.

These two exceptional design concepts are
closely related and are the essential components of
all but a tiny fraction of his later work in mass
housing; they therefore warrant closer examination.
The first is an attempt at an impossible
compromise between the two radical housing
traditions—at least *seemingly* impossible, because

the opposition between the monumental-revolutionary of the phalanstery and the *pavillionisme* of the cottage-cooperative is so deeply and permanently ingrained in French political and civic thought. It surfaced again as late as the run-up to the *événements* of 1968, when the impossibility of compromise seemed to be systematically underlined by the realization that the new *petite bourgeoisie* who had fled the central city for an apparent appliance paradise in individualized apartments in phalanstery-sized but hopelessly underserviced superblocks in the remotest reaches of suburbia had got the worst of all possible worlds, were neither liberated nor given a stake in any tolerable status quo, but were simply locked into a perpetually frustrating routine of *Métro-Boulot-Dodo.* . . .

Yet—to go back to Corbu in the early twenties—the *immeuble-villas* project (or projects, since there are more versions than Corbology commonly acknowledges) was just such an attempt at this compromise: to provide individual family dwellings with their own private outdoor spaces *and* communal services in a single giant block on a densely occupied urban site. The mediating element that was to effect this compromise was the other exceptional design concept, the Maison Citrohan.

This stunningly simple yet architecturally rich device—a two-story room with a sleeping balcony at its back end—is exceptional in that it owes almost nothing to any of the building types with which Corbu experimented before finally coming to Paris. Although the Villa Schwob in La Chaux-de-Fonds had possessed a double-height living room, the Citrohan concept has nothing to do with his early suburban villas, and although it was to be built of concrete, it has nothing to do with the various systems by which he had hoped to profit from reinforced concrete in constructing garden suburbs—except for a conceptual ambiguity that it shares with the Dom-ino system, to wit: is it a continuous architectural system that can be divided into single units, or a unit that could be conjoined with others to form a continuous architecture?

Although Le Corbusier initially presented the Citrohan idea (and built it, at Stuttgart) as a free-standing object on a green-field site, its deep, narrow-fronted plan betrays its urban origins. Whether its exact source of inspiration was the Café Legendre, as Corbu himself insisted, or was the standard Paris *atelier* unit, as his interests and lifestyle powerfully suggest, the type belongs to a tradition of close-packed continuous street-frontage construction and a pattern of urban land occupation that goes back to the late Middle Ages.

Its use in the form of vertically stacked duplex apartments, however, is almost without precedent in Europe. Although such apartments existed in many U.S. cities, at least as luxury variants on conventional apartment types, the pairing of each unit with a duplex-height garden terrace within the shelter of the block was a stroke of pure inventiveness without rival anywhere in the world (though perhaps only because it was not economically feasible in any real-life rental market!).

Yet even though each apartment/terrace unit is effectively a private and separate single-family dwelling, the total block recapitulates many aspects of the monumental revolutionary tradition, such as the "communalization" of at least part of the services and servants and the internalization of some social and recreational facilities in the core of the block. In the latter, of course, Corbu is picking up from the recent past the central communal spaces of the Futurist Sant'Elia's *case a gradinate,* as was Henri Sauvage in his block on the rue des Amiraux of 1924. Little else, however, looks back in this way, and most of the concept looks forward to what was to prove a long-postponed future, for the *immeuble-villas* already contain the essentials of the *unité d'habitation* of twenty-five years later: duplex apartments with open terraces, stacked in a block containing necessary communal and neighborhood services.

The long postponement of that housing future seems largely to have been due to the novelty and size of the concept. In France, if the people were ever to be rehoused by community or governmental effort, it would be through the *pavillionaire* approach represented by the Loucheur legislation of 1929; if apartment blocks were to be built, they would be of the narrow-chested type of Corbu's own Porte Molitor example or the numerous and elegant exercises in refined Art Deco of Michel Roux-Spitz. Only the projects for Edmond & Wanner, partly realised in the Clarté block of 1932 in Geneva, carry Corbu's ideas toward realization.

It might be supposed that in less conservative countries than France these ideas might have taken hold, yet they did not. In Russia they were not needed—until the collapse of Soviet modernism in the early thirties progressive architects there ran ahead of Le Corbusier in both ideas and realizations, although they were clearly aware of his work and the influences were mutual and reciprocative. Germany presents a more surprising contrast, however, since many of the ideals for which Corbu was campaigning—in particular, standardization and the concept of types—had already an established constituency among German architects, and the grinding demands of constructional economics left housing designers no option but to follow the paths of standardization.

Yet even given standardization and a fair degree of acceptance of the need for communal services, the great bulk of the *Siedlungen* built at that time were remarkably conventional in all but their absence of period architectural detail. They were neither structurally nor socially adventurous, and their planning, even when it involved the grouping of very large blocks, remained in touch with the Garden City tradition and even reached back to the quasi-picturesque plans recommended by Camillo Sitte in the previous century—and even these minor aesthetic graces were to be lost when Gropius and others finally perfected the hygienic systems of parallel blocks of *Minimalwohnungen*, in which the traditional bourgeois biological family was left almost totally undisturbed. It is intriguing in this last respect to note that at the Weissenhof exhibition only Corbu's double house, with its

wide-open plans and almost complete lack of privacy between its "freely interpenetrating bedrooms for freely interpenetrating sex lives," implies any serious revisions of traditional family structures; for the rest traditional compartmentation sustains a fundamentally conservative view of domestic life, in spite of the steel tube chairs and tables and standardized door furniture.

Le Corbusier knew of the German *Siedlungen*, of course, and was envious of the sheer size[4] of the German housing achievement (who would not be in those days) but had no ambition to involve himself with the innate social conservatism of the great trade union cooperatives that built most of them. His view of proper social patronage for housing was—as Robert Fishman's studies make clear[5]—of a more elitist and directed trade unionism, something dangerously close to the structure of Mussolini's "corporate state" (admired in those same days by British fascists like Oswald Moseley), in which the social inertia of the masses could be galvanized by innovative action "from above."

In spite of the best hopes of Le Corbusier and the leaders of the specialized brand of revolutionary syndicalism with whom he associated in the thirties (and who were eventually to lead him into his self-deceiving alliances with the Vichy regime after 1940), such leadership and patronage was not to appear in France in the thirties, and up to the point where the Great Depression brought most building to a halt, the nearest he was to come to "social housing" was a pair of commissions for mass dwellings of a more institutional type: the Pavillon Suisse and the Cité de Refuge. Neither could be blocks of apartments—the accommodation in the Pavillon was in separate study-bedrooms, and in the Cité consisted almost entirely of large open dormitories—and for this reason both the circulation patterns and the internalized social spaces of the earlier projects lost their locations and justifications. Neither the single-loaded corridors against the exterior wall of the block at the Pavillon Suisse nor the discharge of staircase traffic directly into the ends of the dormitory spaces at the Cité de Refuge offered a natural location for social or communal activities within the block itself.

In an effort at architectural creativity that has, almost coincidentally, altered the appearance of downtown areas all over the world, Le Corbusier rephrased his original concept of a block with internal services and social areas and produced instead a tight slab of pure (or almost pure) basic residential accommodation in standard rooms or dormitories to which the nonstandardized central and communal functions are attached as external dependencies. Whatever part Russian examples may have played in the sudden evolution of this "second mode" of mass-housing design (as von Moos has suggested[6]), the result was an almost irresistible new style of architecture of such immediate impact that the Pavillon Suisse has been acclaimed as the most seminal building of the twentieth century.

In spite of the Pavillon's diagrammatic clarity in presenting what a later age would call a new "paradigm" of design, the Cité de Refuge offers a more extended, systematic, and instructive exercise in the Second Mode. In front of the glazed cliff of the six stories of standardized accommodation in the dormitory block, unique and ceremonial facilities are arranged in a linear sequence from left (entrance) to right (social offices and entry to dormitories). This compositional device involves a dissolution of the organic conception of the *immeuble-villas* as well as an externalization of these communal spaces, which are deployed in a linear "listing" according to a classificatory system of functional elements that is almost infantile in its simplicity, yet has good academic precedents in the idea of the *programme* (or schedule of accommodation) as understood at the Ecole des Beaux-Arts.

With a literal-mindedness that is either pedestrian or poetic according to one's viewpoint,

Corbu offers a distinct and separate built volume for each named function of the sequence (or very nearly so), and to give form to the volumes he recovers from his own past a still-life aesthetic of regular solids—cube, wedge, cylinder, cube—that gives their diversity an artistic unity. Something aesthetically similar, of course, was done at almost exactly the same time on the roof of the Villa Savoye, but the *programme* there—at once simpler, vaguer, and yet more complex—cannot give the simplistic one-to-one correspondence of forms to functions that makes the Cité de Refuge so effective an object lesson.

It was a lesson in how to design more than just institutional hostels, for among the most seductive aspects of the Second Mode was its apparent universality. Its simple formulae of classification—everything standardized in the slab, everything unique outside—could be applied to practically all building types containing a large amount of one specific function and a minor garnish of others. Modern office blocks were prime examples of this kind of functional breakdown, and Corbu's Second Mode increasingly became the norm as the thirties merged into the forties and—above all—the fifties and sixties, the epoch of the organization man in his grey flannel suit.

With an apparent irony that should provoke some revisionist thoughts concerning the relationship of the Second Mode to conglomerate capitalism, Corbu's first office block in this style was to be in Russia—though the dependency of Centrosoyus on the Second Mode is obscured by the multiplicity of slabs framing the site and concealing most of the unique, common, or ceremonial volumes from outward view. The mode is seen much more clearly in his 1936 sketches for the Ministry of Health in Rio de Janeiro, especially the second version, where the slab has been raised to compensate for the reduced dimensions of the site, while the version actually built by Lucio Costa and Oscar Niemeyer pushes the Second Mode to a condition of diagrammatic simplification that would probably have had little appeal for Corbu himself.

The plain rectangular office slab is raised two stories on dowel-like *pilotis* and exhibits a perfectly regular façade on both main faces (the building is a model maker's dream!), an entrance-cum-auditorium block is tucked under the slab without either being compromised, and minor structures of varied form are placed on the roof but are not allowed to come close enough to the edge to interrupt the continuity of the parapet line that defines the upper edges of the slab.

The result is almost a cartoon of Le Corbusier's intentions, but its diagrammatic elegance, immediately comprehensible to lay eyes, probably did more than anything else to establish or confirm Corbu's international reputation as the modern architect par excellence of the new world that would arise after World War II. Adopted by the liberal consciences of the victorious antifascist alliance as a kind of shining ideal for the architecture of welfare democracy, the Ministry at Rio became the model for the United Nations building in New York (or possibly became the channel by which Le Corbusier's own uncommissioned design could be adopted by the International Commission as the official project). Perhaps more significantly for the future of downtown scenery everywhere, Gordon Bunshaft at SOM used an even more diagrammatic version of the Second Mode for his Lever House design of 1950 and thus created a prototype whose influence is only just beginning to fade.

Yet Le Corbusier himself hardly ever returned to the Second Mode format in his housing designs. A trickle of projects, mostly for North African sites in the late thirties and forties, continue to develop the theme of duplexes interlocked around a central double-loaded corridor; some of these designs stand on larger podia containing parking (prototyped at Clarté in 1932), and some have the stair towers pulled out of the block and set up as separate attached volumes in the classic Second Mode way.

The distillation of much of this unrealized designing is to be found in that strange and disturbing book *La Maison des hommes,*[7] which Le Corbusier wrote in Vichy in collaboration with François de Pierrefeu in 1941. Officially, Corbu did the illustrations and Pierrefeu the text, but there is much evidence of overlapping authorship, and the words often echo sentiments that Corbu had uttered before. What emerges is that these late developments of the Second Mode are set in a context that is very conservative—so much so that one is tempted to say "reactionary." God is invoked; *la maison des hommes* is to be "la maison visible qui incarne la maison spirituelle." In this context the social-control aspects of the Garden City dream take on a less humane air: "The permanence of the family, and thus the stability of the human personality, depends on physical stability of place and occupation." This may be a human truth, but when one discovers toward the end of the book that the whole of the building industry is to be organised into one giant hierarchical corporation under the direction of a single *ordonnateur du domaine bâti de la France . . .* then we realise that Corbu's ancient admiration for the *Roi soleil* is in command once more.

The book ends with what is almost a denunciation of reason and rationalism, which Le Corbusier illustrates with the famous emblem of the sun in confrontation with the Medusa-head that was to become so familiar in his postwar publications. Not only does the book sum up the Second Mode, it also presents for the first time many signs and diagrams, such as the *journée solaire de 24 heures,* that were to become the emblems of his thought in the period that finally delivered the long-postponed promise of the *unité d'habitation de grandeur conforme.*

Yet the physical delivery of that promise involved the creation of a Third Mode, whose most obvious manifestation was *le béton brut,* but whose architecturally crucial aspect was the replacement of the external diversifications of the Second Mode by a new procedure of diversification within the outlines of the rectangular slab. The sources of this device are to be found among the mass of sketches done for the various projects for the replanning of Algiers that had occupied him for a long and barren decade. In one form it appears in the interruptions of the grid of *brise-soleils* that cover the seaward face of the giant office tower over the harbor, but more significantly it makes its decisive appearance in the famous drawing for a *redent* at Fort l'Empéreur. This shows a perspective of the space under an elevated, curving motorway, a space occupied by giant concrete decks at two-story intervals and the spaces between the decks filled with individual duplex dwellings. It is as if the *immeuble-villas* had risen from the dead—except that the dwellings are not standardized and have elevations in varying styles . . . including the Moorish!

The drawing is justly famous, because it is the starting point for Habraken's theory of "supports," do-it-yourself housing within a vast publicly funded frame of concrete decks, and beyond that it has been the perpetual inspiration for the whole concept of local variability within the invariant massive frame of megastructures. For Corbu, however, it was a starting point for the practical reabsorption into the residential slab of all those picturesquely displayed communal elements he had spread on the ground at the foot of the Pavillon Suisse and the Cité de Refuge. As a *solution type*, in which each named function is represented not by a disparate volume but by a unique variation in the elevational treatment of the block, this Third Mode was to be used far beyond the practice of mass housing and makes its most spectacular appearance on a truly heroic scale on the long façades of the Secretariat building at Chandigarh. Yet its definitive elaboration must always be the elevations of the *unité* at Marseille, where it is used to signal not only changes in types of apartment but also the presence of floors of community services within the block.

In this it was the model, not always to be followed in detail, for all the other *unités* that were to be built. But all the *unités* also carry over

one aspect of the Second Mode as well, for the still-life aesthetic of the forebuildings of the Cité de Refuge, somewhat modified by Costa and Niemeyer's final version of the Ministry of Health, is now redeployed along the roof. At Marseille this takes the form of a marvelous sequence of vaults and cubes and stairs and the gigantic tri-lobe funnels through which the ventilation system exhausts. The ground has been cleared around the *pilotis*, and some of what has been cleared has gone, elegantly, to the roof, but the most substantial elements have been reabsorbed into the slab itself.

In effect, the *unités* are recapitulations and variations of many major themes from Corbu's past. When he said of the first of them at Marseille, "This is a building I have wanted to build for twenty-five years," he may well have deserved André Lurçat's acid reply, "So you insult the people by offering them a dwelling which is a quarter-century out of date," because the truth of the matter is written all over the building and is the clue to both its architectural virtues and its residential vices, such as they are.

It stands unequivocally in the monumental tradition; the population of each *unité* was to be around sixteen hundred persons—almost exactly the same as that of a phalanstery, as Peter Serenyi has noted.[8] The form of the block and its craggy detailing would emphasise its sheer bulk in defiance of its conceptual compactness and the reassuring signals of adherence to a concept of "human scale" given by the references to the Modulor dimensions cast into the *béton brut* at conspicuous locations around the block.

The apartments sustain the never long-abandoned theme of cross-over duplexes locked around a central, double-loaded corridor, now dignified with the title *rue intérieure*. The garden terraces of the *immeuble-villas* have shrunk, it is true, but the enormous two-story balconies that front each duplex serve most of the same purposes as well as aggregating into a *brise-soleil* of antique grandeur. The desire to liberate children and women from the tyrannies of the biological family and bourgeois housework is attenuated, but persists: the crèche is within the block, and the provision of extensive built-in furniture in the apartments could have done something to deliver housewives from the *armoire brétonne* and its endless need for dusting.

The communal services are there, too, within the block, but they can be seen to be at the midpoint of its section (the change of façade is clearly visible), and they cannot be in the center of the plan because there is no room for them. For this is—unlike the *immeuble-villas*—a slab, not a hollow rectangle. The aesthetic and technical innovations of the Second Mode are carried forward too: the slab profile has a sharp-edged impact as an image that the *immeuble-villas* on their *rues à redents* could never have, and the experiments in sound insulation begun at the Pavillon Suisse here culminate in the isolation of one apartment from another within the lead-cushioned interstices of the famous bottle-rack frame, though this is hardly equivalent to the individualization that was given by the alternating garden terraces of the *immeuble-villas*.

These resumptions, redefinitions, and restatements of themes from twenty-five years of work make the first unité at Marseille one of the pinnacles of Corbu's architectural career, even if it was an urbanistic and social disappointment because the rest of the cluster was not built. The subsequent *unités*, at Nantes-lès-Rezé, Strasbourg, Briey-en-Forêt, Berlin, and so forth, each offer some further technical or architectural refinement, but the residues of the old revolutionary social aspirations become thinner and fainter with each succeeding project. Even the most modest proposals for cooperative self-help become less and less plausible with conventional trade-union sponsorship, conventional mortgage financing from the HLM, a building industry bent on organizational giantism, and a determinedly consumerist society. Architecture or revolution?

Revolution has been avoided, but it is difficult, as one surveys the incredible landscape of mass housing *style-Corbu* that now surrounds the first *unité*, not to feel that architecture has been in increasing danger of avoidance as well. Corbu may have died only just in time to have been spared confrontation with the inevitable outcome of the dilution of his revolutionary dreams by the pressures of a real world he had helped denounce in *La Maison des hommes*. The *misère des villes* was to persist. Architecture alone is no substitute for revolution.

Missing from the foregoing history is one element that came to be taken very seriously in all discussions of Corbu's mass housing in the last years of his life—the European monastic tradition. As soon as it was known that he was to design a monastic building—the Dominican "house" at La Tourette—many commentators believed that a missing clue had been given to the secret intentions, as it were, of his large-scale residential work. Earlier religious designs, such as those for La Sainte-Baume, were brought under fresh study, and the references to the monastery at Ema in the introductory pages of *Le Modulor* were scrutinized in a new light, as were the sketches of monastic buildings in his early *carnets de voyage*.

At first blush the life of a monastic "rule," with its defined periods of privacy alternating with communal forgatherings and sacraments, might well appear to be a kind of perfected program for the daily routines to be followed in a *unité d'habitation*, and for a time, following Peter Serenyi[9] and certain British commentators with a vested interest in making Christianity appear modish, it was almost received opinion that Corbu's conception of mass housing was at base a fusion of monastery and phalanstery. But this proposition is ultimately a cartoon of his long life's work on *la maison des hommes*. In the monastery too many of the problems of bourgeois society and the biological family have been presolved by decisions that the rest of the human race has little opportunity to make or preempted by withdrawal into a position of defensive privilege that cannot be made available to society at large.

And one does not have to be much of a cynic to observe that just as the monastery may be seen as a caricature of Corbu's intentions in the reform of urban housing, so La Tourette can be interpreted as a satire on the monastery. Certainly it recapitulates many themes from his earlier works, but few of them are architecturally related to his residential designs in any consequential manner. Viewed as a monastery pure and simple, however, it reveals many of those qualities of Dada or Surrealist humor that Sir John Summerson identified long ago[10] as basic to Corbusian design. Here is a building aggressively claustral in form that contains no useful cloister, for its central square is too clogged with miscellaneous structures to be used. And if those structures were to be cleared from the central square, then the claustral form would be revealed as a cruel joke in itself, for the fall of the land and the elevation of much of the building on *pilotis* and buttresses together mean that a large segment of its perimeter, far from being closed, is dangerously open to the distractions and temptations of the world outside.

Corbu never treated housing with such apparent levity—*on ne badine pas avec l'habitat*—because it was for him and all his generation an extremely serious matter. The housing problem, in so many words, was one of the gravest charges laid upon that generation by the reformers, philanthropists, and ideologues of the later nineteenth century. It was a problem considered endemic to liberal capitalist economics and engrained in the structure of all great cities. The reform of housing was seen as an essential component in the cure of *la misère des villes*—the intellectual and civic, as well as economic, poverty that perpetually threatened the good order of urban society in the modern world.

The machinery of society, profoundly out of gear, oscillates between an amelioration, of

historical importance, and a catastrophe.

The primordial instinct of every human being is to assure himself of a shelter.

The various classes of workers in society today no longer have dwellings adapted to their needs; neither the artisan nor the intellectual.

It is a question of building which is at the root of the social unrest of today; architecture or revolution.

The question-begging identification of "architecture" and "housing" may well cause raised eyebrows today, but at least Corbu was not, even in 1923, so naïve as to suppose that mass housing was the sole or sovereign cure for *la misère des villes.* Unfortunately for him and his reputation, the forms and usages of his housing designs were widely pirated by many who thought that it might be. Too many legislators up for reelection, too many bureaucrats, trade unionists, building-industry lobbyists, and real-estate interests to whom the seductive arithmetic of "one dwelling equals two votes" was irresistible tried to remake the world's suffering cities in the image of a *style Corbu* so totally misunderstood that they even proposed that people live in the tall, narrow downtown towers that he goes out of his way, from the *cité contemporaine* onwards, to identify as reserved for business and government.

Occasionally, it is true, the great cities of the world produced a few projects that showed understanding of some real and valuable part of his grandiose, but in its way humane, vision of urban housing: the Cerro Grande and Cerro Piloto projects of Guido Bermudez and others above Caracas, the grimy, awkward bulk of Park Hill above Sheffield. Both were true children of the *unité* and the accumulated lifetime of patient research that went into it. The young architects of Park Hill revealed the depths of their rare understanding by paying the old master the compliment of criticism, and offering to correct the *"rue intérieure* mistake."

Few others show such sympathy for his approach, nor such understanding of his deeply felt desire to save the cities; the tawdriness of the consequences worldwide has become a byword for the failure of modern architecture. It is equally possible, of course, that Corbu too might have failed if his ideas had been put into effect on the scale he demanded. It is perfectly possible, for instance, that the shortcoming of the original *unité* would have been multiplied, not ameliorated, had the ensemble of four been built there as planned on the boulevard Michelet, instead of the present mess. But we don't know and cannot tell. What we do know is that the *unité* is already one of the tourist attractions, perhaps even one of the ancient monuments, of modern Europe.

Notes

1. See the opening chapter of Phillipe Boudon's *Lived-in Architecture* (Cambridge, Mass.: MIT Press, 1972), pp. 7ff.
2. *Le Corbusier: Elements of a Synthesis* (Cambridge, Mass.: MIT Press, 1979), p. 151.
3. These extremes were not necessarily so far apart in architectural concepts; the Russian "cross-over duplex" section, discussed below, was noted by Coates as well as Le Corbusier and used with little alteration in his Prince's Gate Apartments.
4. Conversation with the author, 1956.
5. See the whole last section of *Urban Utopias of the Twentieth Century* (New York: Basic Books, 1977).
6. *Le Corbusier: Elements of a Synthesis*, pp. 152–54.
7. Paris: Librairie Plon, 1942, and later editions.
8. *Le Corbusier in Perspective* (Englewood Cliffs, N.J.: Prentice-Hall, 1975), p. 114.
9. Ibid., p. 115, where La Tourette is described as "his most perfect communal building."
10. *Heavenly Mansions* (New York: Norton, 1963), pp. 190–191.

The Unité d'Habitation at Marseille
by André Wogenscky
translated by Stephen Sartarelli

I. Background

In 1945, the first of the French ministers of the "Reconstruction" proposed to Le Corbusier that he build somewhere in France a *unité d'habitation* (large residential unit) in accordance with the ideas that he had long been advocating. Le Corbusier therefore decided to reopen his 35, rue de Sèvres workshop with three collaborators—Aujame, Hanning, and myself. We had to get down to work immediately, especially as Le Corbusier was then preparing the urban renewal plans for Saint-Dié and La Rochelle-Pallice.

The workshop grew rapidly in size. Many young architects from various countries came to work with Le Corbusier. They formed just the kind of dynamic team that Le Corbusier needed.[1]

This was the starting point, but it was also a return of sorts. The idea of the *unité d'habitation* was not new. Its central principle had already been expounded by Le Corbusier in his books and published projects. It had been the object of numerous theoretical plans drawn up by Le Corbusier and Pierre Jeanneret in their prewar workshop.

The *unité d'habitation* has a source. The idea first came up in 1907 when Le Corbusier, at the age of twenty, visited the monastery of Ema on the outskirts of Florence. He was struck by the harmonious organization of individual life and collective life. In this monastery, these two aspects of living coexist, and though each is pushed to its extreme, each exalts the other. The monks live alone in their cells. They do not even see those who give them meals through a revolving hatch. Their solitude is protected from excessive contact. Nevertheless, their collective life is very intense: they make up a community. Le Corbusier wrote: "From this moment on, the binomial—individual and collectivity—became clear to me; it is an indissoluble binomial."[2]

This marked the beginning of an ever-growing area of research, the organization of housing, and it was first staked out by Le Corbusier's series of projects.

All of these projects, studies, and reflections led to the prototype of the *unité d'habitation de grandeur conforme* (housing unit of adequate size) integral to the plan for the *ville radieuse* (Radiant City).

Their concrete result was the order for the *unité d'habitation* at Marseille.

II. Le Corbusier at Work

The earlier projects, however well developed they might have been, had always remained theoretical, owing to the force of circumstances. Once the order was given, however, it was necessary to elaborate, down to the smallest details, a program of execution.

For a long time Le Corbusier had been concerned with the need to create homogeneous teams among architects, engineers, and specialists in all the techniques involved in the process of building. He had already achieved this sort of teamwork efficiency when he formed the ASCORAL (Assemblée de Constructeurs pour une Rénovation Architecturale—Association of Builders for a Renovation of Architecture). But the main object of the ASCORAL was theoretical research, which eventually resulted in, among others, the books on the Modulor and the Trois Etablissements humains.

Now it was time to build.

At this time, it was not common practice to establish a close relationship of collaboration between architects and engineers. Technical research was almost always under the control of the contracting firms, and the engineers, especially the structural engineers, often intervened on the part of the contractors. With few exceptions, the architect drew up the plans without collaborating with the engineers. The plans served to pass the orders on to the contractors. And it was only after the authorization of expenditures that a collaboration between the architects and the firms' engineers took place, and this collaboration was often a difficult one because the engineer tended to defend the interests of the contractor, his client, over the architect's point of view.

Le Corbusier understood the need to change these common practices. He had always been convinced of the need for the architect to be able to collaborate with all the technicians, starting with the elaboration of the very first drafts. Hence, even in the organization of labor, Le Corbusier was an innovator. He created the ATBAT, the Atelier des Bâtisseurs (Builders' Workshop).

The ATBAT was composed of four sections, each headed by a collaborator appointed by Le Corbusier: the "administrative section" headed by Jacques Lefèvre, the "works management" section headed by Marcel Py, the "technical research" section headed by Vladimir Bodianski, and the "architectural research" section headed by myself.

For a certain period of time the ATBAT functioned well, thanks to the feeling of solidarity that existed among the four teams. But then the ATBAT slowly fell apart. First Marcel Py had to leave, and I took up the works management section on top of architectural research. Then conflicts and disagreements between Jacques Lefèvre and Vladimir Bodianski on the one hand and Le Corbusier on the other created a split. Why did the ATBAT fail? I have always thought that the cause lay in differences among the individuals involved and not in the principle or the organization.

In spite of everything, the preparations were made. In the workshop at 35, rue de Sèvres, where the number of workers reached thirty at one point, more than a thousand plans for the *unité d'habitation* at Marseille were drafted.

The teamwork, although highly developed, should, however, be seen for what it was. And on this matter I should reaffirm a point that was and still is contradicted: some former collaborators of Le Corbusier have claimed that they, more than Le Corbusier himself, were the authors of a number of his projects. This is incorrect. Apart from the interruption caused by the war, I worked continuously with Le Corbusier from late 1936 to early 1956. And I continued to see him often and to assist him in certain projects up until his death in 1965. I can attest that he and he alone was the author of all of his projects. Even for small details, he drew up his own sketches and directions. Because it is they who draw out in full the plans of a project, draftsmen often have the illusory impression of being a project's author. Nothing could be further from the truth when working with Le Corbusier.

Often, after numerous days during which we wondered if Le Corbusier hadn't forgotten a study that had to be done, he would bring in a bundle of typing-size papers covered with colored sketches. When one was just a beginner in his workshop, it was rather difficult to understand anything in these drawings. With a bit of experience one learned how to read them. And one saw how they contained the entire project, in its functional organization as well as in its plastic and aesthetic organization. He himself would spend hours at the drafting table of each draftsman. He and he alone was the creator.

On a large blackboard against one of the workshop's walls, he would have us draw up plans and cross sections in life-size scale. In this way, the loggias of the apartments were designed in their real dimensions. Le Corbusier himself corrected the drawings with chalk. He sculpted his architecture.

The work for the *unité d'habitation* at Marseille was difficult. Our client was the French government, and inevitably we came into conflict with the authorities involved. There were countless meetings, discussions, and formalities. The choice of a plot, and even of the city in which to construct the *unité*, caused long delays. Finally the plot at the Boulevard Michelet in Marseille was chosen as the definitive site.

Difficulties also arose in the form of the project's detractors. At first it was a question of routine and stupidity. Often those who did not understand the project did not hesitate to criticize it. Then jealousy and spitefulness came into play. Certain persons and organizations tried to wreck the project's realization.

They did not succeed. The tenacity of Le Corbusier and the team of young people working with him proved too strong. And their perseverance was greatly assisted by all of the successive ministers of the "Reconstruction" who held office during the time of the preparations and construction. All of them, it should be pointed out, showed confidence in Le Corbusier. The chief one among them, Eugène Claudius-Petit, played a decisive role in the construction and completion of the *unité*, which he solemnly inaugurated in 1952. He forever remained one of Le Corbusier's devoted defenders, and several years later he entrusted to him the task of realizing the Maison de la Culture, the stadium, and the *unité d'habitation* at Firminy.

Le Corbusier's tenacity was one of his strongest qualities. When applied to himself, it took the form of great demands made on himself, and we find this expressed in all his works.

III. Guiding Principles (Idées-Forces)
Although an examination of the plans of the *unité d'habitation* is indispensable, it may not be enough for an understanding of the project's guiding principles (*idées-forces*). Le Corbusier's architecture is never gratuitous. There are always profound reasons behind his organization of space, but they are not always easy to uncover. One should never be content with just "seeing" an architectural work from the exterior, since in the proper sense of the term, and especially in Le Corbusier's understanding of it, architecture is first and foremost an internal organization from which the exterior aspect results. This is not to say that the exterior does not often affect the interior forms, but that in his thought process, Le Corbusier moved from the interior towards the exterior. He thought of a construction as an internal organism of its façades and exterior forms as its expression, its face.

It is also a "seeing" in the figurative sense, for all of Le Corbusier's architecture is the result of profound reasonings on which his thought is based; it is hence their expression as well. This is saying a great deal, since it is in fact a whole philosophy: the cause behind that which he proposes is a conception

of life, the life of societies as well as the inner life of every individual. He told me many times that deep down it was not architecture that interested him—for him this was but a means—but people.

Although they are quite numerous, rich, and interrelated, I think it is possible to summarize briefly the guiding principles that lie at the basis of the *unité d'habitation*. And I believe that one cannot really understand, and by extension appraise, the *unité d'habitation* except in the light of these guiding principles. They are:

1) Individual life. Respecting individual life. Seeking to protect it from excessive contact with neighbors. Within the dwelling itself, seeking to protect each person's possibilities of solitude and self-development. Presenting architectural solutions that harmoniously reconcile individual life and family life.

The traditional designs of family apartments or houses do not exhibit this concern. They are shaped by a juxtaposition of rooms without any concern for the unity favorable to family life. If the number of rooms is sufficient, each person may then perhaps have his own room. But in this case the dwelling does not bring about any unification of family life: there is a danger that the architecture will create a segregation of the family. If there are not enough rooms, which is usually the case given the social and economic habitat, the result is excessive contact among family members. The architecture of the dwelling is such that all live "on top of one another." The individual life of each is not protected. Solitude is not possible. The architecture in this case provokes conflicts.

Le Corbusier would have liked to build apartments where, on the one hand, family unity would be ensured by a large living room favorable to the family's gathering, but where, on the other, each member's independence and right to solitude would still be guaranteed. Le Corbusier would have liked each of the parents to have, in addition to their bedroom, a reserved, perhaps very small place, very much "on a human scale," where individual and solitary life might blossom. And for the children, however small they might be, Le Corbusier proposed a small individual room for each, with the possibility for all of them to come together, especially to play, in a place distinct from the living room. Alongside the collective life of the family there is the collective life of the children: a kind of children's dwelling within the family dwelling.

This "ideal" apartment was never realized for economic reasons. It would have been necessary to build a larger apartment, which was impossible given the limited funds. In the *unité d'habitation* at Marseille, what remained of this idea was the organization of small, "deep-set" (*en profondeur*) children's rooms separated from each other by a sliding blackboard partition that opens up onto a play space. In Le Corbusier's original plan, these rooms would have been separate. Financial constraints also forced us to drop the idea of the personal private space for each parent.[3]

2) Family protection. Same importance, same respect for family life within social life. Isolating the family dwelling. Eliminating all excessive contact with neighbors. To this end, spacing the residences in order to distance the neighbor situated opposite the residence in question. Isolating the construction so that the neighbor next door, or above, cannot be heard. Distancing neighboring families in the abstract sense of the word by creating two conditions: not seeing and not hearing the neighbors and hence knowing that one is not seen or heard.

Here, once again, traditional constructions do not conform to this fundamental idea.

In a residential zone divided into lots, in a horizontally extended garden city, the inhabitants have the illusion of being independent from the other families because they live in a separate house. But this is only the case if one lives in a villa surrounded by a large garden. But obviously one cannot envision, as a resolution to the worldwide housing problem, lodging every family in a villa isolated in a small park. When houses are close to

one another, there is excessive contact between families—one sees and hears one's neighbor and hence one is aware of being seen and heard by him.

In our traditional cities, apartment buildings are aligned along the street. Unless the streets are very wide, there is a lack of privacy between apartments opposite one another but separated by very little space. And the traditional mid-century constructions were built without any concern for soundproofing. Inside the apartment, one hears the neighbors. For Le Corbusier, this lack of privacy is a serious threat to individual and family life that should be protected within the dwelling.

This is an essential principle, and one of the central reasons behind the *unité d'habitation*. The deep-set apartment, extended towards the exterior by a kind of diaphragm formed by the loggia, is conceived in such a way that one does not see the neighbor and is not seen by him. In the Marseille *unité*, Le Corbusier envisioned and realized a highly developed soundproofing to make the neighbors inaudible. And in the plan for the *ville radieuse*, of which the *unité* is one element, the facing apartment is set at a great distance.

What Le Corbusier had in mind when he imagined the *unités d'habitation* was an architectural form that would protect the family within its dwelling. Judging by what the inhabitants of the Marseille *unité* say, this was successfully achieved.

3) Collective organization. Reconciling this protection, this "distancing," with collective organization. If we have a need to develop our individual lives as well as to live in the small community of the family, and if for this reason individual life and family life need to be protected from "others," we also have a need for collective life. We are social animals. We have a need for others, for their assistance, and sometimes for their presence. Le Corbusier refused to acknowledge any dilemma between individual life and collective life; he refused to recognize a conflict between the two. He offered a dwelling that is at once isolated and situated within a collectivity. When one enters the dwelling, one leaves the society from which one is now protected. When one leaves the dwelling, one enters the society in which one plays an active role.

In traditional forms of housing, there is a conflict among individual, family, and society, because these forms tend to favor one of the three factors to the detriment of the other two. In addition, our contemporary society creates a perpetual conflict between individual and society.

Le Corbusier rejected the notion of this conflict. He could not forget the monastery of Ema. Urbanism and architecture must be capable of offering solutions propitious to striking the right balance, the harmony between the individual and society. Though he wanted to protect the family as well as the individual within the family, he sought to integrate the family into a community, just as a village or a small town integrates its inhabitants into a community. Why must the village extend only horizontally across the terrain? Since contemporary techniques make it possible, why shouldn't this "new village" be developed in all three dimensions, that is, in space, air, and light? This is what the *unité d'habitation* proposes.

4) Dwelling extensions. In order to effect this reconciliation between family and society, it is necessary to avoid segregating the dwellings from the collective services. It is especially important to provide at close proximity to the dwelling all services that are daily or very frequent necessities: certain businesses, day care, nursery school, primary school, playing fields and gymnasiums, meeting places, youth centers. Le Corbusier called these things "extensions of the dwelling," a very meaningful term—it connects the dwellings with the collective life.

The dwellings are not complete if they are not "extended" by these services, which must be situated nearby. Single-family dwellings and horizontal garden cities cannot offer these various services in such close proximity to all the houses. The *unité d'habitation* enables them to be provided close to all the apartments.

At Marseille, the nursery school is on the top floor, and the "playground" is on the roof terrace.

Children four and five years old can go to school by themselves, in elevators, without crossing any streets.

Le Corbusier pushed the idea of integrating businesses to the point that he reserved a floor for businesses within the *unité* itself. Together with a specialist in hotel layout, we made some calculations that showed that it was more economical, in terms of the transportation of merchandise, for the businesses to be at a height midway up the building. But this floor of businesses was not utilized in the manner that Le Corbusier had hoped; he had envisioned the development of large supermarkets, so that the entire commercial floor would become a great store supplying the whole community.

5) Integration into unités. One of Le Corbusier's most misunderstood and yet most fundamental guiding principles was the following: the architect should not be content with bringing people and dwellings together under forms of arithmetical accretion. He fully understood that a group of men and women is not a simple accretion, especially when it is linked together by the bonds of everyday life. It is a sociological phenomenon: social units (*unités*) are created, an organic structuring of society. Architectural and urbanistic structures must proceed from, and translate, the preexisting structures of the society. The village is much more than an arithmetical accretion: it is an integration of people into a community. Le Corbusier sought to recover a form of habitation, a "town" that would group dwellings together, not in arithmetical accretions creating only a juxtaposition, but in integrations creating communities or social units in *unité d'habitation*. He had all this in mind when developing, after detailed study with his collaborators, the correct size for the *unité*: three hundred to four hundred families, the number necessary to create this kind of unit. From this derives the expression: *unité de grandeur conforme* (unit of adequate size).

This is yet another fundamental idea behind the *unités d'habitation*.

There has been a lot of criticism of the "great complexes" of housing realized since the Second

World War on the outskirts of large cities in various countries. The main criticism that can be leveled at them, with a few exceptions, is that they responded to a quantitative problem without showing any concern of the qualitative order and without a real sociological understanding of the problem. In them, apartments are simply set alongside one another and not integrated into units of correct size. The number of apartments amalgamated in an apartment building is a function of the area of the terrain and the density often arbitrarily established by urbanistic bylaws and very often results from a calculation of the building's profitability with respect to the land expense that an apartment can support. Thus population density is a function of the value of the land instead of the result of human concerns.

With the intuition that made him so psychologically and sociologically perceptive, Le Corbusier understood this error and wanted to avoid making it. To Le Corbusier the structure of society was made up of units integrated with one another. He believed that architectural structures must reflect social structures and must offer units of appropriate size integrated with one another. This is precisely what was formed by the *unités d'habitations* of the *ville radieuse*.

6) Natural conditions. Another of Le Corbusier's guiding principles is the return to natural conditions. (In certain ways he may be considered one of the first ecologists.) He brought nature back within the confines of the city. He affirmed the human need for contact with nature and made it possible. He refuted the city-country dichotomy by bringing the country into the city. The residences are placed in yards at wide intervals from one another, freed from arbitrary alignment along the circulation routes. In a garden town, a very high population density is possible.

Around the *unité d'habitation* is a park of 3.5 hectares (1 hectare = 2.47 acres). The building, 110 meters long and 20 meters wide, covers a space of 2,200 square meters; 32,800 square meters of free space are left over in the plot. There are 300

apartments, about 1200 inhabitants, a density of about 350 inhabitants per hectare. In spite of this density, the inhabitants live in a park. "Sun, space, and greenery" is one of Le Corbusier's guiding principles.

7) Pedestrians and automobiles. In the face of the major contemporary problem of traffic flow, it is important to separate the pedestrian from the automobile. Between residences in the garden town, avenues are used by pedestrians to get around. The cars are kept apart, no longer circulating in the streets, but on roads and highways laid out not according to the alignment of streets, but according to the places that must be connected. In open spaces, parking lots are a possibility. Thus is the problem of traffic flow resolved.

8) The core of the city. But Le Corbusier was careful not to imagine all the buildings in the city set in gardens at a good distance from each other. He knew that nuclei, centers of gravity, are a necessity. So he created little "downtown" areas and quarters, which are not just intersections and convergence points of major traffic routes, but also gravitational centers of social life. These are the nuclei, the cores. In these centers, Le Corbusier advocated a blend of functions: commerce, private and public administration, the town hall, public services, meeting places, cafés, restaurants, leisure places, places for thinking, theatres, music halls, churches, places devoted to culture, places where one goes, as Montaigne once said, "to polish one's mind against those of others."

9) Biology. Le Corbusier saw society as an organism, made up of cells and individualized yet dependent organs, each a unit integrating constitutive elements, each integrated into a higher unit of which it is a vital element. His architecture and his urbanism reflect this vision.

10) The three human establishments (Les trois établissements humains). Extending this vision beyond cities, Le Corbusier proposed orienting the growth of cities along the major flows of circulation, along the four routes (land, water, rails, and air) so as to form linear industrial towns grafted onto these routes on one hand and onto the countryside on the other. At the intersection of highways and exchanges would be the large crossroad cities. Between the highways would be countryside and agriculture. This broad organic vision includes the development of the land.

11) Beauty and poetry. This brings us to the last guiding principle, without question the most important one in Le Corbusier's thought: every rational organization prepared with intelligence according to the functions of society is unfinished, incomplete, if it is not imbued with the irrational, the sensitive—with beauty and poetry. Contrary to what is often believed and said of him, Le Corbusier never thought that a work of architecture or a functional form was necessarily beautiful. To Le Corbusier, such a notion is ridiculous. Of course, like any architect worthy of the name, he knew that architectural and urbanistic organization must rigorously meet the demands of all functions. For this reason, the process of architectural creation must span all the material problems of functional organization and resolve them in a rigorous manner. But it must overcome them in order to reach, beyond the realm of reason, the aesthetic and poetic state of mind. The goal of architecture is beauty and poetry. It is harmony. It is the play of forms and proportions. In this same vein, Le Corbusier invented the Modulor, a scale of harmonic proportions linked to the human body. He once said: "Architecture is the learned, proper, and magnificent play of volumes in light."[4] Architecture is the base from which life may blossom. It is animated.

IV. The Modulor

It was in the *unité d'habitation* at Marseille that the Modulor was applied for the first time.

Le Corbusier had always been interested in proportion. In a sense, Le Corbusier was a great musician. But rather than unfolding in time, his music unfolds in three-dimensional space. And like a musician, he expressed himself through relationships: relationships between forms; between spatial sizes, that is, between "proportions"; between spatial sizes and our own human measurements, that is, "dimensions"; between sequences of spatial sizes, that is, "rhythms." And since these rhythms imply a "sequence" in space, a dynamism, that is, the feeling of a "crescendo," one could perhaps say that the architecture of Le Corbusier is a music that unfolds in the space-time continuum.

What is the Modulor?

It is not easy to answer this question without once again making a comparison with music. One could say that the Modulor is a scale somewhat comparable to a musical scale, but instead of being a scale of sounds, it is a scale of spatial sizes. These sizes are reduced to lengths of straight lines, but by being multiplied among themselves they can determine not only segments of straight lines but surfaces and volumes as well.

The Modulor is actually a double scale, since it is composed of two series, which Le Corbusier called the red series and the blue series.

Two fundamental options define these two series. The first is that the relation between any two successive lengths in the series is the famous "golden section" ratio, the ratio of 0.618 to 1.000, which has special mathematical and aesthetic properties.

The second option is the a priori choice of human sizes for calculating the Modulor.

Why these two options? And how did the Modulor come into being?

From his youth, Le Corbusier focused much attention on proportions. He understood their importance in architecture and the central role that they play in the quest for plastic beauty, which was always Le Corbusier's ultimate goal.

At first he studied proportions with regulative outlines (*tracés régulateurs*). In his first book, *Towards a New Architecture* (*Vers une architecture*), he devoted an important chapter to regulative outlines.

He studied books on this subject, such as

those written by Matila C. Ghyka, which had a strong influence on him. He became very interested in the celebrated "golden section" and sought to establish golden section ratios in his architectural projects and his paintings.

But although he was interested in philosophy and abstract ideas, Le Corbusier always sought to put his ideas into concrete form, to bring them into reality. And when I began to work under his guidance in late 1936, Le Corbusier, under the double influence of regulative outlines and the golden section, was busy with his attempt to invent a "proportions grid" that would have facilitated the calculation of proportions during the preparation of a project. A man of concrete reality and manual labor, he even wanted to develop a worksite grid, which could be set up at the site itself, next to the construction. It would have enabled everyone, workers as well as engineers and architects, to verify the proportions and to "have an image of them in their mind's eye."

It was for the purpose of developing this grid that Le Corbusier plunged himself into the studies of the double square and the lowering of the diagonal that were described in his first book on the Modulor.[5] He received much assistance in this research from various people, most notably from Mlle Elisa Maillart, curator of the Cluny Museum, who had made her reputation by her research on the golden section and on regulative outlines.

But it should be said that in spite of the help he received, Le Corbusier, a self-taught man without a very advanced background in mathematics, suffered many setbacks in this study. The research resumed at a brisk pace after the Second World War, and it was at this time that, with the help of collaborators and as a result of a slow, tentative process, the worksite grid was abandoned and the Modulor was invented.

The Modulor is, as we have said, composed of two series of sizes. Supposing that we name the successive sizes of a series A, B, C, D, and so on, the essential element constituting the series is the consistent ratio between any two consecutive sizes—the golden section ratio, that is, 1.618 (or 0.618). Hence, A $\times$ 1.618 = B, B $\times$ 1.618 = C, and so forth. In the same way, B $\times$ 0.618 = A, C $\times$ 0.618 = B. In addition, another remarkable property of this ratio is that each size in the series is equal to the two smaller sizes that precede it: C = A + B, D = B + C, and so on.

These series were discovered in the thirteenth century by the Italian mathematician Fibonacci (Leonardo of Pisa). The problem for Le Corbusier was to choose two Fibonacci series that would be applicable to architecture.

To establish a connection between the two scales, Le Corbusier decided that all the sizes of the blue series would be double those of the red series. But in order to calculate the two series, it was necessary to establish a starting point.

It was here that Le Corbusier got the idea of reconciling the golden section with the "human scale." Since the human body contains golden section ratios in its measurements, Le Corbusier was convinced that this reconciliation was possible. He had already been seeking to integrate the human body into his worksite grid.

In order to choose the right Fibonacci series, it was necessary to start with the height of a man. Le Corbusier calculated the first Modulor by starting with a man 1.75 meters tall. This meant 1.08 meters for the height of the solar plexus and 2.16 meters for the height of the man with his arms raised.

But over the course of numerous experiments, one of Le Corbusier's collaborators discovered that by starting with a man 1.83 meters tall instead of 1.75, one could establish a correspondence between the sizes of the Modulor and the measurements of the English system, the foot and the inch. Intrigued by these correspondences, Le Corbusier decided to adopt this principle, and the second, definitive Modulor was formulated on this basis. The man 1.83 meters (6 feet) tall implies 1.13 meters for the height of the solar plexus and 2.26

for the man's height with his arms raised. Since the Modulor was going to serve to measure the proportions of a "container for people," it was best to base it on a tall man.

It was in this way that the Modulor's two scales were adopted, which go from the infinitely small to the infinitely large. And when Le Corbusier met Einstein at Princeton, Einstein said of the Modulor: "It is a scale that makes the good likely and the bad unlikely."

This is exactly what Le Corbusier thought as well. He always insisted that the Modulor be taken as a tool and not as a machine for the manufacturing of beauty. Like all tools, it can be used for better or for worse. Having become accustomed to the Modulor at the rue de Sèvres workshop, we would often respond, when Le Corbusier criticized our drawings, by saying "But it's done according to the Modulor." And then Le Corbusier would answer: "To hell with the Modulor! When it doesn't work, you shouldn't use it."

In reality, the Modulor is a tool that helps one to "tune" dimensions to each other just as one tunes the strings of a piano. It does not help one to determine sizes, but rather to arrange them, to prevent them from being in arbitrary relation to one another, to make them adjust precisely to one another, to bring them together in one single family. It is this "single family" that gives a strange unity to any composition made with the Modulor. With all of the forms that surround us in a disorder that often seems more noise than

music to our visual perception, to employ the Modulor is to create mathematical and aesthetic order.

For bringing all sizes into a single series of equal ratios means ensuring unity and harmony. It also means reducing the number of sizes used. The apartments of the Marseille *unité* were designed with just fifteen different dimensions, and these can be found repeated and harmonized with one another everywhere, as in a living being created by nature.

"To make architecture is to make a creature."[6]

Notes

1. The principal designers making up this team were: Afonso, Andreini, Roger Aujame, Edith Aujame, Badel, Barnes, Candilis, Carellas, Chatzidakis, Creveaux, Doshi, Fenyo, Gardien, Gonzalez de Léon, Genton, Hanning, Hirvela, Hoesli, Kennedy, Kondracki, Kujawski, Lemco, De Looze, Maisonnier, Masson, Mazet, Nicolas, Perriand, Préveral, Provelengios, Rosenberg, Rottier, Sachinidis, Salmona, Samper, Seralta, Soltan, Vaculik, Wogenscky, Woods, Xenakis, Yosisaka, Zalewski.
2. *Unité d'habitation de Marseille* (Paris: Edition Le Point, 1950).
3. For the internal organization of the dwelling, see the analysis published by A. Wogenscky under the influence of Le Corbusier in the first issue of the review *L'Homme et l'Architecture*, July 1945.
4. From Le Corbusier, *Vers une architecture* (Paris: Crès, 1924).
5. *Le Modulor*, collection ASCORAL (Paris, Editions de l'Architecture d'Aujourd' hui, 1950).
6. Le Corbusier, *Poème de l'angle droit* (Paris: Edition Tériade, 1955).

The Chapel of Ronchamp as an Example of Le Corbusier's Creative Process

by Danièle Pauly
translated by Stephen Sartarelli

At the outset of my research on the chapel of Ronchamp, when first exploring the archives and the large corpus of architectural drawings kept at the Fondation Le Corbusier, I found myself face to face with the documents in their rough stages, and it was probably this that most aroused my interest. The relevant documents were all in the state in which they had been left by Le Corbusier or his close collaborators. Thus the first task was to sort, analyze, and classify the material.[1]

To shed some light on the work of exploration I undertook into the written archives, it should be noted that a part of these archives that directly concerned the commission and realization of the project had already been gathered together by the shop staff at the time of the project's execution. Meanwhile, in the course of my research, other documents were found by chance in the various files assembled by Le Corbusier himself. It was most important to respect their order (or apparent disorder), since on numerous occasions we found a seminal idea, the first outline of a form, among these scattered documents. Therefore, at the beginning, a considerable amount of detailed analysis was necessary; it was carried out with the same sense of precaution as required by a fragile assemblage that must not be in any way disturbed. Indeed, it was mainly because of this initial approach to virgin material that it was later possible to reconstruct the different phases of the process of architectural creation and to retrace the genesis of the project.

An analogous method was necessary for the corpus of architectural drawings. Analyzing the project for the chapel of Ronchamp proved particularly revealing; unlike most of Le Corbusier's other projects, for which only a small number of preparatory drawings have been found, in this case it was possible to retrieve almost all of the study sketches, notebook sketches and studio drawings; they give the project's essential characteristics in a few strokes and make it possible to grasp the birth of the architectural object. The earliest notebook drawings, the tracing-paper sketches, and

Le Corbusier's drawings, as well as the studies and plans executed by the rue de Sèvres shop staff, at the time when I began my work, had been neither catalogued nor analyzed.[2] Here, too, it was, above all, a matter of undertaking to identify them and establish their chronology; I was thus able to distinguish the two stages in the genesis of this work, and, by establishing the genealogy of the project, it became possible to situate within it most of the studio drawings and studies.[3]

It should also be mentioned that in the inventory of sources judged essential to my research, Le Corbusier's texts represented a precious help. It is well known that Le Corbusier was an astute observer of his own work; in this case, he made abundant commentaries on Ronchamp. And his discussions of the work and the origin of his references, as well as his own commentary on the architectural object,[4] exercised a significant, determining influence on my work. This discussion authoritatively enriches the ways in which one might read the architectural work.

Finally, it should also be mentioned how essential, as a complement to our investigations of the archive documents and the corpus of architectural drawings, the testimony of individuals—clergymen, public figures, collaborators of Le Corbusier, etc.—was. They took part in the commission or participated in the "architectural adventure." I had the chance to meet some of them.[5]

It is also essential to point out that for my research on Ronchamp, I decided to go back only to those sources that, in my opinion, authorized the "reading of an architecture."

But what is meant by the "reading of an architecture"? It is a matter of retracing the project's genealogy, finding and analyzing the architect's references, and attempting to "decipher" the architectural object. This deciphering consists of considering it in relation to its site, studying it as a whole and in each of its separate elements, and describing and interpreting its forms and its spaces.[6]

This reading is both easy and complex: easy because of the real importance of the documents that we found and the abundance of commentaries by the architect; complex because this architecture is truly imbued with the "phenomenon of the unutterable," caused by its inventive richness and its poetic dimension: Le Corbusier, upon returning to the hill several years after the project, asked himself: "But where did I get all of that?"

In writing this essay devoted to the publication of the drawings and plans for Ronchamp made in studio, I intend to present and describe several of the elements that authorize this "reading of architecture." This said, I should add that it is the preparatory sketches that trace the genesis of the idea that held my interest rather than the more elaborated studies; in a real sense, they "tell the story" of the project's birth. This is why I have chosen to present here several of the first sketches that illustrate the research undertaken: it makes it possible to uncover those references that figure in the project's elaboration and to grasp the architect's creative process. Le Corbusier published a portion of these sketches in a pamphlet entitled *Textes et dessins pour Ronchamp*[7] and explained himself in the following manner:

> Publishing the sketches of an architectural work's genesis may be interesting.
>
> When assigned a task, I am in the habit of storing it in my memory, that is, of not allowing myself to make any sketches for months.
>
> The human brain is made in such a way that it has a certain independence: it is a box into which one can pour in bulk the elements of a problem, and then let them float, simmer, ferment.
>
> Then, one day, a spontaneous initiative of one's inner being takes shape, something clicks; you pick up a pencil, a stick of charcoal, some colored pencils (color is the key to the process), and give birth onto the paper: out comes the idea. . . .

If the first notebook sketches show an already synthesized idea of the project, it is indeed because between the commission and the architect's first contact with the site a fairly long period of time passes, which corresponds to the incubation phase alluded to by Le Corbusier; the gestation during which the idea reaches its maturity is clearly of prime importance. As I have shown in my monograph on Ronchamp,[5] Le Corbusier, as early as his first visit to the hill of Bourlémont where his chapel was to be built, immediately traced the building's plan in four lines and gave its essential volumes. These sketches express a kind of immediate intuition of the answer to be given that is an answer to the site and indicate the building's entry into the landscape: Le Corbusier notes: "Ronchamp? contact with a site, situation in a place, eloquence of the place, word addressed to the place."[8] Elsewhere, in a work that he devoted solely to Ronchamp, he explains: "On the hill, I had carefully drawn the four horizons. . . . [T]hese drawings have been misplaced or lost; it was they which architecturally triggered the acoustic response—acoustics in the realm of forms."[9] The plan's four lines are indeed a response to the site; they are two curves opening up onto a vast landscape and designed to receive the pilgrims; two straight lines that rejoin them and close the figure (Figure 1).[10]

The building's volumes were also defined in the earliest sketches. One of the first notebook pages[11] shows two sketches: one for the elevation of the eastern side, the other suggesting the form given to towers (Figure 2). This elevation is characterized by the bulging mass of the roof, which acts as a hood over the exterior choir. This covering's appearance reminds one of a shell, the crab shell spoken of by Le Corbusier when describing the birth of the project. He tells how, after finding it on a Long Island beach during a trip to New York in 1947, he noticed with surprise how strong it was when he put the entire weight of his body on it; he decided to keep it among the *objets à réaction poètique* that he liked to collect. This shell inspired in him the idea for the form of the chapel's roof—an organic form corresponding to an organic plan—as well as its structure; and just as the hollow and very resistant shell was composed of two fine membranes, the roof would be made up of two thin veils of reinforced concrete:

> Give me some charcoal and some paper; it all begins with a response to the site. The thick walls, a crab shell to round out the plan, which is so static. I bring in the crab shell; the shell will be placed on the stupidly but usefully thick walls; to the south, the light will be made to enter. There won't be any windows—the light will enter everywhere, like a stream.[12]

Thus Le Corbusier at the outset began with a very precise idea of the appearance that the building's roof would take. This done, he did not merely transpose this form into the architectural space; he elaborated the very particular aspect of this shell and transformed its initial appearance by imagining two parallel casings, creating a structure similar to that of an airplane wing (Figure 3).

In the same way, Le Corbusier almost spontaneously came up with the idea for the form of the towers that would overlook and illuminate the secondary chapels. On the same notebook page there is an outline of one of these towers; in this case as well, the source is to be found in Le Corbusier's own store of references. Thus the form and the principle of lighting adopted here derive from one of the many references that the architect accumulated over the course of his voyages. In this particular instance, he visited the villa Adriana at Tivoli, near Rome, in 1911; in the serapeum cut out of the rock, the recess of the apse is lighted by a chimney emerging from the rock to catch the light like a kind of periscope. Le Corbusier retained, in a few drawings, this principle of lighting; several decades later, he considered using it for the project of the underground basilica at La Sainte-Baume, a project that was never realized. He used the sketches made at Tivoli to develop this principle and later published a few of them in his *Oeuvre complète* (Figure 4) to help explain the genesis of this idea.[13] This idea would reach its fulfillment in the "wells of

light" that are the towers of Ronchamp. A note commenting on a small sketch, found in the file "création Ronchamp," points to the source of this idea: "Some light! In 1911, I had noticed something like that in a Roman grotto in Tivoli—no grotto, here at Ronchamp, but the hump of a hill."

The Tivoli example eloquently reveals the role played by references in Le Corbusier's process of architectural creation. My purpose here is not to dig up and describe all the references, conscious or unconscious, that lie at the origins of Ronchamp: for this, the reader should refer to my book on Ronchamp.[5] Rather, in order to attempt to grasp the architect's method, it seems to me essential, with the few examples that I have chosen to present, to understand the manner in which these references figure in the process of creation. And it is essentially through the drawing—the writing-down of "sight"— that they are retained and take their place in the architect's own history; it is also through the drawing that they reemerge at the moment of "invention." Thus, if the memory of the villa Adriana comes back to the architect's mind almost immediately, it is not only because Le Corbusier went to Tivoli and visited at length the impressive site but, above all, because he chose to draw what struck him and what he wanted to remember most. This example shows that drawing served in a real sense as a "memory" for the architect.

We have just established that in the earliest sketches the essential course to follow had already been adopted. Some of these sketches, made in a notebook and dated June 1950, show quite clearly how the initial idea for the plan evolved and became explicit in a few strokes (Figures 5 and 6). The four lines that initially outlined the plan become accurate, and in two sketches the quasi-final plan is realized: the southern and eastern sides come together in an acute angle, and the northern and western sides curl at their extremities, forming three loops designed to contain the secondary chapels. The locations of the window openings and the interior arrangement with the location of the furniture are indicated in a few lines. This plan shows a clear favoring of asymmetry;

the later workshop studies by Le Corbusier and Maisonnier will only confirm the overall course adopted.[14] The same notebook pages show how the elevations are jointed with the organic plan and roof and how the masses are organized among themselves (Figures 5 and 7).[15]

Le Corbusier describes his architectural process in the following terms:

> Three phases to this adventure:
> 1) identifying with the site;
> 2) spontaneous birth (after incubation) of the whole work, all at once, and all of a sudden;
> 3) the slow execution of the drawings, the purpose, the plans and the construction itself.[16]

After this "spontaneous birth," discernable in all of the initial sketches, which follows the fundamental phase of gestation (during which the ideas feel their way and begin to take shape and where the references come into play), the workshop studies are made. These carry out on a larger scale the process of creation introduced in the notebooks and the tracing-paper sketches. I give only one example, but it is significant because it presents an overall vision of the architectural object: it is a study in pencil by Le Corbusier,[17] giving the four elevations of the building. I shall not describe it in detail, but I should, nevertheless, point out that it clearly expresses the major contrast embodied in the overall form of the chapel. Indeed, one can read in the forms the dual function that the architect wanted to give the building: the small chapel providing a shelter for prayer and meditation and the place of worship capable of receiving a vast crowd of pilgrims. On the one hand, there is the idea of the "deep grotto," rendered by the effects of soft, round masses that surround the observer and give a sense of reassurance. On the other hand, we see the intention of creating a welcoming-place expressed in the concave form of the walls opening up toward the horizons; the idea is also shown in the dynamic character of the roof's mass, which acts as a covering over the south entrance and over the exterior choir.

In this way, the chapel's forms conflict with each other and balance each other at the same time: the bold shooting-out of the southeastern corner responds to the solid, squat masses of the towers; the bulging form, like a full sail, of the roof's shell is balanced by the verticality of the large southwestern tower; this tower, solidly anchored in the ground and overlooking the site, acts as a beacon. The walls, which seem to turn their backs on the landscape in order to contain and protect an enclosed space, respond to the walls "opening up" toward the horizons: the building is at the same time an open-air cathedral and a place for Christian mystery.

Thus, this study executed in accordance with the first sketches contains the essentials of the architect's intentions. By starting with these notebook sketches —dated May and June 1950—it was possible to find the sketches and workshop studies that corresponded to the first phase of the work and to establish their chronology[18]; these studies, drawn up between June and November of 1950, constitute the preliminary project and make explicit the course to be followed for the whole.

I then singled out the second phase in the elaboration of the project, which was carried out in the sketches and drawings made after January 1951 (at which time the preliminary project was presented to the Commission of Holy Art). The modifications made were in response to opinions expressed by the patrons; they are the product of the final perfecting of the idea by the architect and his shop staff.[19] They do not alter the overall conception of the building but are concerned mostly with fine details. This is not the place to describe these changes; but let us take note that in the sketches[20] and outlines for the definitive project[24] the overall dimensions are reduced, as a response to the desire to create a more powerful play of volumes and a denser interior space: to this end, the lines of the building are hypertense, "like bowstrings," as the architect explained.

In this second phase of the project, it might be interesting to examine a few examples that provide an understanding of the manner in which the work of research that began with an idea or a form was refined. Therefore, let us consider an example already cited: the form and structure of the roof. We have indicated the primary sources for Le Corbusier's conception of the chapel's roof: the crab shell of which he spoke and the airplane-wing structure that one finds in his drawings. He further developed the initial idea, and in his desire to tighten the lines of the building to the utmost, he makes the eastern side and the large southeast corner fit together with the western side "like a growing wave."[22] It is interesting to discover how he creates this "growing wave" profile for the slope of the roof: during my research, I found in an archive chest a review on which was written, in Le Corbusier's hand, "Ronchamp préparation documents"; he had noticed an illustration representing the cross-section of a hydraulic dam (Figure 8). The similarity between this cross-section and the curve given to the slope of the roof is quite evident; we should bear in mind that the plan required that it be possible to collect rainwater, since such was rare on the hill. The architect therefore imagined the roof's incline—starting with its highest point at the southeastern corner, down to its lowest point to the west—with a profile analogous to that of a dam's outfall. He used a form that evokes and corresponds to a very specific function.

This requirement in the plan that appears in the building's overall form is also taken into account in certain details. For example, the architect was also inspired by the dam profile in the ski-jump look that he gave to the gargoyle through which the rainwater flows to the west, toward the water tank. The dam cross-section (Figure 8) bore a note by Le Corbusier: "See *Propos d'urbanisme*." We find in the *Propos* a sketch made by the architect in 1945 depicting a dam (Figure 9). I have, moreover, discovered other sketches of this same dam,[23] one of which (dated May 14, 1945) bore the following note by Le Corbusier: "A simple straightforward perspective—the outfalls are a hydraulic form that must be deter-mined through experiments." In this instance, he tested the form by applying it to the gargoyle of

Ronchamp several years later (we should note that the earliest sketches for the gutter date from February 20, 1951, and clearly belong to the second phase of research sketches).[24]

These two examples are representative of the work carried out during this phase of research, which followed the work of giving shape to the original idea. Of course, this research was carried on throughout the process of the project's elaboration and not just during this second series of sketches; this second series only completes and refines the research done by Le Corbusier in his studio.

The example of the dams sheds light on the architect's creative method: starting with an initial idea—in this case, to create an organic form corresponding to an organic plan—and with an intuition—to use the crab shell—he "invents" an original form that will characterize the chapel of Ronchamp in a decisive way. The initial form of the shell is developed, revised, and takes on the structure of an airplane wing; and the necessity of collecting water, which is rare on the hill, leads to the architect's adoption, for the mass of the roof, of a profile of a hydraulic outfall. From this synthesis of ideas and forms is born the "prow," the "full sail" of Ronchamp.

Thus, in order to find the sources of inspiration that would complement his work, the architect drew on a very diverse store of references, as much the product of travel reminiscences (such as Tivoli) and personal memories (like the crab shell found on Long Island) as borrowings from the language of contemporary technology (the airplane wing, hydraulic dams, etc.). It is obviously not a question of compiling a kind of catalogue of forms or models to be directly transposed into a project. It is rather a question of retaining ideas and solutions, of noticing analogies of forms attributable to analogies of function, as is the case with some of the sources that I should like to cite at present. Unlike the direct influences that I have just described and to which Le Corbusier explicitly refers, these sources reveal instead, to my mind, the workings of an unconscious process.

Indeed, parallel to the explicit references that come into play in the process of the creation of the architectural work, there are a number of unconscious influences that enter into the work process either during the gestation of the work or during the elaboration of the project. But before discussing these influences, it would be useful to dwell for a moment on this incubation phase, which is to my mind of utmost importance in Le Corbusier's creative process. It seems, moreover, to be one of the constants of his work method, as much in painting as in architecture. He explained, as we remember: "When assigned a task, I am in the habit of storing it in my memory, that is, of not allowing myself to make any sketches for months"; he added further on that the "human brain" is like a "box" in which one lets the "elements of a problem simmer." During this phase, even if indeed he does not draw, some part of the work of research and documentation necessary to master the elements of a given problem is nevertheless being carried out. In our particular instance, that of Ronchamp, the architect informed himself about the site, the tradition of pilgrimage associated with the place, and its devotion to the Holy Virgin; he looked into the rituals of the Catholic religion, spoke with ecclesiastics; he studied and annotated a monograph devoted to the site of Ronchamp, consulted reviews of religious art, etc. . . . Thus, before anything else, he gathers information, accumulates documents, takes notes. Then these various elements are sorted out, analyzed, assimilated, perhaps reused, sometimes forgotten. Only then does the idea become precise. Enriched by sources emanating from his unconscious, the idea emerges, clearly formulated by the drawing: only then does Le Corbusier "invent."

Among the implicit sources that I was able to discover,[25] and for which I was able to establish a clear relation with the Ronchamp project, one seems to be particularly revealing; it is found, like a number of others, among the architect's travel souvenirs. During a 1931 trip to northern Africa,

Le Corbusier visited the valley of the M'zab in the Algerian desert.[26] I found several drawing notebooks[27] marking out the whole itinerary of this voyage and showing in particular the fascination that Mozabite architecture held for the architect: he gave attention to urban sights, street scenes, the effects of volumes, plays of light and shadow, as well as to relationships of proportions, details of the organization of dwellings, the layout of patios and indoor spaces, and principles of light admission. He notes in particular how the openings are distributed with parsimony in the thick walls; he remarks that this sort of loophole with deep splays preserves an indispensable freshness inside the building and diffuses the light in a very precise and restrained manner. The similarity between this kind of opening and those of the southern wall of Ronchamp is certainly remarkable (Figure 10); here, too, this principle makes possible a very exact control of the amount of light inside the chapel, creating that atmosphere of semidarkness so conducive to meditation. Le Corbusier notes that some of these loopholes also act as placement niches. Later we see this same idea at work at Ronchamp, in the thickness of the southern wall, to the east, where hollows designed to hold objects of worship during open-air services are cut out. At Ronchamp, as at M'zab, we find the same whiteness of the material, a whiteness of lime serving to catch the light and exalt the purity of the forms: ". . . there, the volume of things appears clearly; the color of things is explicit. The whitewash is absolute: everything stands out, everything is absolutely etched in, black on white: it is honest and direct."[28] In both places, we find walls of the same thickness; in the one case, this serves to protect from heat and retain shadow; in the other, the deep splays make possible the calculated and attenuated diffusion of the light; and the thickness of the southern wall serves to buttress the mass of the roof.

We cannot claim a direct and conscious influence of the Mozabite architecture analyzed by

Le Corbusier on the chapel of Ronchamp. Here instead we are dealing with that kind of reference that the architect retains through the drawing, over the course of his travels and throughout his experiences and his research. And there is another example that seems sufficiently demonstrative to be also cited. Over the course of my research, I found by chance, among the vast mass of documents amassed by the architect,[29] a reveiw from 1930 with a photograph of the funerary steles of a Jewish cemetery in the Middle East:[30] the form of these steles disturbingly evokes that of the chapel's towers. There is nothing that really allows us to see a relation, even unconscious, between the two; let us say that it is an image, among so many others, that he saw and perhaps preserved in his memory.

These references are far from being purely formal. They involve a multitude of observed and assimilated facts, "spatial facts" and "architectural facts": these are plays of volumes, ideas for arrangement, approaches to the site, proportional relationships, lights and shadows, colors, effects of building materials, *modenaturas*; they are also solutions that respond ingeniously to a particular problem, forms of knowhow, of "ways to make." Didn't Le Corbusier take pleasure in repeating that "art is the way to make"?

This constant enrichment of what constitutes the architect's knowledge came about, for Le Corbusier, as much through his voyages and his visiting of buildings as by his visiting museums and libraries, particularly in his formative years. And all of the data that he garnered along the way and that become his own will sometimes reemerge, without being really visible or conscious, at the moment in which he "invents," in which he creates his own architectural language.

This process is marked with hundreds, even thousands, of sketches, innumerable annotated notebook pages that constitute, throughout his life, his "long, patient search," for—and I must insist on this point—it is fundamentally through the constant

practice of drawing that Le Corbusier is able to retain all those references representing possible sources for the architectural project: and here, to my mind, lies the key to his creative process.

In a work published during the last years of his life, *L'Atelier de la recherche patiente*,[31] Le Corbusier explains the importance of the drawing as "memory":

> When one travels and is a practitioner of visual things, architecture, painting, or sculpture, *one sees with one's eyes, and one draws in order to take inside, into one's own history, the things that one sees.*[32]
>
> Once things have been interiorized through the work of the pencil, they remain within for the rest of one's life; they are written there, inscribed.
>
> To draw oneself, to follow outlines, to fill up spaces, to explore volumes, etc., is first of all to see; it is being perhaps qualified to observe, perhaps qualified to discover . . . at this moment the phenomenon of invention may arise. One invents, and one even creates; one's whole being is brought into the action; this action is the central issue.

Thus, the drawing enables one to see better, to glean the essentials of a form or an idea, to establish relationships, to make note of details; it is a way of making observations, of registering information, of singling out a problem or a solution; it is a way of "understanding things," as the architect gives us to understand. The numerous drawings that are not part of the corpus of architectural drawings published here constitute in themselves an exceptionally rich collection. I undertook the study of these drawings a number of years ago[33] because they seemed to me of essential importance to understanding the artist's method. These drawings, those from the period of his youth and formative years—life-studies, building surveys, portraits, landscapes, sketches made in museums, etc.—as well as those that mark all of his production—still-lifes, studies for paintings or sculptures, drawings of women, sketches made during his travels—give us a glimpse of the architect's vast curiosity, his powers of observation, his understanding of the world, and his powers of invention. It is by starting with this "sedimentation," with a plurality of things seen and retained through drawing, that the phenomenon of invention can occur. It is with this knowledge that Le Corbusier sustains the work of creation. And the drawing thus serves to concretize this invention, to express the idea.

Indeed, if the drawing is "memory" for the architect, it is also, during the project, the instrument of research and creation. We cited earlier these comments of Le Corbusier's: "Then, one day, a spontaneous initiative of one's inner being takes shape, something clicks; you pick up a pencil. . . ." The drawing is thus the immediate transcription of the idea that is taking shape: "To see first of all the project in one's mind"; he goes on to explain, "The drawing is useful only in contributing toward the synthesis of ideas already thought out."[34] In the same way, the notebook sketches that we mentioned above make plain how, in a few strokes, the essentials of the idea are given. The drawing, made in ink, is linear, concise, synthetic; at the same time it is a research tool that, in the detail studies, for example, helps the idea to become manifest, to formulate itself definitively. Though ink is the preeminent material permitting the architect this lively and rapid writing that characterizes the notebook sketches, it is with charcoal that he gives forth, in the studio, the first expression and traces in broad strokes the first outlines (". . . give me some charcoal and some paper; it all begins with a response to the site . . ."). Color helps to determine choices; it is the "key to the process," as the architect indicated. Finally, he sketches out the more advanced studies in pencil; the pencil allows for a more precise rendering and makes it possible to present details and to represent the density of the masses, the plays of light and shadow, the "life of the forms." As he himself explains, the overall conception of the

project is always, for him, defined at the start, and one may assert that for Le Corbusier the drawing is in a real sense *cosa mentale*.

The vast production of drawings existing alongside the architectural drawings is, to my mind, the most eloquent illustration possible of Le Corbusier's relationship with history. We have seen how the multitude of remembered images and ideas comprising the architect's personal history and experience nourish his creativity and enrich his architectural vocabulary and how he feeds the project with the study and knowledge of history, even though this is not immediately discernable. If I have been able to cite some of the sources that seemed essential to an understanding of the genesis of the project, it is because I made the effort to seek them out or because the architect chose to reveal them in explaining his procedure and commenting on his work. It is also in order to demonstrate that creation, far from being the fruit of inspirational genius, depends much more on a long and minute work process, a "long, patient search," as the architect liked to repeat. This said, the manner in which his relationship with history is registered in the work of architectural creation lies rather in the realm of the inexplicable, the "unutterable." In a work entitled *Le Territoire de l'architecture*, Vittorio Gregotti explains:

It is, however, necessary to know that the whole experience, as history, tends toward becoming presence and signification at the moment of the project; that is, becoming action for the subject; and then, anew, becoming historical experience.[35]

I believe that, for Le Corbusier, history intervenes in a real sense as a dynamic element in the creative process. And in the project that I have chosen to analyze, I have been able to ascertain to what degree this is confirmed at various stages and levels. I have dealt at length with the role of references in the gestation phase and in the research phase. I also mentioned the importance that the architect attributed to knowing the history of the site where his edifice would be built, here, the devotion to the Virgin Mary and the tradition of pilgrimage associated with the place, with which he imbued his projects. Finally, through the forms he imagines and the spaces he creates, he firmly establishes the chapel in architectural tradition. In fact, as surprising as this work may have appeared to his contemporaries, its users found that it had certain affinities, and even a certain intimate resemblance, to Roman churches, for example: the same sacred atmosphere, the same bulky volumes, the same thick walls, the same deep splays, the same semidarkness conducive to meditation . . . In this way, the building expresses a kind of intimacy, an implicit bond with the past.

The architect's language has the basis of its originality in a "creative" and dynamic vision of history; he speaks of the links existing between "architectural invention" and knowledge of the past in the following terms:

> . . . carried away by the defense of the rights to invention, I used the past as a witness, this past which was my only master and which continues to be my permanent counsel.
>
> Every level-headed man, once cast into the unknown of architectural invention, can really only sustain his impetus by looking to the lessons provided over the centuries. The testimonies provided by the ages have a permanent human value. One may consider them folklores—a notion expressing the flower of the creative spirit in folk traditions—by extending their realm beyond man's home to that of the gods.
>
> Flower of the creative spirit, chain of traditions which embody it and each link of which is and can only be a work that is innovative, and often revolutionary, within its working; a contribution.
>
> The history that bases itself on reference points preserves only these faithful testimonies; the imitations, plagiaries, and compromises fall behind them, abandoned, even destroyed.

> Respect for the past is a filial attitude natural to every creator.[36]

This text seems particularly to reveal an "intimate and profound harmony with the past" that determines Le Corbusier's attitude. For him, history is truly "the mark of human presence,"[37] and architecture is the "memory of peoples," to use Ruskin's terms. In a profound sense, it is a relationship of "sympathy" toward history that most authoritatively characterizes his development. He says, ". . . but we who intensely experience the current epoch of modern times . . . we have extended our sympathy to the entire earth and to all the ages. . . ."[38] It is essentially through the constant, unfailing practice of drawing that this fundamental relationship to history is expressed.

Notes

1. I was associated with the Fondation Le Corbusier from 1973 to 1977, and after having worked on the archives, I was assigned the research work on drawings.
2. That is, about ten years ago. I was able at the time to distinguish the studies executed or revised by Le Corbusier from those made by his collaborators, especially Maisonnier.
3. I was able to establish the chronology of the studies and drawings, but this chronology does not figure in this publication.
4. Le Corbusier, *Ronchamp, les carnets de la recherche patiente*, notebook 2 (Zurich: Girsberger, 1957); and *Textes et dessins pour Ronchamp* (place not given: Forces Vives, 1965).
5. See Danièle Pauly, *Ronchamp, lecture d'une architecture* (Strasbourg: A.P.P.U.; Paris: Ophrys, 1980), p. 24ff.
6. We shall not treat this matter here; see above-cited work.
7. Unpaginated.
8. Le Corbusier, *Textes et dessins pour Ronchamp*, unpaginated.
9. Le Corbusier, *Ronchamp, les carnets de la recherche patiente*, p. 89.
10. Outline of the plan made from the first notebook sketches: Fondation Le Corbusier (FLC) No. 7.470 (charcoal and red pencil on tracing paper, signed "L.C." and dated June 6, 1950; 0,75 X 1,185).
11. Sketchbook D 17, p. 15.
12. Le Corbusier, in the file "création Ronchamp" (FLC archives)

13. Le Corbusier, *Oeuvre complète, 1946–1952* (Zurich: Girsberger, 1967), pp. 28–31.

14. For example, FLC Nos. 7.435, 7.369, 7.415, among others.

15. Sketchbook E 18, pp. 7 and 9.

16. Le Corbusier, *Textes et dessins pour Ronchamp,* unpaginated.

17. FLC No. 7.433, black pencil and colored pencil on tracing paper, 1,10 X 0,75.

18. For example, FLC Nos. 7.470, 7.417, 7.433, or 7.412 and 7.414.

19. Le Corbusier's studies were taken up again in the workshop by Maisonnier above all; I was easily able to distinguish Le Corbusier's studies from the rest (see Pauly, p. 40).

20. Sketchbook E 18, sketches dated February 1951.

21. For example, FLC No. 7.324.

22. See in Pauly, Figure 20, p. 49.

23. Investigations into various archive chests.

24. Sketchbook E 18, pp. 18 and 19.

25. See Pauly, pp. 132ff.

26. For my part, I was able to take the "M'zab voyage" and retrace part of Le Corbusier's itinerary. I did the same for the villa Adriana at Tivoli.

27. These notebooks of drawings are distinguished from the sketchbooks by their format; they are larger than the latter and consist of drawing paper; they are spiral notebooks whose pages we have numbered according to the drawings of Le Corbusier's (cf. Notebook C 12).

28. Le Corbusier, cited in Maurice Besset, *Qui était Le Corbusier?* (Geneva: Skira, 1968), p. 17.

29. An analysis of the contents of the numerous portfolios of Le Corbusier enabled me to uncover the richness and diversity of the material gathered to stimulate his creativity. In addition to the drawings and sketches, these portfolios contained many magazine clippings, photos, reviews, and documents of a great variety.

30. In VU, No. 137, December 1930 (FLC archives).

31. Le Corbusier, *L'Atelier de la recherche patiente* (Paris: Vincent, Fréal, 1960), p. 37.

32. My emphasis.

33. To this end I am preparing a descriptive catalogue of some of these drawings.

34. Le Corbusier, cited in Jean Petit, *Le Corbusier lui-même* (Geneva: Editions Rousseau, 1970), p. 30.

35. Vittorio Gregotti, *Le Territoire de l'architecture* (Paris: L'Equerre, 1982), p. 88.

36. Le Corbusier, *Entretiens avec les étudiants des écoles d'architecture.* (Paris: Editions Minuit, 1957).

37. See Manfredo Tafuri, *Teorie e storia dell'architettura* (Roma: Laterza, 1968), pp. 62–63.

38. Le Corbusier, *Quand les cathédrales étaient blanches* (Paris: Plon, 1937), p. 16.

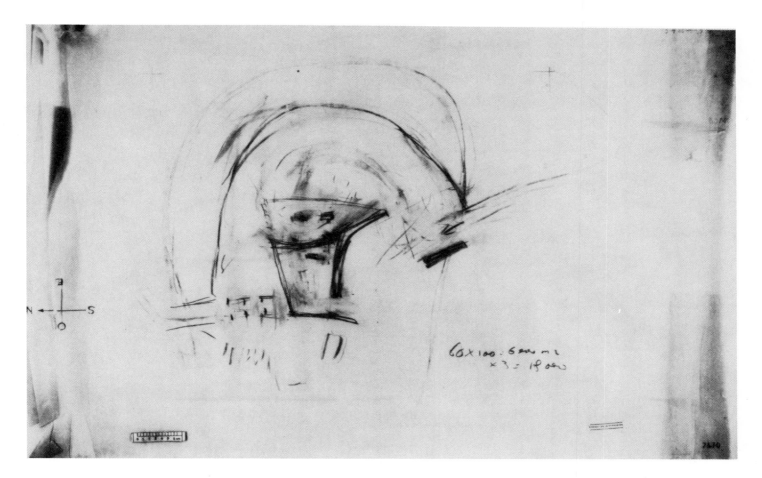

Figure 1. Early plan of building, Fondation Le Corbusier #7.470.

Figure 2. Eastern elevation and calotte of tower, Sketchbook D17, p. 15. Reproduced by permission of the Architectural History Foundation and the Fondation Le Corbusier.

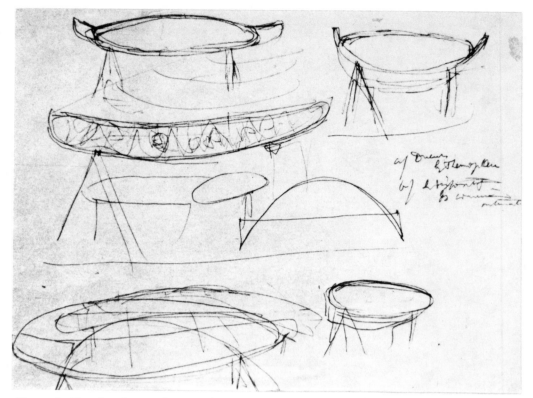

Figure 3. Sketches for roof.

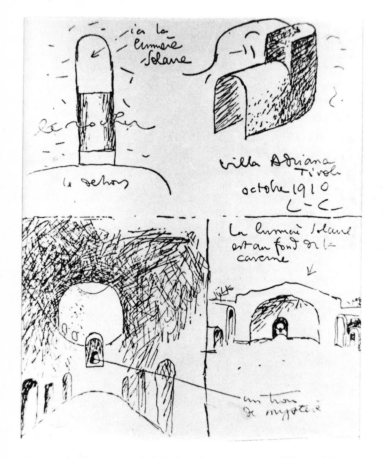

Figure 4. Sketches of lighting in serapeum, Villa Adriana, Tivoli.

Figure 5. Southeastern elevation and plan, Sketchbook E18, p. 7. Reproduced by permission of the Architectural History Foundation and the Fondation Le Corbusier.

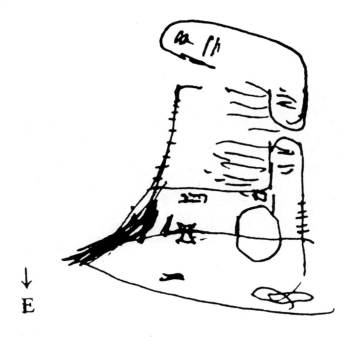

Figure 6. Plan, Sketchbook E18, p. 8. Reproduced by permission of the Architectural History Foundation and the Fondation Le Corbusier.

Figure 7. Southeastern elevation, Sketchbook E18, p. 9. Reproduced by permission of the Architectural History Foundation and the Fondation Le Corbusier.

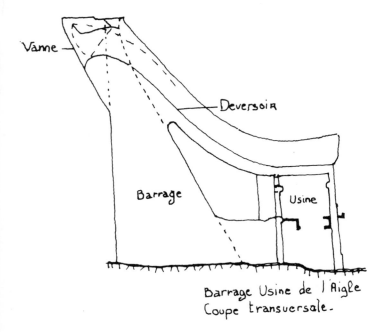

Figure 8. Hydraulic dam, cross-section. From *Reconstruction*, October 1948, p. 12.

Figure 9. Dam at Chastang, pen-and-ink sketch.

Figure 10. Mosque of Sidi Brahim at El Atteuf, M'zab. Photograph courtesy of Danièle Pauly.

The Monastery of La Tourette: general view.

The Monastery of La Tourette
by Iannis Xenakis

By 1953 Le Corbusier had already separated from Vladimir Bodianski, the head engineer of ATBAT (Atelier des Bâtisseurs: Builders' Studio) in charge of the *unité de'habitation* of Marseille, and had kept André Wogenscky, for the time being, as administrator and studio foreman. Le Corbusier was working on several projects at the same time. Each project was entrusted to one of the young collaborators with whom he worked several hours each week, in the mornings after reading his mail, because in the afternoons he stayed at home to work on his painting. Between work sessions the collaborator designed the plans while trying to respect as much as possible the guidelines that Le Corbusier had laid down in the work sketches, which he colored for easier readability. Here it should be pointed out that in general he made these sketches while conversing with the collaborator of the project in question, making suggestions and often accepting those of his collaborator. He benefited thus from a dialectic of thought with the young and inexperienced, but at times generous and inventive, mind of his interlocutor, who would give away, in all innocence, his thoughts, in case that he had any! I must also say that it was very rare for his young collaborator to give him any truly new and interesting ideas.

Having graduated in engineering, I was in charge, for all the current projects under way, of technical considerations and of making calculations, even if provisional. Of all the young collaborators, who at that time were no more than five or six in number, no one understood very well, if at all, the principles of strength of materials—which is what transformed me into an arbiter even of architectural aesthetics. This is how I started getting into the work of an architect, little by little, through the act itself, in depth and with responsibility, and all the while acquiring a taste for it, though in fact my deep-seated vocations were music and science, not architecture. Thus one fine midday in 1953, while accompanying Le Corbusier to Rue de Sèvres, I asked

him abruptly if I could work with him personally on a project. "Yes," he told me without hesitation, "I have a project that will suit you perfectly; it is pure geometry—a Dominican monastery."

In the face of this project I had to struggle against my atheism rooted in ancient civilizations and, having been an orthodox Christian, against the "schismatic" reflexes buried in my psychic unconscious. As a matter of fact, I felt suited to create as if I were a believer, since I had escaped twofold from religion—from the ancient religion with which I had been impregnated as well as from Christianity. I possessed the necessary critical distance. But of course never during my collaboration with Le Corbusier was the religious or ideological side brought up by him, nor by me or the monks, our interlocutors. Besides, it was neither a question of revolutionizing the faith of the Dominicans nor of disrupting their habits. It was necessary to follow their planning of the physical spaces, of circulations and functions, and to organize them in the best possible way into receptacles that were stark but resonantly architectural. To discover, to create a different, other architecture, unique and original in its essential nudity—that was our goal.

As always, it took a percussive idea to get the project started—just as in the music composition that I was doing at the same time. It was Le Corbusier who, when bringing me the plan-sketches of the Reverend Father Couturier, initiator of this new monastery, also furnished me with the key idea that he had seen in a church near Moscow—a sort of box standing on end with a ramp giving access to its center, powerfully plastic in its simplicity. But how could this be done in keeping with the plan? I shall come back to this in a moment.

The general design of a closed rectangle was copied exactly from the model for monasteries of all times, which itself was copied from ancient dwellings: life inside walls around a garden, like in the house at Delos, itself in all probability a successor of the Mycenaean megaron (see also 315c—

316b in Plato's *Protagoras*). Meditative and contemplative life unfolds as one walks about inside the enclosure, the cloister. With the all-inclusive rectangle, Le Corbusier brought in the cell plan of the Charterhouse of Ema in Italy. But Le Corbusier wanted to give it a loggia and to open the cell toward the exterior of the monastery. The hotel room/apartments of the *unité* at Marseille became the prototype of the ready-made cells that were to occupy the upper levels of the monastery; the monastery itself was conceived as a *stadium*, that is as a college for the Dominican monks. The total necessary area required by the Dominicans' plan turned out to be around five thousand square meters: two upper levels of cells, one level of classrooms and common rooms, and a partial level of kitchens and communal services. The church had its own characteristics and closed one of the sides of the overall rectangle. On the map Le Corbusier chose to situate the monastery in the lap of a hill on the vast property not far from an old guest house of the Dominicans of the Monastery of Lyon. One of the sides of the rectangle, the west facade, was turned toward the valley, which gave the monastery the appearance of a monastery of Athos or of Tibet, because of the great overhang due to the sharp slope of the terrain (Figure 1).

The cloister, a covered passageway, was originally placed on the terrace roof of the monastery. But in the interim Le Corbusier's idea of a ramp's giving access to the nave of a church sparked my imagination, and I presented him with two types of solution. The first was a spiral, covered ramp around a vertical concrete core providing access to the terrace from all four levels of the monastery and to the church as well as to the entrance of the monastery (Figure 2). The project that I conceived on February 26, 1954, was rejected by Le Corbusier on March 19, 1954. I then presented a second project to him with variants in which a covered ramp placed against the south face of the church received, like a commutator, the covered ramps of the other levels (Figures 3, 4, and 5). These covered ramps, besides being an attempt to preserve the initial idea of

Le Corbusier, took the place of the cloister walk leading to the real cloister of the more conventional terrace roof, but from where there was a view of the west valley. Moreover, to speed up the exchanges between the four sides of the rectangle, Le Corbusier had the idea of making two covered ramps in the form of a rampant cross from east to west connecting the bodies of the buildings and as well as running from north to south. In the end, of all these tremendous ideas, there survived, due to lack of funds, only the cross-shaped covered ramps, to which would be added a covered "atrium." Le Corbusier left it to me to organize architecturally the spaces, the functions, and the circulations both on the drawing table and in the comings and goings between Lyon and Paris for the work meetings with the Dominican fathers. After each elaboration I asked Le Corbusier for a meeting, and he accepted or modified my drawing. As soon as he accepted it, I marked it with the initials L. C. and the date. I cannot enter into all of the details, and besides, time has erased many of my memories. I will therefore speak only of a few salient points of which I am proud or which seem to me interesting both in terms of this study and in this battle of wits with architecture, Le Corbusier, the fathers, and the construction prices.

Hence the "atrium." The fathers had called for a surface area at the intersection of the cross-shaped covered ramp. I traced an oblique line on the interior facade. Le Corbusier accepted it, and the atrium received its roof (Figure 6). Then, since I planned to hold it up by two parallel north-south sides, made of concrete blind veils, I lowered these veils to the natural ground level, and to lighten them visually I tore them into rather free-form combs and into curves, which Le Corbusier accepted with a smile (Figure 7). I also added, afterward and at the request of the fathers, a spiral staircase to link the cells of the professorial fathers to the level of the atrium, which was accepted as well.

Undulating Glass Panes
In June of 1954 I was studying the glass openings, 366 centimeters high, for the level of the common

rooms and the classrooms. I found out the vertigo of combinatorics in architectural elements, after having experimented with them in music. In fact, in *Metastasis* for orchestra, which I was finishing at about the same time (1953–54), the median part was constructed on a combinatorial organization of melodic intervals ±1, ±2, ±3, ±4, ±5, ±6, expressed in semitones. Furthermore, *Metastasis* was the source of another much more radical work of architecture that I conceived two years later. This was the Philips Pavillon at the 1958 Brussels World's Fair, which I designed and made out of ruled surfaces much like my fields of string glissandi, which suddenly and for the first time in the history of music opened the way to the continuity of sound transformations in instrumental music. Moreover, on the occasion of the world premiere of *Metastasis* in Donaueschingen, Le Corbusier published in 1955 the first page of the score at the end of his book, *Modulor 2*, with an explanatory text of mine. Then I made several studies of the three facades, which did not satisfy me. I had chosen four elements, *a, b, c, d*, of the golden section and their twenty-four permutations, which I arranged on the unfolding of the facades like a variation on a single theme in time (Figures 8 and 9). But the play was too subtle to catch the eye. It was only in November 1954 that Le Corbusier made a kind of synthesis of my attempts and created the glass walls that are today the inside facades of the monastery (Figures 10, 11, and 23). But not everything could be put into glass in the same way. In the spring of 1955, on returning from Chandigarh, Le Corbusier called me into his office and gave me a sketch, by Pierre Jeanneret I believe, of a glass partition made of regularly spaced vertical casings containing glass panes of variable heights but identical widths, piled one on top of the other for the entire height of the story so as to lessen the glass wastes. Le Corbusier asked me to work on this for the glass facades of the Assembly at Chandigarh. The obsession of combinatorics had not left me, but right away I chose several distances in golden sections drawn from the Modulor. My problem was how to distribute these concrete upright casings (for

which I defined a standard rectangular section with rabbets to receive the glass panes) on the facades. In other words, how to distribute points on a straight line. This problem may elicit an infinity of answers, but two are extreme poles. One is to choose points without any periodicity whatsoever, that is by following a stochastic (probability) distribution. The other is to follow a strict periodicity. But at that time I was only catching a glimpse of the stochastic music that I invented a year later, and therefore I missed this solution in architecture. I regret it very much, because it was a unique occasion to introduce probabilities into architecture. Thus, I chose to follow a strict periodicity. But there the pitfall of the aridity of the permutational variation was amplified, this time thanks to the greater number of elements that I wanted to use. For if one is still able to "control" the twenty-four permutations of four elements, it is impossible to do so with ten of them (10! = 3,628,800 permutations). It was thus necessary to choose another criterion on a more general level, situated above the permutations. I had already treated this problem in music by creating a magnetic tape with blips at distances defined by the golden section and by even writing an unpublished score for percussion.

The criterion was that of the fluctuations of the densities of the points (blips) on a straight line (time). Density is a macroscopic perception, an instantaneous unconscious calculation that we make visually as well as aurally. This faculty originates in our mind and seems to be statistical. We make statistical analysis (synthesis) without knowing it. Thus, in traditional music the movements—adagio, largo, presto, vivace—are related to the criterion of density (the number of events per unit of time or length), which thus assumes an aesthetic weight. The chiaroscuros are akin to density, as is intensity. Thus the problem on the level of density is simpler, since in being situated on a more general plane, it contains fewer elements than the set of the distances between the upright casings. Control is easier. So the solution is to juxtapose on the facades patches containing dense, upright casings of reinforced concrete with patches containing rarefied ones. Naturally, here it is necessary to define the degrees of density and their respective lengths (durations). But, moreover, another problem that springs up is that of the passage from one density to another, either in a continuous progression or brutally, in jerks. The problem of continuity in the transition as well as its speed and/or form plays a fundamental role in musical aesthetics or in visual arts and architecture.

After several attempts I designed a first composition, notably of the west facade, on three or four levels in counterpoint, which Le Corbusier approved (Figures 12 to 19). He was so pleased that he wanted to call them "musical glass panes," and he asked me to describe them in his book *Modulor 2*. I suggested calling them "undulating glass panes" because of the undulation of the densities. He accepted this, and that is how I designed them for the Assembly of Chandigarh, the Maison des Juenes of Firminy, the Brazilian Pavillon in Paris, and for other buildings.

The parallelepipedical church posed several serious problems concerning its use, acoustics, lighting. It was supposed to contain the monks' choir, space for the laic faithful, with a high altar separating the two, and altars for the concelebration, which, during the 1950's, was an idea dear to the Dominicans. The width of the nave was defined by the necessity of having two rows of stalls on each side and in the middle a space large enough to permit two to lie down completely head-to-head in prostration on the floor. I designed a high altar that was judged by the monks to be too abrupt, too high, too, separative. In fact I had conceived it a little like a place for terrible sacrifices. It was too dramatic, too Aztec. Christ sacrificed himself, as did Dionysos, but the drama had to remain internal and luminous. In the end, just a few steps separated the two levels, that of the faithful from that of the monks, with great enough visibility in both directions and with the high altar able to be used from all sides (Figure 20).

It was obvious that the twelve small altars could not fit into the principal nave. I proposed a volume joined to the north side in the form of a piano, noncylindrical with a ruled conoidal surface with a flat terrace roof (Figure 21). Seven altars would be set up on the ground level and five on the level of the high altar. For lighting I made three cones which I called "light-cannons," tilted in various ways on the plane of the terrace roof. In order to study them I made a model with little aluminum cans of Algerian olive oil and obtained Le Corbusier's approval (Figure 22). Other small altars were added beneath the sacristy. A passage beneath the church provided access to the seven small altars of the piano form. I decided on the spot in a four-hour meeting with fathers Prisset, Belot, and de Couesnongle at Lyon to open and link the piano volume with the volume of the central nave. Fortunately, Le Corbusier, in Paris, found fault with none of this. The merging of these two volumes provided a spatial aeration and moreover allowed the light of the "light-cannons" to pass into the church, thus creating a lower, lateral lighting while leaving the upper part of the church in shadowy light. To make the south part of the church symmetrical, I added on the terrace roof of the sacristy, irregular, pentagonal prisms of concrete, tilted in such a way as to let the sun at the equinoxes pass into the principal nave by way of a slit in the church's concrete wall along the length of the sacristy. These were the "light-guns" (Figure 23). There, Le Corbusier added a final touch by imagining, beneath this slit, a slightly inclined plane, like an invitation to the light. Thus was the church joined to the cosmos like the pyramids and other sacred edifices. After this, I studied the luminosity of the church with a light meter and found it to be not entirely sufficient. This is why Le Corbusier then opened a whole vertical slit in the northeast corner with a concrete shell marking it on the exterior (Figure 24) and then a partial slit between the ceiling and the walls in the nave, which created a glow of light in the darkness high up in the nave. The openings behind and directly above the choir went through quite a few adventures. Indeed, the problem was to light, without dazzling the opposite stalls—contradiction that found a most simple expression, but perhaps not an interesting one (Figure 25).

Suddenly we realized that the Dominicans made use of an organ but that there was no place for it in the church. I designed a kind of concrete "knapsack" on the exterior of the church's west side, at the end of the choir. Le Corbusier accepted the solution but changed the curves of the knapsack into straight lines (Figure 26).

The problem of acoustics was never settled, due to a lack of money. Initially I had planned, with the consent of Le Corbusier, concrete diamond shapes on the long north and south walls. On seeing them, Le Corbusier, ironically kind, commented that it was German Expressionism of the 1920's, but he did not forbid them (Figures 27 and 28). It was only the lack of funds that doomed them. The ceiling sound treatment (flockage) met with the same fate.

There was also the idea of installing electronic bells (real bells being too expensive) that would bathe in sound the valley far off. I drew my inspiration from sound louvers and shaped them in the form of an ellipsoid or paraboloid by revolution. The Dominicans, however, rejected this project (Figures 29 and 30).

Perhaps the most brain-racking difficulty was the belfry for local use in the monastery. A church must, of course, have a belfry. Le Corbusier set me on the track with a sketch from his youth of the belfries of the small, all-white Greek churches. A crop of multiple belfries ensued (Figures 31 and 32), but Le Corbusier found finally a "plagal" solution rich in simplicity and elegance (Figure 24).

One day Le Corbusier designed the oratory for the youth, not yet included for lack of space, in the form of a cube inside the monastery rectangle. He asked me to cut a pyramid out of paper, which he stuck on top of the cube on the study model that I had made of the monastery. I argued that this pyramid was not of the same family as the other forms. He disregarded my objection and kept the pyramid, to which he then added a light hood, since the cube had no other opening.

It must also be added that I calculated in a first approximation all the dimensions and all the concrete sections of the building as an engineer in such a way that the whole monastery displayed a harmonious lightness. So it was to our surprise when the calculations of exterior engineers practically doubled all the concrete sections and even declared some parts (such as the terrace roof of the piano) impossible to build. I must say that Le Corbusier backed me up to the hilt in this disagreement and that finally we did find another contractor who recalculated the whole of it, and precisely according to my dimensions. The terrace roof of the piano came to be realized in prestressed concrete, which was used also for other parts of the structure.

In concluding these succinct recollections, almost thirty years later, I realize to what a great extent this collaboration was a perpetual and rich exchange between me, with admiration for him and his ideas, and him, Le Corbusier—understanding, cooperative, creative, free and independent, quick-thinking— never trying to crush me or to reject my own discoveries, but on the contrary always respecting them, discussing them, accepting them as they were or modifying them. A certain kind of fraternal joy united us in this project, not always the case in other projects on which I worked with him during these years—years during which architecture gradually became as important to me as the music that I was relentlessly working on at the same time. The monastery has remained for me a luminous memory. A few years ago the French government finally declared the Monastery of La Tourette as a historical monument of France.

Figure 1

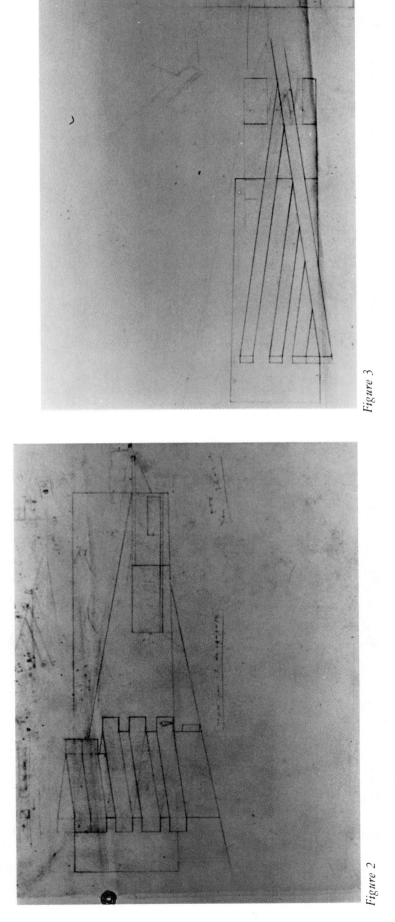

Figure 3

Figure 2

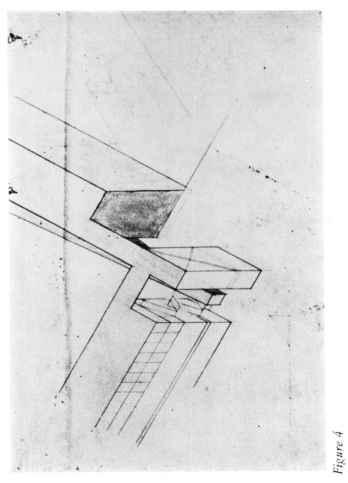

Figure 5

Figure 4

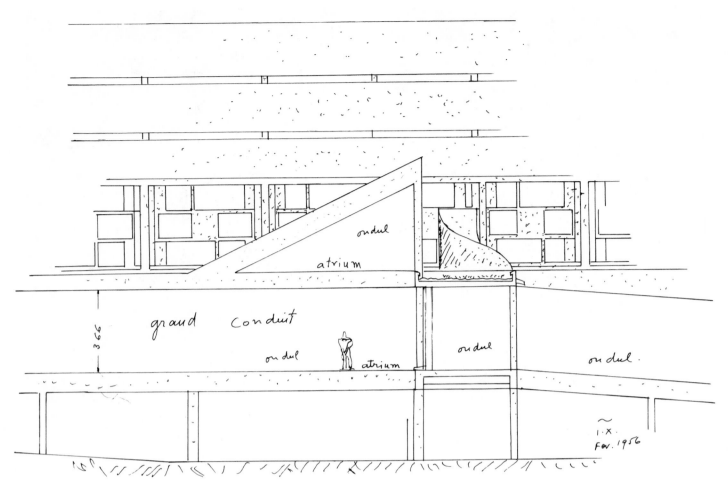

Figure 6

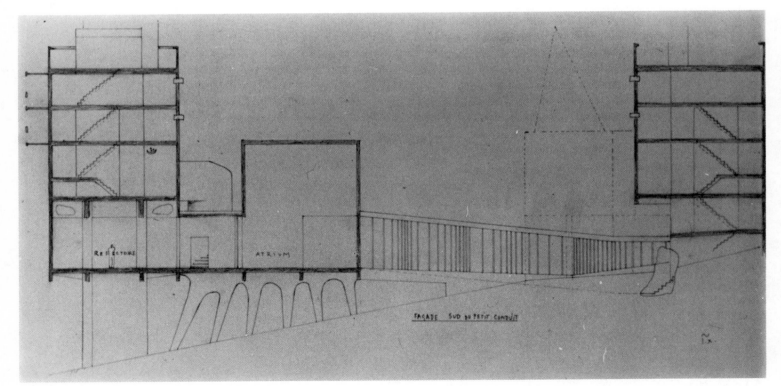

Figure 7

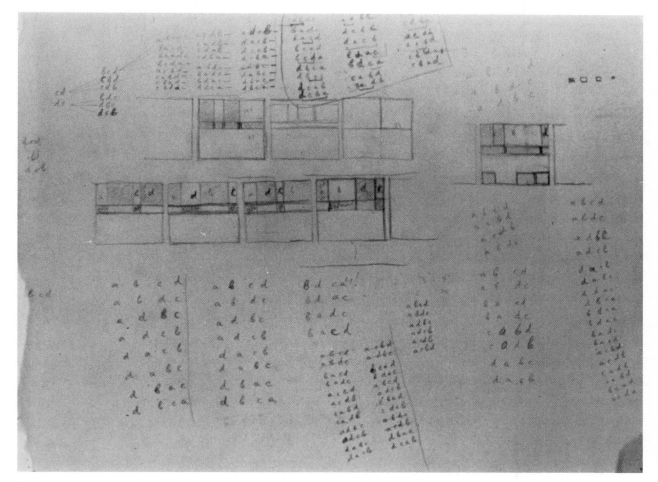

Figure 8

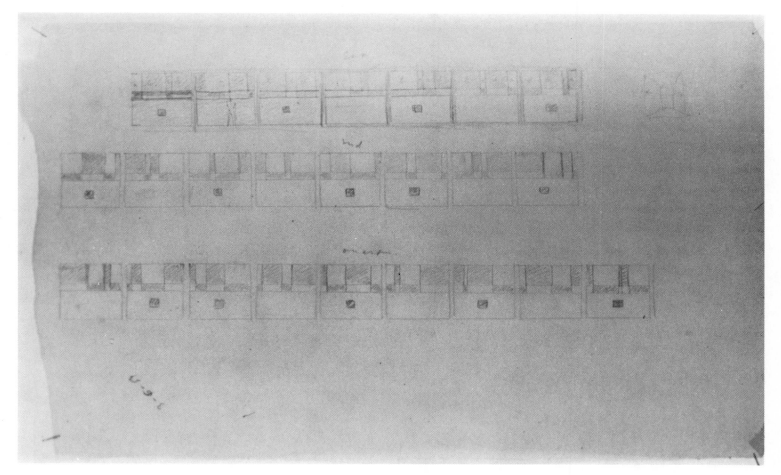

Figure 9

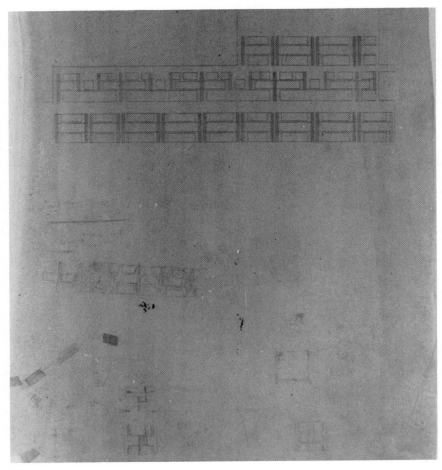

Figure 10

Figure 11

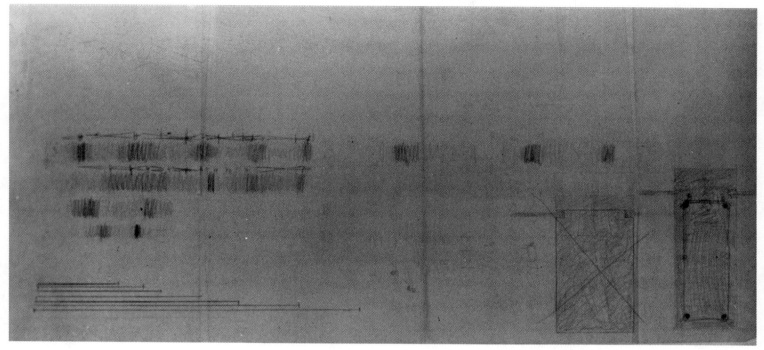

Figure 12

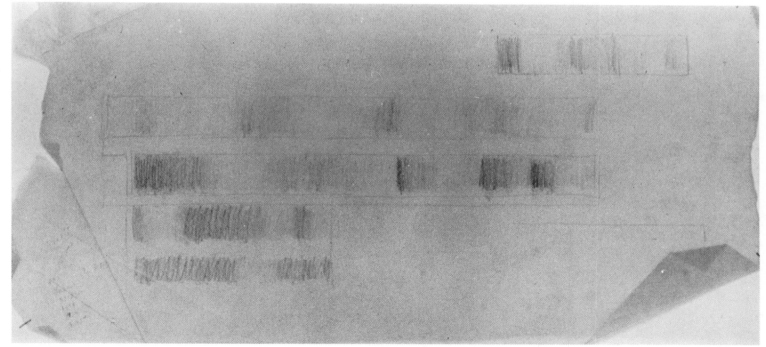

Figure 13

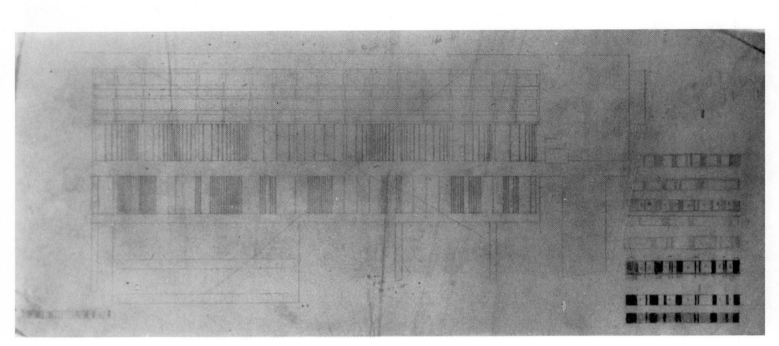

Figure 14

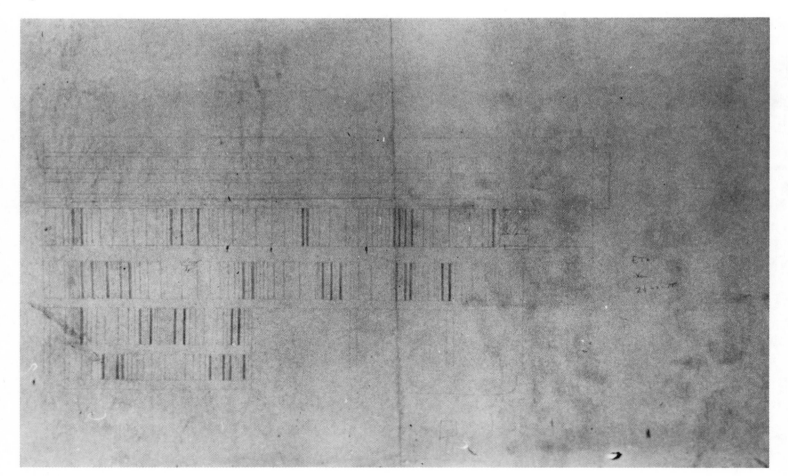

Figure 15

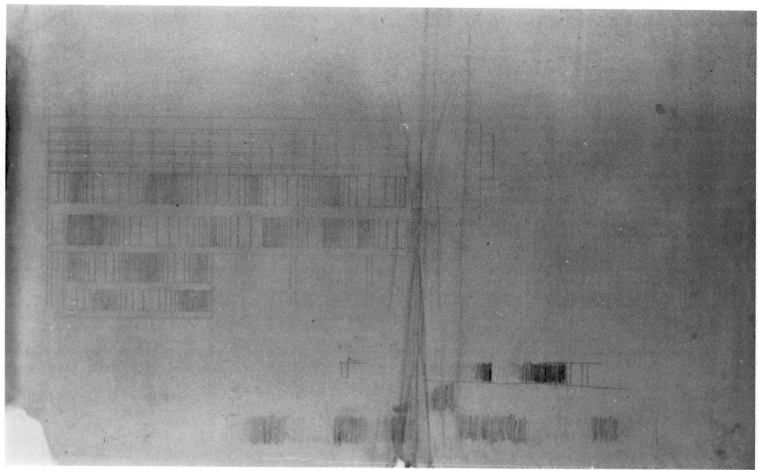

Figure 16

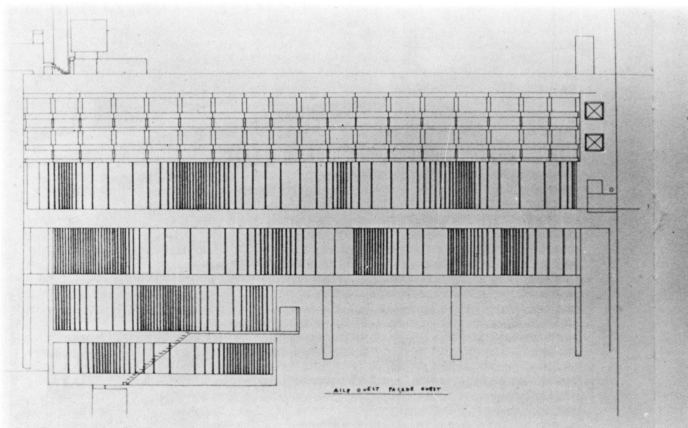

AILE OUEST FACADE OUEST

Couvent de Sainte-Marie-de-la-Tourette à Eveux sur l'Arbresle, 1955. Pans de verre ondulatoires, façade ouest. Voir p. 150

Figure 17

Figure 18

Figure 19

Figure 20

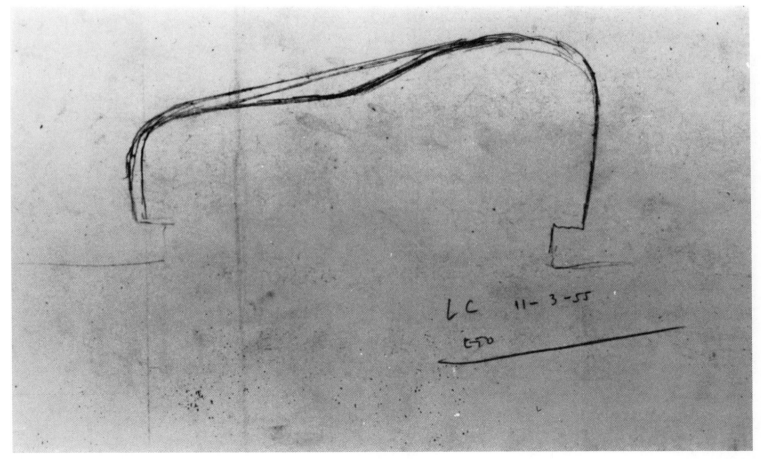

Figure 21

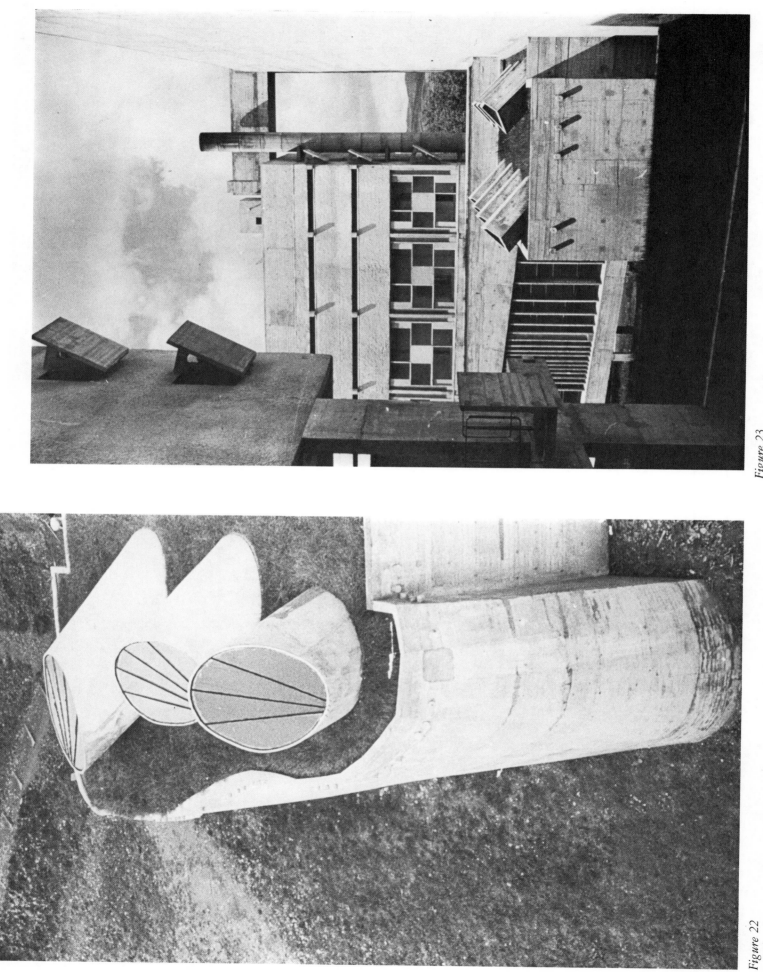

Figure 23

Figure 22

Figure 24

Figure 25

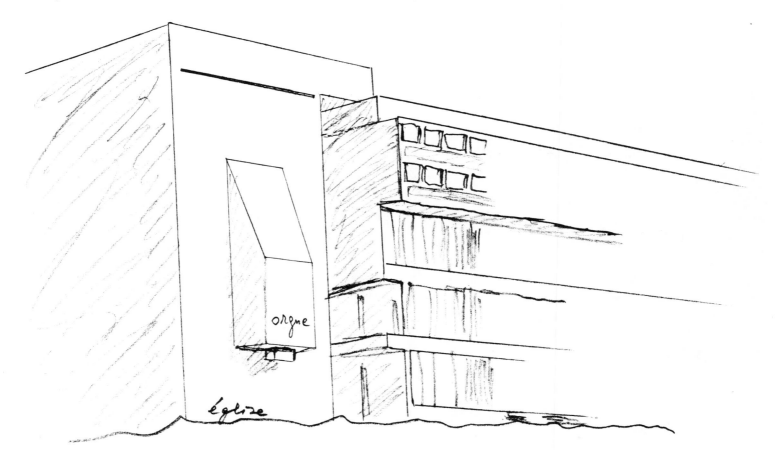

Figure 26

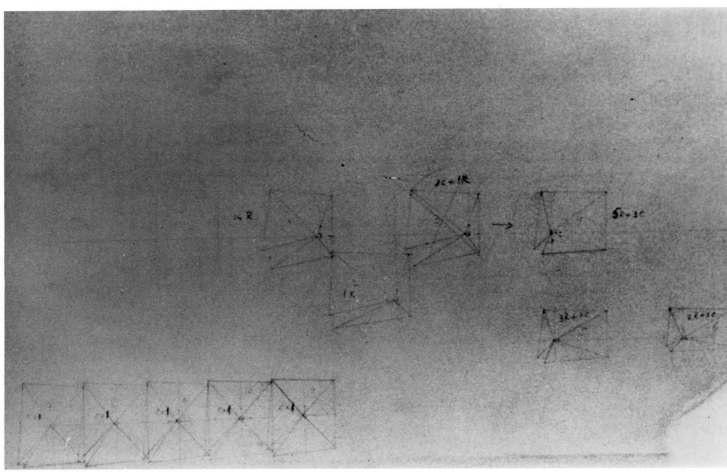

Figure 27

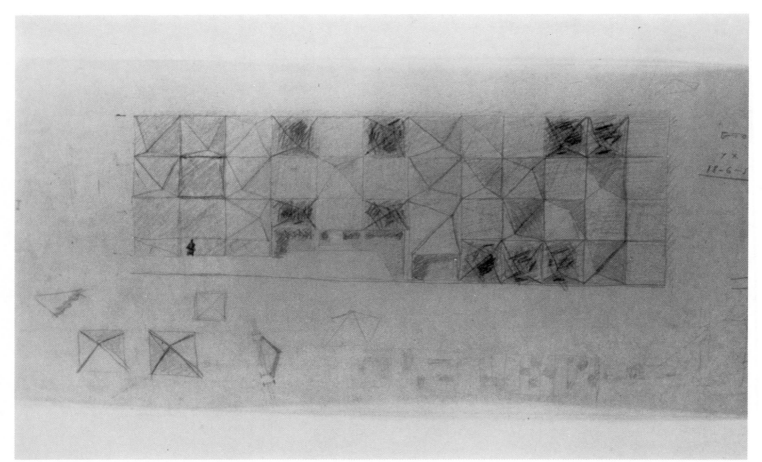

Figure 28

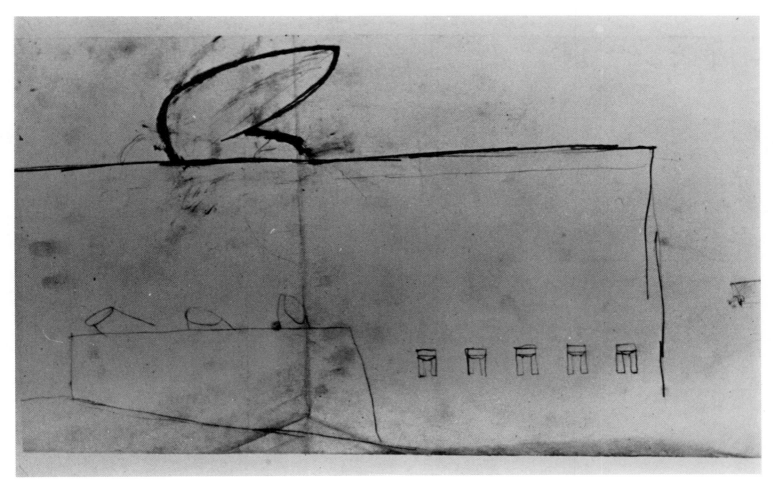

Figure 29

Figure 30

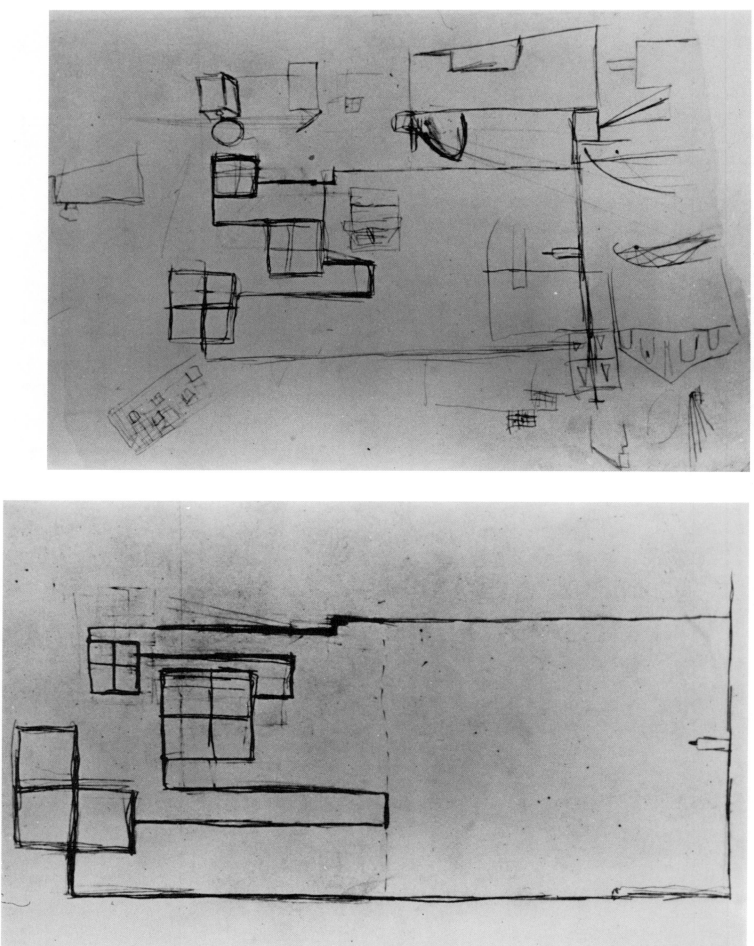

Figure 32

Figure 31

Timeless but of its Time: Le Corbusier's Architecture in India

*by Peter Serenyi**

For Le Corbusier the resolution of opposites was a deeply felt need that elicited some of his most heroic architectural responses. He was certainly not alone among twentieth-century architects in this respect, for some of his greatest contemporaries, Frank Lloyd Wright and Mies van der Rohe, were equally obsessed by it. To create a resolution of opposites, Wright fused, whereas Mies neutralized, a building's constituent parts. This resulted in a state of inter-dependent individuality in the work of Wright and a state of anonymity in the work of Mies. Le Corbusier, on the other hand, used juxtaposition as a means of attaining a resolution of opposites. In so doing, he succeeded in preserving the identity and at times even the separateness of a building's constituent parts.

For Le Corbusier the juxtaposition of diverse and often seemingly contradictory architectural elements was not merely a formal exercise, but rather a manifestation of a new kind of synthesis that brought together images of diverse cultural, historical, environmental, sociopolitical, and psycho-logical forces while permitting each to maintain its identity. He interpreted these forces in terms of a series of polarities that include: history and modernity, Mediterranean and Northern, mechanistic and folkloristic, utopian and pragmatic, puritanical and hedonistic, male and female. Although the resolution of these polar and often contradictory forces had obsessed Le Corbusier since his formative period, most notably since the creation of the Villa Schwob in 1916, this complex process found its richest and most subtle realizations in his late work, of which India received the largest share.

As is well known, Le Corbusier's name is linked with two cities in India: Chandigarh, the newly built capital of the state of Punjab, and Ahmedabad, the textile capital of India located in the state of Gujarat.

Both cities are intimately tied to two of modern India's greatest statesmen: Mahatma Gandhi and Jawaharlal Nehru. Gandhi, a native son of Gujarat, had spent fifteen years in Ahmedabad laying the groundwork for India's independence. It was from here that he led the famous Salt March in 1930 that initiated the second phase of national nonviolent resistance. Prime Minister Nehru, who supported Chandigarh both morally and financially, viewed the city as "symbolic of the freedom of India, unfettered by the traditions of the past . . . an expression of the nation's faith in the future."[1]

The price India had to pay for its independence from the British in July, 1947, was the loss of what is now Pakistan and Bangladesh. The people most affected by the partition of India were the Hindus of West Punjab and East Bengal who elected not to remain under Moslem rule but to resettle in India. In addition, Punjab lost not only its western part to Pakistan but its old capital, Lahore, as well, whose population was fifty-six percent Hindu. What set the stage for the creation of Chandigarh was independ-ence and partition, exhilaration and tragedy. Naming the city in honor of Chandi, the Hindu goddess of power, must be seen in this context.

Once the decision was made to build a new capital for East Punjab, Prime Minister Nehru seized the opportunity to make it the city of *his* India, liberated from the traditions of the past. As an initial act of commitment, Nehru recommended to the Punjab government that the American planner, Albert Mayer, whom he had known personally, be asked to draw up a master plan for the city. Although Mayer's plan was not carried out, Le Corbusier adopted many of its features when he prepared his own plan in Simla in February 1951. This plan was created only three months after P. N. Thapar and P. L. Varma, representatives of the Punjab government, had approached Le Corbusier in Paris to become the architectural advisor for Chandigarh.[2] Le Corbusier's biannual trips to India resulting from his contractual agreement made with Thapar and Varma started on February 18, 1951. He left a permanent record of his thoughts and

*The research for this paper was made possible by an initial grant from the Graham Foundation for Advanced Studies in the Fine Arts. A senior research grant under the Fulbright-Hays Act enabled Professor Serenyi to study Le Corbusier's works in India.

observations about India in his sketchbooks, which he carried with him during his many trips. These sketchbooks also contain visual imprints of his creative process, giving us a rare glimpse of his buildings in their formative stages.[3]

The two sketchbooks in which Le Corbusier recorded his first stay in India, extending from February to April 1951, give us the best indication of what he found most compelling and timely in the country's built environment.[4] It is revealing that the very first observation he made about India refers to Sir Edwin Lutyens and the Jantar Mantar, the astronomical observatory in Delhi built by Maharajah Jai Singh in 1719. He considered the observatory as "leading the way: linking mankind with the cosmos." In contrast, he found even the "best qualities" of Lutyens' work in New Delhi less successful.[5] Yet both touched a familiar chord in his heart, the observatory being an example of what he described in *Towards a New Architecture* as "pure creation of the mind" and Lutyens' New Delhi, with its axes and broad boulevards, being an evocation of Paris. It is not surprising that both reappear in Chandigarh.

Beyond this initial observation, these two sketchbooks encompass a wide yet predictable range of images of the Indian environment: the seventeenth century Pinjore gardens near Chandigarh, Hindu and Jain temples in Ahmedabad, the Mogul-style Viceroy's garden by Lutyens in New Delhi, Bombay's Gateway of India of 1911, aerial views of Rajasthani villages near Jaipur, old courtyards in Ahmedabad, a water tower near Ambala, and a factory in Ahmedabad. These and similar examples included in Sketchbooks E 18 and E 19 suggest that Le Corbusier's approach to absorbing a new culture had remained unaltered since his early travels spanning the years 1907–11, when he classified his observations into three categories: culture, folklore, and industry.[6]

The first two Indian sketchbooks also shed light on Le Corbusier's itinerary, which in turn sets the stage for initiating contact with all but one of his future Indian clients.[7] After his arrival in New Delhi on February 19, his first destination was Chandigarh and Simla. Already on March 19, he left for Delhi to fly from there to Ahmedabad. After a brief stay in Ahmedabad on March 22 and 23, he flew to Bombay to meet Bhabha Tata, the steel magnate and major owner of Air India.[8] On his way back to Chandigarh, he stopped in New Delhi on March 25 to be entertained in the presidential palace. Six days later he left Chandigarh to fly from Delhi to Bombay, whence he returned to Paris on April 2.

During these first six weeks in India, Le Corbusier gained a deeper understanding of the country's cultural, vernacular, and industrial tradition, met most of his future clients from Pandit Nehru to the Sarabhais, and initiated ambitious projects ranging from the master plan of Chandigarh to a cultural center for Ahmedabad. But why Ahmedabad? Such a question happily no longer needs to be raised about Chandigarh,[9] but still requires an answer with regard to the commissions he received in India's textile center. There are few cities in the world that can claim more than three buildings by Le Corbusier, and Ahmedabad is one of them (after Paris, Chandigarh, and La Chaux-de-Fonds), with the Museum, the Millowners Association Building, and the Sarabhai and Shodhan houses to its credit. Such major commissions, all initiated during Le Corbusier's first visit to the city, attests to Ahmedabad's intellectual climate and economic prosperity unrivaled in India for a city of its size. The events that contributed to these favorable circumstances have a long history whose highlights are worth mentioning here.[10]

Since its founding by Sultan Ahmed Shah of Gujarat in 1411 A.D., Ahmedabad had been a city of commerce and industry centered around textiles. After a period of great prosperity during the first hundred years of its existence, the city declined but recovered again when Akbar annexed it to the Mogul Empire in 1572. Its recovery prepared the way for Sir Thomas Roe's visit in 1618, which initiated the first commercial ties between Ahmedabad and England. The disintegration of the Mogul Empire during the eighteenth century brought in the Maratha from the south, who ruled it until 1817.

During that year, and almost two hundred years after Sir Thomas' visit, Ahmedabad's ties with Britain were forcibly reestablished by the East India Company.

Yet the British presence in Ahmedabad during the next hundred and thirty years was never too pervasive, largely because the economic base of the city's highly developed culture had always been trade and industry rather than agriculture. Hence, long before the advent of the modern era, the leading citizens of Ahmedabad were businessmen rather than landowners or men in the service of a court. This enabled the Ahmedabadis to take up the British on their own terms by offering them stiff competition through mechanizing the city's textile industry.

With the help of the city's Jain financiers, the modern textile industry of Ahmedabad was founded in 1861. One of the key factors behind the success of this industry is that since its founding it has been largely run by a closely knit group of Jain families who valued cooperation rather than competition among themselves. Thus, as Kenneth Gillion has pointed out, "the caste system and joint family system found new avenues of expression in a modern context."[11] In addition to the social cohesion of the Jains, it was also their work ethic, their puritanical and frugal character, not to mention their entrepreneurial spirit, that contributed greatly to the success of Ahmedabad's modern textile industry. No wonder that by the turn of the century the city had become known as the "Manchester of India."

The economic growth Ahmedabad enjoyed since the 1860s was given a further boost by World War I, when the termination of British imports allowed the city's textile mills to supply India's needs more fully. After the war the city utilized its unprecedented economic power by becoming, in Gillion's words, "a financial and political base for the Indian National Congress and a leader and prototype of New India."[12] While it was the mills that supplied the financial base for this new political movement, it was Mahatma Gandhi who provided the leadership.

The fact that Ahmedabad became Gandhi's home between 1915 and 1930 had powerful conse-quences for the city's political development, both in terms of its own affairs and in terms of its influence on the nation as a whole. Enjoying the respect of both industry and labor, Gandhi proved to be an effective arbitrator between the wealthy millowners and their workers during the city's labor unrests in the late teens and twenties. Moreover, through his teachings Gandhi disseminated those very ideals which made Ahmedabad such a success: puritanism, frugality, and the ethic of hard work.

When India's independence was won in 1947, Ahmedabad could rightly claim an important share in its realization. More importantly, however, it could claim that its unique blend of traditional values and modern technology could serve as an appropriate model for independent India. Conscious of this potential, the leaders of the city pursued a two-pronged approach to shaping its future: by strengthening the achievements of the past and by moving into new directions. In pursuit of the former, they diversified the city's industry and helped make it, even if only temporarily, the state capital of Gujarat. In pursuit of the latter, they established it as one of the foremost cultural centers of India. In so doing, they revived an aspect of the city's past that had been lost since the seventeenth century.

Among the key leaders of the new Ahmedabad, four Jain textile millowners stand out: Kasturbhai Lalbhai, Chinubhai Chimanbhai, Surottam Hutheesing, and Gautam Sarabhai. Mr. Lalbhai, the wealthiest of the Ahmedabad industrialists, spent a considerable part of his fortune on establishing and supporting the city's new cultural and educational institutions through such organizations as the Ahmedabad Education Society and the Ahmedabad Textile Industry's Research Association. Chinubhai Chimanbhai, a nephew of Mr. Lalbhai, was the city's energetic mayor, who, during his tenure between 1950 and 1962, was instrumental in building such major undertakings as libraries, playgrounds, a stadium, an auditorium, and a cultural center. It was the mayor in fact who was largely responsible for inviting Le Corbusier to the city. Surottam Hutheesing, another nephew of Mr. Lalbhai, was the president of the Millowners Association, the textile industry's powerful organization, and it was he who was responsible for commissioning Le Corbusier to build the Association's new headquarters. Gautam Sarabhai, a leading member of a family that had distinguished itself in the arts and sciences, was the founder, designer, and first director of the National Institute of Design in Ahmedabad, which under his leadership became one of the foremost art schools of India. And it was Gautam Sarabhai's sister-in-law Manorama—a niece of Mr. Lalbhai—who entrusted Le Corbusier with her house.

During Le Corbusier's first visit to Ahmedabad in March 1951, Mayor Chinubhai Chimanbhai had given him two commissions, the building of a cultural center overlooking the Sabarmati river and a house for himself.[13] Although the Chimanbhai house was never built by Le Corbusier and the cultural center was only partially realized according to his plans,[14] he was at least given the opportunity to build the center's museum according to ideas he had developed since 1929 (Figure 1).[15] In the museum of Ahmedabad Le Corbusier combined two concepts at once: the notion of an environment that is both interdisciplinary and unlimited. Even if neither of these concepts was realized in the building literally, both are inherent in its design. The best explanation of these concepts can be given by citing their first visualizations.

The concept of an interdisciplinary cultural environment was first proposed by Le Corbusier in the project for the Mundaneum's World Museum of 1929. In this ziggurat-shaped building the visitor could have surveyed the physical manifestation of man's diverse achievements in a historical and geographical context.[16] The Museum of Unlimited Growth was first developed by him in 1931, when he envisaged such a building as a flattened-out ziggurat spiraling outward in squares with the potential of being extended ad infinitum. Both of these proto-types find a partial realization in Ahmedabad, where the museum's exhibition space is treated as a continuous volume revolving around a central

courtyard. This makes it possible to present works representing the broadest range of human activity in a contextual setting and in a continuous manner.

For the roof of the museum, Le Corbusier had planned a Mogul garden which he intended to fill with flowers, shrubbery, and forty-five shallow reflecting pools arranged in straight lines. Had it been realized, this garden would have combined Le Corbusier's longstanding fascination with roof gardens with his admiration of India's own cultural tradition. Regrettably, however, only the concrete frames of the pools give the visitor a hint of the architect's original vision.

Although the cultural center was not completed as originally planned and the museum is still under-utilized, Le Corbusier's original proposal—the creation of a stage where the arts could not only interact among themselves but could also relate to a broader contextual setting—is still a provocative concept. It is not surprising that it had such an appeal for Ahmedabad's energetic mayor, who was determined to make the city a symbol of the new India, not unfettered by the past as Nehru proposed but rather continuing its past through its cultural institutions.

The second public building Le Corbusier designed for Ahmedabad is the headquarters of the Millowners Association, commissioned by its presi-dent, Surottam Hutheesing, in March 1951 (Figure 2). Planned for a site overlooking the Sabarmati river, the building was to serve a unique organization whose essence Le Corbusier seems to have under-stood very well. Since its founding in 1891, the Millowners Association had provided an institutional framework for the close family ties that existed among the city's largely Jain textile millowners. Here Le Corbusier encountered a public institution whose very existence depended on personal relationships that resulted from caste and family ties. His response to this unique commission was to express the institution's dual character—the private and the public—through his concept of the house as a palace, which he developed during the

1920s and given clearest expression in his book, *Une Maison—un palais*, published in 1928. There he defined the palace as "a house endowed with dignity", which for him meant monumentality achieved by "pure forms composed according to a harmonious law."[17] One of the houses Le Corbusier singled out in his book to exemplify his concept of the house-palace was his Villa Cook of 1926, which offers important clues for understanding the internal organization of the Millowners Association Building.[18]

The Millowners Association Building, like the Villa Cook, is defined by a richly symbolic front and back placed between two blind end walls. Within this exterior shell the Millowners Building contains a partly open ground floor for service and circulation, as did its antecedent. The second floor in both is intended for more private functions: the bedrooms in the Villa Cook and the board rooms and offices in the Millowners Association. The third and fourth floors in both buildings are treated as double floors and intended for public functions: living room, dining room, and kitchen in the Villa Cook and lobby and auditorium in the Millowners Building.[19]

The lobby and the auditorium are the climactic points of the interior of the Millowners Building. It is here that Le Corbusier created the greatest dramatic tension by treating the lobby as an open space defined by harsh, angular forms and the auditorium as an enclosed space delineated by soft, curvilinear forms. "This prodigious spectacle has been produced by the interplay of two elements, one male, one female: sun and water. Two contradictory elements that both need the other in order to exist."[20] There are no better words than these, written by Le Corbusier many years before this building was ever conceived, to best sum up the essence of these antithetical spaces. Here, as in most of his buildings, Le Corbusier achieved a resolution of opposites by juxtaposing rather than fusing diverse architectural elements so that each part retains its identity and separateness. With the male/female correlation as the central theme here, Le Corbusier

imbued these spaces with a meaning that is analogous to the Indian attitude toward the sexes. Viewed in this light, the relationship between the lobby (male) and the auditorium (female) based on the notion of a strong sense of identity and separateness acquires a special significance.

Besides the Millowners Building, Surottam Hutheesing also commissioned Le Corbusier to build him a house in the spring of 1951 (Figure 3).[21] The architect's task was to respond to the life-style of a wealthy bachelor, about to marry, who needed a variety of spaces to allow entertaining on a grand scale. After the plans were completed, however, Mr. Hutheesing decided to sell these to his fellow millowner, Shyamubhai Shodhan. Notwithstanding the change in the site and the dissimilarity in his life-style, the new client wanted Le Corbusier to build him the very same house he had designed for the former client.[22] Hence, in assessing it, the original functions intended for the house must be kept in mind.

For Le Corbusier the Shodhan house represented the culmination of his efforts in the field of domestic architecture that evolved over a period spanning more than forty years. In order to understand its nature and meaning, we must examine the house in a dual context: how it grew out of the architect's own works and how it is related to the traditional architecture of Ahmedabad.

The house is a cubical concrete frame structure whose exterior surface unfolds from a severe and forbidding entrance façade to an open and welcoming garden façade (Figures 3, 4). By treating each side of this classical cube differently, Le Corbusier juxtaposed the formality of the Mediterranean with the flexibility of the Northern approach to architectural design. The classical aspects of the house find their antecedents in Le Corbusier's earlier houses, going back to the one he designed for his parents in La Chaux-de-Fonds in 1912. Apart from its sharp and clear cubical mass, certain important details of the first design for the Jeanneret house find their way into the Shodhan house, as for example its flat roof defined by strong projecting cornices and the continuous band of windows beneath it. These are reinterpreted as the parasol roof and the continuous openings of the terrace in the Shodhan house.

Le Corbusier's most important house built in La Chaux-de-Fonds, the Villa Schwob of 1916, serves as a point of departure for the structure and personality of the Shodhan house. As one of the first concrete framed houses in Europe,[23] the Villa Schwob marks the beginning of Le Corbusier's use of this structural system, which reached a high degree of complexity in Ahmedabad. More interesting, however, is the way in which these houses reveal Le Corbusier's own personality. He was known to have had an "impressive demeanor seemingly built for defense, behind which he appeared to withdraw."[24] On the other hand, he was considered by his friends to be "uncommonly generous and unselfish."[25] Both houses convey these personal characteristics by the stark and almost forbidding demeanor of their street façades and the generous and accessible quality of their garden façades. As a result, they effectively ward off strangers while at the same time they welcome those who have been allowed to enter.

Although the Schwob and Jeanneret houses are important precedents for the Shodhan house, they play a far less significant role in this capacity than Le Corbusier's houses designed after 1919. In fact, in 1919 Le Corbusier initiated a new direction in architecture which he never abandoned afterward. In the realm of domestic architecture the Maison Citrohan of 1920–22 and the Maison Monol of 1919 mark the beginning of this new direction.[26] The former, angular and firm, stands erect on the ground, dominating the setting, while the latter, undulating and soft, rests on the ground, absorbing the setting. Le Corbusier's description of what for him represented the masculine and feminine characteristics in architecture succinctly sum up the essence of these two projects.

In the one, strong objectivity of forms, under the intense light of a Mediterranean sun: *male*

architecture. In the other, limitless subjectivity rising against a clouded sky: *female* architecture.[27]

Having thus set the stage for a dual approach to domestic architecture, Le Corbusier used these two projects as the basis of all his later houses. When in 1951 he was called upon to design a house for Surottam Hutheesing, a bachelor wanting to entertain extensively, he understandably followed the Citrohan model.

Among the many sources of the Maison Citrohan, two provide the best clues to an understanding of its nature and meaning. The inspiration for its exterior came from such Parisian artists' studios as those built by François Le Coeur in the rue Cassini in 1906, which Le Corbusier admired greatly.[28] Its double-storied interior, on the other hand, was based on the spatial organization of the Café Legendre in Paris, which Le Corbusier frequented with Amédée Ozenfant (Figure 11).[29] The fusion of the artist's studio with the restaurant resulted in a new kind of house which so appropriately expresses the lifestyle of a growing segment of the urban population in the industrialized world: uprootedness and transience. The former is embodied in the artist's studio, the latter in the restaurant, and Le Corbusier understood both these states of mind from personal experience, for when he conceived the Maison Citrohan he was an uprooted artist whose family table became the restaurant table.

The most important link between the Maison Citrohan and the Shodhan house is the first project for the Villa Baizeau in Carthage, Tunisia, designed by Le Corbusier in 1928.[30] The significance of this design lies in two areas: a new approach to climate control and a fuller use of de Stijl vocabulary. The former is exemplified by the parasol roof and the interlocking interior spaces providing shade and ventilation; the latter is expressed by the façade where the studio and ribbon windows—hallmarks of Le Corbusier's style of fenestration—are fused with the help of de Stijl vocabulary. As in Mondrian's paintings or especially as in Rietveld's Schröder house of 1924, the composition of the facade is based on compensation rather than symmetry achieved by a strong interplay between lines and planes, between verticals and horizontals, and between different colors.[31] All of these elements were given a more complete realization in the Shodhan house. The design that provides the key connection between the villa at Carthage and the Shodhan house is Le Corbusier's house in Lannemezan of 1940 (Figure 5). This project was conceived as a cubical structure of exposed stone and wood. Here, as in his houses designed during the 1930s, Le Corbusier abandoned his favored structural device, the steel or concrete skeletal frame, in favor of load-bearing walls to be constructed of natural materials. Moreover, instead of putting the house on stilts, he anchored it to the ground, thus imbuing it with a sense of rootedness which was so clearly lacking in his houses of the 1920s.

The decade of the 1930s and 1940s represents a turning point in Le Corbusier's architecture for reasons that are too numerous to list, but mention must be made of the economic depression of the period, his questioning of the supremacy of technology, and his marriage to Yvonne Gallis in 1930. The direction he began to pursue in 1930 found its clearest architectural expression in his designs for houses ranging from the project of the Errazuris house to the house in Lannemezan. In them Le Corbusier reestablished a closer relationship with nature, the site, and the vernacular tradition in a manner that recalls his first three houses in La Chaux-de-Fonds.[32] These changes in fact paved the way for the formal and structural innovations made in his later buildings such as the Shodhan house.

As seen from the point of view of Le Corbusier's later buildings, the decade of the 1930s stands out for an entirely different reason as well: the invention of the sunbreaker, or *brise-soleil*. This device makes its first appearance in 1933 with the project for an apartment house intended for a site in Algiers.[33] But it is only in his design for an office building conceived for Algiers between 1938 and 1942 that Le Corbusier gave it his first imaginative

interpretation (Figure 25). From this project forward, sunbreakers began to fulfill a number of complex functions in his design, ranging from the utilitarian to the symbolic: they provide protection from the sun, they help give scale and proportion to the building, and they serve as major conveyors of the building's symbolic significance.

In the Shodhan house the sunbreakers act in all of these roles. Dominating the southwest or garden façade of the house and forming an irregular concrete grille, they provide an effective screen against the summer sun without blocking out the winter sun on the most open side of the house. They also serve as visual connections between the observer and the house, between inside and outside, between the various parts of the house ranging from the very large to the very small. Most important, however, is the fact that they embody a major part of the personal and cultural significance of the house.

Le Corbusier likened the sunbreaker to a portico as well as to the aperture of a camera.[34] As a portico it acts as a container and definer of human action and as an opening it links the outside with the inside in a defined and sequential way. As a photographer focuses the camera on a given target, Le Corbusier zeroes in on a specific view by giving a desired aperture and orientation to each concrete frame. Furthermore, if taken together, sunbreakers serve as conveyors of the life pattern that unfolds within the building. In their role as porticoes, the sunbreakers of the Shodhan house provide a more intimately scaled architectural environment within the framework of a palatial house; they act as houses within a house. As cameras, they focus on the sensuous shape of the swimming pool and the soft, grass-filled mound surrounding it; as such, they act as apertures between the angular interior and the soft exterior. Taken together, they convey a playful, spontaneous, almost dollhouse-like quality, thus effectively counteracting the formal setting. In all three roles, they help express the function Le Corbusier intended for the house: to be like a "Château of the Loire . . . for an intelligent prince."[35]

On a cultural level, the sunbreakers link the

Shodhan house with the architectural tradition of Northern Europe, whose asymmetrical, irregular, and flexible design elements they incorporate. In a sketch of primitive huts of Ireland published in 1928, Le Corbusier captured these elements by highlighting their structural frame, which in turn foreshadows the sunbreakers of his later buildings.[36] More important, however, is the connection between the sunbreakers of the Shodhan house and a more recent manifestation of Northern architecture: de Stijl. As a comparison between Theo van Doesburg's project for an artist's house of 1923 and the sunbreakers reveals, Le Corbusier incorporated in his design such de Stijl elements as asymmetry, flexibility, and plasticity (Figure 6). In the Shodhan house, however, these Northern elements are held in check by the restraining power of the classical cube, whereas in van Doesburg's project they are expressed more freely. Having always remained a classicist at heart, it is not surprising that in this house, as well as in most of his other buildings, Le Corbusier allowed the Mediterranean rather than the Northern tradition to dominate the design.

Le Corbusier's Mediterranean formalism and Northern flexibility served him well in India, where both of these cultural traits are manifested in the country's indigenous architecture. In the context of the exterior of the Shodhan house, two examples of traditional architecture in Ahmedabad stand out: the Hutheesing Jain temple and the old town house of the Shodhan family (Figures 7, 8). The temple was commissioned by the wealthy Jain merchant Sheth Hutheesing in 1850, and Le Corbusier made reference to it in one of his sketchbooks during his first visit to Ahmedabad.[37] The temple is distinguished by its openness and flexibility, largely achieved by its numerous porches that are grouped around the main hall of worship. Like the sunbreakers and terraces of the Shodhan house of a hundred years later, the porches of the temple offer shade in the summer, sun in the winter, and breezes in every season.

The old town house of the Shodhan family located in the heart of the city provides an interesting clue to an understanding of the client's willingness to accept Le Corbusier's design exactly as it was intended for Surottam Hutheesing. Having been raised in a house which had *pilotis*, terraces, roof gardens, and open façades, Shyamubhai Shodhan must not have found the designs for the house he was to buy too unusual. Coming from such an architectural environment, he was in fact better prepared to accept Le Corbusier's ideas than a Parisian client. One of the reasons why Le Corbusier's architecture was welcomed by his Indian clients was because they were accustomed to seeing classical buildings that, in addition to being open, are often characterized by irregularity and flexibility. Hence, in evaluating Le Corbusier's success with his Indian clients, the Northern element in his architecture is just as important to bear in mind as its more obvious Mediterranean element.

The focal point of the interior of the Shodhan house consisting of the great double-storied living room is also in keeping with Ahmedabad's own architectural tradition (Figure 9). The large houses of old Ahmedabad were usually built around a double-storied entry hall, or *chowk*, which signifies their symbolic and ceremonial center. As seen in the eighteenth-century Chunilal house, this space was given the greatest artistic attention in terms of spatial organization and decorative treatment (Figure 10). When Shyamubhai Shodhan first saw the designs for the double-storied interiors of his future house, he must have recognized in them a modern reinterpretation of a familiar symbol of status and wealth.

Apart from the coincidental connection between the Shodhan house's living room and the entry halls of Ahmedabad's old houses, the roots of Le Corbusier's double-storied space go back to his earlier architecture. As mentioned before, the inspiration for this space, according to the architect, originally came from the Café Legendre, where a balcony provided additional seating space (Figure 11). His first literal interpretation of this spatial arrangement occurred in the Maison Citrohan of 1920, whose interior can best be visualized through the Pavilion of L'Esprit Nouveau of five years later. As with the Café Legendre, the balcony does not merely connect two parts of the house as in the Villa Schwob, but instead functions as an actual room.

During the 1920s, Le Corbusier gave the double-storied interior space a wide range of interpretations, but the one that stands out in relationship to the Shodhan house is the great entry hall of the Villa La Roche of 1923. Here, as in his later house, Le Corbusier organized the interior volume in terms of polarities that include public and private, formal and informal, and impersonal and personal, allowing each to preserve its discreet identity. In the living room of the Shodhan house the strong contrast between the public level of the main space and the private level of the balcony best exemplifies the architect's polarization of spaces. The balcony, as in the Villa La Roche, functions as the study and den and provides an ideal setting for intimate gatherings enlivened by a striking view of the space below.

The most dramatic part of the house is the triple-storied terrace where Le Corbusier's definition of architecture as "the masterly, correct, and magnificent play of forms in light" was fully realized (Figure 12). Created largely in response to Ahmedabad's intense sun, the terrace functions as a major part of the house's natural climate control system by cooling the bedroom units during the day and serving as bedrooms during hot summer nights. Beyond this, it provides a stage where man, architecture, and nature meet as active partners. Following a precedent established in the recessed terraces of the Immeubles-villas project of 1922 and first realized in the Villa Stein-Monzie of 1927,[38] Le Corbusier created a setting here where nature is invited to penetrate the body of the house through light, air, and water while being compelled to respond to the power of architectural form to shape nature. In the midst of this orchestrated interaction between architecture and nature, Le Corbusier engages the observer as an active participant so that he/she can develop a heightened awareness of the experience of living.

As Le Corbusier's most ambitious example of domestic architecture, the Shodhan house represents a highly complex synthesis of forms and spaces that resulted from a long process of selection, absorption, and transformation. Although the constituent elements of his architecture have undergone major changes to suit new functions and express new meanings, they have retained their original identity. As the Shodhan house's double-storied living room illustrates, the key formal solutions that Le Corbusier developed during the 1920s have remained an essential part of his late work. Yet notwithstanding the continuity of such forms and spaces, their characteristics and qualities have changed dramatically over the years. As a comparison between his houses of the 1920s and the 1950s indicates, the frail, transient, and uprooted qualities of the former were reshaped by Le Corbusier into the strong, durable, and rooted qualities of the latter. This process was in no small measure reinforced by his encounter with India, where he found the right cultural and climatic setting for strengthening the direction he had initiated in the 1930s.

The second house Le Corbusier built in Ahmedabad was commissioned by Mrs. Manorama Sarabhai in March 1951, who, after the death of her husband, wanted a secluded place for herself and her sons, aged ten and thirteen.[39] The site chosen for the house was a tree-filled area on the large Sarabhai estate located in the Shahibag district of the city. In response to the site and his client's needs and personality, Le Corbusier designed an open and flexible house whose spatial organization was determined by its dual function: to provide maximum comfort for adults and children alike. To this end, he planned a double-storied block for Mrs. Sarabhai and a single-storied block for her children; these blocks, although adjoining, are divided by a built-in carport and a slide. The exterior of these blocks is defined by load-bearing concrete walls, while their interior is organized in terms of parallel bays crowned by low concrete barrel vaults (Figure 13). This structural solution ingeniously combines both of Le Corbusier's approaches to domestic architecture by utilizing the angularity of the Maison Citrohan for the exterior and the undulating quality of the Maison Monol for the interior.

By giving the Sarabhai house a hard, angular exterior and a soft, undulating interior, Le Corbusier juxtaposed what for him represented the masculine and feminine characteristics in architecture, without allowing either to lose its identity. To this end, he visually separated the exterior shell from the interior, so that when seen from the outside the "feminine" interior seems incomprehensible and when seen from within the "masculine" exterior becomes unintelligible. The separation between the two is reinforced by the materials and colors: mostly grey concrete on the outside and mostly red brick and multicolored on the inside. For a house intended for a widow with two sons, the archi-tectural imagery embodying the male/female symbolism seems most appropriate, especially as it was handled by Le Corbusier. Unlike the Shodhan house, whose masculine exterior is as important as its equally masculine interior, in this house everything emanates from within, making the feminine interior the *raison d'être* of the house. No wonder that its masculine exterior is reduced to a quasi-autonomous shield that offers some physical and psychological protection to the interior without, however, interfering with it.

The focal point of the interior is the open multipurpose public space which occupies most of the first floor of the main part of the house (Figure 13). Serving as a living/dining room and hall, this space is defined by low tile vaults resting on exposed concrete beams which in turn are supported by brick walls that are either exposed or covered by plaster or plywood. To add to this rich orchestration of materials, Le Corbusier used the three primary colors, plus black and white, for the walls covered by plaster. Hence, each major part of the interior stands out visually, if not necessarily structurally, as an independent element. But to

counteract this, he forged a spatial connection among the bays and between the inside and outside so as to achieve a greater sense of openness. To gain a clearer understanding of this spatial and formal organization, we must examine, however briefly, some of its sources.

As we have seen, the interior of the Sarabhai house grew out of the project for the Maison Monol, which was planned as an earth-hugging structure with an undulating concrete roof held up by concrete columns. The first built version of this project was designed by Le Corbusier in 1935 for a suburban site in La Celle-St.-Cloud, near Paris.[40] This weekend house represents the most important link between the Maison Monol and the Sarabhai house largely because of the way in which the architect handled its form, space, and materials. As in the Monol house, the space is anchored to the ground by low barrel vaults, yet the interaction between inside and outside is far greater here than in its prototype. These spatial characteristics were further developed in the Sarabhai house, where they acquired a sense of sheltered openness. In terms of form, the weekend house offers striking juxtapositions between the angular and curvilinear and between the smooth and the rough, yet the greatest amount of contrast is to be found in the handling of materials. Such diverse materials as concrete, stone, brick, glass, and plywood are placed side by side so as to give each constituent part of the house a high degree of independence. This brings us only a short step away from the Sarabhai house, where form, materials, and colors are juxtaposed in an even more uncompromising manner.

The role fulfilled by the weekend house in preparing the way for the Sarabhai house is comparable to that played by the house in Lannemezan in relationship to the Shodhan house. The spatial and formal innovations made in both of these "transitional" houses greatly facilitated Le Corbusier's encounter with India, where he was compelled, more than before, to respond to conditions set by nature. It is not surprising, therefore, that the weekend house's low, earth-hugging form, channeled space, and roof garden reappear in the Sarabhai house, where they were eminently suited to the prevailing climate.[41] This leads to the question of whether the Sarabhai house was at all inspired by India's traditional architecture.

A comparison between the Sarabhai house and the royal apartments of Delhi's Red Fort shows that both are low, dark, and sheltered architectural environments which shut out the summer sun yet let in the cooling breezes. Moreover, both spaces are primarily intended for the sitting position (Figures 13, 14). Yet the close kinship that exists between these two interiors is not necessarily the result of a direct influence from India's own architectural tradition; instead, it is largely the outcome of a long creative process that was decisively shaped by the natural and built environment of the Mediterranean world.[42] What India did offer to Le Corbusier was the right climatic and cultural setting for bringing his Mediterranean style to a full fruition.

If the formal and spatial qualities of the Sarabhai house are Indian only by coincidence, is there anything about the house that can be called uniquely Indian? The answer is yes: its naturalness. And this is precisely the quality that is so greatly valued by the followers of the Jain religion. The belief in the overriding importance of nature constitutes in fact a central tenet in Jainism. This is most eloquently manifested in the avowed commitment not to harm any living being and to interfere with nature as little as possible. In the Sarabhai house, Le Corbusier paid a profound tribute to Jain beliefs by making it his most natural house.

In the concluding lines of *Le Poème de l'angle droit* (1955), Le Corbusier writes:

With a full hand I have received
With a full hand I give[43]

There are no better words to sum up what Le Corbusier and Ahmedabad owe to each other, for what he created there is just as much the result of his clients' vision as it is of his genius.

Whether the intention was to enrich the cultural life of the city or the personal life of a client, it took courage and insight to engage Le Corbusier in the process of restoring Ahmedabad's eminence in the cultural life of India. The most immediate effect of the reciprocal relationship between Le Corbusier and his Ahmedabadi clients was that it made the city aware that modern architecture can be used as a means to express its aspirations. Those who benefited from this were India's own younger architects, most notably Achyut Kanvinde of New Delhi, Balkrishna Doshi of Ahmedabad, and Charles Correa of Bombay, who later became the country's foremost architects. Thanks to the patronage they received in Ahmedabad from the mid-1950s on, they built some of their finest buildings there, making the city the birthplace of India's indigenous modern architecture.

However important Le Corbusier's work is in Ahmedabad, it was Chandigarh that brought him to India, and it was there that he created his most profound architectural statements. Thanks to the pioneering work of a number of scholars, it is possible today to offer a brief evaluation of Le Corbusier's achievement there without doing injustice to the subject.[44]

As indicated earlier, Le Corbusier was invited by the representatives of the Punjab government to become the architectural advisor for Chandigarh. In this capacity he was primarily responsible for the master plan of the city and the capitol complex. Later he undertook to design a major portion of the business center and a few additional buildings for the city.[45] My discussion will focus on only a few salient characteristics of the executed buildings of the capitol complex: the Secretariat, the Assembly Building, and the High Court, serving the executive, legislative, and judiciary branches of government.[46]

The first of these to be erected was the High Court, a concrete structure defined by a large rectangular frame within which the different functions of the building are inserted, from the highest court on the left to the lowest on the right (Figure 15). The significance of the Supreme

Court is underscored by its separation from the rest by a giant portico whose massive pillars are painted green, yellow, and red. Clues to an understanding of the nature and meaning of this building can be found in its sources and the development of its design.

The first sketch of the High Court that appears in Le Corbusier's sketchbooks shows that he envisaged the building as a monumental vaulted structure set against the backdrop of the Himalayas (Figure 16).[47] The spatial and formal configuration proposed here recalls two sketches the architect made fifty years apart, the first representing the Basilica of Constantine and the second the pavilion of the Pinjore gardens (Figures 17, 18). Appearing next to the High Court in his sketchbook, the sketch of the pavilion and its surroundings sets the stage for the siting of the capitol complex and the spatial relationships established in it.[48] Like the pavilion, the High Court is placed in a wide-open space linking the mountains with the observer. Although the position intended here for the High Court was soon given over to the Governor's Palace, Le Corbusier retained in the completed building the sense of isolation inherent in the sketch. In fact, a comparison between the High Court and the pavilion of the Pinjore gardens shows that the isolation of Le Corbusier's building is far greater than that of the pavilion. As in most Mogul palace gardens, the individual buildings at Pinjore are interconnected by landscaped processional spaces unmarred by overscaling. Le Corbusier, on the other hand, not only over-scaled his processional spaces but he also replaced landscaping with paving, thus forcing the High Court into an even greater sense of isolation (Figure 15). The High Court, more than the Assembly and the Secretariat, became in fact the victim of Le Corbusier's heroic attempt to fuse Parisian scale with Mogul processional spaces. But mating the two without the mitigating power of Mogul landscaping resulted in failure.[49]

If the Pinjore gardens gave the impetus for the initial siting of the High Court, it was the

Basilica of Constantine as sketched by Le Corbusier during his first visit to Rome in 1911 that provided the point of departure for the design of the building (Figures 16, 17). As can be seen from his early sketches, Le Corbusier used the great barrel vaults of the Basilica as the most dominant element in his preliminary designs.[50] However, as the building evolved in his mind, the importance of Constantine's law court gradually diminished to give way to influences emanating from the North. Hence, in the final design the lower parts of the massive Roman vaults were largely replaced by sunbreakers whose irregular concrete grille was inspired by de Stijl architecture (Figures 15, 6).

The façade of the High Court, consisting of a flexible framework of sunbreakers placed within a single monumental frame, sheds an important light on the symbolic significance of the building. As a classicist at heart and as a citizen of a country whose law still reflects the basic principles of Roman law, Le Corbusier first turned to a great example of Roman judicial architecture, whose most essential elements he retained even in the final design. He did so by joining the Basilica's arcuated and trabeated system in the building's exterior frame. By placing all the law courts within this all-embracing Roman frame, Le Corbusier reaffirmed the fundamental role that Roman architecture and Roman law have played in Western culture. Moreover, by imbuing the building in general and its great frame in particular with clarity, constancy, and logic, he gave the High Court a sense of majestic unity. And it is precisely such a unity that constitutes the essence of Roman architecture and Roman law.

Yet within the High Court's formal, classical frame, Le Corbusier allowed the sunbreakers to act more freely and flexibly, in keeping with the archi-tectural tradition of the North. He did so not only to provide better protection from the sun and give scale to the building but also to convey a major part of the building's symbolic significance. Although Roman law remained the primary basis of Western law, it was English common law that was brought into India by the British. As opposed to the codified law of Rome, common law has developed in England gradually and organically since the early Middle Ages. Based on custom and precedent, this law is known not for constancy and logic but rather for variety and flexibility. And these are precisely the qualities that characterize the sunbreakers of the High Court's façade.

In the High Court Le Corbusier juxtaposed the Mediterranean and Northern traditions of architecture by making the former the anchoring point and primary frame of reference of the building without, however, minimizing the prominence of the latter. He embodied the Mediterranean tradition primarily in the clarity and constancy of the building's monumental frame, while he expressed that of the North in the variety and flexibility of the sunbreakers. In so doing, he created architectural forms that possess the very same qualities that characterize Roman law and English common law: majestic unity and organic quality, respectively. Hence, in the High Court the two great systems of Western law, Roman civil law and English common law, find, unwittingly perhaps, a most eloquent visual interpretation.

Facing the High Court across the 400-meter-wide capitol square is the Assembly, whose exterior consists of three main elements: a square block, a portico, and a superstructure, each of which has a distinct identity (Figures 19, 20). As early sketches of the Assembly indicate, Le Corbusier first envisaged it as a great arcuated building evoking the memory of such Roman structures as the Basilica of Constantine and the Pont du Gard.[51] But as the building evolved in his mind, the arcuated system was replaced by a trabeated system exemplified largely by a regular grille of sunbreakers.

The sources of the three main constituent elements of the Assembly's exterior provide important clues to an understanding of the nature and meaning of the building. Enfronting the building is the monumental portico whose most dominant feature is the upward swooping curvilinear canopy that functions both as an umbrella and gutter. This canopy rests on eight tautly stretched walls that cut the portico into clearly defined cubical bays whose distinctness is reinforced by the compositional organization of the back wall. The climactic point of this wall is the large enameled ceremonial door twenty-five feet square, which depicts a complex set of images dominated by the sun.

The Assembly's monumental portico incorporates the spatial and formal qualities of two distinctly different strains of India's architectural past: the palatial and the folk. As a comparison with the Red Fort's Hall of Public Audiences shows, the repetitive rhythm, the sheltered openness, and the ceremonial dignity of this Mogul palatial building reappear in Le Corbusier's portico (Figures 19, 21). However, the surface treatment of his forms, whether in the Assembly's portico or in his other concrete buildings in India, shows a greater affinity to the country's folk architecture. He was fond of visiting the villages around Chandigarh to study their low, moundlike huts constructed of mud brick; these visits found their way into his handling of rough concrete, or *béton brut* (Figure 22). Even before his contact with India, Le Corbusier was fascinated by the possibility of making concrete look more like a natural material, and his work there greatly enhanced this process.

Le Corbusier reinforced the meaning of the portico with the enameled doorway that links the outside with the columnar lobby. The primary function of this door is to provide a ceremonial entryway for the governor when he opens the assembly once a year. Both sides of the door are decorated with a rich range of images that convey multiple meanings. The door's pictorial composition facing the portico is divided into two halves: the upper, representing the paths of the sun, and the lower, representing rivers, vegetation, and animals; and both are interpreted in a spontaneous, almost childlike, manner. Hence, the function and scale of the ceremonial doorway convey a formal and ritualistic order, while the imagery on its surface evokes the world of fantasy and folklore.[52] And both of these meanings are inherent in the portico.

Treating the great portico as a gateway to the building that houses the two legislative bodies of the Punjab government—the assembly and the governor's council—it is fitting that Le Corbusier incorporated in it a broad range of India's architectural tradition: from the stately and ritualistic to the informal and rustic. In so doing, he expressed in it, unintentionally perhaps, some of the most salient characteristics of Indian society.

The main body of the Assembly Building is defined on three sides by large grilles of sun-breakers arranged in repetitive rows. This organization reveals the nature of the spaces that lie behind them: scores of offices and committee rooms serving the members of parliament and their staff (Figure 20). On top of the Assembly's classical block is a super-structure which consists of three separate yet interrelated parts: a tower in the shape of a hyperbolic paraboloid, a tilted pyramid, and a service tower (Figure 19). The basic function of the first is to provide light for the assembly hall and that of the second to help illuminate the council chamber. The relationship between the hyperbolic tower and the main body of the building evokes the memory of French industrial architecture as exemplified by Züblin's coal-washer for the Société des Mines de Carmaux of 1928–29 (Figure 23). The Assembly's tower, like the funnel-shaped receptor of the coal-washer, is dramatically juxtaposed with the main part of the building, producing a strong sense of tension between the two. Juxtaposing a building's constituent parts in such a manner is not uncommon in industrial architecture but is quite exceptional in an honorific building. In fact, one of the most remarkable qualities of the Assembly is the daring contrasts created by Le Corbusier among the building's three major parts: the portico, the main block, and the superstructure. Without his deep admiration for the compositional solutions established in industrial architecture, this could hardly have been accomplished.[53]

The striking contrast between the Assembly's main block and the hyperbolic tower tends to suggest that the two are not functionally interrelated. Yet a closer examination reveals that the building's crowning feature is in fact a continuation of the large hyperbolic shell that serves as a container for the assembly hall. As Le Corbusier's sketch of June 1953 shows, the inspiration for this shell came directly from the cooling towers of the Sabarmati Power Plant in Ahmedabad.[54] By using the form of the cooling towers for both the interior shell and the protruding part of the assembly hall, Le Corbusier not only preserved the building's consistency but also reinforced a key aspect of the building's symbolic significance.

In the Assembly's interior the building's underlying theme of juxtaposing quasi-autonomous architectural elements is best exemplified in the way in which the hyperbolic shell of the assembly hall is related to its setting. Instead of treating this shell as a continuous part of the interior, Le Corbusier handled it as a building within a building. He did so by placing it inside a large hypostyle hall known as the forum, which in turn is surrounded by offices facing the outside. As a result, the assembly hall is just as clearly separated from the rest of the interior as the Assembly's tower is from the rest of the exterior, thus ensuring consistency in the building's formal organization.

On the symbolic level, the isolation of the hyperbolic shell highlights the importance of the legislative assembly. Following the parliamentary system inherited from the British, the assembly, like the Lower House in Britain, enjoys a prime decision-making power in the government. Le Corbusier gave this political reality a powerful architectural interpretation by making the hyperbolic shell the focal point of the interior and the crowning point of the exterior. In so doing, he not only expressed the nature of the legislative assembly's power in Chandigarh, but also proclaimed the role that the Lower House fulfills within a parliamentary system. In fact, never before has the role of the Lower House been given such a forceful and eloquent architectural interpretation as in Le Corbusier's Assembly Building.

However, the inspiration emanating from the cooling towers of the Sabarmati Power Plant served Le Corbusier in other ways as well. With its obvious references to technology, the image of the cooling towers offered him an opportunity to pay tribute to one of Prime Minister Nehru's most fundamental beliefs summed up in one of his lectures: "The essential and most revolutionary factor in modern life is not a particular ideology, but technological advance."[55] Nehru put these general principles into practice by establishing a five-year plan whose primary aim was to develop industry and produce electricity on a large scale. Thus, the cooling towers of an electric power plant must have seemed to Le Corbusier a particularly appropriate symbol for expressing the social and political aspirations of his friend and patron. As a Ruskinian at heart, he may even have believed that by placing the legislators in the architectural environment that strongly resembles the cooling towers of a power plant, he could influence them to follow Nehru's commitment to technology.

The Assembly's conspicuously visible symbol of technology should not give the impression that Le Corbusier paid tribute to only one of India's great modern leaders, for in addition to Nehru, Gandhi's presence can also be found in the building. Gandhi's philosophy of rejecting technology and focusing on the importance of agriculture, handicraft, and cottage industry finds many direct and indirect references in the Assembly. The hand-made quality of the *béton brut*, the folk imagery on the ceremonial gateway, the wall decorations based on imprints made by the workmen, and the juxtaposition of the oxcart with the building in one of Le Corbusier's sketches all attest to a world view that shared a great deal with Gandhi's own. For Le Corbusier, Gandhi's philosophy of rural rejuvenation offered a felicitous balance to Nehru's technological bias, and how he agreed with both can be seen in two statements he made in his early Indian sketchbooks: "Atomic energy is now a fact. Put it in the countries and in the homes." But elsewhere he wrote: "How the earth remains a primary, primeval, primitive in spite of the works of Men."[56] And one of Gandhi's aims was to keep it that way.

The Assembly Building represents a culmination of Le Corbusier's heroic efforts to give the most

meaningful architectural interpretation to political institutions. This effort has a long history in his own career, going back to his projects for the League of Nations Building in 1927 and the Palace of the Soviets of 1931. In the former he combined Beaux-Arts composition with a technologically perfected structural system, while in the latter he allowed technology to triumph throughout the entire design. Intended for an international political body of the modern world, it is fitting that Le Corbusier imbued his project for the League with a sense of history and modernity. And by giving technology such a prominent presence in the Palace of the Soviets, he highlighted one of Soviet Russia's most deeply felt ambitions: to achieve technological superiority in the world. But to express the social, political, and economic aspirations of newly independent India, Le Corbusier not only had to invent new forms but he also had to develop a new formal organization that could convey architecturally the complexity of the issues at hand. He did so by turning to India's rich past and evolving present while fertilizing these with his own creative memory. No wonder that the Assembly became one of the most probing and compelling architectural manifestations of the human spirit.

Looming behind the Assembly, the Secretariat is an eight-hundred-foot-long concrete slab consisting of six eight-story blocks interconnected by a massive grille of sunbreakers (Figure 24). Originally Le Corbusier had envisaged it as a high-rise building, but when this was rejected he proposed the present solution. As an early sketch of the building shows, the architect first visualized it as a tall concrete slab defined by arches on its narrow ends. In a more developed design, he presented it as an even taller slab resting on *pilotis* and sheathed by a repetitive grille of sunbreakers.[57] The project that links this design with the final version is his Admiralty Building planned for Algiers between 1938 and 1942 (Figure 25).

Intended as an office building and hotel for Algiers' marine district, the Admiralty represents a major point of departure in Le Corbusier's approach to skyscraper design. Here he abandoned his earlier skin-and-bone technique in favor of achieving firmness, scale, and functional clarity. This dramatic change is directly attributable to his encounter with the skyscrapers of New York in 1936. In his account of his American journey he wrote:

> In New York, then, I learn to appreciate the Italian Renaissance. It is so well done that you could believe it to be genuine. It even has a strange, new firmness which is not Italian but American! The maritime atmosphere and the potential of the American adventure have lifted Tuscan graces to a new tone. The oldest skyscrapers of Wall Street add the superimposed orders of Bramante all the way up to the top with a clearness in molding and proportion which delights me.[58]

The praise that Le Corbusier lavished on New York's skyscrapers may seem surprising after the diatribes against them in his earlier books, most notably in *Urbanisme*. But even during the 1920s he singled out a few American skyscrapers as worthy of emulation, for example, Albert Kahn's First National Bank Building in Detroit of 1922 (Figure 26). Illustrated in his book, *L'Art décoratif d'aujourd'hui*, he used the building as a frontispiece for a chapter devoted to utilitarian design.[59] But he had to come to America to appreciate its qualities fully.

The qualities that Le Corbusier ascribed to New York's Beaux-Arts Renaissance skyscrapers in the passage quoted above—clarity, firmness, and proportion—can also be found in Kahn's building. Hence, it can be used as a frame of reference for discussing the "Americanization" of Le Corbusier's approach to skyscraper design. Following the principles of the Beaux-Arts Renaissance style popularized by Daniel Burnham, Kahn divided his building into three major zones: the public for the lobby, the semi-private for the offices, and the private for the top executives. These three functional zones are clearly revealed in the building's exterior design with the help of columns, cornices and windows. Moreover, the building's firmness and proportion are expressed in its mass and articulation of parts, respectively.

In the Admiralty, Le Corbusier incorporated some of the key principles of the American Beaux-Arts Renaissance skyscraper style, most notably its emphasis on mass, proportion, and hierarchical organization. As a comparison between the Admiralty and the First National Bank Building in Detroit shows, he interpreted these principles with the help of large frames and sunbreakers to be built of concrete. In fact, from this project forward, sunbreakers became the key conveyors of his design principles based on the American Beaux-Arts skyscraper. They gave his projects and buildings clarity by externalizing the spatial and hierarchical organization of the interior; they imbued his works with firmness by the sheer weight of their mass; and they helped achieve proportion by the articulation of their forms. And all of these principles were fully realized in Chandigarh.

When it became clear to Le Corbusier that he could not build the Secretariat as a tall slab, he offered a horizontal version of it without, however, abandoning the principles he had developed in the Admiralty Building. The Secretariat, like its precursor, is divided into large rectangular blocks which are shielded by a massive grille of sunbreakers whose shape ranges from the simple to the complex. The simple, repetitive sunbreakers covering most of the building enfront the endless rows of bureaucratic offices, while the complex ones concentrated in the central block largely define the ministerial offices. The unprecedented complexity and monumentality of the ministerial block show that Le Corbusier wanted the sunbreakers to serve there as powerful witnesses to the functional and symbolic role fulfilled by the spaces that lie behind them.

If the Secretariat's firmness, proportion, and functional clarity must be seen in part as a continuation of American Beaux-Arts skyscraper design principles, the form and composition of its sunbreakers should not. To find precedents for these one must turn to Le Corbusier's books, where illustrations of file cabinets will provide the clues. The two that stand out appear in his *L'art décoratif d'aujourd'hui*, the first of which represents a Ronéo file cabinet system (Figure 27) and the second a file cabinet drawer.[60] Discussing these and other examples of office furniture, Le Corbusier singled out their efficiency, suitability, and flexibility, qualities that he also expected of buildings. No wonder that he incorporated these when he designed an office building such as the Secretariat, whose overall composition shares a great deal with the built-in file cabinets (Figures 24, 27), while the sunbreakers enfronting the bureaucratic offices reveal a striking similarity to the file cabinet drawer. As a result, the building looks like a huge file cabinet system, with most of its "drawers" lined up in an orderly fashion while its "shelves" (porticoes) are left open in a random fashion.

By juxtaposing the firmness, proportion, and functional clarity of the American Beaux-Arts office building with the efficiency and flexibility of the office cabinet system, Le Corbusier developed a new approach to the design of office buildings. The experience that had a decisive role in making this possible was his first visit to New York in 1936, when he saw the city's skyscrapers at first hand. Notwithstanding his oft-quoted statement that the skyscrapers of New York are too small, he learned to value them once he saw them. His most consequential immediate response to New York was embodied in the project for the Admiralty, in which he launched a new direction of skyscraper design. But the only country that benefited from this was India, by giving him the opportunity to put his ideas into concrete form and thus enabling him to realize his most eloquent architectural interpretation of modern bureaucracy.

In his first Indian sketchbook Le Corbusier wrote: "Calm, dignity, contempt for envy: perhaps India is capable of *standing by them*, and establishing herself at the head of civilization."[61] These words clearly sum up what for Le Corbusier represented India's most lasting values: her moral force and potential for moral leadership. In the buildings of Chandigarh's capitol complex, Le Corbusier offered a powerful architectural interpretation of the moral force inherent in India's executive, legislative, and judicial branches of government. He also expressed in them India's aspiration

to become the foremost moral leader in the world, as envisioned by Gandhi and Nehru. No wonder that in his outline of the city's program he noted that "responsibilities of aesthetics and ethics equally dominate the work."[62]

Le Corbusier believed that he was in an exceptional position to interpret India's needs and aspirations, for he was not bound by the issues of the day in which political leaders—including Gandhi and Nehru—are often enmeshed. In his third Indian sketchbook he wrote:

> Life has placed me in the position of an observer, giving me incomparable—and exceptional—means of judgment. I believe that this order of thought is not available to political leaders and that they live *in* the problem and hence do not see it.[63]

Viewing his role in this light, he spared no effort in giving the three great buildings of the capitol complex the most memorable form and the richest possible meaning. In so doing, he offered the newly independent India an architecture intended to outlast the contribution made even by the country's two greatest modern political leaders. Hence Le Corbusier's architecture there can justly be called timeless but of its time.

Notes

1. Quoted by B. P. Bagchi, *Chandigarh* (Chandigarh: New Horizons Press, 1965), p. 1.
2. For an account of the birth of Chandigarh, see Norma Evenson, *Chandigarh* (Berkeley: University of California Press, 1966). For an interpretation of the city's symbolic significance, see Stanislaus von Moos, "The Politics of the Open Hand: Notes on Le Corbusier and Nehru at Chandigarh," in *The Open Hand: Essays on Le Corbusier*, ed. Russell Walden (Cambridge, Mass.: The MIT Press, 1977), pp. 412–57.
3. There are seventy-three sketchbooks covering the period from 1914 to 1964 in the Archives of the Fondation Le Corbusier in Paris. These have been published by the Architectural History Foundation, New York, as *Le Corbusier Sketchbooks Volume 1, 1914–1948* (1981); *Le Corbusier Sketchbooks Volume 2, 1950–1954* (1981);

Le Corbusier Sketchbooks Volume 3, 1954–1957 (1982);
Le Corbusier Sketchbooks Volume 4, 1957–1964 (1982).

4. These are Sketchbooks E 18 and E 19. See *Le Corbusier Sketchbooks Volume 2, 1950–1954*, No. 309–414.

5. Ibid., No. 329–330. It must be kept in mind, however, that Le Corbusier's reservation about Lutyens' work is made here in the context of an exceptional example of earlier Indian architecture. Elsewhere he was unequivocal in his praise of this British architect/planner. "New Delhi (in Tuscan inspired style), the capital of imperial India, was built by Lutyens over 30 years ago, with extreme care, great talent, and with true success. The critics may rant as they like, but the accomplishment of such an undertaking earns respect." (Le Corbusier, *Oeuvre complète, 1952–1957* [Zurich: Girsberger, 1957], p. 51). For Lutyens' influence on Chandigarh, see Allan Greenberg, "Lutyens' Architecture Restudied," *Perspecta 12* (1969): 129–52.

6. Le Corbusier, *Le Voyage d'Orient* (Paris: Forces Vives, 1966). For an earlier published account of Le Corbusier's trip to the East, see "Confession," in his *L'Art décoratif d'aujourd'hui* (Paris: Crès, 1925), pp. 197–247, esp. p. 246).

7. The client whom he was to meet only in the fall of 1951 was Shyamubhai Shodhan.

8. During the next few years Le Corbusier repeatedly tried to convince Bhabha Tata to let him build the headquarters of the Air India Company, but without success. I am indebted to Charles Correa for this information.

9. L. R. Nair, *Why Chandigarh?* (Simla: Publicity Department, Punjab Government, 1950).

10. For the best study of Ahmedabad in English, see Kenneth L. Gillion, *Ahmedabad, A Study in Indian Urban History* (Berkeley: University of California Press, 1968).

11. Ibid., p. 94.

12. Ibid., p. 153.

13. Except during the monsoon season, this river is reduced to a trickle, leaving the large riverbed exposed. For the project of the Chimanbhai house, see the drawings in this volume (FLC 6.313–6.397).

14. The unexecuted buildings include the Spontaneous Theater, The Magic Box, the Library, and the Art Studios. See *Le Corbusier, Oeuvre complète, 1946–1952* (Zurich: Girsberger, 1960), pp. 160–61. Balkrishna Doshi's Tagore Theater and Gautam Sarabhai's National Institute of Design were subsequent additions to the still incomplete cultural center.

15. The Museum of Admedabad was first adumbrated in Le Corbusier's World Museum planned for his Mundaneum of 1929 (see "Mundaneum," in *The Le Corbusier Archive*, ed. H. Allen Brooks (New York: Garland Publishing; Paris: Fondation Le Corbusier, 1982–), vol. 7, *Villa Savoye and Other Buildings and Projects, 1929–1930* [forthcoming]). However, the most direct prototypes for this museum are the projects for the Museum of Contemporary Art, Paris,

1931 (see "Centre d'Art Contemporaine," in the *Le Corbusier Archive*, vol. 10, *Urbanisme, Algiers and Other Buildings and Projects, 1930–1933* [forthcoming]), the Pavilion for the Paris International Exhibition of 1937 (see *The Le Corbusier Archive*, vol. 13, *Pavillon des Temps Nouveaux and Other Buildings and Projects, 1936–1937* [1983], pp. 557 ff.); and the Museum of Unlimited Growth planned for Philippeville, Algeria, in 1939 (see *The Le Corbusier Archive*, vol. 14, *Buildings and Projects, 1937–1942* [1983], pp. 577 ff.).

16. See "Mundaneum," in *The Le Corbusier Archive*, vol. 7, and Paul Otlet and Le Corbusier, *Mundaneum* (Brussels: J. Lebégue, 1928).

17. Le Corbusier, *Une Maison—un palais* (Paris: Crès, 1928), p. 52.

18. Before the Millowners Building acquired its present form, it had undergone major changes during its lengthy design process, which included an earlier project with stone facing and only a few sunbreakers. See FLC 6.781, 6.788, and 6.789 in this volume.

19. In the Villa Cook Le Corbusier reversed the traditional organization of the interior of a house by placing the public over the private floors. This concept was first realized in his Ozenfant house built in Paris in 1922, where the double-storied studio occupies the top two floors.

20. Le Corbusier, *The Radiant City* (New York: The Orion Press, 1967), p. 78 (originally published as *La Ville radieuse* in 1933).

21. *Le Corbusier Sketchbooks Volume 2, 1950–1954*, E 18, No. 359.

22. Le Corbusier, *Oeuvre complète, 1952–1957* (Zurich: Girsberger, 1958), p. 134; and Balkrishna V. Doshi, *Le Corbusier, Sarabhai House and Shodhan House, Ahmedabad, India* (Tokyo: A.D.A. Edita, 1974), n.p.

23. Reyner Banham, *Theory and Design in the First Machine Age* (New York: Praeger Publishers, 1960), p. 221.

24. Maurice Jardot, "Sketch for a Portrait," in Le Corbusier, *Creation is a Patient Search* (New York: Praeger Publishers, 1960), p. 9.

25. Ibid., p. 11.

26. For the importance of these two projects, see my article, "Le Corbusier's Changing Attitude Toward Form," *Journal of the Society of Architectural Historians* 24 (March 1965): 15–23, and reprinted in my *Le Corbusier in Perspective* (Englewood Cliffs, N.J.: Prentice-Hall, 1975), pp. 68–73.

27. Le Corbusier, *The Modulor* (Cambridge: Harvard University Press, 1958), p. 224.

28. Le Corbusier, *Oeuvre complète, 1910–1929* (Zurich: Girsberger, 1960), pp. 13–14.

29. Ibid., p. 31. Located at 32 rue Godot-de-Mauroy, off the boulevard des Italiens, the Café Legendre is now called the Café Le Mauroy.

30. For the first critical discussion of this project, see my article

mentioned in note 26. Le Corbusier makes reference to this project in Sketchbook E 18, No. 360, by saying, "Brother's villa roofing in manner of Baizeau Tunis." Here he refers to the unexecuted house designed for Chinubhai Chimanbhai, which was almost identical with the early design for the Hutheesing/Shodhan house. Compare FLC 6.313 in the Villa Chimanbhai drawings with FLC 6.444 in the Villa Shodhan drawings, in this volume.

31. For the most thorough discussions of the Schröder house in Utrecht, see Theodore M. Brown, *The Work of G. Rietveld Architect* (Utrecht: A. W. Bruna & Zoon, 1958), pp. 35–74, where he writes that, according to Mrs. Schröder, "Le Corbusier visited the house within a few years of its completion." p. 74.

32. These are the Villa Fallet, 1906 and the Villas Jaquemet and Stotzer, both of 1908. See Charles Jencks, *Le Corbusier and the Tragic View of Architecture* (Cambridge: Harvard University Press, 1973), pp. 21–23.

33. See "Maison locative," in *The Le Corbusier Archive*, vol. 11, *Immeuble, 24, rue Nungesser-et-Coli and Other Buildings and Projects, 1933* (1983), pp. 485 ff.

34. See Le Corbusier, *Oeuvre complète, 1946–1952*, p. 109. For the camera analogy, see Christopher Rand, "City on a Tilting Plain," *New Yorker*, April 30, 1955, p. 56.

35. *Le Corbusier Sketchbooks Volume 3, 1954–1957*, J 39, No. 451.

36. For this and other drawings of primitive architecture, see Le Corbusier, *Une Maison—un palais*, p. 39.

37. *Le Corbusier Sketchbooks Volume 2, 1950–1954*, E 18, No. 357.

38. For the Immeubles-villas project, see *The Le Corbusier Archive*, vol. 1, *Early Buildings and Projects, 1912–1923* (1982), pp. 353 ff.; for the Villa Stein-Monzie, see *The Le Corbusier Archive*, vol. 3, *Palais de la Société des Nations, Villa les Terrasses, and Other Buildings and Projects, 1926–1927* (1982), pp. 365 ff.

39. *Le Corbusier Sketchbooks Volume 2, 1950–1954*, E 18, No. 361 and E 23, No. 689.

40. See *The Le Corbusier Archive*, vol. 12, *Buildings and Projects, 1933–1937* (1983), pp. 391 ff.

41. Although a discussion of the roof garden of the weekend house lies outside the scope of this paper, it should be noted that it is there that Le Corbusier began to treat the roof garden as a more freely landscaped space. This new direction was given its fullest manifestation in the roof garden of the Sarabhai house.

42. In the context of the Sarabhai house the folk element of the Mediterranean tradition stands out. For earlier manifestations of this element in Le Corbusier's architecture, see his project for the Peyrissac house, near Cherchell, Algeria, 1942 (in *The Le Corbusier Archive*, vol. 14, *Buildings and Projects, 1937–1942* [1983], pp. 733 ff.), which is an important link between the weekend house and the

Sarabhai house; and the projects for La Sainte-Baume, near Marseille, 1948 ("La Sainte-Baume," in *The Le Corbusier Archive*, vol. 18, *Palais des Nations Unies and Other Buildings and Projects, 1946–1948* [forthcoming]), and Roq and Rob, Cap Martin, 1949 (in *The Le Corbusier Archive*, vol. 19, *Projet Roq et Rob, Roquebrune-Cap Martin, and Other Buildings and Projects, 1948–1950* [1983], pp. 47 ff.).

43. Translation by Mary Patricia May Sekler, "Ruskin, the Tree and the Open Hand," in *The Open Hand: Essays on Le Corbusier*, ed. Russell Walden, p. 73.

44. The most important scholars include: Norma Evenson, Stanislaus von Moos, Mary Patricia May Sekler, and Alexander C. Gorlin. For Evenson and von Moos, see note no. 2; for Sekler, see note no. 43; and for Gorlin, "An Analysis of the Governor's Palace of Chandigarh," *Oppositions* 19/20 (Winter/Spring, 1980): 161–183.

45. These are: the Museum and Art Gallery with the adjacent Lecture Hall (1964–68); the School of Art (1964–69); the School of Architecture (1964–69); and the Boat Club on Sukhna Lake (1963–65). For the best illustrations of these and the Business Center, see *Le Corbusier: Last Works*, ed. Willy Boesiger (New York: Praeger Publishers, 1970); for drawings, see *The Le Corbusier Archive*, vol. 25, *Chandigarh: City and Musée* (forthcoming).

46. The original plan of the capitol complex also included the Governor's Palace, which was abandoned and replaced by the Museum of Knowledge in 1960. The museum has not yet been built. In addition to the buildings, Le Corbusier also planned certain monuments for the capitol complex, which are: the Monument of the Open Hand, the Tower of Shadows with the Trench of Consideration, and the Monument to the Martyrs of the Indian Partition. Only the last one has been built so far. See *Le Corbusier: Last Works*, pp. 64–75, and Gorlin and Sekler. For the drawings, see *The Le Corbusier Archive*, vol. 24, *Chandigarh: Capitole, Volume III: Palais du Gouverneur and Other Buildings and Projects* (forthcoming).

47. *Le Corbusier Sketchbooks Volume 2, 1950–1954*, E 19, no. 391.

48. Ibid., no. 392. The Pinjore gardens date from the 17th century and are located ten miles from Chandigarh at the foothills of the Himalayas. The Patiala gardens to which Le Corbusier makes reference here are the Baradari gardens in Patiala, which he visited on February 25, 1951. See Ibid., E 18, No. 331.

49. However, Le Corbusier applied the principles of Mogul landscaping in general and that of Pinjore in particular to the project for the garden of the Governor's Palace. See Le Corbusier, *Oeuvre complète, 1946–1952*, p. 143.

50. For additional early sketches of the High Court, see Le Corbusier, *Oeuvre complète, 1946–1952*, p. 126.

51. Le Corbusier referred to the Pont du Gard as "among the very great works of architecture, and going far beyond mere

mathematical formulae." Le Corbusier, *The City of Tomorrow* (Cambridge, Mass.: The MIT Press, 1971), p. 57.

52. For a discussion of other aspects of the door's symbolic significance, see Richard A. Moore, "Alchemical and Mythical Themes in the Poem of the Right Angle 1946–1965," *Oppositions 19/20* (Winter/Spring, 1980): 111–39, esp. pp. 129–32.

53. Le Corbusier's reliance on the compositional solutions found in industrial architecture was preceded by the work of many architects, most notably by the Russian Constructivists.

54. For the sketch, see Le Corbusier, *Oeuvre complète, 1957–1965*, p. 80.

55. Quoted by Stanislaus von Moos, p. 418.

56. *Le Corbusier Sketchbooks Volume 2, 1950–1954*, E 23, No. 662 and E 18, No. 361.

57. See "Capitole," FLC 5.144, in *The Le Corbusier Archive*, vol. 22, *Chandigarh: Capitole, Volume I: Assemblée and Other Buildings and Projects* (forthcoming).

58. Le Corbusier, *When the Cathedrals Were White* (New York: McGraw-Hill Book Co., 1964), p. 60 (originally published in 1947).

59. Le Corbusier, *L'Art décoratif d'aujourd'hui* (Paris: Vincent, Fréal, 1959), p. 83 (originally published in 1925).

60. Ibid., pp. 74 and 70.

61. *Le Corbusier Sketchbooks Volume 2, 1950–1954*, E 18, No. 362.

62. Le Corbusier, *Oeuvre complète, 1946–1952* (Zurich: Girsberger, 1961), p. 115.

63. *Le Corbusier Sketchbooks Volume 2, 1950–1954*, E 23, Nos. 662 and 663 (Translation by Agnes Serenyi).

Figure 1. Le Corbusier, Museum of Ahmedabad, 1951–56. Photograph courtesy of Parmanand Dalwadi, Ahmedabad.

Figure 2. Le Corbusier, Millowners Association Building, Ahmedabad, 1951–56. Photograph courtesy of Parmanand Dalwadi, Ahmedabad.

Figure 3. Le Corbusier, Shodhan House, Ahmedabad, 1951–56. Photograph courtesy of Peter Serenyi.

Figure 4. Le Corbusier, Shodhan House, Ahmedabad, 1951–56. Photograph courtesy of Peter Serenyi.

Figure 5. Le Corbusier, project for house in Lannemezan, 1940 (Fondation Le Corbusier #31.807).

Figure 6. Theo van Doesburg, project for an artist's house, 1923 (from Theo van Doesburg, *Grundbegriffe der neuen gestaltenden Kunst*).

Figure 7. Hutheesing Jain Temple, Ahmedabad, 1850 (from *Souvenir Volume, Annual Convention, Indian Institute of Architects, Gujarat Chapter*, 1968).

Figure 11. Café Legendre (now Café Mauroy), Paris. Photograph courtesy of Fondation Le Corbusier, Paris.

Figure 8. Old Shodhan House, Ahmedabad, 19th century. Photograph courtesy of Peter Serenyi.

Figure 9. Le Corbusier, Shodhan House, Ahmedabad, 1951–56, living room. Photograph courtesy of Peter Serenyi.

Figure 10. Mohanlal Chunilal House, Ahmedabad, 18th century (from R. K. Trivedi, *Wood Carvings of Gujarat*, 1965).

Figure 12. Le Corbusier, Shodhan House, Ahmedabad, 1951–56. Photograph courtesy of Peter Serenyi.

Figure 13. Le Corbusier, Sarabhai House, Ahmedabad, 1951–55. Photograph courtesy of Peter Serenyi.

Figure 14. The Red Fort, Royal Apartments, Delhi, 1639–48. Photograph courtesy of Peter Serenyi.

Figure 15. Le Corbusier, High Court, Chandigarh, 1951–55. Photograph courtesy of Peter Serenyi.

Figure 16. Le Corbusier, sketch of High Court, 1951, Sketchbook E19, p. 32. Reproduced by permission of the Architectural History Foundation and the Fondation Le Corbusier.

Figure 17. Le Corbusier, sketch of the *Basilica of Constantine*, Rome, 4th century A.D. (from Le Corbusier, *The City of Tomorrow*).

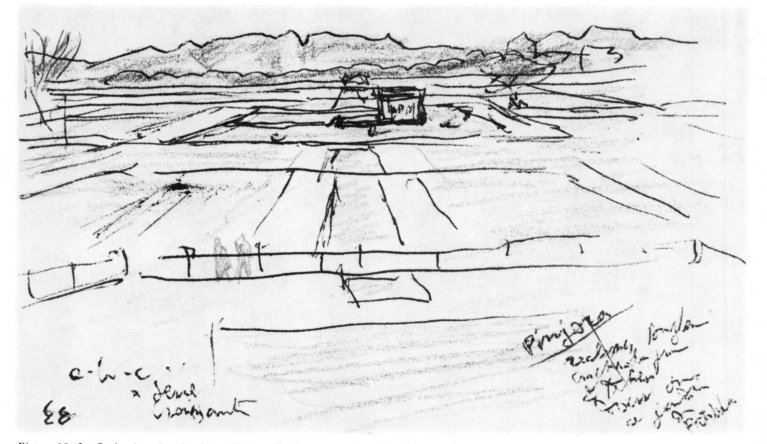

Figure 18. Le Corbusier, sketch of the Pinjore Gardens, near Chandigarh, 17th century, Sketchbook E19, p. 33. Reproduced by permission of the Architectural History Foundation and the Fondation Le Corbusier.

Figure 19. Le Corbusier, Assembly Building, Chandigarh, 1951–61. Photograph courtesy of Peter Serenyi.

Figure 20. Le Corbusier, Assembly Building, Chandigarh, 1951–61. Photograph courtesy of Peter Serenyi.

Figure 21. Delhi, The Red Fort, Diwan-i-Am (Hall of Public Audiences), built by Emperor Shah Jahan between 1639–48. Photograph courtesy of Peter Serenyi.

Figure 22. House in Punjabi Village, near Chandigarh. Photograph courtesy of Suresh Kumar, Chandigarh.

Figure 23. Coal-washer (under construction), Société des Mines de Carmaux, France, by Züblin, 1928–29 (from Roger Ginzburger, *Frankreich: Die Entwicklung der neuen Ideen nach Konstruktion und Form*).

Figure 24. Le Corbusier, Secretariat, Chandigarh, 1951–58. Photograph courtesy of Lucien Hervé.

Figure 25. Le Corbusier, project for the Admiralty Building, Algiers, 1938–42 (from Le Corbusier, *Oeuvre complète 1938–1946*).

Figure 26. Albert Kahn, First National Bank Building, Detroit, 1922 (from Le Corbusier, *L'Art décoratif d'aujourd'hui*).

Figure 27. Ronéo Office Cabinet Systems (from Le Corbusier, *L'Art décoratif d'aujourd'hui*).

Chandigarh: The View from Benares
by Charles Correa

O, Chandigarh. Brave new Chandigarh. Born in the harsh plains of the Punjab without umbilical cord. . . .

The 1950s were indeed a heroic time. India had just won independence and, with Nehru as prime minister, was all set to invent the future. Into a mosaic of development strategies for village *panchayats* and handloom cooperatives, atomic energy and steel plants, came Chandigarh.

It proved to be a catalyst of staggering effectiveness. All at once, India was catapulted to center stage on the world architectural scene. Overnight the things we couldn't possibly build in our climate and within the constraints of our economy (i.e., paper-thin Miesian glass boxes) were OUT. What was IN was exactly what we could do best: in situ concrete, handcrafted form work, an architecture of hot, vivid color, deep shadow, and tropical sun.

The direction of architecture throughout the world swung around abruptly, following Le Corbusier. In bitterly cold, sunless, high-tech societies, people went to enormous expense to produce one-off concrete buildings, complete with sun breakers. But what was an expensive affectation for them appeared rational and economical in the context of our own lives. Here Le Corbusier seemed to raise the most impassioned issues. His buildings were great gestures, evocative of our past: not the Hollywood image that permeated Edward Stone's Delhi embassy like a cheap perfume, but a truer India, an India of the bazaars, sprawling, cruel, raucous, with a dimension all its own.

In part it was the extraordinary decibel level at which Le Corbusier's buildings came at you. Compared with the bland, sotto voce tone of most 1950s architecture, his had the brutal, primordial (yet elegant, urbane!) thunder of Stravinsky in the concert hall. Thus the ramp of the Ahmedabad mill-owner's building, stretching out like a great hand to pick pedestrians up off the road; the (unbuilt) governor's residence in Chandigarh with its incredible silhouette ("I am a Governor's Palace!!"); and the Sarabhai house in Ahmedabad, using barrel vaults similar to those in the Jaoul houses in Paris

and yet so totally different in expression—a masterwork as complex, as amorphous, and as open-ended as a banyan tree, as an Indian joint family, as India herself.

It seemed that on every visit to Chandigarh (which was an annual pilgrimage for many of us in those days) one learned something new. Each time, the old magician had a new rabbit to pull out of his hat. Just when one was certain that structural integrity was crucial and that the plan was "the generator," he produced the High Court: one great crazy, spaced-out entrance, and to hell with everything else (i.e., courtrooms broiling in the sun, lawyers' chambers in the basement, and so forth). Or the Secretariat: a monumental façade that was its own justification, the ramp on the roof acting as an immense backbone, holding the marvelously long, fractured, ungainly heap together. The building as façade: a thesis straight out of the Beaux Arts, one that seemingly turned the fundamental tenets of the Modern movement upside down.

Needless to say, the effect was electrifying—and the arguments were endless. But as Nehru would often say, "It doesn't really matter whether you like Chandigarh or whether you don't like it. The fact of the matter is simply this: it has changed your lives." He was right.

Because of Le Corbusier and because of the questions that arose from his work, a spine of architecturally conscious communities sprang up in the north and west of this country, from the Punjab all the way across to Delhi and down to Ahmedabad, Baroda, and Bombay. Today much of the Chandigarh vocabulary has become standard vernacular for public works departments all over this subcontinent, and a number of private practices—including my own—have probably survived only because of the interest in architecture triggered by that city.

India was indeed lucky to get Le Corbusier—and we knew it.

*   *   *

Thus far, the good news. Now for some of the bad. Over the past two decades, it has become evident that many of Le Corbusier's ideas don't work.

For instance, sun breakers: they are really great dust-catching, pigeon-infested contrivances, which gather heat all day and then radiate it back into the building at night, causing indescribable anguish to the occupants. They are not nearly as useful as old-fashioned verandahs, which are far cheaper to build, protect the buildings during the day, cool off quickly in the evenings, and, furthermore, double as circulation systems. Neither have the great parasol roofs (as in the High Court) proved much more useful. Was Le Corbusier perhaps more concerned with the visual expression of climate control than with its actual effectiveness? In any event, his enthusiasm seemed to lie not in solving the problem but in making the theatrical gesture—assuming the heroic pose—of addressing it. One recalls Steen Eiler Rasmussen, who likened Le Corbusier and his buildings to a child playing with chairs and boxes. The child sets these up in a certain way and then cries out gleefully: Look at my motor car! You say: How can that be a motor car? Does it move? But the child cannot understand. To him it *is* a motor car.

And there seems to be a curious lack of concern for the actual users. This leads to a lot of inadequate planning and much gross detailing. For instance, throughout the office halls of the Secretariat there are files piled high on clerical desks. You can blame the clerks, but surely it was the architect's responsibility to analyze the program and identify the area (at least thirty percent in any government office!) needed for filing. Or take the cafeteria on the roof: it has an exposed concrete counter from which even an animal would refuse to eat. So the food is kept on the floor! When you think of the chaos and disorder of much of India, you realize that Le Corbusier's buildings were really beamed at us aesthetes. To the average government employee, it's just more of the same. Oh, for a single building by, say, S.O.M.! It would have raised a lot of irrelevant questions, but perhaps also some of the right ones.

Then again, however fine the perceptions of Le Corbusier about the visual world, his Chandigarh buildings were never really concerned with the Indian psyche. After all, he was a Mediterranean man, and the capital buildings were part of that astonishing series of consecutive steps that make up his *oeuvre complète*. Thus, both as an architect and as a person, Le Corbusier remained one whose deepest instincts were intensely European. Take, for example, the High Court in Chandigarh with its great entrance recalling, among other things, the fantastic "Buland Darwaza" at the entrance to Fatehpur-Sikri. With these monumental, superscaled spaces and volumes, Le Corbusier (perhaps unconsciously) projects an ambiance conducive not to any Indian sense of justice but to the Napoleonic Code: i.e., justice that is suprahuman, justice that is blind, justice that is beyond the individual. Compare this with the decisions that the Emperor Akbar might have reached atop the pillar in the center of his Diwan-i-am (also in Fatehpur-Sikri), a small masterpiece, exquisitely scaled to human dimensions. I am not saying that the justice of Akbar was preferable, only that if, like the code of Manu and the wisdom of Solomon, sprang from a completely different set of instincts and mode of understanding and that architecture, unconsciously and at a deep level, reflects these differences.

When we put aside the buildings of Chandigarh and examine its planning, the questions become even more evident. Perhaps, as Sibyl Moholy-Nagy used to say, Le Corbusier was never really interested in urbanism. He only turned to it when he couldn't get enough commissions as an architect. Certainly Chandigarh as a town plan never was the brave new world that Nehru presumed it to be. Far from being a futuristic city, it isn't even a contemporary one; it is positively feudal in its ironclad separation of rulers and ruled, in the caste-ridden pattern of its sectors, and so forth. Most perplexing of all is its antic heirarchy of roadways, with V1s and V2s intersecting along a grid every half mile or so. By 1950, anyone who had ever driven a car knew that wouldn't make for speedy traffic. (But perhaps in Paris Le Corbusier took taxis?)

Even more serious was the low density of building adopted for the city, especially in those sectors where the richer people stay. Far from the kind of carpet housing so prevalent in Le Corbusier's beloved Greek islands (and all over the villages and towns of India), Chandigarh exhibits the meaninglessly large plots found in the military cantonments of the British Raj. These criminally low densities involve large per capita subsidies that get progressively higher as a person rises in government! Worst of all, they make a viable public transport system a near impossibility, so that in the middle of a scorchingly hot afternoon you will see hapless Indians plodding along on foot or bicycle down mercilessly long straight roads, between brick walls, to infinity.

But the 1950s must have been a very naïve time, and many of our planners took Chandigarh to be a portent of the future, with the result that scores of new towns were built in its likeness. (One of them, Bhilai, houses the biggest steel complex in India, built with Russian collaboration. When Khrushchev visited the town he asked to see the chief planner. An Indian stepped forward proudly. "In the USSR," Khrushchev said pleasantly, "we would take you out and shoot you.") Like their prototype, all of these new towns assume a middle-class pattern of living totally unrelated to the actual income profile of the population; thus many of the sectors in Chandigarh have two or three families crowding into single dwelling units, and thousands of desperate squatters have eked out miserable crevices for themselves all over the city.

For India is a poor country, and the human condition is brutal for more than half the inhabitants of our spaceship Earth. These facts are palpable today; perhaps they were not so vivid twenty-five years ago. Or perhaps, as was suggested earlier, Le Corbusier was not really a planner at all, but an architect manqué. When he was given the twin assignment of planning the city and designing the capitol complex, he seems to have spent minimal time on the former, modifying only marginally the plan prepared by Albert Mayer; the capitol complex, on the other hand, demanded and obtained his most complete attention. He forthwith decoupled the four buildings of the capitol complex from the city and

placed them against the foothills of the Himalayas, thus setting himself an intriguing architectural exercise, perhaps *the* most exquisite architectural exercise of all, one that took him back to his student voyages to Greece and to the Acropolis at Athens.

The imbalance between the quality of effort brought to bear on the capitol complex and that on the town plan as a whole was obviously Le Corbusier's own decision, taken by him unilaterally. And this brings us to a crucial aspect of his influence, one that even now, twenty-five years later, is difficult to judge: it concerns the role of the architect in society and his responsibility to the client. This is a question of fundamental importance in India and, by extension, in most of the developing world as well.

Now, Le Corbusier always brought the very highest integrity to bear on his task as designer. Despite certain ambiguities in his writings (for instance, in "The City Of Tomorrow," in which he seems to be signaling his availability to large-scale developers and the "captains of industry!"), he was never one to compromise his design objectives; never in *that* sense was he a gun for hire. For us in India in the mid-1950s, that itself was a revelation. For with one or two exceptions, the majority of architects we knew went about their business with the most mundane objectives. Le Corbusier changed all that. He gave us a sense of the dimensions of history and the kind of task—and standards—an architect could set himself. There is no lesson in architecture more important than that.

Yet it is precisely this search for excellence that can become a two-edged sword, for it implies that you act alone, independent of—and often despite—your client (not to mention the rest of society). The resultant building is, at best, a sort of "mad jeweler's act"; more often than not, it degenerates into a pointless ego trip. In any event, however well (or badly) done, it always involves essentially the same equation: one in which the client is cajoled, charmed, dazzled, threatened—in brief, conned—into doing it *your* way. This adversary/confrontation syndrome was something Le Corbusier sought out, fostered, reveled in; it reinforced what Charles Jencks calls his tragic view of architecture.

Yet it is an architect-client relationship fundamentally different from that which produced the masterpieces of the past, from the Katsura Palace in Tokyo to the great cathedral at Chartres. Golconda is exquisite, but its architect surely didn't make any unilateral decisions against the wishes of the emperor. In fact I doubt if you could ever win an argument with an emperor. You'd get your head chopped off. No, the reason why Golconda is so exquisite is precisely because the architect *wasn't* trying to "con" the emperor into anything. He didn't have to. They both shared the same aesthetic. They were both on the same side of the table.

Thus there were enormous advantages to the traditional Indian relationship of architect and client. It was an arrangement that as recently as 150 years ago could produce a masterpiece as magnificent as the desert town of Jaiselmer. This traditional relationship was deeply eroded by British influence during the Victorian era, but in any event, any possibility of it regenerating took a great leap backward when Le Corbusier appeared on the scene. In the hearts and minds of architects throughout the country, he embodied the prototype ("I am the prima donna; I sing alone!") for many decades to come.

But hindsight is always unfair, and twenty-five years is a long time. In fact, almost none of these issues had arisen in the 1950s. There were a number of laymen (philistines!) who didn't like Chandigarh, but simply because they thought it "too modern," not because they eschewed the social and economic attitudes it implied. We were all too naïve and innocent to see the writing on the wall. Yet in ten short years all that had gone. By 1965, when Louis Kahn started building his new capital in Dacca, the issues had surfaced.

Poor Kahn! His monumental brick boxes with their giant pop-out circles appeared much too late: vain, willful mannerisms in an ocean of desperate poverty. In the 1950s life was different; you went to Chandigarh and saw buildings that were a great exaggeration of concrete, and you came back to your own office and wanted to use nothing but concrete on all your projects as well! In the 1970s you visit Kahn's Management Institute in Ahmedabad and see monuments that are a great exaggeration of brick, and you never want to see another brick again; they keep pouring out of your ears.

Obviously the difference is not just one of time scale, it is also visual. Kahn (who in his research laboratories in Philadelphia created one of the great icons of the twentieth century) failed in Ahmedabad and Dacca—for me at least—on the level of poetic invention. This is a shortcoming of which Le Corbusier can never be suspect. Even today, almost three decades later, his buildings are stunningly beautiful. Thousands of imitators haven't managed to devalue their impact. ("The artist goes ahead in a private car," wrote Cocteau, "the public follows in a bus.")

The anticipation starts as one approaches Chandigarh. One drives through the town, past the houses spread out in the dust, endless rows of foolish confidence tricks. Then suddenly in the distance, like an aircraft carrier floating above the flotsam and jetsam of some harbor town, there appears the Secretariat. From miles away one sees it, white in the sunlight, racing along with the car, riding high above the rows of houses that make up the foreground. Gradually this proscenium clears, the other two actors—the Assembly and the High Court—in the melodrama appear, and all three ride together against the grey-blue foothills of the Himalayas. Ride together, swinging sometimes in front of each other and sometimes behind enormous banks of earth. One approaches closer and closer, and the bleached whiteness deepens slowly into the grey-green of concrete, the simple outlines of the masses dissolve into an astonishing, voluptuous complexity of shadow and substance.

"I have seen the future—and it works!" cried Lincoln Steffens, the American author, in 1922 on his return from the USSR. A statement so optimistic, so naïve, so poignant as to be almost incomprehensible to us in the 1980s. Today, architects and planners are an extremely cautious tribe, our heads bloody and very much bowed. Hence much of postmodernism says, "We have seen the past, and it appears to have worked . . . maybe."

This is indeed ironic. For it is countries like India that *live* with the past all around and accept it as easily as a woman drapes a sari that are also the most impatient to invent the future. They see the past every day, and much of it doesn't work, any of the time. Thus we have Mao Tse-tung, with a kind of divine impatience, restructuring China through his concept of communes. And we have the great manifestos of the 1920s. And we have Chandigarh.

What is amiss: these ventures or our own lives? I remember being caught in New York in 1962 during the Cuban missile crisis. All over the city there was a mounting alarm about possible nuclear attack, endless talk of air raids, and so forth. After three harrowing days, my wife and I decided to return to Boston. The highway was crowded with cars, jamming all the great cloverleaf intersections. It was wretched. I thought to myself: Damn Sant'Elia and all those Futurists! Couldn't they see that their visions wouldn't work? We were listening to the car radio when suddenly we heard an announcement: the Russian ships had turned back! All at once we realized that America and Russia were not going to fight after all, that this marked a turning point in the cold war, that there would probably be world peace for a decade or more. It was an enchanted moment. I looked out the window at the beautiful highway, at the marvelous cloverleaf intersections and the myriad cars arching gracefully through the night, red taillights aglow. Our misery, dear Brutus, lies not in our buildings, but in ourselves.

We have been diminished because our perceptions have become small. We can never be bigger than the questions we define. What made the architects of the twenties exceptional was not so much their talent as the import of the issues they tackled. For, as Stendhal wrote about Napoleon, "There are no great men; there are only great events." The attitudes and values of the 1920s, which

Peter Smithson calls "the Heroic Age of Architecture," had receded; with Chandigarh they burst forth again, like an Indian summer.

The venture remains unique in our minds, not only for what it accomplished but also *for what it conceived of doing.* This is what generated the enthusiasm and the dedication of the team around Le Corbusier. To them, the building of the city was the central fact of their lives. They gave the task everything they had. Le Corbusier demanded no less. Architecture was for him a deeply moral act, and to us in India this was comprehensible; he was right. Certainly without such a commitment even architects of enormous talent can be vitiated, as witness the buildings that are going up all over the Gulf today. Ironically enough, it is the poor countries of this world, like India and Bangladesh, that go to Le Corbusier and Kahn for their buildings. Rightly or wrongly, they believe that architecture is a passionate, nearly sacred, undertaking. I sometimes wonder what would have happened to Le Corbusier if he had landed a commission in the Gulf! Would he have accepted? (Remember "The City Of Tomorrow.") And would he have survived?

India was lucky to get Le Corbusier; Le Corbusier, too, was lucky to get India.

* * *

When all is said and done, twenty-five years is not such a long period; it is a mere eyeblink in history. Over the decades to come, new issues will arise and Chandigarh will have to measure up to them. Perhaps the future will be even harsher than we have been on Le Corbusier's abilities and insights as a city planner. But to the incredible power of his architecture, Chandigarh will always bear steadfast and unique testament—and to something far more important than even his talent: his temperament. His was the kind of commitment Hinduism has always respected and understood.

India, in its turn, brought out the best in Le Corbusier. It was as though the warm sunlight and the life-accepting patterns of the people loosened up the Swiss in him. As in his earlier visit to Brazil, he changed. His buildings grew more exuberant, more tropical, which is to say they became more pluralistic, less rigidly predetermined. Old temples and cities in India (like their counterparts elsewhere) are a collection of a good many decisions—some transparently rational, others opaque—that makes them as equivocal, as unfathomable, as music that you want to hear again and again. Thus, perhaps, the Vedic saying "An architect should not finish all his building; he should know how to leave forty percent to God."

India is an ancient land. Over the centuries there have been other new cities like Chandigarh and other prophets like Le Corbusier: Fatehpur-Sikri, Patrick Geddes, Edwin Lutyens, Golconda, Mandu. Today many of them are not perceived at all as foreign elements but as an integral part of the Indian landscape. Yet when, for instance, Fatehpur-Sikri was first built, it must have seemed as exotic as IBM technology, as outlandish as something landed from the moon. Today we see it as a very Indian city. For this timeless civilization has never fretted over labels like old and new, indigenous and foreign; it establishes affinities far more fundamental than that. And Hinduism has developed a truly amazing pluralistic schema where new and old, light and dark, can coexist, be absorbed, endure. . . .

India as blotting paper. Who knows? A hundred years from now, perhaps Chandigarh will also fit seamlessly into the Punjabi ethos; perhaps it will be perceived as a famous old Indian town, and Le Corbusier will be acknowledged . . . as the greatest Indian architect of them all?

"*Machine et mémoire*": The City in the Work of Le Corbusier

by Manfredo Tafuri
translation by Stephen Sartarelli

In designing the Beistegui penthouse on the Champs-Elysées (1929–1931), Le Corbusier was well aware of giving life to a place that could not be standardized. If the Pavillon de l'Esprit Nouveau of 1925 was conceived as a "maison de série pour un homme courant" (standardized house for the contemporary man), the penthouse for Charles de Beistegui was merely a place for extravagant receptions for a social circle anxious to absorb every avant-garde, which it consumed as the latest fashion.[1] Le Corbusier, in a letter of July 5, 1929, to his client, declares his interest in the subject "parce qu'il est un programme-vedette (Champs-Elysées)" (because it is a star project) and "parce qu'il propose une solution des *toits de Paris*, dont je parle depuis 15 ans" (because it offers a solution for the *roofs of Paris,* that I have been talking about for 15 years).[2] In this apartment, for which no electric lighting was originally planned—only candles, which, according to de Beistegui, alone gave off "living" light[3]—Le Corbusier used technology to make hedges disappear, operate the movement of doors and partitions, and project cinematographic images onto the mobile screen in the living room. Thus we have technology in the service of a game. But de Beistegui's guests were condemned to this game: it is no accident that it is only by remaining "entombed" in the upper cockpit and by using a periscope that one might enjoy the entire Parisian panorama.

Moreover, on the uppermost terrace the high walls give a view only of fragments of the urban skyline, such as the tops of the Arc de Triomphe and the Eiffel Tower. But this is not merely an adoption of Surrealist poetics: this square space, this "chambre à ciel ouvert" (room with open sky) is free of the game—it is a final landing place where *le silence* and *le grand large* (the wide-open space) dominate, a gathering place that no longer has anything to do with the desires aroused by the *boîte à miracles* situated below. Its message will have to pass through the dance of forms on the Algerian hills in order to shape the "listening spaces" of the capitol of Chandigarh. The Beistegui penthouse is not part of any urban planning program: on the contrary, it is a precious coffer for a worldly elite, a group quite different, in its sociological and cultural characteristics, from that to which Le Corbusier would have preferred to dedicate his solutions for reforming the modern universe. And yet, this very project gives many hints of Le Corbusier's positions regarding urban themes, a subject on which his theoretical writings remained, not accidentally, silent.

First of all, there is the detachment from the metropolitan spectacle: the forced separation in the Champs-Elysées penthouse, a deliberate obstruction of the aerial panorama—a notion as dear to Le Corbusier as to his friend Saint-Exupéry. Detachment is prerequisite to dominance over universal laws: the eye frustrated by Le Corbusier's penthouse is the same eye that wishes to gaze with the sublime and passive indifference of the *flâneur* who contemplates the great theater of merchandise without compromising himself by buying and who makes a show of the passing riff-raff.

The distance interposed between the penthouse and the Parisian panorama is secured by a technological device, the periscope. An "innocent" reunification between the fragment and the whole is no longer possible; the intervention of artifice is a necessity. But no technological artifice mediates the discourse between man and *le grand large*, that vast ocean of the whole revealed above the final terrace. The sea of grass and the great ocean of sky are carefully delimited by sacred walls: Le Corbusier here dictates the terms of a discourse that suspends the customary dimensions of space and has as its precondition a metaphysical separation, the rupture of all usual connections. The attitude of mind implicit here is not one that projects, but rather one that waits.

In the Beistegui penthouse, this poetics of listening is presented as the final stage of the "journey" through architectonic and technical apparatus, and, more importantly, as an alternative to the unobstructed view of the metropolitan panorama. Above all of this is the "great void," the place that does not come into contact with the space of human trade, that is not part of the universe of ends. The silences that may be experienced in it inexorably detach themselves from the theoretical landscape to which Le Corbusier relegates his social messages. The importance of the fact that Le Corbusier placed this space of separation in the heart of a metropolis should not be underestimated. Because of its location, the Beistegui penthouse serves as an excellent litmus test for revealing the hidden motives that guide—and not always consciously—Le Corbusier's approach to the urban phenomenon. Indeed, in this work unsettling metaphors predominate, metaphors that build up to a *chambre à ciel ouvert* that speaks the language of myth: the suspenses, absences, and expectations inhabiting that empty space express the very meaning of the phrase *objets à réaction poétique*. But how can one reconcile this *poiesis* with the necessities imposed by the fashionable myth of rationalization? In other words, is it possible to incorporate into such *poiesis* a theory of the "new city"? Le Corbusier avoids answering such questions, at least until 1929, the year of his trip to Latin America. And in any case, he makes no reference in his vast literary polemical output to these issues in relation to the subject of urbanism. Traces of the universe presented in the *chambre à ciel ouvert*, on the other hand, would later appear, as has been suggested, in the Plan Obus for Algiers; but this universe would also shape, in full, the realization of the capitol of Chandigarh.

This does not, however, mean that Le Corbusier was of two different minds. Rationalization must be carried out in order to be surpassed, in order to recuperate other universes of ends. Such a perspective can be gleaned from more than a few passages of Le Corbusier. But even in examining his early urbanistic models, it is necessary to clear the ground of certain prejudices that have become common fare.

Too often, indeed, Le Corbusier's urbanism has been viewed as the ultimate goal of his research.[4] According to this interpretation, in all of Le Corbusier's works—from the Maison Dom-ino to the Citrohan cell to the Immeubles-villas, with first the *Ville Radieuse* and then the *Trois établissements humains* as the final syntheses—the architect's idea of city gives us a picture, on a small scale, of the entire process of his research. But clearly this is an inevitably reductive interpretation. Not only is it difficult to grasp from this standpoint the full richness of a plan such as the Obus for Algiers, but it is also impossible to appreciate the fundamental distance between Le Corbusier's theory and his production. Thus one might attack Le Corbusier for what his writings and urban plans seem to say— perhaps judging individual projects to be incoherent and contradictory—by refusing to see, in those contradictions, "faithful" discrepancies and essential differences. What is certain, on the other hand, is that Le Corbusier's notion of the city is directly related to the long and laborious development of the nineteenth-century strategies aimed at controlling social behavior. An examination of the *fiches* of the young Charles Edouard Jeanneret at the Bibliothèque Nationale of Paris (1914–1915) makes it possible to trace the sources of his later elaborations: we find Le Corbusier familiar with *Der Städtebau* of Stübben, with the texts of Unwin, with Hénard's *Études sur les transformations de Paris,* with the volume by the mayor of Brussels, Charles Buls, *L'Esthétique des villes* (1893), with the writings of Émile Vandervelde (*Les Villes tentaculaires,* 1899), Luigi Einaudi (*La Municipalisation du sol,* 1898), and Charles Lucas (*Habitation à bon marché,* 1899)—not to mention his marked interest in Anatole France, Zola, and Benoit-Lévy, as well as in the tradition of French Classicism from Tiercelet to Cordemoy, to Blondel, Laugier, Bélidor, and Patte, and an explicit rejection of Piranesi.[5]

Do we, therefore, have in Le Corbusier a synthesis of classical tradition and nineteenth-century models? Thus far we are still in the realm of the general, at the periphery of the problem. But we move a step forward with the discovery of the theoretical formulation of the house as *machine à habiter* in an 1853 writing by Adolphe Lance. "Would it not be possible," writes Lance in his review of the *Traité d'architecture* by Léonce Raynaud,[6] "to go even further and plan our buildings and houses by taking into account the person who frequents or inhabits them, not only to determine their general arrangement and distribution, but also to introduce thousands of specific comforts, services, and time- and energy-saving devices that the adaptation of new procedures from science and industry could provide for domestic life? *A house is an instrument, a machine so to speak,* that not only serves as a shelter for Man, but . . . must conform to his activity and multiply the production of his work. Industrial constructions, workshops, plants of every kind are, from this viewpoint, almost fully achieved models worthy of being imitated." *Comfort* is, from this perspective, to be found in the mechanization of services, necessitating new spatial apparatuses: what we have here is an ideology that assumes the primacy of human labor by economizing time and energies. The affinity between this and similar propositions of Le Corbusier is immediately evident.

But Lance's theories are not the only ones in the air in nineteenth-century France. It is useful to see them rather as segments of an ensemble of propositions and strategies that include César Daly's ideas on the transformation of architectural programs and the later proposals for domestic environments regulated by "flows," as well as the experiments prompting the realization of such *cités ouvrières* as the one near Le Havre (1847) which Daly himself approved, and the Cité Napoléon, jointly developed by the architect Veugny and the administrator Chabert (1849), which was the first to be state financed. Nor should we forget the Cité Napoléon of Lille (1860), also the product of collectivistic and Saint-Simonian inspiration, built for approximately one thousand poor people. In this project the theme of the flexibility and adaptability of the units appears—the partitions within a space of 4 meters square assigned to individual families are mobile, while numerous other housing projects of the time, more or less inspired by the phalanstery, familistery, and the Panopticon, seem fully to exemplify cardinal points of Le Corbusian theory. Thus, corresponding to Théodore Charpentier's project for an economically autonomous Cité de l'Union near Paris (1849) are the projects for *cités de chemins de fer* dispersed across the land and linked to the natural environment (1857)—foreshadowings of the Roadtown of Chambless

and the "technological picturesque" on which the linear utopias of the twentieth century would be based—and the aérodomes of Jules Borie (1865), which, along with the models of Fourier and Godin, were already hailed by Serenyi as precedents of Le Corbusier's "impossible reconciliation" of the individual with the collective.[7]

But we must not let ourselves be confounded by purely formal aspects. Georges Teyssot has shown, through pointed analysis, that in the nineteenth-century projects of collectivistic inspiration in which vanguard technologies aim at creating "exact environments" the defense of progress and of the myth of associationism is subordinated to the creation of perfect machines,[8] machines above all capable of controlling and guiding, through types of dwelling, the social existence of the "dangerous classes." The theme of hygiene is thus wed to themes that proclaim—through the use of the new technologies—the inevitability of a form of progress that must see the working classes as participants. The collectivism expounded by the physicians and hygienists of the nineteenth century is infused by a plurality of disciplines, technical developments, and ideologies, not the least of which are Bentham's "happiness for all" and Gérando's "balanced" intervention,[9] which see in the politics of services a condition for the spreading of wealth; in the ubiquitous control of behavior, the premise of stability; and in the invention of residential models, valuable politico-economic strategies.

The Saint-Simonian "colonies," the projects born as filiations of the Panopticon, the phalanstery, barracks, refuge homes, and monasteries, all delimit, enclose, and separate. Only by creating heterotopias did the collectivists—many of them Catholic socialists—believe they could rationalize, arrange, and individuate. The proletarian "Noah's arks" are "cities of refuge" for "guided existence", the fact that they derive from the barracks and the hospital thus has a rather eloquent metaphorical value.

Brian Brace Taylor has irrefutably demonstrated that in his Cité de Refuge Le Corbusier—in adhering to the strategies of General Booth and to the programs of the Salvation Army of the late 1920s—

creates a device that claims to be perfectly heterotopic.[10] Collectivist ideology in the use of spaces and in the artificial and standardized control of the environment inevitably gave rise to a fragment, in itself complete, of the totality of existence as planned and ordered by an all-inclusive and ubiquitous technical design, an *exemplum*, on a reduced scale, of the possible benefits of the "plan." And the fact that the technical installations proved to be unworkable was due less to the clients than to the considerable strains of idealism contained in Le Corbusier's poetics.[11] The instruments of mechanical reform for the creation of a regulated society and the principles behind the devices put to use by nineteenth-century reformers seem, according to Foucault's interpretation,[12] to reach their fulfillment in the propositions set forth by Le Corbusier in the early 1930s. This fulfillment is, however, a hindered, defective, imperfect one. This, of course, is due to the sidesteppings necessitated by dynamic realities that challenged the rigidity of the "social engineering" in which Le Corbusier placed his trust. The "imperfect machine" of the Cité de Refuge is, nevertheless, an allusive heterotopia: the strategy contained therein expects to be able to expand eventually to the entire surrounding space.

Teyssot himself, however, has shown how the collectivist strategies came to be defeated, around 1850, by a more refined approach based on industrial *cités* composed of workers' cottages that went beyond the militarized conception of labor still visible in the ironworks and mining settlements of the first half of the nineteenth century (Le Creusot and Anzin). This new strategy involved such models as those that emerged victorious at Mulhouse and at Guebwiller and that, via the ideas of Frédéric le Play, paved the way for the ideologies affirmed by the Parisian Expo of 1867.[13] The private worker's cottage united the plan for eliminating the proletarian "disease" with the myth of the hearth and the land as the antidote for lost individual and social "health." In the ideology of the private worker's home nineteenth-century philanthropy focused on an instrument of social reform and

extensive control of mass movements: the determination of needs, indeed their very production, takes the shape of a project to stablize the family cell in places that are themselves predetermined by the demands of production. Moreover, as a service apparatus, this house "produces production": such can be surmised from the results of an inquiry by Alfred de Foville into housing in rural France, a study with which Le Corbusier was quite familiar.[14]

It is significant that from the start the young Jeanneret—influenced by the teaching of Howard and Unwin—attempted to experiment with housing models related to the second strategy mentioned above in his studies on Hampstead and Hellerau, in the garden suburb at La Chaux-de-Fonds (1914), and the projects for Saintes and Saint-Nicholas d'Aliermont (1917), and that later he experimented with models from the collectivist tradition. It is equally significant that in the Cité contemporaine trois millions d'habitants (1922) he strove to make the two models coexist. But what seems to me most important here is that, in the early 1920s, his reading of these same sources could have bracketed their underlying strategies. This was not the result of analytical myopia. The fact is that when the new instruments of mass information began to take hold, urbanistic strategies were articulated and then fragmented, which tended to reduce the significance earlier attributed to the form of housing installations. It was this overall rearrangement that Le Corbusier mistook for a power vacuum. His plan to educate the *civilisation machiniste* presupposes authoritarian decision making, but it also calls for participation from below: the differential space that opens up between the two is filled by an apologia for technology that nevertheless assumes exquisitely formal features. The synthesis of eighteenth-century tradition and nineteenth-century models occurs precisely in the following way: only formally may the results of strategies in which power and knowledge are concealed and in which central importance is assumed by praxis-oriented vocabulary and the units of discourse insinuated into the discourses practiced by the subjects be traced back to schemata that reveal the allegory of plans radiating out from a center. This center later proves to be a center of power, an *auctoritas* that incorporates the *esprit de système* of the *ancien régime*; and this center is presupposed by a place, the architect's laboratory, where technology becomes "transparent" due to its ability to assign form (a form hence ordered, legible, and connected to a system of hierarchies) to the multiplicity of languages into which the old syntheses have disintegrated.

Hence, there is a bipolar relationship between that urbanism that is understood to be a "home of technology," in which the "accursed" multiplicity of languages is "forced" to find a hearth common to all, and the centerless *multiversum* of the contemporary metropolis; it is one among a number of bipolarities, including those between the individual and collective, nature and artifice, Apollo and Dionysus, the archaic and "futurable," that reflect a Manichean representation of reality that hopes to build bridges toward the "subversive intentions of Surrealism."[15]

However, our interpretation of the Beistegui penthouse brought us face to face with a poetics comprised of "differences." Is it not perhaps possible to interpret the illuministico-authoritarian valences present in Le Corbusier's ideological formulations as consoling compensation for the irreparable contradiction between the call for synthesis and the infinite multiplication of the forms of knowledge and power?

The portrait of technology painted by Le Corbusier is indeed an ambiguous one. Though the following observation has already been made regarding the "five points" on which his architecture is supposedly based, it might also be applied to Le Corbusier's rules of urbanism: by replacing codes previously believed to be natural with arbitrary ones, he effects a series of negations and nullifications—nullifications of the hierarchies imposed on the relationship of edifice to nature and edifice to road, nullifications of street axes as elements of functional and visual coordination, nullifications of traditional zoning mechanisms. His first gesture is therefore one of nullification; the Dom-ino plan is rather

explicit in this respect.[16] The will behind the new act of creation is *founded upon nihilism*—a good reason to reexamine the young Jeanneret's relationship to and attitude about the work of Nietzsche.

The open terrain cleared by nihilism becomes arbitrarily repopulated by "constructions." Values—those of the intellectual elite pointed to by men such as L'Eplattenier, Schuré, Provensal[17]—and ethics—even those of Ruskin, if we go by the interpretation of Mary Patricia May Sekler[18]—are invoked to fill the void left behind by the nothingness on which the metaphysics of technology is based. A synthesis of nihilism and synthetic principles: such, apparently, is the impassable trail that Le Corbusier hoped to blaze through the stifling forest of the modern universe. All of which presupposes a crisis of modernity: the inability of this universe to create the instruments of redemption necessary to save it from its own nihilism. For this reason, such instruments must be founded on something other; they will have to speak the language of the nihilism of technology, in a classical synthetic mode.

But where is the synthesis of Le Corbusier? Is it to be found in that schematics, classificatory and finally naïve, embodied in the urban models of 1922 and 1923, in the *Charte d'Athènes* and the *Trois établissements*; or is it to be found in that dialectics that worked its way through his painting phase of 1928–1932,[19] reached a high point in the Villa Savoye, and was broadened to the territorial scale in the Plan Obus? Certainly, both these instances are matters of synthesis.

Before Ronchamp, Le Corbusier never placed his trust in a language comprised of pure differences. However, there is no doubt that the messages expressed by his architecture speak metaphorically of a representation of the metropolitan *multiversum* in a manner much richer and more problematic than is reflected in his urbanism: we saw this in the Champs-Elysées penthouse, and the same could be demonstrated for the spatial dialectics of the villas of the 1930s.

Indeed, after 1922, his urbanism, with the partial exception of the plans for Algiers and for the capitol of Chandigarh, is dominated by a conceptual poverty that inevitably minimizes the complex problems inherent in the contemporary city and countryside. Le Corbusier's main concerns, in fact, are all of an anachronistic nature: delimiting, classifying, differentiating, and standardizing are all operations that lead up to the absolute of the planned unit. Given these premises, it is not surprising that Le Corbusier should have placed his hopes in the prophecies of decision-making authorities whose power would be unequivocal and centralized: moreover, it is significant that such authorities would eventually become incarnate in Lenin and Mussolini, in the circle of Hubert Lagardelle, Philippe Lamour, Pierre Winter, and François de Pierrefeu, in the Front Populaire and the Vichy government.[20] The *auctoritas* dreamed of by Le Corbusier, in fact, takes the form of a ghost to whom he gives the name of Colbert.[21] The synthesis that forces together the banal materials of the Purist paintings, which resists, in the paintings and drawings made after 1928, the divisive presence of the feminine figure—bearer of "differences," which imposes itself as the primary figure of a calculability-predictability announced in the urbanistic plans—this synthesis may in fact be justified only in relation to that phantom of power. Rather than acknowledge the action of a plurality of fluxes, a plurality of practices that necessarily defy any unified representation, Le Corbusier prefers to entrust to the irreality of a phantom an ephemeral guarantee of totality for his own ideas. This explains why he looked back to classical sources—Greece, *le grand siècle*, Abbé Laugier—to confirm hypotheses of the machine age that had nevertheless been applied, or at least dreamed, over the course of the nineteenth century. Thus, given his extreme conflict with the nineteenth century, we can say that only the forms of the strategies and devices developed in that century are of interest to Le Corbusier; this is what was meant when we spoke of the "bracketing" performed by the architect in this regard.

Simplification and will to synthesis: we are dealing here with tools that can hardly be called modern. And yet, it was with precisely such tools

that Le Corbusier confronted the explosion of interconnections and the disintegration of all "organicity" occurring in the modern metropolis. The *Ville radieuse* is not a future-oriented proposition, but rather an idea cast abroad on an ark built outside space and time and run aground on the shoals before the island of utopia. Of course, the *Ville radieuse* claims its language to be absolutely transparent, claims to be able to say all that can be said about the irreconcilable dimensions that intersect without forming recognizable centers, claims to be able to establish the primacy of a logos for the innumerable languages of technology. But it is a stranger to the game of chance and the arbitrary on which the negative avant-gardes were founded, though they too were in search on an "iconography of the shattered." In this light, the substance of Le Corbusier's anti-avant-gardism, his attacks on the Futurists and Surrealists, becomes more visible. With his urban models, Le Corbusier opposes the "magnificent illusion"—so called by Barthes[22]— "which enables one to conceive of a *langue* outside of power, in the splendor of a permanent revolution of *langage*," to the authority of an assertive *langue* that demands repetition (in Moscow as well as in Paris or Rome).[23]

Is it any wonder, then, that this assertive *langue*, made up of signs that gravitate toward the stereotype, should show itself to be closely linked to a monotheistic idea of power, represented as *in-dividuum*? Le Corbusier lets his ideologies oscillate between the Saint-Simonian tradition, an obscure syndicalism, and a corporativism containing within itself a theory of elites; they are very much part of the current of ideas circulating among technocratic groups, such as the *Redressement francais*,[24] in the 1920s.

The "industrial symphony," according to Le Corbusier, can only be founded on a *novum organum*, on an organic body of decisions, on an internally solid pyramid, a pyramid opposed to the destructive cacophony of real conflicts, but also alternative to atonal constructions.

Given these premises, it is no surprise that Le Corbusier's urbanism avails itself of slogans taken from Laugier; that it adopts types such as the *à redent* types already developed by Hénard; that it draws from the morals-hygiene-aesthetics triad so dear to the nineteenth-century strategies and proposes this again as a principle for the salvation of the modern city; or that it borrows, from a 1913 text by Robert de Souza, procedures for the perfect sunning of buildings.[25] The postliberal city prefigured by the Ville Radieuse points to a surpassing of the *civilisation machiniste* itself through the acceleration of development processes ensured by the machine plan. But such a machine must continually strive for more: the "illness" of modern times will be vanquished when technology shapes the entire universe as a whole; therefore, technology must point to a continuous and perfect process of becoming.

Only by their total immersion in the flow of this process, according to Le Corbusier, can conflicts be eliminated: "la ville, devenue une ville humaine, sera une ville sans classes" (the city, once it has become a human city, will be a classless city).[26] Participation in the plan will ensure its perfect functioning; in this we even hear an echo of the voluntary and universal alienation foreseen by Jean-Jacques Rousseau.

However, the technology that is supposed to cure the "ills of civilization," that is supposed to crush the egotisms of the nineteenth century, rests on synthetic representations, on devices that attempt to translate into reality the dreams of the modern century par excellence, the nineteenth. Furthermore, it can also be said that technology, for Le Corbusier, as well as for the technocratic ideologues on whom he leaned for support in the 1920s, does not admit political reality as an external limit. On the contrary, technology lays siege to the political realm, claims to appropriate its languages, and presents itself as a form of knowledge endowed with power. To politics is left only the task of execution.

But it should be repeated that there is more to Le Corbusier than this *reductio ad unum* of the serpentine ubiquity of power, this naïve overdetermination of the authority of the plan—*le despote*[27]—as logocentric synthesis. Interpreting Corbusian architecture in the light of the evolution of his urbanism is not only reductive, as stated above, but distorting as well. We should try rather to consider the architect's research as an investigation into the limits of a utopia of language. (N.B.: the utopia of language is not the language of utopia.) It is, in fact, within the limits of the architectonic object that Le Corbusier succeeds in creating theater out of the game of slippings that he plays while combating codes as they establish themselves.

Hence, we are dealing with an architecture situated in a conceptual framework that has painting and urbanism as its upper and lower boundaries: that which may be tested within these limits assumes the form of residuum or trace; in the architectonic object it becomes the open margin. In the latter, the materials brought together problematically—and ever more problematically—over the course of Le Corbusier's study in painting come into conflict with the assertive demands of his urbanistic theory. The villas of the 1930s, as well as the Cité de Refuge and the project for the Palace of the Soviets, constitute the theaters of this conflict: the language here aims not at totality, but rather at bringing into discussion the battle that the different hypotheses of space are waging among each other. It is this side of Le Corbusier that acted as director and strategist of these dramas of conflicts that should be seen as a lasting interpreter of the "age of poverty" and not that other side, which prefigured and made apologies for inevitably anachronistic forms of dominion over this age.

But does our argument still prove valid when confronted with the plans for Algiers, which are closely connected, as is known, to the ideas formulated for the cities of Latin America?[28] In the Plan Obus, Le Corbusier seems to want to shatter all disciplinary barriers: the figurative world of this painting directly invades the structuring of the urban machine, which is, nevertheless, represented as a single architectonic object. Indeed, precisely because architecture here finds itself devoid of its own limits as object, it is capable of exploding, of liberating itself from the constraints that forced it to remain within arbitrary margins. All the metaphors that had previously been forced to speak allegorical languages now find themselves able to spill over into the spatial environment, to take full possession of nature, to reshape it, to subdue it. The desires that were frustrated in the Beistégui penthouse irrupt in Algiers, twisting before the sea, swiftly flowing in a stream of fluxes, clenching in their coils both nature and history, joyously and victoriously dancing upon the hills of Fort-l'Empéreur.

It is significant that this victory over "differences" comes about through a structural organization that assimilates both the perfection of the machine and the unexpected, chance, mutability: the whole is an organic exaltation of the forms. By spreading like magma into reality, technology—or its image—subsumes it, dominates it wholly: speed, which acts as protagonist in the lanes installed on the roof of the zigzag block, forces the observer to make accelerated and simultaneous readings, which correspond to the interchangeability and mobility of the residential cells below. The public is invited to take part in the festivity prepared by this fragment of perfect productivity devoid of residua—it in fact embraces even the "bad taste" of its users—and the feast coincides with a radical estrangement from all sense of place, with a "being torn away," with an acceptance of the laws that rule the immense biomorphic machine.[29] And this machine, in spreading out and contracting, metaphorically revealing its functioning, becomes charged with mythical values. The new Acropolis contemplates, from above, the battle of technology against nature: it is no mere chance that one grasps its signifying signs with a sense of vertigo.

Le Corbusier seems already to know what Heidegger would later say on this subject, namely, that technology is in essence poetic, that production and *poiesis* share common roots. And wherever the productive fully discloses itself in striving for absolute dominance over the future, myth reappears.

But why does Le Corbusier reserve this reconciliation between technology and myth only for cities of developing countries? And why such insistence on Algiers, where Le Corbusier attempted to create for himself a nonexistent clientele in the years of the great crisis?

Le Corbusier did make an "official" response regarding the world role he assigned to Algiers within the Mediterranean sphere: a pivotal element in an *entente latine*—Paris, Rome, Barcelona, Algiers—according to the political programs of the *Prélude* group,[30] this city was intended by Le Corbusier to become the *tête de l'Afrique*. But Algiers is also a place where another civilization is expressed, a culture in some way similar to that explored by Le Corbusier in the *Voyage d'Orient* of his youth. In Moslem culture, in the customs and habits of "simple men," Le Corbusier seeks not so much the signs of the "noble savage" as those of a primeval mode of existence, a cosmic disposition, a trust in the order of the great ocean of being, now lost, but which the plan is called upon to recuperate at higher levels. This prerational existence is charged with eros: von Moos was correct in pointing out the symptomatic nature of the drawings made by Le Corbusier on the theme of Delacroix's *Femmes d'Alger*.[31]

The case that encloses this model of existence, which must be singled out as a memento to the colonizers, is the Casbah. It assumes, in Le Corbusier's eyes, a value not unlike that which he attributed to the Charterhouse of Ema or to the monastery on Mount Athos. And yet, a very carefully preserved Casbah is inserted into that image of the machine as perfect process, the Plan Obus: the Casbah is the antithesis of this perfect process, but it is thus necessary and invoked. It is no accident that in the 1931 project the Casbah is passed over by the new city: the figure of the bridge here appears in all its metaphorical substantiality. A bridge, in fact, connects two extremes: the residences on the hill and the command post facing the sea. The Casbah is isolated, untouched, and untouchable, a timeless model that paradoxically cannot be reproduced. The "modern" is forced to "flow" over this structure, which possesses a language that cannot be reduced to that of the routine and acceleration expressed by the "machine" that tightly surrounds it. And yet, the metaphors of ephemerality and acceleration need to be related back to the Casbah, to the metaphor of an ancient time that knew no crisis. The bridge in this way takes on unsettling meanings. Thrown over an anthropological relic that the activity of colonization could not destroy, it accentuates the fundamental "difference" that secretly undermines the unity of the overall "machine." Le Corbusier himself is insistent about this difference: the Casbah, in its absolute otherness, cannot be subjected to the logic of the new signs that convulsively interlink themselves on a territorial scale; it can only remain what it is, foreign to time, foreign to the modern, indifferent to its destinies. As silent witness, its function is to grant mythical depth to the conflict between the immobile and the transient that it itself initiated and that runs through the entire plan.

The fact that the plan for Algiers is conceived as an act of extreme violence against nature and as an attempt to build time and space *ab imis*—and hence as an act of cosmic refoundation—is not unrelated to the role Le Corbusier attributed to the preservation of the Casbah. "La Casbah n'est qu'un immense escalier, une tribune envahie le soir par des milliers d'adorateurs de la nature" (The Casbah is nothing but a vast stairway, a platform invaded every evening by thousands of worshipers of nature),[32] writes Le Corbusier, who went on to note, in a section drawing of the Casbah itself: "chef d'oeuvre urbanistique—cellule, rue, et terrains" (a masterpiece of urbanism—cells, street, and grounds). The terracing system of the Casbah would later serve as inspiration for Le Corbusier's "amphitheater" of the urbanization of Nemours (1934–1935) and—with the mediation of the models of Sauvage and Sarazin, studied after 1915[33]—for the Durand development project near Algiers (1933–1934). But the Casbah is not a model that can be standardized. It is a symbol of perfect "rest" in a maternal interior, in the fullness of an embrace, symbol of a humanity that still remembers a time of happiness. The Casbah's time is an eternal present. The time of the "new Algiers" is that of the total uprooting from all here

and now, the time of unsuturable wounds, of a moving-ever-onward that renders all lingering impossible: a time when happiness can no longer be even remembered. (There is no "time" for remembering.) For this very reason, the two structures, both of them integral, are juxtaposed. Between them there can be no intercourse, nor even a clash, at the limit. The void extending beneath the bridge that separates the two is the visible residue of the unfathomable space that occupies the rupture generated by the monumental "difference" staged by Le Corbusier.

One cannot fail to reflect upon the fact that Le Corbusier so carefully isolated his urbanistic experience in Algiers. Only a shadow of it appears in his plan for Stockholm; thereafter, there are no signs of even the memory of that complex research: in terms of method, the classifications of the "Athens Charter" resort to troubling simplifications;[34] the plans for Barcelona, Antwerp, and Buenos Aires constitute more or less academic applications of already tested models; and the urban plan for the Zlín valley is given over to the repetitiveness of standardized objects, affording a glimpse of the later, postwar plans.[35]

The eros discovered in Algiers makes its mark instead on Le Corbusier's painting and sculpture: in the "Ubu" and "Ozon" series, for example, biomorphic, metaphysical envelopments dominate. But the *Stadtkrone* of the Plan Obus was also an envelopment, with surrealistic characteristics, and it too made anthropomorphic allusions to the memory of Arabic writing and to primitive dolmens (the same that would reappear at Ronchamp). What in the Plan Obus is designed to go inside a "machine" ensuring its significations is destined to reemerge, isolated, as an enigmatic fragment. But it is precisely the rupture of all fictional unity that Le Corbusier experiments with in the 1940s: the sculptures made in collaboration with Joseph Savina bear witness to this. Hence, eros is seen as laceration, rupture, tendency toward an otherness—the universe of absolutes and totality—that is necessarily and continuously elusive: while Le Corbusier is renouncing the immanence of his totalizing hypotheses, the *multiversum*, the overwhelming plurality of the forces that penetrate the subject as well as intersubjective relations, falls upon his formal world. All that remains is to give expression to this battle. Le Corbusier's architecture thus becomes a kaleidoscopic theater in which cyclopean wars are staged. His late architecture is a gigantomachia: fragments of certitude heroically battle figures born out of the "listening" to "unutterable" languages. The fact that the result of the clash cannot be decided prevents this architecture from falling into "sickness."

All this is not without consequence for urbanistic theory. Already the *unité* of Marseilles presents itself as an enclosed whole in exaltation of a "second language" that penetrates the interstices of this extreme homage to the collectivist dream: and this second language expresses the conditions that bind the object to its solitude, force it to pretend to be a "type," and chain it to its condition as fragment of a totality destined to remain merely thinkable.

If the Cité de Refuge is a heterotopia that tends to exceed its own limits, the *unité* is a solution that makes a fundamental refusal to exceed the limits fixed for it: it is no coincidence that the first work exalts transparence and the second opacity (*pan de verre* versus *béton brut*). Both the transparent and the opaque render "experience" impossible. But the opacity of the *unité* accentuates the isolation of the community brought together within it, nullifies all utopian features, brings the project back to the present that it contains. A transatlantic monastery and familistery, the *unité* is rooted to the soil by means of its monumental *pilotis*, but this anchoring does not let us forget that we stand before a fragment, a slice, isolated, of the linear system that once confronted nature and brought it back to itself in Le Corbusier's urban dreams for Algiers and South America. Behind the brutal assertiveness of the *unité*'s forms hides a declaration of demystification.

It is at Chandigarh that the deeper subject of the Marseille *unité*, that which cannot be "standardized" or reduced to figurative formula, reaches its culmination. It is no longer the figures of unity, process, and the projectile launched against the future but rather those of isolation, finiteness, and interruption that form the basis of the capitol of Chandigarh. The differences that appeared in the Beistegui penthouse reappear here: but where they coalesce in the penthouse into a single object juxtaposed with "Paris, capital of the nineteenth century," in Chandigarh they go on to surround with emptiness an entire complex inexorably separated by an urban hypothesis formulated for a country still at the threshold of a contradictory development.

In fact, it is well known that at Chandigarh Le Corbusier merely corrected, regularized and standardized—the Seven Vs, zoning units, etc.—the already existent plan of Albert Mayer.[36] Moreover, though he repeatedly and loudly proclaimed that the Ville Radieuse, the city of the new age, of optimism, and technological planning, would rise up as the capital of the Punjab, it is difficult not to have misgivings about his assigning to Maxwell Fry and Jane Drew the nodal points of the urban body, and his bestowing upon Pierre Jeanneret, after rescinding the three-year contract of the two Britishers, the office of Chief Architect and Town Planner.

Le Corbusier seems to treat the planning of the city as a purely professional matter: it should be enough, he thinks, to apply the previously elaborated theoretical corpus, appropriately revised and adapted to the Indian situation; he refuses, having completed the plans for the capitol, to enter into a discourse that cannot be expressed with these means. But this gives rise to a separation that we should not hesitate to see as being consciously sought. On the one hand is the city in which urbanism and architecture speak common, everyday, inevitably conventional tongues; on the other, the Acropolis, where a modern "builder of symbols" seeks to converse with time, nature, and being. The separation wrought by Le Corbusier in the body of Chandigarh is perfectly classical.

But the new Acropolis does not, like its Greek

ancestors, contemplate the *apeiron* from the safety of its finite components, even if in it the solitude to which objects are bound does take on cosmic connotations.

Nothing in fact joins together the gigantic volumes of the Secretariat, the Parliament, and the High Court of Justice: nothing—neither roads, perspectival allusions, nor formal triangulations— helps the eye to situate itself with respect to these three "characters," which weave among themselves a discussion from which the human ear is able to gather only weak and distorted echoes. Indeed, the modeling of the terrain, the dislocation of levels, the mirrors of water, especially the Pool of Reflection,[37] are all there to accentuate discontinuities and ruptures. The observer is presented with a space comprised of absences, an impassable, alienating space: as one climbs up to the prominences designed (and not completely realized) by Le Corbusier—the artificial hillocks, the Monument to the Martyrs, the Tower of Shadows—these absences become even more unsettling; descending into the Pool of Reflection, the absence and multiplication of enigmatic echoes turn into silence.

All that remains is to run through and across the three immense objects, first testing their radical heterogeneity and then trying to burst their compactness. But heterogeneity and compactness already are words from a coded language that speaks through differences. It is difference, and not dialectics, that holds the three volumes together: they speak through their distortions, revealing that the space separating them functions to prime the multiple electric arcs. Those three objects, indeed, can be said to be "desirous" in a real sense. Above all, they desire to overcome the condition that chains them to this form and this place; they desire to come into contact with each other and, further, to interlink with each other in a single tangle of forms. (The role given the governor's palace seems, in fact, to be a peripheral and interpretative one.)

The harmony of relationships, of which Le Corbusier speaks in his letters to Nehru and which supposedly resides in the symbol of the open hand,

assumes problematic overtones in the realized work. The allegories with which the work is sprinkled allude to a course of initiation at the culmination of which the language of archetypes is supposed to link up indissolubly with a hypothetical catharsis. But no "thread of Ariadne" is provided for such a course as this. With eyes fixed on the elusiveness of the origin, the structures by which the capitol of Chandigarh is disarticulated "will the future"; but they no longer dare to predict the forms of this future. The objective is rather to fuse the memory of the origin with the tendency toward surpassing the present: their desire for eternity arises from their being situated at the center of divergent temporal fluxes restrained within a single place; and the fact that this place contemplates from afar the Himalayan range is certainly not insignificant.

The capitol of Chandigarh is indeed situated at the limits of space and time. This very fact legitimates its metamorphic games. The truncated cone of the skylight of the Assembly Hall recalls ancient minarets—in a 1953 sketch Le Corbusier designed a truncated cone with a spiral staircase— but it is also an echo of an industrial cooling tower. On the other hand, in the profile of the roofing of the Parliament's gigantic pronaos one recognizes the palm, here truncated, of the *main ouverte*.

This truncated allegory is significant, surreptitiously inserted as it is by Le Corbusier into the body of his architectonic structure. Interruptions, slippings, and distortions indeed pervade the language of the later Le Corbusier: at Chandigarh they are essential to the dramatization of the forms. The three great "desiring objects" seek to shatter their own solitude: the Secretariat through its inclined ramp and the broken meshes of its façade gradations; the Parliament through the distortion of the geometric solids that dominate it like hermetic totems; the High Court of Justice through the bending of the *brise-soleil* and the giant entrance stairway. But the interchange takes place only at a distance: tension informs this dialogue among symbols that have lost the codes that once gave them the value of names. It should now become clearer why the capitol complex is so definitively isolated from the body of the city. In it, everyday language is not spoken; the "words" of the architecture do not play among themselves. In it, we find rather the sacredness of names remembered by Le Corbusier.

In suspending his desire to bring to fulfillment the universe of technology, Le Corbusier is seeking at Chandigarh the essence of technology itself, linking its emblems—diffraction, displacement, plurality—to the *poiesis* of the primeval. Of the "project" of the Ville Radieuse not a trace remains; the construction of myth, which at Algiers was united with the machine's song of victory, here presents itself in its pure state.

For Le Corbusier, none of this implies a return to esoteric culture. At Chandigarh, the culture of the "great initiates"—of Schuré, Provensal, Péladan—which had nourished in the young Charles-Edouard Jeanneret the myth of an intellectual minority to whom the artist might reveal the "word" of his inner self, to be later poured out as a "gift" to the great masses, clashes with the memory of the eternal return announced by Zarathustra, the protagonist of the book that Le Corbusier picked up again in 1959 (August 1) for the first time since his initial reading of 1908.[38] Le Corbusier had attempted to go beyond the "cancer" of the great city: like Zarathustra, he had not listened to the invitation to stop at its gates. But his "going beyond"—as Georges Bataille would later note—had been vitiated by an "Icarus complex." Le Corbusier had "flown" over the great city: the flight is very often invoked to avoid "crossing." And yet, in his very observations "from above" Le Corbusier encountered still another Nietzschean metaphor, that of the eternal return, the eternal recurrence of peace and war, as well as the intersection between the infinite past—that which shines at the moment when the *mémoire involontaire* is working—and the will of the future.[39] And we know well that in Nietzsche the unutterable, the very theme of the later Le Corbusier, appears at the crossing of time and timelessness.

The Open Hand, too, speaks of this. Beyond the explanations of it offered by its author, this symbol announces the opening up of infinite possibilities,

left in a nascent state, in waiting. The hand is the mediator, as regards the world, of every human project. Open, it is no longer operative; in this position it is restrained. But perhaps it assumes a second meaning, one that eludes Le Corbusier himself, despite its continual reappearance in his formal universe from the monument to Vaillant-Couturier on. The *main ouverte* does not in fact express only a "will to power" left indeterminate. In its ambiguity it also expresses a "will to cessation," a *halt*. In order to modify the rules of the game that governs the destinies of the world, it seems to say, one must make a strategic move capable of breaking up the game itself, of stopping the "bewitched flow" of events. It is no accident that Le Corbusier established a direct relation between the Open Hand and the Pool of Reflection.

But none of this is an invitation to retreat into asceticism: it is, rather, a search for new frontiers for the space of the utterable. On the near side of such new frontiers there is urbanism, an instrument that has become conventional, now devoid of the cathartic potential previously accorded it.

Thus were the impracticable utopias of the 1920s and 1930s shattered; Le Corbusier's critique has now come to exert itself on disciplinary limits as well. In this sense, the *main ouverte* is the outermost limit the "will to planning" runs up against. "There exists a modern tragic emblem", wrote Aragon in *Le Paysan de Paris*: "it is a kind of great steering wheel that turns and turns, unguided by any hand." A steering wheel without a hand: technology assumed as destiny, as the "infernal" foundation of "what is most modern," the limitless calculability and organizability of all that lives. The Ville Radieuse wanted to guide such a mythological steering wheel; its ceaseless motion is what the Open Hand opposed with its oscillating metaphors, which are endowed, to use Walter Benjamin's phrase, "with a feeble messianic strength."

Notes

1. See *L'Architecte*, October 1932, pp. 100–104: Paolo Melis, "Il 'cadavere squisito' di Le Corbusier, Pierre Jeanneret

e Charles Beistegui," *Controspazio* 9, No. 3 (1977): 37; Pierre Saddy, "Le Corbusier chez les riches: L'appartement Charles de Beistegui," *Architecture, Mouvement, Continuité* 49 (1979): 57ff.; Saddy, "Le Corbusier e l'Arlecchino," *Rassegna* 2, No. 2 (1980): 25–32.

2. Letter from Le Corbusier to Charles de Beistegui of July 5, 1929, Fondation Le Corbusier, Paris.

3. See Charles de Beistegui to Robert Baschet in *Plaisir de France*, March 1936.

4. On Le Corbusier's urbanism, leaving aside what has been written in general monographs or in texts concerning single projects, see, among others, H. Allen Brooks, "Jeanneret and Sitte: Le Corbusier's Earliest Ideas on Urban Design," in *In Search of Modern Architecture: A Tribute to Henry-Russell Hitchkock*, ed. Helen Searing (Cambridge, Mass.: MIT Press, 1982), pp. 278–297; Paul Hofer, "Le Corbusier und die Stadt," *Bauen und Wohnen* 15 (1961): 67–72; Lewis Mumford, "Yesterday's City of Tomorrow," *Architectural Record* 132 (1962): 139–144; Claude Parent, "Le Corbusier et l'urbanisme moderne," *L'Architecture d'Aujourd'hui* 113/114 (1964): v–vi; Harry Antoniades Anthony, "Le Corbusier: His Ideas for Cities," *Journal of the American Institute of Planners* 32 (1966): 279–288; Anthony Vidler, "The Idea of Unity and Le Corbusier's Urban Form," *Architect's Year Book* 15 (1968): 225–237; Norma Evenson, *Le Corbusier: The Machine and the Grand Design* (New York: George Braziller, 1969); Kenneth Frampton, "The City of Dialectic," *Architectural Design* 10 (1969): 541–546; Martin Pawley, "A Philistine Attack," *Architectural Design* 4 (1972): 239–240; Ernesto d'Alfonso, "Dalla cellula alla città (Le Corbusier 1920–1925)," *Parametro* 5 (1977): 40–45; Anthony Sutcliffe, "A Vision of Utopia: Optimistic Foundations of Le Corbusier's 'Doctrine d'urbanisme,'" in *The Open Hand: Essays on Le Corbusier*, ed. Russell Walden (Cambridge, Mass.: MIT Press, 1977), pp. 216–243; Thilo Hilpert, *Die funktionelle Stadt: Le Corbusiers Stadtvision—Bedingungen, Motive, Hintergründe* (Braunschweig: Vieweg, 1978); Frampton, "The Rise and Fall of the Radiant City: Le Corbusier 1928–1960," *Oppositions* 19/20 (1980): 2–25.

5. See Philippe Duboy, "Charles Edouard Jeanneret à la Bibliothèque Nationale," *Architecture, Mouvement, Continuité* 49 (1979): 9–12. On Piranesi, Le Corbusier writes: "All the reconstructions of Piranesi, the Rome plan and the tight-rope compositions that have so dreadfully served the Ecole des Beaux-Arts are nothing but porticoes, colonnades and obelisques! It's crazy. It's ghastly, ugly, imbecilic. It is not grand, make no mistake about that. In this sense the law of Péladan and the 5 orders would indeed be welcome" (Fondation Le Corbusier, Paris, Box BN). For the texts of the Le Corbusier library from before 1930, see Paul Turner, "Catalogue de la Bibliothèque de Le Corbusier avant 1930," Fondation Le Corbusier, Paris, 1970 (16 pages mimeographed).

6. Adolphe Lance, summary of the *Traité d'architecture* of Léonce Raynaud, in *Encyclopédie d'architecture*, May 1953,

cited in F. Béguin, "Savoirs de la ville et de la maison du début de 19ème siècle," in *Politiques de l'habitat (1800–1850)*, ed. Michel Foucault (Paris: Corda, 1977), p. 306.

7. See Peter Serenyi, "Le Corbusier, Fourier, and the Monastery of Ema," *The Art Bulletin* 49, No. 4 (1967): 277–286, reprinted in *Le Corbusier in Perspective* (Englewood Cliffs, N.J.: Prentice-Hall, 1975), pp. 103–116. On the strategies concerning workers' housing in France, see, aside from *Politiques de l'habitat*, Roger Guerrand, *Les Origines du logement social en France* (Paris: Editions ouvrières, 1966), Italian edition (Rome: Edizione Officina, 1981) revised and enlarged, with an essay by Georges Teyssot, "'La casa per tutti': per una genealogia dei tipi." Among the influences on Le Corbusier's residential architecture we should not forget the *familistère*, with twenty-four lodgings and a carefully studied air circulation, dug up in 1868 by G.E. Boch in the equestrian arena built in 1855 at La Chaux-de-Fonds. Marc Emery, who called attention to the edifice to ensure its survival, observed that it is one of the first constructions influenced by the *familistère* of J.-B. Godin and that, as it is situated only a few meters from the Grenier restored by the students of the Ecole d'Art, it could have had an influence on the ideas of the young Jeanneret. See Marc Emery, "SOS: un familistère a La Chaux-de-Fonds: le manège," *Werk/Archithese* 29/30 (1979): 75.

8. Georges Teyssot, "'La casa per tutti,'" in particular pp. xli and following (see Note 7). Teyssot also established here (p. xlviii) an "essential continuity among the objectives of all that which contributed to the formation of the disciplinary corpus of architecture from . . . the first hygienist and technological arguments of around 1830 up to those recapitulated in a fixed and totalizing form in the 'Athens Charter' of 1933."

9. In his manual on "social relief," the Baron de Gérando writes: "There are two obstacles which public administration must beware of: it must avoid doing too much and doing too little. . . . But public beneficience . . . above all needs the concurrence of this active charity which seeks, examines, surveys, and adds to its material assistance the benefit of moral comfort." J.-M. de Gérando, *Le Visiteur du pauvre* (Paris: L. Colas, 1820), p. 383. On the nuclear family as social mechanism, see Lion Murard and Patrick Zyberman, "Le petit travailleur infatigable ou le prolétaire régénéré," *Recherches* 25 (1976): 195–228, and Gilles Deleuze, "L'ascesa del sociale," *Aut aut* 167/168 (1978): 108–114.

10. See Brian Brace Taylor, "Technology, Society and Social Control in Le Corbusier's Cité de Refuge, Paris 1933," *Oppositions* 15/16 (1979): 169–185, and the more complete treatment by the same author, *La Cité de Refuge di Le Corbusier* (Rome: Officina edizioni, 1979).

11. Shedding light on this matter are the works by Brian Brace Taylor mentioned above; see also Taylor, *Le Corbusier at Pessac* (Paris: Spadem, 1972), and Eleanor Gregh, "The Dom-ino Idea," *Oppositions* 15/16 (1979): 61–87.

12. See Michel Foucault, *Discipline and Punish: The Birth of the Prison*, trans. Alan Sheridan (New York: Pantheon, 1977).

13. Georges Teyssot, "'La casa per tutti,'" pp. lix and following (see Note 7).

14. Alfred de Foville, *Enquête sur les conditions de l'habitation en France: les maisons-types* (Paris: Noël, 1894). See also Brian Brace Taylor, *Le Corbusier at Pessac*.

15. Kenneth Frampton, Editor's Introduction, *Oppositions* 15/16 (1979): 11, but see also the propositions set forth on this matter by Charles Jencks in *Le Corbusier and the Tragic View of Architecture* (Cambridge, Mass.: Harvard University Press, 1973).

16. Useful sources on the "five points" as a catalogue of negations are as follows: Laurent Israël, "Les pilotis"; Fernando Montes, "L'Hypothèse lumineuse: la fenêtre en longueur"; Patrick Germe, "Pureté et liberté: plan libre—façade libre"—all in *Architecture, Mouvement, Continuité* 49 (1979): 39ff. An interpretation of the Maison Dom-ino as a reflection of a "modernist or self-referential condition of sign" may be found in Peter Eisenman, "Aspects of Modernism: Maison Dom-ino and the Self-Referential Sign," *Oppositions* 15/16 (1979): 119–128. On the other hand, I find unacceptable the relations established between the "transgressed grids" of Le Corbusier and the oscillating rhythms of seventeenth-century Mannerism in the article by Barry Maitland, "The Grid," *Oppositions* 15/16 (1979): 91–117.

17. See Paul Turner, "The Beginnings of Le Corbusier's Education, *The Art Bulletin* 53 (1971): 214–224; Turner, "Romanticism, Rationalism, and the Dom-ino System," in *The Open Hand*, pp. 15–41; and Turner, *The Education of Le Corbusier* (New York: Garland Publishing, 1977).

18. See Mary Patricia May Sekler, *The Early Drawings of Charles Edouard Jeanneret (Le Corbusier), 1902–1908* (New York: Garland Publishing, 1977); Sekler, "Le Corbusier, Ruskin, the Tree and the Open Hand," in *The Open Hand*, pp. 42–95.

19 See Maurice Jardot, *Le Corbusier, dessins* (Paris: Editions Mondes, 1955); Stephen A. Kurtz, "Public Planning, Private Planning," *Art News* 71 (1972): 37–41, 73–74; but more important, see Danièle Pauly, "Dessins et peintures 1928–1932," in *Le Corbusier, la ricerca paziente* (Lugano: Federazione Architetti Svizzeri, 1980), pp. 181 ff. See also Katherine Fraser Fischer, "A Nature Morte, 1927," *Oppositions* 15/16 (1979): 157–165; Stanislaus von Moos, "Le Corbusier as Painter," *Oppositions* 19/20 (1980): 89–107; and the book by Luisa Martina Colli, *Arte, artigianato e tecnica nella poetica di Le Corbusier* (Rome and Bari: Laterza, 1982).

20. It is hardly necessary to underline that our analysis has nothing to do with the criticisms of Le Corbusier as prophet of the "inhumanity" of metropolitan centralization and the *grands ensembles*. See, as an example of such inaccurate attacks, Jacques Riboud, *Les Erreurs de Le Corbusier et leurs consequences* (Paris: Editions Mazarine, 1968) (also published earlier in *Revue politique et parlementaire*, February 1968);

but see also Martin Pawley, "A Philistine Attack." The ties between Le Corbusier and the various political groupings from which he drew support have been repeatedly analyzed in recent years. On his relations with regionalist syndicalism, technocratic and right-wing French groups, the Front Populaire, and the Vichy government, see Kenneth Frampton, "The City of Dialectic"; Anthony Eardley, "Giraudoux and the Athens Charter," *Oppositions* 3 (1974): 83–90; Roberto Gabetti and Carlo Olmo, *Le Corbusier e "L'Esprit Nouveau"* (Turin: Einaudi, 1975); Robert Fishman, "From the Radiant City to Vichy: Le Corbusier's Plans and Politics, 1928–1942," in *The Open Hand*, pp. 244–283; and Thilo Hilpert, *Die funktionelle Stadt*. This last work is important for correcting some earlier interpretations. See also Giuliano Gresleri and Dario Matteoni, "La naturalità logica degli eventi: Le Corbusier da Vichy a 'Propos d'Urbanisme,'" introduction to the Italian translation of Le Corbusier's *A propos d'Urbanisme* (Bologna: Zanichelli, 1980), pp. 7–24, and the article by Mary McLeod, "*Plans*: Bibliography," *Oppositions* 19/20 (1980): 185–189 (with summary and index of the magazine *Plans* at pp. 190–201). Concerning the relations between Le Corbusier and Italian fascism, see Mimita Lamberti, "Le Corbusier e l'Italia," *Annali della Scuola Normale Superiore di Pisa*, Classe di Lettere e Filosofia, series III, vol. 2 (Pisa, 1972), pp. 817–871, with abundant previously unpublished documentation; and Giorgio Ciucci, "A Roma con Bottai," *Rassegna* 2, No. 3 (1980): 66–81. For Le Corbusier's relations with the Soviet Union, see Jean-Louis Cohen, "Cette mystique: L'URSS," *Architecture, Mouvement, Continuité* 49 (1979): 75–84, and Christian Borngräber, "Le Corbusier a Mosca," *Rassegna* 2, No. 3 (1980): 79–88.

21. Le Corbusier, *Une Maison, un palais* (Paris: Crès, 1928), p. 228; *Précisions sur un état présent de l'architecture et de l'urbanisme* (Paris: Crès, 1930), p. 187; Le Corbusier, *La Ville radieuse* (Boulogne/Seine: Editions de l'Architecture d'Aujourd'hui, 1935), p. 249.

22. Roland Barthes, *Leçon inaugurale de la chaire de Sémiologie Littéraire du Collège de France, prononcée le 7 janvier 1977* (Paris: Seuil, 1978).

23. See Jean-Louis Cohen, "Cette mystique"; Giorgio Ciucci, "A Roma con Bottai"; and Ciucci, "Le Corbusier e Wright in URSS," in *Socialismo, città, architettura: URSS 1917–1937* (Rome: Officina edizioni, 1971), pp. 173–193.

24. It should be pointed out that it was for the group *Redressement français*—an organization of technocrats devoted to a revitalization of the country through the efforts of an "industrial elite of intelligence, talent, and character"—that Le Corbusier published his pamphlet *Vers le Paris de l'époque machiniste* (supplement to the group's bulletin of February 15, 1928).

25. Robert de Souza, *Nice, capitale d'hiver* (Paris: Berger-Levrault, 1913). See also Pierre Saddy, "Le Corbusier chez les riches."

26. Le Corbusier, *La Ville radieuse*, p. 38.

27. Le Corbusier, *La Ville radieuse*, p. 154.
28. Regarding the impact of Latin America on Le Corbusier, see Le Corbusier, *Précisions*. Regarding the plans for Algiers, see Le Corbusier, "Le plan d'aménagement de la ville d'Alger," *L'Architecture Vivante*, October 1932; Le Corbusier, *La Ville radieuse*, pp. 226–240; Giorgio Piccinato, "Metodologia di Le Corbusier," *Casabella* 274 (1963): 16–25; Stanislaus von Moos, *Le Corbusier: Elements of a Synthesis* (Cambridge, Mass.: MIT Press, 1979), pp. 200–206; von Moos, "Von den 'Femmes d'Alger' zum 'Plan Obus,'" *Archithese* 1 (1971): 25–36; Edmond Brua, "Quand Le Corbusier bombardait Alger de 'Projets-Obus,'" *L'Architecture d'Aujourd'hui* 167 (1973): 72–77; Manfredo Tafuri, *Architecture and Utopia* (Cambridge, Mass.: MIT Press, 1976), pp. 125ff.; Marcello Fagiolo, "Le Corbusier 1930: progetti per l'America Latina e per Algeri," *Ottagono* 44 (1977): 21–41. See also the important essay by Mary McLeod, "Le Corbusier and Algiers," *Oppositions* 19/20 (1980): 55–85, which gives a complete history of Le Corbusier's adventure in Algiers.
29. Interesting observations on the anthropomorphism in the architecture of Le Corbusier, which may also be relevant for his urbanistic projects, may be found in Timothy Benton, "Le Corbusier's 'propos architectural,'" in *Le Corbusier, la ricerca paziente*, pp. 23ff.
30. The program for a "Latin entente" was published in the first issue of *Prélude*, the motto of which was: "The true man is the Craftsman. The expression of the Craftsman is the labor union integrated into the State." An explanation of the meaning of this use of the term "prelude" is offered by Pierre Winter: "Therefore, since we are in a Prelude between Fascism and Collectivism, we claim our place along this line of demarcation." (Pierre Winter, "Formations nouvelles," *Prélude* 7 [1933]: 3.) The call to the authority of the group behind *Prélude*, an organ "of regionalist and syndicalist action," is hence anything but concrete, as Thilo Hilpert has correctly observed in *Die funktionelle Stadt*, note 4.
31. See Stanislaus von Moos, "Von den 'Femmes d'Alger' zum 'Plan Obus.'"
32. Le Corbusier, *La Ville radieuse*, p. 233.
33. On the residential amphitheater of Nemours as a "Casbah of modern times, in steel and cement," see *La Ville radieuse* p. 315. Le Corbusier's interest in the *maisons à gradins* of Sauvage and Sarazin is documented by a *fiche* of ca. 1915. See Philippe Duboy, "Charles-Edouard Jeanneret à la Bibliothèque Nationale," p. 12. As Mary Patricia May Sekler tells us in *The Early Drawings*, p. 326, Sauvage offered work to Le Corbusier in 1908.
34. On the Athens Charter and the problems concerning its drafting, see Reyner Banham's review of Le Corbusier, *The Athens Charter*, trans. Anthony Eardley (New York: Grossman, 1973), in *Journal of the Society of Architectural Historians* 33 (1974): 260–261. See also A. Eardley, "Giraudoux and the Athens Charter"; Martin Steinmann, ed.,

CIAM: Dokumente 1928–1939 (Basel and Stuttgart: Birkhauser, 1979); the sole issue of *Parametro*, 1976, No. 52 (*Da Bruxelles ad Atene: la città funzionale*), and the essay by G. Ciucci, "Il mito Movimento Moderno e le vicende dei CIAM," *Casabella* 463/464 (1980): 28–35.
35. On Le Corbusier's project for the Zlín valley and his relations with the Bat'a industry, see Jean-Louis Cohen, "Il nostro cliente è il nostro padrone," *Rassegna* 2, No. 3 (1980): 47–60. Le Corbusier did not "discover" Tomáš Bat'a (1876–1932), the "Ford of Central Europe," until 1935, though both Tretjakov and Hyacinthe Dubreuil, propagandist of Taylorism with ties to Le Corbusier, had taken an interest in him. Le Corbusier's interest was the result of a letter from František Gahura, architect of the Bat'a industrial buildings. Le Corbusier's plan for the valley is polemical as regards the garden cities planned by Gahura, but it did not sufficiently impress Jan Bat'a. The same sort of failure was in store for Le Corbusier's plan for Hellocourt (Bataville) in 1936 as well as for the Bat'a pavilion project for the Paris Expo of 1937. Le Corbusier got his revenge in 1957, when he refused to support Jan Bat'a for the Nobel Peace Prize. Le Corbusier's failure regarding the Bat'a industry is significant: Tomáš and Jan Bat'a both seem to have had all the characteristics of the "leader" so dear to Le Corbusier's ideology, just as their production and propaganda strategies seem to have great affinities with Le Corbusier's planning ideas. But Bat'a is not Frugès.
36. Of the vast bibliography on Chandigarh, we should like to mention the *Oeuvre complète,* vols. 5–8, passim; Norma Evenson, *Chandigarh* (Berkeley: University of California Press, 1966); Sten Nilsson, *The New Capitals of India, Pakistan, and Bangladesh* (Lund, 1973); Maxwell Fry, "Le Corbusier at Chandigarh," in *The Open Hand*, pp. 351–363; Madhu Sarin, "Chandigarh as a Place to Live In," in *The Open Hand*, pp. 375–411; Stanislaus von Moos, "The Politics of the Open Hand: Notes on Le Corbusier and Nehru at Chandigarh," in *The Open Hand*, pp. 413–457.
37. The connection between the Pool of Reflection and the Open Hand is established from the start by Le Corbusier. See his letter to Nehru of July 21, 1955, in *Le Corbusier lui-même*, ed. Jean Petit (Geneva: Editions Rousseau, 1970), pp. 116–117. In many ways, the Pool of Reflection seems to be a further development of the metaphors contained in the "chambre à ciel ouvert" of the Beistegui penthouse: descending into it, rather than ascending to the height of a penthouse, one is supposed to remain in the company of one's own solitude, while the symbols of the great values disappear. Better yet, one is supposed to contract into the final and unitary symbol of the Open Hand.
38. In his copy of *Thus Spoke Zarathustra,* Le Corbusier noted on August 1, 1959: "I have not read this book since 1908 (quai St.-Michel, Paris) = 51 years = my life as a man. Today, having plundered these pages, I discover situations, acts,

decisions, destinations, which are the achievements of a man. I have decided to mark their pages."

39. It is, therefore, possible to assert a close connection between the Jeanneret who in the years of La Chaux-de-Fonds perceived the modern as crisis, tending to group together the *secrets* of the machine and of nature, and the Le Corbusier who built, in the works of his mature adulthood and old age, a "language of crisis." Casting light upon the theme of the *wait* in the young Jeanneret, Jacques Gubler concludes a penetrating essay in the following manner: "Le Corbusier will sing of the deed of the violent restoration of the ancestral heritage, built with calm and reason." And the symbol of this heritage—at La Chaux-de-Fonds as well as at Chandigarh—is *la vache*. Gubler, "Jeanneret et le regionalisme: du sentiment à la raison," *Archithese* 3 (1981): 31–38.

Urbanism and Transcultural Exchanges, 1910–1935: A Survey
by Stanislaus von Moos

The Beginnings

The basic facts concerning the period 1910 to 1935 are revealed—and at the same time elaborately concealed—by Le Corbusier's own books *Urbanisme* (1925), *Précisions* (1930), *La Ville radieuse* (1935), *Quand les cathédrales étaient blanches* (1937), and the first three volumes of *L'Oeuvre complète*. We are told that the logic of urban form had been one of Charles-Edouard Jeanneret's concerns since 1910. And in the first volume of the *Oeuvre complète* (1910–1929) we find quite a few early travel sketches and drawings of historic squares and fortified towns, mostly taken from books. Indeed, the first Dom-ino studies (1914) are arranged in compounds that reach the scale of whole neighborhoods.

Yet we are left with the impression that the leap from occasional study and speculation to systematic urbanistic invention occurred only after 1920, the moment the architect had established his official identity as Le Corbusier. The actual story is a rather different one. As a matter of fact, as early as 1914 Charles-Edouard Jeanneret submitted a project for a garden city to be built "Aux Crétets," on the outskirts of his hometown, La Chaux-de-Fonds. The project consisted of no less than 120 houses, partly detached and partly combined in rather long rows and grouped in a picturesque manner along curved streets. A semicircular terrace planted with a bosket forms the center of the compound and overlooks the land (Figure 1).

A scheme as elaborate as this one is not imaginable without previous extensive studies of contemporary urban design in general and the garden city movement in particular. The symmetrical group of houses flanking the entrance to the compound is almost literally taken over from the one-family row houses "Am Schränkenberg," a part of the artists' colony at Hellerau near Dresden designed by Heinrich Tessenow (1910–11). The houses situated higher up the hill in turn are free variations on the theme of Barry Parker and Sir Raymond Unwin's designs for Hampstead Garden City, with occasional reminiscences of Jeanneret's own juvenile

works at the Chemin de Pouillerel thrown in (Figure 2[1]).

The project as such is proof enough of Jeanneret's direct involvement in the planning discussions of the years around 1910. His *Etude sur le mouvement d'art décoratif en Allemagne* (1912), a short report he had written for the La Chaux-de-Fonds art school during his 1910–11 stay in Germany, offers additional clues as to the situation in Germany that is the natural background for his early urbanistic proposals. Although the subject of the report is the state of the applied arts in Germany, it does contain interesting observations on Peter Behrens's workers' housing for the AEG in Berlin and on the Werkbund colony at Hellerau, which Jeanneret knew well. Among other things, the author praises the famous *Städtebau* exhibition, organized by Werner Hegemann in Berlin (1910), for having clearly established that streets have to be arranged in curves and according to the structure of the landscape.[2]

"La Construction des villes"

But that is not all. Quite recently H. Allen Brooks discovered Jeanneret's unfinished manuscript, hitherto unknown, of a book that he planned to publish under the title "La Construction des villes" (The Building of Cities).[3] The first table of contents dates from 1910 and reveals that the structure of the proposed book was to be modeled after Camillo Sitte's *Der Städtebau* (Vienna, 1889). In a note addressed to Charles L'Eplattenier, his master and also the intended coauthor of the book, Jeanneret is even more explicit and says that he intends to "cite plans and views in the manner of Camillo Sitte."

All that may come as a surprise to anyone who is familiar with the later Le Corbusier's contempt for Camillo Sitte, this "intelligent and sensitive Viennese who simply stated the problem badly."[4] Yet there are more such surprises, for instance, in the chapter on the street ("Des rues"). I am quoting H. A. Brooks's summary of this section: "Streets should be curved, their width and slope should vary, views along them should be closed, and asymmetrical or geometric layouts must be avoided." More precisely, Jeanneret urges planners to learn from the donkey how to design roads that respect and enhance the landscape: "The lesson of the donkey is to be retained," he insists.[5]

Even if after 1915 Jeanneret seems to have turned away from Sitte's *Städtebau* in favor of more classical and monumental concepts of urban space like those exemplified in Pierre Patte's *Monuments érigés en France à la gloire de Louis XV* (1765), a book he studied extensively, bits and pieces dating from his early involvement with Sitte later found their way into *Urbanisme*, such as the drawing after a seventeenth-century veduta of an unidentified medieval town (Rottweil im Allgäu?, Figure 3).[6] After 1917 Tony Garnier's *Cité industrielle* had started to "rationalize" Jeanneret's urbanistic vocabulary, as can be seen in his industrial and housing proposals for Saintes (1917).[7] And by the time that *Urbanisme* appeared, his positions on practically all pertinent issues of urbanism seem to have been completely reversed. The new book, conceived on the waves of France's national rebirth after World War I, returned full steam to the urbanistic axes and symmetries characteristic of the French mythology of reason and *grandeur*. And whereas in "La Construction des villes" Jeanneret had condemned the grid system *à l'américaine* for its monotony, Le Corbusier in *Urbanisme*, using the words of Abbé Laugier, postulates a city that displays "du tumulte dans l'ensemble, de l'uniformité dans le detail."[8] In part, this emphasis on monumental order may be attributed to the shift in scale from the Swiss suburb to the French metropolis now chosen as the object of study. As radically as Le Corbusier seems to have departed from the atmosphere of the picturesque garden city and artists' colony, the theme, architecturally purified, was soon to re-emerge in his later projects of workers' housing, especially at Pessac.

L'Esprit Nouveau

In fact, the saga of Le Corbusier as an urbanist begins only after his final move to Paris and his establishment as one of the editors of *L'Esprit Nouveau* in 1920 (together with Amédée Ozenfant and Paul Dermée). The direction his architectural thought now took is indicated in his first articles written for the magazine, especially in his "Trois rappels à MM. LES ARCHITECTES" (Three reminders to architects, Figure 4), which ended with the well-known Olympian statement: "here are American silos and factories, magnificent BEGINNINGS of a new age, AMERICAN ENGINEERS DESTROYING A DYING ARCHITECTURE WITH THEIR CALCULATIONS."[9]

The point of view that emerges here is Neoplatonic and idealist. Technology and engineering were not really what mattered. The point was that, in Le Corbusier's view, technology seemed to have found, in accordance with its own rules, its way to the primary forms: cubes, cones, spheres, cylinders, and pyramids, and that was proof enough that it was in agreement not only with the "lesson of Rome" (the theme of the article in *L'Esprit Nouveau* that later became a chapter in the book *Vers une architecture*), but also with the beauty of the elementary forms referred to by Plato in his Philebos dialogue. A pseudo-Darwinian law of mechanical selection seemed to have brought about the premises of a new harmony within the sphere of man-made forms. The ideals of classical discipline seemed to have come unexpectedly close to the agencies of mechanization.

The argument as such owes much to the German Werkbund of the years around 1910, to Peter Behrens's work for the AEG in Berlin, and to the writings of Hermann Muthesius. That the illustrations Le Corbusier used for his first article in *L'Esprit Nouveau* are partly taken over—not without slight adjustments to the Purist taste—from the *Werkbund Jahrbuch* of 1913 is certainly no coincidence.[10]

Technology and its Cultural "Ready-Mades"

Yet there is a significant step from the Werkbund pleas for aesthetic purity in industrial building to Le Corbusier's claim that architecture's salvation on the whole depends on the adoption of the aesthetic principles of engineering. Artists like Marcel Duchamp or Francis Picabia must have played a liberating role in this polemical radicalization of Werkbund thought. For them too—as was the case for Le Corbusier himself (even if he was not to travel there until 1935)—America was the decisive eye-opener. Upon his arrival in New York in 1915 Duchamp had declared that the city was "a complete work of art"; later he added that "the only works of art ever produced by America are its installations and its bridges."[11] Picabia, whose paradoxical biomorphic manipulations of machine-age imagery didn't fail to irritate the editors of *L'Esprit Nouveau*, had pushed this Dadaist reversal of the classical hierarchy of the arts to an extravagant extreme by presenting the drawing of a spark plug as "portrait d'une jeune fille américaine dans l'état de nudité" (portrait of a young American girl in the nude, Figure 5).

The first episodes of the official story of Le Corbusier as an urbanist—and especially his project for a *Ville contemporaine*—is not to be understood outside the context of the Parisian avant-garde and its polemical interest in the "ready-made" culture of the machine age. On the other hand, Paris itself, its dramatic conditions of overcrowding, and the measures taken after World War I to decentralize the city and to coordinate it with the newly defined *région parisienne* provided the immediate context and background for his proposals. In fact, the official master plan for Paris, drawn by Bassompièrre, de Rutte, and Servin, which generated satellite towns like Drancy and the "Butte Rouge," was established at the same time as Le Corbusier's *Ville contemporaine*—in 1922.

From the *Ville contemporaine* to the Plan Voisin
The story itself—or rather Le Corbusier's version of it—is well known. In 1922 the architect was invited to submit an urbanistic project to the Salon d'Automne of that same year. Asked by the architect what he meant by "urbanism," Marcel Temporal, the organizer of the exhibit, explained that he was inter-

ested in benches, kiosks, streetlights, signposts, and billboards. "Look, why don't you design a fountain for me?" Le Corbusier accepted. "All right, I will make a fountain, but behind it, I will place a city for three million inhabitants" (Figure 7).[12] The project was entitled *Ville contemporaine* (contemporary city) in order to emphasize that it was not intended for a distant future, but as a solution to the present problems based on present possibilities: "It is this that confers boldness to our dreams: the fact that they can be realized."[13]

Next to the grandiose scheme of the *Ville contemporaine* Le Corbusier exhibited a smaller plan proposing an adaptation of the plan to the specific situation of Paris.[14] In 1925 the reorganization of Paris became the great issue. In a side wing of the Pavillon de L'Esprit Nouveau at the Art Deco exhibition Le Corbusier displayed the sixteen-meter-long diorama of the *Ville contemporaine* facing another, similar diorama of what he called the Plan Voisin of Paris. This Plan Voisin relegated the *Ville* to where it originated: to the city of Paris, "eye of Europe."

A few lines must suffice to describe the dominant characteristics of this plan. To render Paris habitable, Le Corbusier recommends massive surgery and makes the total razing of the area between the Seine and Montmartre a preliminary condition of any renewal. Only a few isolated buildings—the Louvre, the Palais Royal—and the place des Vosges, the place de la Concorde, the Arc de Triomphe plus a few selected churches and town houses are to be spared. The architect declares, "the historical past, a universal patrimony, will be respected. More than that, it will be saved."[15]

With a sweeping gesture Le Corbusier's city is inscribed into the landscape: its axes reach out towards the four corners of the horizon. At the beginning of *Urbanisme* we are given a grandiose moral reason for this return to the urbanistic space conception of Versailles or of Baron Haussman's Paris: "Man walks in a straight line because he has a goal and knows where he is going."[16] The straight line is the line of man, the curved line that of the donkey; the choice to be made was thus an obvious one. Jeanneret's earlier picturesque preferences are not forgotten, they are simply turned upside down. In the introduction to *Urbanisme* Le Corbusier admits having been affected by Sitte in earlier years:

> Sitte's demonstrations were clever, his theories seemed adequate; they were based on the past, and in fact WERE the past, but a sentimental past on a small and pretty scale, like the little wayside flowers. . . . Sitte's eloquence went well with that touching rehabilitation of "the home" which was later, paradoxically enough, to turn architecture away, in the most absurd fashion, from its proper path ("regionalism").[17]

In order to articulate the system of the axes in the *Ville contemporaine* and in the Plan Voisin the architect reverts to the most classical means. The main axis of the *Ville* is a superhighway laid out between two triumphal arches. A closer look at the obelisks, columns, and monumental domes along the main traffic arteries as well as the general layout reveals a composition worthy of any Beaux Arts student.

Once again the ideals of the classical tradition are intermingled with those of the machine age. We are reminded of the quasi-magical character that Le Corbusier ascribed to speed. "The city that has speed has success," he claims. This sounds like a futurist slogan; indeed Antonio Sant'Elia's projects of about a decade earlier were based upon an analogous worship of velocity. Whether one wants to claim Sant'Elia's *Città Nuova* of 1914 as an actual inspiration for the *Ville contemporaine* is an academic question; Le Corbusier hardly ever refers to the Italians at this time (which may or may not be attributed to his habit of covering up his sources). But he liked to refer to the rhetoric of French automobile advertisements. In *Urbanisme* he quotes an article by one of the directors of the Peugeot plant, Phillipe Girardet, who saw in the automobile the vigorous and brilliant confirmation of an age-old dream of humanity. Girardet describes man as one of the slowest animals in creation:

> a sort of caterpillar dragging himself along with difficulty on the surface of the terrestrial crust. Most creatures move more quickly than this biped so ill-constructed for speed, and if we imagined a race among all the creatures of the globe, man would certainly be among the "also rans" and would probably tie with the sheep.[18]

It was, of course, motorized traffic that ultimately enabled man to triumph over this deplorable condition.

Attempts at Gaining a Mass Audience: the Michelin Episode

In the framework of *L'Esprit Nouveau*, where some among the chapters that were later assembled under the title *Urbanisme* first appeared, such references to the French automobile industry are usually to be understood as courtesies directed towards potential advertisers in the magazine. And one of those advertisers, the Voisin automobile factory, turned out to be the sponsor of the plan for Paris itself. In fact, the cars that race down the main axis of the *Ville contemporaine* published in the final issue of *L'Esprit Nouveau* are the same ones that in a Voisin advertisement several pages later are shown at their arrival, covered with dust, after a Paris-Nice race in which Voisin took six prizes (figure 8).

Of course, Le Corbusier's urbanism is not only a simple extrapolation of the automobile industry's secret wishes. But it *is* that as well, and in a much more explicit way than could be guessed from the fine drawings in *L'Esprit Nouveau* or the well-known slogans such as "La ville qui dispose de la vitesse dispose du succès" (The city that has speed has success). In a letter addressed to the advertising departments of Voisin, Delage, and Citroën, the editor in charge of the magazine's public relations—Le Corbusier—insists:

Today's automobile industry finds itself confronted with the fact that its progress has
become quite questionable owing to the present
conditions in cities and metropolitan areas,
where the basic layouts are no longer adequate
to the demands of traffic. . . . Cars will soon
not be able to circulate in today's downtown
areas. The businessman's car will be a thing of
the past, as is already the case in New York
City.[19]

It was thus perfectly appropriate that Voisin gave its
name to the revised version of the plan that was
exhibited at the 1925 international arts and crafts
exhibition in Paris. Le Corbusier, however, was well
aware of the aura of exclusivity that was associated
with the Voisin trademark. In a letter dated April 3
of that same year he tried to involve the Michelin
tire factory in the project. Such an involvement, so
he thought, might secure the plan a more popular
dimension. If Michelin were to come into the
project, the title would then read, "Le plan Michelin
et Voisin du Centre de Paris" (The Michelin and
Voisin Plan for the Paris City Center).

> Through association of the name "Michelin"
> with our plan, the project will acquire
> considerable mass appeal. It will become
> possible to motivate public opinion in a much
> more fundamental way than would be possible
> through books, for example.[20]

Even though, despite these efforts, the little tire man
was never drafted into service to win over the public
at large for the cause of the "shining city," Le
Corbusier's plan reveals itself as the exact urbanistic
dramatization of those principles of industrial
rationalization Michelin had put to work in its plant
(Figures 6, 7).

Transatlantic Cross-Pollinations

As to the office towers that constitute the center of
the *Ville contemporaine*—a first version had

appeared in *L'Esprit Nouveau* as early as in 1921—
Le Corbusier credits Auguste Perret for having
suggested to him the idea as such. But when Perret's
first drawings were published in August 1922, the
difference between the two concepts was striking.
While Perret's proposal is an elaborate Beaux Arts
variation on the theme of the setback skyscraper that
might easily pass as an American submission to the
Chicago Tribune competition of the same year,
Le Corbusier's is a categoric redefinition of the office
tower as a type: cruciform in plan, with straightforward cubic elevations and fully glazed surfaces. In
order to provide good lighting of the interiors, the
surfaces are organized *à redents*, that is, in terms of
bays and recesses that guaranteed maximum sight
and lighting.

None of these characteristics were, strictly
speaking, Le Corbusier's invention. American
precedents can be claimed for all of them. The
cruciform plan is already present in Louis Sullivan's
design for Fraternity Temple in Chicago (1891), and
the glazed bays are an essential feature of such
landmarks of Chicago School architecture as the
Reliance Building by Burnham & Co. (1895, Figure 9)
or the Tacoma Building by Holabird and Roche
(1887–89) in Chicago's Loop. Le Corbusier's
alternative to the "chaos" of Manhattan, which in his
early articles is constantly evoked with spectacular
photographs (Figure 10), is "European" only to the
degree that it is based on an aesthetic idealization of
structural possibilities empirically put to work almost
half a century earlier by the pioneers of the Chicago
School without, however, being a primary preoccupation in their "architectonic potential" so much
praised, a posteriori, by the historians of the Modern
Movement.[21]

Yet not only the "rationalized" skyscrapers that
constitute the core of the *Ville contemporaine*, but
the very principle of an overall gridiron plan based
on axes and diagonal thoroughfares can and perhaps
must be traced back to American precedents. It is
quite unimaginable that the splendid publication of
Burnham's Chicago Plan of 1909 should have

escaped Le Corbusier's attention (Figure 11).[22] Yet while Burnham's plan, as a demonstrative attack on the urbanistic imagery of capitalist laissez faire, had sacrificed the early steel-and-glass architecture of the Chicago School (of which Burnham himself had been a protagonist!) to the bombastic unity of the "City Beautiful," Le Corbusier reinstalled it at the expense of the neoclassical monumentality of Burnham's street façades and public buildings. In short, if Burnham's plan for Chicago celebrates Baron Haussmann's Paris, Le Corbusier's metropolis dramatically idealizes the business skyscrapers of Chicago's heroic years.

Not all the elements of Le Corbusier's early urbanistic vocabulary can be attributed to trans-atlantic cross-pollination. His urge to separate automobile traffic from pedestrian circulation and to layer the different levels of mechanical transporta-tion according to function, range, and speed stays in line with myriads of earlier, widely publicized urbanistic proposals for cities like Paris, Berlin, London, New York, or Chicago.

In Paris it was Eugène Hénard who, as early as 1903, suggested a number of important urban changes in order to cope with the increasing dangers of traffic. His *carrefour à giration*, probably the first traffic roundabout in the modern sense, was designed for horse-drawn carriages; the concept was published by Le Corbusier in *Urbanisme*, and it obviously served as an inspiration for the great central station in the heart of the *Ville contemporaine*.[23] While Hénard proposed two levels of circulation, vehicles on the surface and pedestrians underneath, the author of the *Ville contemporaine* suggested no fewer than six superimposed layers. At the lowest levels, the terminals for the main lines; above, the suburban lines; then the subway; above that, all pedestrian circulation; then the throughways for rapid motor traffic; and last, at the top, the airport (Figure 12). This latter idea of an airport placed in the heart of a metropolis seems to have preoccupied many designers at that time; that Le Corbusier kept a press photograph showing André Basbevant's

extravagant project of an airport with a movable runway circling above the center of a metropolis (1924) comes as no surprise (Figure 13).[24]

Housing Proposals *à redents*

The housing proposals follow more immediately Parisian patterns. On the whole, the residential "greenbelt" that surrounds the downtown area of the *Ville contemporaine* is an attempt at combining the garden city idea—which had inspired Jeanneret's urbanistic proposals for La Chaux-de-Fonds—with the more urban type of the apartment block. Earlier Parisian studio houses like the one built around 1908 at the rue Campagne Première near Montparnasse anticipate in many ways the Corbusian type of the *immeuble-villas* with their double-height, split-level living rooms and little balconies accentuating the middle axis of the large picture windows. Between the two types of apartment blocks indicated in the Plan Voisin—the blocks of the cellular principle and the blocks with setbacks—it is the latter that will remain an established element in the architect's urban code (Figure 14). The principle is similar to that of the Louvre embracing the Tuileries—an image that Victor Considérant had already chosen as appropriate for his Fourierist phalanstery (1840, Figure 15); Le Corbusier himself refers to the Palais Royal and its garden. Yet both the form and the term *à redents* are directly from Eugène Hénard's *Etudes sur les transformations de Paris* (1903).[25]

Urbanism as Alarm System?

As to social and economic aspects of the scheme, Le Corbusier was well aware of which card to play. He left no stone unturned in order to prove the great virtues of the *Ville contemporaine* as a guarantor of business profits and social peace: "Paris, capital of France, must build up in this twentieth century its position of command,"[26] he announces. The whole urbanistic imagery of the *Ville contemporaine* as well as of the Plan Voisin—the huge, eight-hundred-foot-high steel and glass office towers lined up on the flat and between the superhighways like figures on a chessboard—is indeed a glorification of big business and of centralized state control.

"But where is the money coming from?" Le Corbusier was enough of a business-man himself not to be embarrassed by such a question; his closest friends from the Swiss colony in Paris were, after all, bankers. "To urbanize means to increase value," he proclaims. "To urbanize is not to spend money, but to earn money, to make money".[27] How? The key word is density: the greater the density of land use, the greater the real estate value. And again the reassurance: the colossal towers are not "revolutionary," they are a means of multiplying business profits.

The Plan Voisin thus characterizes itself as the ideal city of capitalism and not of French big business alone; foreign capital should have its share in it too. Le Corbusier argues that the distribution of land among French, German, and American trusts would minimize the danger of possible air attack. A downtown made of glittering office towers reflecting the power of multi-national corporations—it took a few decades for Europe to catch up with this vision. Yet in economic terms, if not in those of urban imagery and planning procedure, the quartier de la Défense north of Neuilly and other recent large-scale developments inside Paris are based on the very forces with which Le Corbusier had hoped to put his Plan Voisin into action.

Marshall McLuhan once compared the function of avant-garde art to that of a radar system. Art, he suggested, has the prophetic capacity of anticipating under laboratory conditions what might one day actually become an everyday experience, as soon as the conditions hypothetically chosen by the artist for his experiment turn out to be conditions of the social and technological reality of a given society at large. In fact, it is tempting to think of Le Corbusier's *Ville contemporaine* as an "early warning system," and Norma Evenson can hardly be contradicted when she claims, in the context of Le Corbusier's early urbanistic utopia, that this architect was "the

messenger who brought a certain type of bad news. He did not present an ideal city, but the city that might logically result given certain circumstances."[28]

To the degree that the circumstances of advanced industrial society turned out to be in many instances those anticipated by the *Ville contemporaine*, reality has caught up with Le Corbusier—or at least the Le Corbusier of 1922–25. And so he will—and with good reason—continue to be blamed or admired, according to the critic's own philosophy, for having accepted modern technology and centralized bureaucracy as guidelines of action and for having elevated these realities to the level of universal and natural laws, as indeed he did in his early projects. These qualify him as a protagonist of the ideology of the modern welfare state, and part of his personal fate was that his first large-scale renewal projects were developed some twenty-five years before their underlying ideology became universally accepted in the industrialized world.

South America and North Africa, Visions of the Vernacular

Paris provoked Le Corbusier's urban utopia, but at the end of the twenties new factors intervened. First of all, there was his trip to South America and his involvement with Africa; second, his increasingly frequent contacts with Russia, the promised land, with its rational architecture and large-scale planning policy. While the sudden contact with the nonindustrialized world—South America and Africa—generated a new awareness of the vernacular roots of building, Russia seemed to bring Le Corbusier's view into a context of technical feasibility and of immediate social need.

In the summer of 1929 Le Corbusier made his first trip to Latin America at the invitation of the magazine *Stil* and a group called Amigos del Arte. He traveled in a Zeppelin and delivered ten lectures in Buenos Aires, two in Montevideo, two in Rio de Janeiro, and two in Sao Paulo. In December, on his way back on board the ocean liner *Lutetia*, he wrote a summary of these talks. The outcome was a book, *Précisions sur un état présent de l'architecture et de l'urbanisme,* which was published after his return. Besides summarizing his architectural and urbanistic vision in extremely animated prose, the author pays tribute to the country and the people of South America. Unlike *Vers une architecture*, the book is not didactic. Inspired by the scale and splendor of the South American landscape, it is the epic of an architecture and an urbanism that responds to the turbulent skyline of the mountains and to the great expanses of the plains, rivers, and seas. The wide plains crossed by waterways and rivers meandering majestically toward the sea—a view Le Corbusier observed from the plane and described with Balzacian eloquence—added a new verve to his urbanistic ambitions.

In the light of South America's realities the earlier schemes developed for Paris proved to be too rigid. For instance, how could a business center be established on the steep coast of Montevideo? Ever since the *Ville contemporaine* of 1922 Le Corbusier had regarded the central traffic artery as the backbone of an urban plan. Given a hilly coastal site, however, he is obliged to change his views: in order to have a straight main traffic artery, it is necessary to elevate it from the ground and place it at the crowning point of the city. Thus, from the top of the coastal hill three viaducts reach out toward the horizon, forming three platforms that overhang the port by 250 feet. Here the offices of the business center are to be suspended underneath. What is needed is not a skyscraper, as Le Corbusier put it, but a "seascraper."[29]

His "solutions" to the problems of Rio de Janeiro are no less adventurous. He arrived there in October 1929, and at first he seemed to have been speechless: "To urbanize here is like trying to fill the barrel of the Danaides."[30] In a landscape as imposing as that of the Pao de Acúar, the Corvocado, the Gàvea, and the Gigante Tendido, architecture even on an urbanistic scale no longer has a chance. A few weeks later, however, he had recovered from the

shock, and the solution to the problem was ready. Just before returning to Europe in December, he explained his ideas in a lecture:

> From far away, I saw in my mind the vast and magnificent belt of buildings, crowned horizontally by a superhighway flying from mount to mount and reaching out from one bay to another.

Thus Corbusier's response to the challenge of this landscape is an immense elevated viaduct winding between the hills like a gigantic folding screen of glass and metal (Figure 16). The idea received further elaboration in 1936, when Le Corbusier was back in Rio again, but in the meantime it had become the basis for no doubt one of his most interesting proposals, the Plan Obus for Algiers.

Algiers: The Plan Obus

Between 1931 and 1942 Algiers was the focus of Le Corbusier's town-planning endeavors. He seems to have found in Algiers what he had looked for in his youth in Constantinople and Athens: the white city under the sun, facing the sea. In his eyes Algiers not only outdid all the cities of the French mainland as a center of business and trade, it also preserved the remnants of an authentic and centuries-old folk tradition. The Casbah, unspoiled by nineteenth-century industrialization and taste, was a lively cluster of folk architecture and preindustrial forms of life.

The first contact had taken place around 1930. In 1931 Le Corbusier was invited to deliver two lectures on modern architecture at the recently opened Casino of Algiers. In 1932 he returned in order to present his first projects to the public as part of an exhibition on town planning. He called his masterplan "Plan Obus."[31]

The concept is reminiscent of the plan for Rio. Downtown in the quartier de la Marine close to the harbor an office skyscraper was to be built upon a site that had been due for demolition for some time. From its roof terrace an immense road bridge leads to the elegant apartment blocks on the hills of Fort l'Empereur. Thus the seat of public administration would be safely linked to the quarters of the ruling class. Just below, parallel to the coast and at right angles to the bridge, the great traffic artery serving the entire region was to be built as a viaduct forming an enormous hairpin bend in the west. The underlying principle of the plan is simple. First of all, the highway department would build this system of viaducts crossing the coastal landscape at a height of 350 feet; later, the population of the overcrowded center would gradually move into the levels underneath the road. Thus the building of superhighways would not reduce but actually multiply the built-up surface of the city—and the Casbah could remain physically intact.

A well-known drawing by Le Corbusier demonstrates how he planned the utilization of the filled-in land gained through the plan. On each level individual houses would be built side by side, each according to the desires of the occupants. Instead of the rigorous visual hygiene of the Plan Voisin and its implicit dictatorial "freedom through order," we have a kind of open planning, founded on broad-based participation and initiative.

It may be easy to ridicule the plan's guiding idea, but it is hard to refute its underlying logic: in a capitalist economy public funds for automobile highways are more easily available than funds for housing or urban renewal. Here, then, is a proposal that shows how to improve the housing situation in downtown areas with the help of an urban superhighway. In the light of recent urban history, where superhighways have usually played the opposite role, it is hard to say which is more surprising: the ingenuity of the physical plan itself or the paradox of its supposed economic base.

Sources and Premises:
Automobile and Airplane

There are historic precedents for Le Corbusier's combination of viaduct and habitat: the medieval "urbanized bridges" of London, Paris, and Florence; Edgar Chambless's "Project for Roadtown," of 1910;

and some contemporary Russian schemes more or less directly based on the concept of the linear city introduced almost a century before by Arturo Soria y Mata. In fact, with the Plan Obus Le Corbusier extends his field of action as an urbanist to the region as a whole—the countryside, not the metropolis, is now the proposed object of urbanization. If seen in the context of the traditional discipline of urban design, Le Corbusier's method once again recalls the principle by which Marcel Duchamp declared a bottle rack or a toilet bowl as a work of art. Through a simple inversion of the classical hierarchy of architecture and engineering, the architect declares the highway viaduct that follows the coastline as the raison d'être of the new urban form.

Giacomo Mattè-Trucco's FIAT factory at Turin (1920–23) with its test track installed on the roof is the most immediate precedent that comes to mind.[32] Le Corbusier had praised the factory in *L'Esprit Nouveau* and in *Vers une architecture*. Finally, in 1934, he had an opportunity to visit the site and to use it with the latest sports model (Figure 17). This was, for him, the ultimate proof that the Plan Obus was feasible:

> The Fiat factory has gained a lead over the urbanism of our machine age. The superhighway on the roof, for instance, actually proves the possibilities of modern technology. It is no longer a dream but a reality: certain cities like Genoa, Algiers, Rio de Janeiro could thus be saved from the impending disaster.[33]

Yet the Rio plan and the Plan Obus are connected with the fine arts not by the Dadaist principle of the decontextualized technological "ready-made" alone. The bold curves that make up the structure of these plans recall the outlines of the figurative studies of the years after 1930 (Figure 18). The title of a painting of 1949, "Alma Rio 36," where a symphonic rhythm of outlines and an interplay of depths and heights seem to evoke rivers, peninsulas, mountain ranges, and hills, very explicitly refers to an earlier visit to Rio (Figure 19). If in turn in Rio and Algiers the large coastal outlines of South America and Africa with their curving rivers had become the starting point of a new urbanism, then such an urbanism could only have been dreamed up in an airplane. And, in fact, the architect often described how, during his journeys in South America and in North Africa, the view from the plane had revealed to him the chaotic state of human habitation and how the broad contours of the coast-line and the meanderings of the rivers provided him with guidelines for a new urban aesthetic, which he thought should be conceived with regard to the "fifth façade," that is, the view from above.

During a flight over the Atlas mountains in 1933 he wrote:

A flight in a plane is a drama with a message—a philosophy.

Not a sensual delight.

From five feet above the ground, flowers and trees have a proportion: a scale which is related to human activity and to human proportions.

But in the air, from above?—A wilderness, without relation to our thousand-year-old ideas, a fatality of cosmic advents and events.

I can understand, and measure it, but I cannot love it; I feel that I am not prepared for the joy of this drama from on high.

The non-professional flier, who flies (and knows nothing), is led to thought: he finds refuge only in himself and in his works. But once he is down on the ground again, his aims and intentions will have achieved a new dimension.[34]

A few years later, in 1939, Antoine de Saint-Exupéry summarized his flight experience in the following words:

Thus we are changed into physicists, biologists, surveying these civilizations which embellish valley bottoms and sometimes, miraculously,

spread out like parks when the climate is favorable. Here we are, judging mankind on a cosmic scale, observing man through our port-holes, as through a microscope. Here we are rereading our history.[35]

But Saint-Exupéry also experienced the world aloft as a world unrelated to human destiny; after describing a cyclone, he adds, "It would certainly have been more of a thrill if I had told you the story of an unfairly punished child."

I need not discuss here how praiseworthy or questionable Le Corbusier's desire to design a city as a sculpture seen from outer space may have been—apart from the fact that the plan cannot of course be appropriately judged from the model photographs alone, however epic. Yet flight seems to confirm one of this architect's basic intellectual tenets: nature and the world are both to be grasped as the nameless expression of cosmic laws. Unquestionably, the avant-garde's attempts to redefine the city as a work of art are reaching an extreme in the cosmic vision of architecture and urbanism so enigmatically embodied in this plan.

The Cartesian Skyscraper and the Promise of the Revolution

The numerous proposals by which Le Corbusier tried after 1930 to introduce the urban future into the reality of existing cities are all based on an estab-lished catalogue of building types. Apart from his extensive studies for Paris and Algiers, he had in fact developed renewal projects for Barcelona, Stockholm, Antwerp, Geneva, Buenos Aires, and various other cities, usually without any commission from those concerned. It is noteworthy that he eliminated, around 1930, the cruciform tower from his vocabulary. It was replaced by the so-called "Cartesian Skyscraper": Y-shaped in plan, "like a hen's foot."[36] The principle is obvious: like a reflector, the building is oriented toward sun and light (whereas in the cruciform skyscraper fifty percent of the façades remain in the shade during the whole year). The new type shows up for the first time in the master plan for Barcelona by José Luis Sert and the GATEPAC group, a study made in collaboration with Le Corbusier and Pierre Jeanneret (1932–1935). Later, it appears in the Antwerp master plan as well as in that of Hellocourt, not to mention the Plan de Paris of 1937 and finally the project for Buenos Aires (1938) with its five glass skyscrapers lined up like soldiers standing at attention and facing the sea (see also Figure 20).

Among these international contacts it is appropriate to single out those with the USSR and with the United States. Le Corbusier made at least three trips to Moscow between 1928 and 1930. Having won the competition for a large office building (Centrosoyus), he was obliged to visit the city from time to time in order to supervise the development of the project. Like most Western European architects in the twenties, he realized that Russia around 1930 was the "New World," where the concepts of modern town planning were most likely to be realized on a grand scale and where the architect was in the long run most likely to be assigned a leading role in the transformations of society.

In fact, whereas the economic crisis in Western Europe had jeopardized the prospects of radical architects and planners, Russia with its first five-year plan (1928) had established a program of nationwide industrialization and urbanization that surpassed the most utopian projects of the West. A number of avant-garde architects from Germany, Holland, and Switzerland moved to Russia, where they remained for a number of years and were put in charge of important planning projects. These architects included Ernst May, Erich Mendelsohn, Bruno Taut, Mart Stam, Hannes Meyer, Hans Schmidt, and others. During his visits Le Corbusier met the leaders of the architectural avant-garde, including the Vesnin brothers and, in 1930, Moses Ginsburg, who was then working on his project for the deurbanization of Moscow. Later, in 1931, he submitted a master plan for Moscow that, although rejected by

the Russians, became the basis for his book *Ville radieuse* (1935).[37]

The impact made by the Soviet avant-garde on Le Corbusier's oeuvre as an architect is not our subject,[38] but it should be recalled that the Plan Obus owes much to Moses Ginsburg's linear city project of 1930 and that Le Corbusier's later attempts at establishing instruments of planning on a regional, even international, scale are elaborating themes established in Russia, for example, by N. Miljutin's proposals for industrial cities, particularly for Tractorstoy (1928). The linear industrial cities proposed after 1940 by the ASCORAL group (*Assemblée des constructeurs pour une rénovation architecturale*), which was headed by Le Corbusier, are directly based on these experiences.[39]

More Transatlantic Cross-Pollinations: New York

Although the USSR had appeared to be the "promised land" for the new architecture for some time, the Western avant-garde quickly lost track of Soviet developments once the Stalinist bureaucracy returned to the dogma of socialist realism (1934)—particularly since the United States began to adopt at least some of the ideals of "modern architecture" at about the same time. In 1931 New York received its first "modern" skyscraper—the McGraw-Hill building by Hood, Godley, and Fouilhoux. In 1932 the Museum of Modern Art drew the attention of the élite to what it called the "International Style"; Rockefeller Center was under construction at the time, and George Howe and William Lescaze were supervising the completion of the PSFS Tower in Philadelphia. The principles of rational design, as demonstrated and advertised by these buildings, were suddenly regarded by many architects as the only possible approach to the vast social and economic issues of the Depression years. American interest in European urban utopias grew in intensity, and on January 3, 1932, the *New York Times* published a long, lavishly illustrated article on Le Corbusier's

"Ideal Metropolis," in which the architect pays a tribute to what he calls the American "juvenility":

> The United States is the adolescent of the contemporary world, and New York is her expression of enthusiasm, juvenility, boldness, enterprise, pride and vanity. New York stands on the brink of the world like a hero.[40]

It is interesting to compare this generous, if rather patronizing, homage to the New World with the growing anti-Americanism that had found a favorable response in large parts of the French public, especially after the Wall Street crisis of 1929. Typical of this wave of French anti-Yankeeism was a book like Robert Aron and Arnaud Dandieu's *Le Cancer américain* (The American Cancer, 1931), in which that "cancer" was defined as "not only a physical and economic decay, but an aberration of the spirit," namely, as the authors continued, "the supremacy of industry and banking over the entire life of the epoch."

> In fact, the Yankee spirit is nothing but the mass exploitation on a gigantic scale of the most lamentable mistake ever committed by Europe, the rationalist mistake. Descartes is not to be blamed. . . .[41]

Obviously, Le Corbusier didn't quite share this view. More or less at the same time he baptized a new type of skyscraper the "gratte-ciel cartésien"; for him to ask the rhetorical question "Descartes était-il américain?" (Was Descartes American?) was meant as the highest possible praise of the "American spirit."

On the other hand, among the concerns that inspired the corporatist and fascist *redressement* in which Le Corbusier was to participate quite actively, anti-American resentment seems to have played a considerable role. Not by coincidence, the magazine *Plans*, whose editorial board counted Le Corbusier among its members, picked up the line of thought indicated by Aron and Dandieu's book, and in May

1932 it published an article by A. Alexandre that opens with the following statement: "Aujourd'hui nous ne croyons plus en l'Amérique (Today we don't believe in America anymore).[42] Whatever Le Corbusier's share in these discussions may have been, they reinforced the violent ambiguity with respect to the New World that had already characterized his numerous references to American engineering and to American office towers in the early issues of *L'Esprit Nouveau*.

It was not until October 1935 that Le Corbusier sailed on the *Normandie* to the United States, whose skyscrapers and grain silos had so often served to illustrate or clarify his arguments in his articles and books. On the evening of his arrival in New York he surprised the local press by stating that "the skyscrapers [of New York] are too small.[43] Later he added:

> It is a catastrophe, but a beautiful and worthwhile catastrophe . . . America is not negligible! Compared with the Old World, she has established, after twenty years, the Jacob's ladder of modern times.

His prose reaches a climax of enthusiasm when he attempts to evoke the "violent silhouette" of the city as it appears to him at sunrise on a clear day: "like a fever chart at the foot of a patient's bed."[44]

His book entitled *Quand les cathédrales étaient blanches*, which bears the subtitle *Voyage au pays des timides*, summarizes Le Corbusier's violent and contradictory response to the American reality and the American dream.

> I return from the United States. Good! On the example of the USA, I want to show that although the times are new, the houses are uninhabitable. The table has not yet been cleared after the meal; the leftovers of the departed banquet guests remain—congealed sauces, carcasses, wine stains, bread crumbs and dirty dishes.[45]

With a characteristic mixture of fresh insight and a patronizing display of cultural superiority this ambassador of the Old World offers his advice on traffic congestion and sprawl, downtown development, and regional planning. Much of what the book contains is a repetition of what Le Corbusier had said earlier in articles, lectures (of which he gave twenty-three in twenty cities during his travels through the United States), and interviews.

In fact, the coverage given by the press to his visit to New York was extraordinary and may have disturbed some of his American colleagues (Figure 21).[46] Despite this, the hoped-for flood of important commissions never occurred. The New Deal had no use for a Colbert from the Old World; it ascribed more importance to good technicians and managers. Le Corbusier's New York proved to be yet another crusade that ended in disaster, for it was based on a tragic misconception of the possible role of the architect in an advanced industrialized society governed by liberalism and big money.

Notes

1. For illustrations, see Brian Brace Taylor's important study, *Le Corbusier at Pessac, 1914–1928* (Paris: Spadem, 1972), pp. 6–7. On Hellerau, see Kristiana Hartmann, *Deutsche Gartenstadtbewegung: Kulturpolitik und Gesellschaftsreform* (Munich: H. Moos, 1976), pp. 46–101, and on Charles-Edouard Jeanneret's early houses in La Chaux-de-Fonds, see S. von Moos, *Le Corbusier: Elements of a Synthesis* (Cambridge, Mass.: MIT Press, 1979), pp. 6–20; figs. 2–6, 10–26.

2. Charles-Edouard Jeanneret, *Etude sur le mouvement d'art décoratif en Allemagne* (New York: Da Capo, 1968, c1912).

3. See H. Allen Brooks, "Jeanneret and Sitte: Le Corbusier's Earliest Ideas on Urban Design," in *In Search of Modern Architecture: A Tribute to Henry-Russell Hitchcock,* ed. Helen Searing (Cambridge, Mass.: MIT Press, 1982), pp. 278–297. I am grateful to Professor Brooks for having allowed me to consult his article before it went to press.

4. Le Corbusier, *Quand les cathédrales étaient blanches* (Paris: Plon, 1965, c1937), p. 58. On the role of Sitte's book, see George R. Collins and Christiane Crasemann Collins,

Camillo Sitte and the Birth of Modern City Planning (New York: Random House, 1965).

5. Quoted in H. Allen Brooks, "Jeanneret and Sitte," p. 282.

6. Le Corbusier, *Urbanisme* (Paris: Crès, 1925), p. 25.

7. Brian Brace Taylor, pp. 14ff.

8. *Urbanisme,* p. 65; the Laugier quotation is from *Observations sur l'architecture* (Farnborough: Gregg, 1966, facsimile of 1765 edition), p. 312f.

9. *L'Esprit Nouveau* 1, reprinted in Le Corbusier, *Vers une architecture* (Paris: Crès, 1923), p. 20.

10. See S. von Moos, p. 62f.; figs. 35f.

11. In *The Blindman* 2 (May 1927), quoted by Bernhard Schulz, "Made in America," in *Traum und Depression, 1920–1940* (exhibition catalogue), Berlin, 1981, pp. 72–137.

12. Le Corbusier, *L'Atelier de la recherche patiente* (Paris: Vincent, Fréal, 1960), pp. 62–64.

13. *Urbanisme,* p. 135.

14. Ibid., p. 265.

15. Ibid., p. 272. Le Corbusier suggests here, in other words, treating the important monuments of the past as "objets trouvés" or, to quote his own terms, as "objets à réaction poétique" within the vast open spaces of the new city. The cultural and ideological implications of this approach were discussed by Manfredo Tafuri in *Teorie e storia dell'architettura* (Bari: Laterza, 1970, c1968), pp. 68ff.

16. *Urbanisme,* p. 3.

17. Ibid., quoted from the English translation, *The City of Tomorrow* (Cambridge, Mass.: MIT Press, 1971, c1929), p. 5.

18. P. Girardet, "Le règne de la vitesse," *Mercure de France,* 1923; quoted in *Urbanisme,* p. 182.

19. Fondation Le Corbusier, box A1 (7).

20. Fondation Le Corbusier, box A2 (13). See also in this context S. von Moos, "Standard und Elite. Le Corbusier, die Industrie und der 'Esprit Nouveau,'" in Tilmann Buddensieg and Henning Rogge, eds., *Die nützlichen Künste* (Berlin: Quadriga, 1981), pp. 306–323. I am grateful to the Fondation Le Corbusier for having allowed me to consult its archives. They, in fact, contain a great deal of interesting advertising material from the Michelin factory. The role of Michelin as a promotor of Fordist and Taylorist ideology in postwar France and Le Corbusier's response to these issues have been studied by Thilo Hilpert, *Die funktionelle Stadt. Le Corbusiers Stadtvision—Bedingungen, Motive, Hintergründe* (Braunschweig: Vieweg, 1978), pp. 39–50.

21. I am, of course, referring to Sigfried Giedion's famous chapter on the Chicago School in *Space, Time, and Architecture* (Cambridge, Mass.: Harvard University Press, 1974, c1941), pp. 368–396. For a more recent and less partial assessment, see Wiliam H. Jordy, *American Buildings and their Architects. Progressive and Academic*

Ideals at the Turn of the Twentieth Century (Garden City, N.Y.: Doubleday, 1972).

22. D. H. Burnham and E. H. Bennett, *Plan of Chicago* (New York: Da Capo, 1970, c1909).

23. See Peter M. Wolf, *Eugène Hénard and the Beginnings of Urbanism in Paris, 1900–1914* (The Hague: Ando, 1968), pp. 49–60. Hénard's plan is illustrated in *Urbanisme*, p. 111.

24. See in this context H. Altvater's scheme of a huge wheel resting on the roofs of skyscrapers (1931) in Martin Greif, *The Airport Book: From Landing Field to Modern Terminal* (New York: Smith, 1979), p. 77.

25. Hénard's term, however, is *boulevard à redans*. He gives two versions of this type: the *boulevard à redans* with alternating rectangular blocks and squares along the boulevard and the *boulevard à redans triangulaires*. It is perhaps no coincidence that Le Corbusier's respective renderings follow so closely the layout of Hénard's. See S. von Moos, fig. 147, p. 225.

26. *Urbanisme*, p. 270.

27. Le Corbusier, *Oeuvre complète, 1910–1929* (Zurich: Girsberger, 1929), p. 111.

28. Norma Evenson, "Yesterday's City of Tomorrow Today," in *Le Corbusier Archive*, ed. H. Allen Brooks (New York: Garland Publishing, 1982–), vol. 15, *Le Modulor and Other Buildings and Projects, 1944–1945* (1983), p. xv. See also her earlier assessment of Le Corbusier's critics in *Le Corbusier: the Machine and the Grand Design* (New York: George Braziller, 1969), pp. 120–122. On avant-garde art as an "early warning system," see Marshall McLuhan, *Understanding Media: The Extensions of Man* (New York: McGraw-Hill, 1965), introduction.

29. Le Corbusier, *Précisions sur un état présent de l'architecture et de l'urbanisme* (Paris: Crès, 1930), p. 238.

30. Ibid., p. 244.

31. For a critical discussion of the project see Giorgio Piccinato, *L'architettura contemporanea in Francia* (Bologna: Cappelli, 1965), pp. 62–66, and Manfredo Tafuri, *Progetto e utopia* (Bari: Laterza, 1973), pp. 115–137. The most encompassing study on the project is Mary McLeod's article on "Le Corbusier and Algiers," *Oppositions* 19/20 (1980), pp. 55–85.

32. See Marco Pozzetto, *La Fiat-Lingotto. Un'architettura torinese d'avanguardia* (Turin: Albra, 1975).

33. *Oeuvre complète 1929–1934* (Zurich: Girsberger, 1934), pp. 44–65.

34. Le Corbusier, *Aircraft* (London: The Studio, 1935), introduction.

35. Antoine de Saint-Exupéry, *Terre des hommes* (Paris: Gallimard, 1957, c1939), p. 72. See S. von Moos, "Le Corbusier as Painter," *Oppositions* 19/20 (1980), pp. 89–107, for more references.

36. *Oeuvre complète 1934–1938* (Zurich: Girsberger, 1938), pp. 74–77.

37. See in this context Kenneth Frampton's study "The City of Dialectics," *Architectural Design* 10 (October 1969), pp. 541–546, and Robert Fishman, "From the Radiant City to Vichy: Le Corbusier's Plans and Politics, 1928–1942," in *The Open Hand*, ed. Russell Walden (Cambridge, Mass.: MIT Press, 1977), pp. 244–283.

38. See Jean-Louis Cohen, "Cette mystique, l'URSS," *Architecture, Mouvement, Continuité* 49 (1979), pp. 75–84, and "L'Architecture en France entre le spectre de l'urbanisme et le halo des recherches soviétiques," in *Paris-Moscou* (exhibition catalogue), Paris, 1979, pp. 272–285. For references to earlier studies, see my *Le Corbusier*, pp. 143–154, 206f.

39. The following three books were to summarize these experiences: Le Corbusier, *Sur les 4 routes* (Paris: Gallimard, 1941), *La Maison des hommes* (Paris: La Palatine, 1965, c1942), and *Les Trois établissements humains* (Paris: Denoël, 1945).

40. *The New York Times,* January 3, 1932, magazine section. Rem Koolhaas's book *Delirious New York* (New York: Oxford University Press, 1978), pp. 199–233, gives a brilliant interpretation of Le Corbusier's reaction to New York.

41. R. Aron and A. Dandieu, *Le cancer américain* (Paris: Rieder, 1931), p. 82; the earlier quotes are from pp. 16 and 17.

42. A. Alexandre, "USA 1932," *Plans*, May 15, 1932, pp. 12–16.

43. *Quand les cathédrales étaient blanches*, p. 61. The incident is actually reported by the *New York Herald Tribune*, October 22, 1935. But the *New York Times* of the same day reported that "Of New York in particular Mr. Le Corbusier was not able to speak, having seen the city so far only from the ship's deck and hurrying taxicabs."

44. *Quand les cathédrales étaient blanches*, p. 52.

45. Ibid., p. 7.

46. See in particular H. I. Brock, "Le Corbusier Scans Gotham's Towers. The French Architect, on a Tour, Finds the City Violently Alive, a Wilderness of Experiment Towards a New Order," *The New York Times*, November 3, 1935.

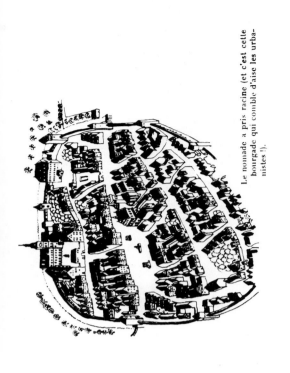

Figure 1. Cité-jardin aux Crétets, 1914. Photograph courtesy of H. Allen Brooks.

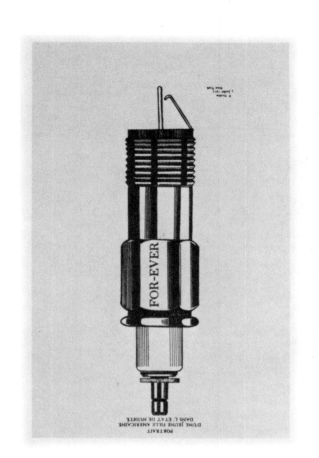

Le nomade a pris racine (et c'est cette bourgade qui comble d'aise les urbanistes!).

Figure 3. Charles-Edouard Jeanneret, view of a medieval town (from *Urbanisme*).

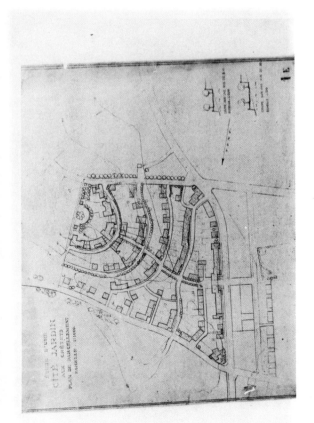

Figure 2. Charles-Edouard Jeanneret, Villa Fallet, La Chaux-de-Fonds, 1906–1907. Photograph courtesy of H. Allen Brooks.

Figure 5. Francis Picabia, "Portrait d'une jeune fille américaine dans l'état de nudité." From *291*, 5/6.

Figure 6. Michelin advertisement.

Figure 7. Le Corbusier, *Une ville contemporaine*.

trois rappels à
MM. LES ARCHITECTES

L'architecture n'a rien à voir avec les « styles ».

Les Louis XV, XVI, XIV ou le Gothique, sont à l'architecture ce qu'est une plume sur la tête d'une femme ; c'est parfois joli, mais pas toujours et rien de plus.

L'architecture a des destinées plus graves ; susceptible de sublimité elle touche les instincts les plus brutaux par son objectivité ; elle sollicite les facultés les plus élevées, par son abstraction même. L'abstraction architecturale a cela de particulier et de magnifique que se racinant dans le fait brutal, elle le spiritualise, parce que le fait brutal n'est pas autre chose que la matérialisation, le symbole de l'idée possible. Le fait brutal n'est passible d'idées que par l'ordre qu'on y projette. Les émotions que suscite l'architecture émanent de conditions physiques inéluctables, irréfutables, oubliées aujourd'hui.

Figure 4. Title page of Le Corbusier's first article in *L'Esprit Nouveau* 1 (1920).

Figure 8. Advertisement in *L'Esprit Nouveau.*

Figure 9. Burnham & Co., Reliance Building, Chicago, 1890, 1894–1895 (from S. Giedion, *Space, Time, and Architecture*).

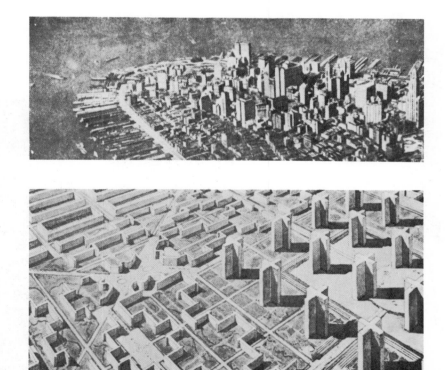

Figure 10. The "Contemporary City" and Manhattan compared (from *L'Esprit Nouveau* 28).

Figure 11. Burnham Plan for Chicago.

Figure 12. Le Corbusier, "Contemporary City," 1922.

Figure 13. André Basbevant, project for an airport to be built on top of the center of Paris, 1924. Photograph courtesy of Fondation Le Corbusier.

236

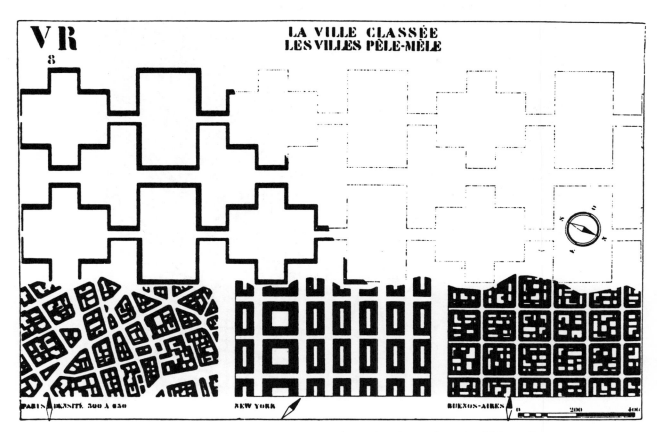

Figure 14. Le Corbusier and Pierre Jeanneret, apartment blocks *à redents* (from *La Ville radieuse*).

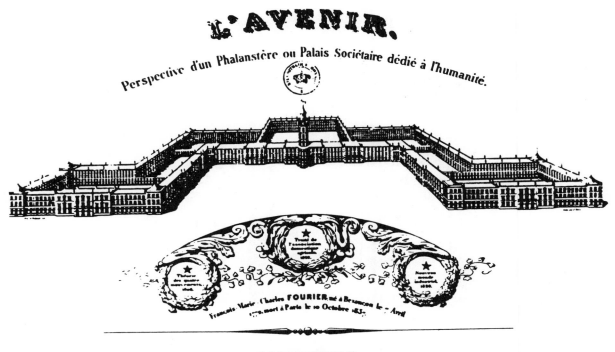

Figure 15. Victor Considérant, a phalanstery after Charles Fourier's Theory, 1840.

Figure 16. Le Corbusier, sketch plan of Rio de Janeiro (from *Précisions*).

Figure 17. Le Corbusier's "Plan Obus" for Algiers and the
Fiat test track compared (from *Oeuvre complète*, 1929–1934).

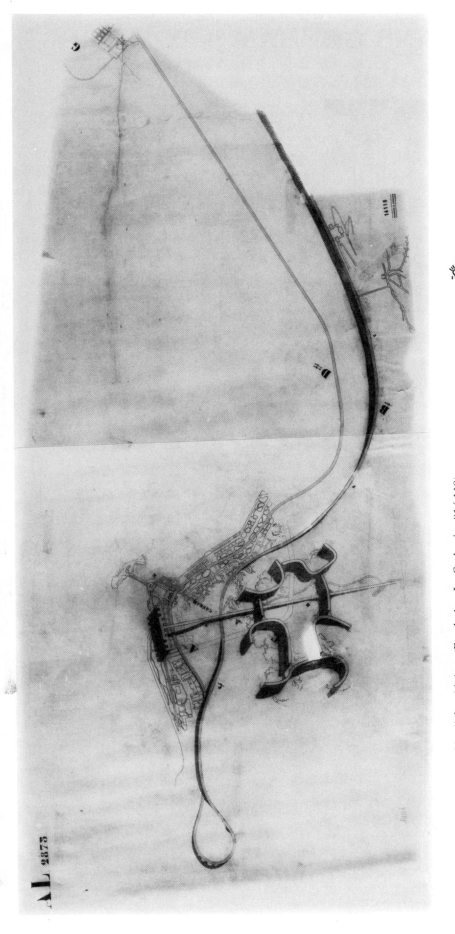

Figure 18. Le Corbusier, "Plan Obus" for Algiers (Fondation Le Corbusier #14.118).

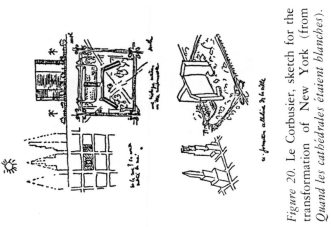

Figure 20. Le Corbusier, sketch for the transformation of New York (from *Quand les cathédrales étaient blanches*).

Figure 19. Le Corbusier, *Alma Rio 36*, oil on canvas, 1949. Photograph collection Heidi Weber, Zurich.

LE CORBUSIER SCANS GOTHAM'S TOWERS

The French Architect, on a Tour, Finds the City Violently Alive, a Wilderness of Experiment Toward a New Order

The City of the Future as Le Corbusier Envisions It.

By H. I. BROCK

THE citizen of the French Republic who is known as Le Corbusier—he was born Jeanneret and his given name is Charles-Edouard—is just now paying his first visit to America and has had his first eyeful of the man-made miracle which is New York. In circles where disputing about art is a major sport, Le Corbusier is identified as the founder and public exponent of the mood in architecture which has been labeled the International Style and which certain stiff conservatives insist does not look like architecture at all.

The basic principle of this style is to regard the architect's function as primarily one of household efficiency engineering. His job is to furnish human creatures with a convenient "machine for living in." As stated, the principle applies specifically to the family dwelling. But it applies also to the multiple arrangement of buildings which takes care of the composite employments and the complex human activities of a city where great numbers of people must live and most of them attend to business.

Since the modern dwelling and the modern city have each new demands to meet, since each has at command a service of machinery and materials which no dwelling and no city has ever had before, Le Corbusier and his school begin by discarding traditions and dismissing prejudices which would perpetuate formulas of building evolved from conditions of life that have ceased to exist.

* * *

THE rough idea is that the machine age, with its vast concentrations of population and its prodigious accumulation of mechanical devices for quantity production and for mass movement of goods and men, has created problems which the older architecture is incompetent to solve. The new architecture must face these problems squarely and find a solution on a sound mechanical basis, let the chips of academic estheticism fall where they may.

New York City, for example, is planted thick with skyscrapers—filing cases of millions of human beings at work or stowed away for the night. The streets of New York are jammed with automotive vehicles engaged in distributing the quantity-production output or moving these millions of people about, back and forth between home and business, and generally where they want to go, creating in the process no end of traffic tangles and even seriously endangering in life and limb those who still have to get about on their own feet.

Le Corbusier has built in France and other European countries machines for living in—machines also for doing business in. Whether these machines are, in fact, more efficient than the houses other architects build is a question which will not be argued here. But it is true that, at three years short of 50, he is more famous as the articulate

Too Small?—Yes, Says Le Corbusier; Too Narrow for Free, Efficient Circulation.

voice of the new architecture than as the executant of its projects. He represents a vision of the future rather than a proved practice of the present.

* * *

MODERN architecture—that is, machine-made architecture—was born, as even its most ardent European advocates admit, in this country. The Europeans who have taken it up have made it much more "modern" than we have dared or cared to make it. Nevertheless, New York—the part of it, at least, which enjoys high visibility—is the creation on the greatest scale that the world knows of the new architecture which is our own. That architecture pierces the sky with pinnacles that lift the level of our rocky little island (which in a state of nature could not boast a really respectable hill) into rivalry with the lesser mountains.

Le Corbusier, from the deck of the giant liner Normandie, looked up the harbor and saw (as he says) afar off a dream city hanging in the blue sky above the horizon of the water—a vision of enchantment. He went below for déjeuner and came up again with the solid substance of the vision right on top of him. He was appalled by the brutality of the great masses—the "sauvagerie"—the wild barbarity of the stupendous, disorderly accumulation of towers, trampling the living city under their heavy feet, like a herd of mastodons.

As the ship moved up the river and he got the city broadside on, as the clutter of bunched towers of the stronghold of finance thinned out and other towers began to stand out separate, gleaming in the sunlight in the open space above their lowlier neighbors, his dispondency abated. Hope revived for the future which the first bright vision had seemed to embody. That vision might not, after all, be a mirage.

* * *

LATER, while touring the city in the company of the writer, he stood at the base of the steep sheer cliff of Raymond Hood's slat in Rockefeller Center and said that it was good, then began ruefully to rub the crick out of the back of his neck that was the result of trying to look up to the very top of anything so tall and uncompromisingly perpendicular.

He found the smaller buildings on the Fifth Avenue front—dedicated to France and the British Empire—out of scale, both with the upreared mass and the human beings walking about the central plaza. That plaza itself, all bare (as it is apt to be when the tourist season is on the wane), struck him as decidedly dull—in spite of Prometheus and his fountain.

Then he was shot in an elevator (at the rate of 1,200 feet a minute) to the very top of the big slat—the deck under which lurks the Rainbow Room—and looked out upon the map of the city, by that time half veiled in a soft gray mist, which cut off the horizons far short of the two extremes of our narrow island but revealed the bounding ribbons of water on either side.

North, south, east and west, the skyscrapers nevertheless stood out boldly. Now and again the sun thrust through the thin clouds and bathed their faces in a brief glory of high light or gilded the fancy tops which some of them have borrowed from all the styles—unimportant to M. Le Corbusier—that came before the steel skeleton revolutionized large-scale building. It was excellent theatre—spectacular drama.

* * *

BUT the modern architect was not particularly impressed. He was looking for architecture, not theatre, and shy, besides, of succumbing to drama so melodramatic. Moreover, he was looking for architecture in his own sense of the word—in this case, the city that is a machine for living in—not merely frightfully expensive scenery built to knock the beholder's eye out.

"They are too small," he said, looking straight at the Empire State Building, tallest in all the world of filing cases for men and standing on one of the biggest pieces of ground devoted to that purpose in the city.

Somebody pointed out a building with "modern" horizontal lines, belting continuous windows about it, down by the Hudson, and a building with "modern" vertical lines, stacking up windows in parallel slits, over toward the East River.

"I am not interested," said Le Corbusier, "in that sort of thing—both sets of lines are all right as expressing the idea of horizontal and vertical circulation respectively. But what counts is the actual existence in the building of the two kinds of circulation and their efficient coordination. That is the combination which creates adequate machines for business for swarms of people—human beehives—if it is joined, of course, with free circulation among the buildings."

The skyscrapers that thrust up

(Continued on Page 23)

New York Times Studios

© Andre Steiner

Le Corbusier Looks—Critically

Figure 21. "Le Corbusier Scans Gotham Towers," *New York Times Magazine*, November 3, 1935.

Yesterday's City of Tomorrow Today
by Norma Evenson

Depending on one's point of view, the years following World War II may be regarded as a time of notable failure or a period of resounding success for Le Corbusier's urban concepts. Although in Europe and elsewhere a period of rapid urban growth and renovation was underway, Le Corbusier's career as a city planner seemed marked by continuing frustration. Yet, ironically, while Le Corbusier himself was denied important urban commissions, a wave of new construction swept the world, sufficiently evocative of his visionary schemes as to be widely attributed to his influence.

During the 1920s and 1930s, Le Corbusier had come to be associated with the image of a geometrically ordered, open-textured urban fabric characterized by motor freeways, widely spaced office towers, and apartment housing set amid expansive areas of greenery. Having formulated these concepts in the 1922 exposition project, The Contemporary City for Three Million (Figures 1 and 2), Le Corbusier provided variations on the same theme in the Voisin Plan of 1925, the Radiant City of 1930, and a series of unbuilt projects. When his book *Urbanisme* was published in 1925, Le Corbusier had assured his readers, "I do not propose to bear witness in the highways and byways as though I belonged to the Salvation Army."[1] This, however, is precisely what he did with unflagging conviction for the length of his career, tirelessly entering every available competition, repeatedly offering his services to government officials, and promulgating his ideas through writing and lecturing.

Resuming practice after the interruption of the war years, Le Corbusier sought to adapt his favored design formula to the rebuilding of several towns damaged during the fighting. For the bombed town of Saint-Dié, he produced a plan in 1946 incorporating a new civic center flanked by a series of large apartment houses and combined with a rebuilt industrial district. Although the scheme was exhibited and praised in the United States and Canada, it found no official acceptance in France. According to Le Corbusier, the plan was "unanimously rejected by the upper, middle, and lower classes, the socialists, the communists, etc. The Ministry of Reconstruction did not press the matter."[2] Similar fates met plans for the redevelopment of La Rochelle-Pallice (1945–1946), Saint-Gaudens (1945–1946), and Meaux (1956–1957). Included in Le Corbusier's unbuilt projects was a competition design submitted in 1958 for rebuilding the center of Berlin. "The time had come," Le Corbusier believed, "to take advantage of forty years of study and experimentation in architecture and planning."[3] The proposal, which included widely spaced slab buildings and a system of separated motor and pedestrian circulation, was, according to the architect, "an excellent design conforming with the principles advocated by CIAM for thirty years."[4] Le Corbusier was convinced that its rejection was based on his insistence that Unter den Linden be restricted to pedestrians. "But the jury decreed that the 'Linden' be covered with automobiles as in all the rest of the world."[5]

Persisting in his conviction that urban housing needs could best be served by apartments, rather than by single-family houses, Le Corbusier incorporated such blocks (sometimes termed "vertical garden cities") in all of his schemes. One such plan was developed for Marseille, the site of his well-publicized *unité d'habitation*. The *unité* had initially been projected as one of a series of apartment slabs, accompanied by tower blocks, clusters of row houses, and communal facilities. An expanded version of this concept was developed for South Marseille in 1952.

Included in the Marseille project was a system of street classification based on function, which Le Corbusier termed the *sept voies*, or "seven V's," and which he considered to be universally applicable. In the seven V sequence, the V1 represented a regional road, and the V2 a major urban artery. The V3 was intended to carry fast motor traffic around residential superblocks, while the V4 would provide a shopping street. The V5 and V6 streets would give access to individual dwellings. (The V6 could take the form of an "internal street," or corridor in an apartment house.) Situated within parkland, the V7 would provide pedestrian circulation to schools, clubs, and sport grounds.

The seven V system was also embodied in a planning study for Bogotá in 1950. This scheme included the creation of a civic center combining new high-rise administrative buildings with existing historic monuments and surrounded by districts of high-rise apartments. Incorporated in the plan was a schematic residential superblock 800 by 1200 meters in dimension, containing a grid pattern of streets combined with cruciform park bands. A master plan based on Le Corbusier's study was developed by José Luis Sert and Paul Lester Wiener. Although initially granted official approval, execution of the scheme was hampered by changes in political administration.

In general, Le Corbusier's postwar efforts added little to his reputation as an urbanist. They introduced no new ideas and in presentation lacked the verve and imagination of his earlier schemes. The plans with which Le Corbusier had first achieved renown had been purely visionary designs conveying a seductive overall impact free from utilitarian concerns. Le Corbusier as an artist had taken an olympian view of urban form, and his early schemes portrayed not cities, but ideas about cities. Allowing himself a certain poetic license, he outlined possibilities, simplifying the complexity of urban function for dramatic effect and frequently leaving unfilled the gap between image and reality. The postwar proposals, envisaged for specific sites and developed with the hope of realization, seem, in comparison, rather pedestrian—even boring. Nowhere in these proposals does one find the lyrical response to site embodied in the elevated roadway schemes projected for Rio de Janeiro in 1929 or Algiers in 1930. Nowhere is there the comprehensive vision reflected in the Contemporary City or Radiant City projects. During this period, Le Corbusier's career as an architect provides a notable contrast to his career as an urbanist.

Departing dramatically from the aesthetic of the International Style, Le Corbusier's postwar architecture was infused with a new plasticity of form and emotional expressiveness, and his innovative use of exposed concrete inspired a major trend in modern building. His postwar urban designs, however, merely rework his old ideas of spatial composition and building type.

Ironically, when Le Corbusier finally got a chance to participate in a large-scale, fully realized urban project, it was in circumstances totally removed from the ambient for which he had normally projected his schemes. This opportunity occurred with the creation of Chandigarh, the new capital of Punjab in India. His contribution to Chandigarh, however, was primarily as the designer of the major monumental buildings. A master plan for the city had been completed in 1950 by the American firm of Mayer, Whittlesey, and Glass, and Le Corbusier had been engaged in 1951 as an architectural consultant, together with his cousin Pierre Jeanneret and the British architects Maxwell Fry and Jane Drew. The existing plan, as developed by Mayer, represented a synthesis of currently accepted design concepts and incorporated functional zoning of major activities, residential superblocks comprising neighborhood units, and a system of pedestrian and motor separation. A government complex was projected at the outer edge of the city. Le Corbusier and his colleagues had been engaged to execute this plan, not to create a new one.

As to what Le Corbusier might have produced in Chandigarh had he been involved in the initial planning, one may only speculate. Certainly it would be hard to find an environment more alien to his characteristic urban vision. The means for large-scale mechanized transport did not exist, economic factors and technical limitations would make high-rise building unfeasible, and both climate and traditional living patterns militated against apartment housing. The principal building material of the city was to be brick, with reinforced concrete a luxury material to be used only in major buildings. Although early drawings by Le Corbusier for Chandigarh show attempts to insert high-rise building into the government complex and also into the commercial center, there was no possibility at the time for such structures to be realized. Relatively low in density and dominated by two-story brick terrace houses, Chandigarh bears a resemblance to the British New Towns of the immediate postwar period (see Figure 3).

While he concentrated his efforts on the creation of the capitol complex, Le Corbusier attempted some modifications in the Chandigarh master plan. He geometricized the major streets, which, in the Mayer plan, had exhibited a slightly curving grid, and classified streets according to the seven V system. Although this system had been devised for a motorized environment, it was deemed suitable as a device to separate the varied conveyances and speeds of Indian transport. As the volume of motor traffic in Chandigarh has continued to be low, however, the segregation of transport implied in the system has yet to be put into effect (see Figure 4).

By coincidence, the residential district included in the Mayer plan had essentially the same dimensions as the 800 by 1200 meter superblock Le Corbusier had projected for Bogotá. This dimension, together with the population densities projected by Mayer, was retained in the Chandigarh plan, although Le Corbusier made some alterations in sector layout. Each sector was to be bisected by a bazaar street (the V4) instead of containing separate bazaar areas as in the Mayer plan. A loop road (the V5) would serve as the main distributor of internal traffic, while linear parks would create continuous bands of greenery through the central portion of the sectors.

In addition to projecting the schematic outlines of the street system and residential sectors, Le Corbusier also concerned himself with the planning of the central commercial sector of Chandigarh. This district was developed to include a series of broad pedestrian promenades focusing on a large central plaza. The architectural character of the district was unified through a standardized four-story concrete building carrying external balcony corridors.

While reflecting a low-rise, unmechanized ambient, Chandigarh embodies certain qualities long associated with Le Corbusier's work. The city is a controlled environment with a disciplined unity of building form. In Chandigarh, government housing follows a pattern of standardized designs, and private housing is architecturally controlled. Neighborhood shops are built to prescribed designs, and in the central commercial district, a potentially competitive and varied architecture has been contained within a regimented envelope (see Figure 5). The relative monotony of the Chandigarh townscape, while not directly attributable to Le Corbusier, may be seen to exemplify many of his concepts. As the most celebrated member of the planning staff, Le Corbusier, perhaps inevitably, is often credited with the total design of Chandigarh and blamed for every flaw.

In view of Le Corbusier's long concern with urban design, it may seem strange that, having at last been given the opportunity to realize a city plan, he would largely abdicate responsibility for its development. Just as in his earliest schematic designs he had placed emphasis on the large-scale generalized aspects of the city, making little attempt to develop the more intimate texture, so in Chandigarh Le Corbusier restricted his efforts to delineating the major outlines of the plan and to creating the monumental government complex. He may have found the programmatic and technical restrictions of the project too hampering to justify a total involvement on his part. He had been unwilling to abandon Paris for an uninterrupted residence in India and may have felt that his associates, residing on the site, would be better qualified to establish the small-scale urban pattern. He may have sensed that his talents and predilections were primarily those of a monumental architect and thus chosen to dedicate himself to the sphere in which he excelled.

244 Yesterday's City of Tomorrow Today

The design of Chandigarh has been abundantly criticized, but whether the city would have been better or worse had Le Corbusier directed personal attention to the details of its planning remains unclear. It could be argued that his fondness for baroque expansiveness combined with his long-term obsession with the industrialized city had rendered him unsympathetic to the functional workings and aesthetic subtlety of the traditional Indian environment. Yet there is evidence that Le Corbusier was not totally insensitive to the indigenous building practices of hot, dry climates. In his North African travels he had admired and sketched Arab towns and houses, observing the dense ground coverage, the narrow streets, the buildings with blank external walls and sheltered internal courtyards. While his schematic designs consistently portrayed an open pattern of building, in Algiers he had praised the "pure and efficient stratification of the Casbah," pointing out that "among these terraces which form the roof of the city, not an inch is wasted."[6] One cannot predict with certainty what Le Corbusier might have produced in Chandigarh had he elected to study local conditions and develop detailed sector layout and housing design. As Chandigarh now exists, it owes to him only its skeletal outlines, while the flesh and substance have been created by others.

Although Le Corbusier felt resentment throughout his career because of the failure of officialdom to recognize and adopt his planning concepts, his greatest bitterness seemed always directed toward the authorities of his adopted home, Paris. When *The Radiant City* was reissued in the 1960s, a drawing of the Voisin Plan (see Figure 6) contained the following addition to the caption: "Since 1922 (for the past 42 years) I have continued to work, in general and in detail, on the problem of Paris. Everything has been made public. The City Council has never contacted me. It calls me 'Barbarian.'"[7]

Le Corbusier had always berated Parisian officials for their timidity and failure to attempt truly bold achievements. In 1935 he had written, "Paris fills me with despair. That once admirable city has nothing left inside it but the soul of an archaeologist. No more power of command. No head. No powers of action."[8] As the postwar era progressed, however, Parisian planning policies underwent a notable change, and by the mid-1960s, Paris may have been a source of despair to some, but not because of stagnation. Municipal planners were at last acting boldly and enthusiastically embracing the concept of urban renewal as a means of revitalizing the city. The rhetoric of the CIAM even found its way into official planning documents. The 1967 Paris master plan made specific references to "the doctrines of the Athens Charter, which introduced *urbanism of the ensemble*, where individual works form part of large development plans" and where projects would be oriented toward "structures of great height, with deliberately simple lines. . . ." It was predicted that *"the aspect of the city will change.* One will no longer go about between parallel walls, in these corridors, the streets, but in spaces alternating with buildings and greenery."[9]

Le Corbusier's Voisin Plan had proposed the redevelopment of a portion of central Paris into a new high-rise business district. This was to be accompanied by a motor expressway cutting through the city from east to west. Although in 1925 such a proposal might have seemed an improbable fantasy, by the time of Le Corbusier's death in 1965 the scheme might have been viewed as prophetic. Le Corbusier's Voisin Plan had incorporated the old market site of Les Halles. Contemplating a redevelopment of the same site in 1967, city officials commissioned a group of architectural studies including skyscraper proposals of such a scale as to make Le Corbusier's plan look rather commonplace.

By the mid-1950s, a wave of major transformation was underway in Paris, and in succeeding decades the traditional urban scale of many districts would be obliterated by high-rise apartment and office clusters. The tallest building in Europe appeared in the form of a glass-walled tower in Montparnasse, and the Port Maillot, for which Le Corbusier had envisaged a skyscraper complex in 1929, was punctuated by a hotel tower in 1971 (see Figures 7, 8, 9). The monumental axis of Paris was culminated at Le Défense by a new skyscraper business district, while mammouth new apartment communities, the *grands ensembles*, burgeoned in the populous suburbs. Motor expressways began to ring the city and cut through the center, sending speeding vehicles along the banks of the Seine.

Poor Le Corbusier. No wonder he was bitter. Everyone got a chance to build Le Corbusier's city but Le Corbusier himself.

The most thoroughgoing evocation of the Contemporary City for Three Million appears in Brasilia, the new capital of Brazil, designed by Lucio Costa and begun in 1956. This city comprises a cross-axial plan in which a sweeping motor freeway intersects a classically ordered government axis by means of a multilevel transport center. Bordering the central motorway are residential superblocks containing standardized apartment slabs raised on *pilotis* and situated amid open spaces (see Figures 10, 11, 12). The business center flanking the transportation hub provides clusters of unified high-rise building. To some, Brasilia seems a synthesis of all the weaknesses of a formalist approach to city planning, although the unusual circumstances of its creation may have made the conception of the city primarily as a large architectural project inevitable. In spite of the criticism leveled at the plan, moreover, the overall imagery of the city may be appropriate to its founders' intentions. The motorized scale of Brasilia, with its visual emphasis on freeways and traffic interchanges, must be seen against the prevailing lack of technical advancement in Brazil in the 1950s. Brasilia visually symbolized a degree of mechanization that Brazil had not achieved but sought as a national goal. (It was President Kubitschek, the founder of Brasilia, who had promoted the automobile industry in Brazil.) The architecture of Brasilia embodies many of the surface qualities associated with the International Style, an easily acquired and popularly recognized symbol of up-to-dateness. With its wide motor roads and glossy buildings, Brasilia is the apotheosis of the glass box, presenting an image that even the most unsophisticated can proudly identify as "modern."

Seen without prejudice, moreover, Brasilia has its moments of beauty. Le Corbusier once stated, "The materials of city planning are sky, space, trees, steel and cement."[10] These are the basic ingredients of Brasilia and seem, in certain ways, appropriate to its expansive setting on the great central plain of Brazil. Le Corbusier wrote of the joys of rapid driving on motor expressways, of the perception of "immensity of space," of "vast architectural perspectives, with the sky everywhere, as far as the eye can see."[11] Brasilia reflects an effort to settle and subdue a wilderness, visibly evoking Le Corbusier's description of a city as the "grip of man on nature."[12] Oscar Niemeyer, the chief architect of Brasilia, acknowledged Le Corbusier's inspiration by including in the government complex a grove of palm trees dedicated in his honor. Le Corbusier, in turn, assured Niemeyer that "I think often of you and your magnificent work. Bravo."[13]

Brasilia is, of course, not everyone's cup of tea and can be criticized on a variety of grounds. The questionable social segregation of the Contemporary City, which concentrated the elite in the central city and the workers in so-called *cités-jardins*, is reflected in Brasilia, where the poor are segregated in "satellite" towns outside the center. The result is onerous commuting for many, as well as a Potemkin-village quality in the city itself. The rigid zoning of building types and activities that enhanced the visual impact of Le Corbusier's drawings has obvious weaknesses when consistently applied in a real city. Brasilia, like the Contemporary City, appears to the eye as a single work of art, each part subordinate to the whole. Yet the result may be a serious sacrifice of urban function to the fetish of visual unity. Both the Contemporary City and Brasilia reflect a certain naïveté with regard to the automobile. Freeway driving may have its charms, but only under ideal conditions. Brasilia's expressways by no means solve the problem of traffic circulation, and the accompanying problem of parking worsens daily. And yet, generally speaking, Brasilia works. Which is to say, it works the way all cities work, which is to say, badly. Life somehow goes on, and in spite of its vast spaces and antiseptic architecture, Brasilia is not a dead city. Although many traditional elements of urban form are lacking, Brasilia does not want for human vitality.

Although the most thoroughgoing, Brasilia is not the only example of a type of design characterizing the postwar period. A rapid pace of urban renovation all over the world has reflected the concepts of Le Corbusier's visionary schemes, and although unable to realize his own projects, he has attracted increasing blame for everything monotonous and overscaled in the urban environment. The drawings of the Contemporary City, the Voisin Plan, and the Radiant City are more widely reproduced than ever before, and Le Corbusier's ideas, often deliberately garbled, are repeatedly invoked by critics in order to be denounced.

Lewis Mumford observed that Le Corbusier's "Cartesian elegance" had been counterbalanced by his "Baroque insensitiveness to time, change, organic adaptation, functional fitness, ecological complexity, . . . his sociological naïveté, his economic ignorance, and his political indifference. These very deficiencies were, as it turned out, what made his City of the Future such a successful model for world-wide imitation; its form reflected perfectly the financial, bureaucratic, and technological limitations of the present age."[14]

Writing in 1962, Mumford declared the imagery of the Contemporary City, which he termed "Yesterday's City of Tomorrow," to have been the dominant influence in architecture and planning schools for thirty years. According to Mumford, "The chief reason for Le Corbusier's immediate impact lies in the fact that he brought together the two architectural conceptions that separately have dominated the modern movement in architecture and city planning: the machine-made environment,

standardized, bureaucratized, 'processed,' technically perfected to the last degree; and to offset this the natural environment, treated as so much visual open space, providing sunlight, pure air, green foliage, and views." Deeming the result of this fusion a "sterile hybrid," Mumford concluded pessimistically that "perhaps the very sterility of Le Corbusier's conception was what has made it so attractive to our age."[15]

Similar denunciations of Le Corbusier's influence appeared in the writing of Jane Jacobs. "Le Corbusier's dream city has had an immense impact on our cities. It was hailed deliriously by architects, and has gradually been embodied in scores of projects . . . His city was like a wonderful mechanical toy. Furthermore, his conception, as an architectural work, had a dazzling clarity, simplicity and harmony. It was so orderly, so visible, so easy to understand. It said everything in a flash, like a good advertisement. This vision and its bold symbolism have been all but irresistible to planners, housers, designers, and to developers, lenders and mayors too."[16]

Although Le Corbusier has been a convenient target for critics, the extent of his personal influence on the course of urban development is not easy to assess. Certainly Le Corbusier did everything he could to promote his concepts during his lifetime. Yet it should be remembered that within the modern movement, he never stood completely alone. No architect, however persuasive and determined, could single-handedly mold the sensibilities of an entire profession throughout the world. One is sometimes led to believe that Le Corbusier is directly responsible for every present-day example of misapplied functional zoning, destructive motor expressways, insensitive urban renewal, overscaled urban parkland, regimented apartment housing, and monotonous glass-walled skyscrapers. Le Corbusier, after all, originated none of these things. He was a synthesizer, rather than an inventor. His visionary urban designs reflected prevailing currents in the thinking of architects and urbanists.

Le Corbusier produced his seminal schemes at a time when the apparent problems of spontaneous urban growth seemed to call for comprehensive planning. In this context, many modern architects conceived their legitimate role as organizing the large-scale urban environment. Perceiving a growing cultural unity within the industrialized world, they sought to develop universal prototypes, favoring a simple geometric ordering and standardized building types. Modernists tended to see the high-density centralized city as the natural habitat of contemporary society and to view tall buildings as the inevitable result of technical advancement and concentrated populations.

Many of the attributes of Le Corbusier's design could be seen in the work of other architects during the 1920s and 1930s. Regularly aligned, uniform slabs and towers appeared in the projects of Bauhaus designers and many of the Soviet architects. The haunting images of Hugh Ferris, based on widely spaced skyscrapers and multilevel roadways, ignore the niceties of intimate urban scale fully as much as Le Corbusier's projects. Americans who had never heard of Le Corbusier could have seen many of his concepts in the General Motors exhibit by Norman Bel Geddes at the 1939 World's Fair. Le Corbusier was not the only architect, moreover, to propose skyscrapers in Paris. Auguste Perret had suggested a tower at the Port Maillot as early as 1905, and during the 1920s and 1930s, suggestions for high-rise complexes in the French capital recurred periodically in the popular press.

If Le Corbusier's visionary urban designs became better known, and thus more influential, than those of other modernists, it is because they were more comprehensively developed and had far greater visual appeal. Le Corbusier may, perhaps, be blamed for his skill in making bad ideas look good. While some observers condemned Le Corbusier's over-simplification of urban form and function, others found his designs a convincing balance of essential urban ingredients. The modern city had been widely deplored for its congested building patterns and chaotic mixtures of activity, the residue of a century of untrammeled growth. To architects seeking an alternative to laissez faire development, the superficial lucidity of Le Corbusier's city may have looked almost all right.

The relative palatability of Le Corbusier's visionary designs compared to those of other modern architects, however, by no means explains the impact that he is widely acknowledged to have had. Why does so much of the contemporary environment look as though it had been directly inspired by his drawings? It may relate less to conscious imitation than to the prophetic qualities Le Corbusier's designs possessed. Le Corbusier was the messenger who brought a certain type of bad news. He did not present an ideal city, but the city that might logically result given certain circumstances. These circumstances included economic prosperity, technical advancement, expanding urban population, rising space standards in housing, increase in automobile usage, a belief in the benefits of open space, an acceptance of high-rise building, and above all, faith in the virtues of large-scale urban planning. If Le Corbusier had never lived, would the contemporary environment be vastly different? One is inclined to doubt it.

If the physical formula associated with Le Corbusier has found wide application, it may be in part because his schemes anticipated an economic transformation that has come about in many modern cities. Le Corbusier envisaged the city as the focus of a white-collar elite, an administrative center from which industry was exiled. The simplification of building type seen in his work implied a reduction in the complex balance of productive activity that previously characterized the urban fabric. Le Corbusier's prototypical city was a city of office workers, and the ease with which his vision was adapted in Brasilia may correspond to the capital city's restricted function as an administrative center.

Viewed in retrospect, Le Corbusier's visionary schemes seem to epitomize that optimistic peak of the modern movement marked by confidence in the splendors of a dawning new age. As the honeymoon of man and machine persisted, it remained possible to derive a romantic excitement from automobiles, airplanes, and tall buildings. It was possible for architects to imagine that redesigning the city would accord with progress, and the new architectural imagery was accepted by many as a symbol of both technical and social advancement.

In our own time, characterized by an increasing disillusionment with the benefits of unrestricted technical development and industrial growth, yesterday's symbols of modernity may understandably fail to seduce. As images of technical advancement, moreover, Le Corbusier's visions were surpassed, in the 1960s, by the striking concept of the megastructure, far more daring in its technical implications, physical scale, and population density. At a time when avant-garde architects were contemplating the housing of urban populations in towers of prefabricated capsule units or in underwater colonies, Le Corbusier's urban schemes might have been seen to embody a traditional, relatively permanent order and manageable size. Le Corbusier had always stressed that he was no Futurist and that his ideas were immediately realizable. Like the modern architecture of the 1920s, Le Corbusier's urban concepts gave existing technology a new symbolic packaging. The success of his imagery lies in part in the relative ease with which it could be built.

The ubiquitousness of urban design reflecting Le Corbusier's ideas supports the contention of early modernists that they had achieved a universal mode of design. Although Le Corbusier had been deemed a bourgeois formalist in the Soviet Union and a communist by some western critics, his conception of urban environment has in the long run proved equally appealing to both socialist bureaucrats and profit-mad capitalists. Le Corbusier had projected his visionary schemes for a highly industrialized society. The visual qualities of his urban plans can, however, be reproduced without technical underpinnings. The standardized forms of Brasilia do not come from standardized components; the machine aesthetic is

achievable without machines. It seems apparent that although Le Corbusier's open-textured urban form was initially conceived for northern Europe, it can be erected, however inappropriately, in any geographic area and inhabited, however awkwardly, by any cultural group. One of the most commonplace observations of international travelers is that the world looks more and more the same.

The apparent persistence of Le Corbusier's influence on the built environment has been accompanied by increasing condemnation of his concepts. In the literature of postmodernism, he has emerged as a semilegendary figure, a monomaniacal Frankenstein who, with virtually superhuman powers, directed the course of urbanism toward a mechanistic formalism and populated the earth with life-destroying monsters.

Le Corbusier's work has offered something for almost every type of critic, has attracted unfavorable mention from both decentrists and centrists, aesthetes and pragmatists, and has been attacked on visual, functional, and social grounds. Ignoring the wider aspects of city planning, Le Corbusier attempted to fit a complex social and economic organism within a simplified physical package, and the results have led many to reconsider the role of the architect in the formation of the city. Jane Jacobs, in her analysis of the workings of American cities, insisted that *a city cannot be a work of art. . . . To approach a city, or even a city neighborhood, as if it were a larger architectural problem, capable of being given order by converting it into a disciplined work of art, is to make the mistake of attempting to substitute art for life.*[17]

Although architects hold as an article of faith that their work closely conditions human life, not much is really known about the effect on people of their physical surroundings. Le Corbusier developed his concepts of urban form in response to the city as he knew it in Europe, especially Paris. He wished to provide an antidote to the familiar pattern of densely built, overcrowded, dilapidated, and disease-ridden structures that constituted the Paris slums. Convinced that his designs held the key to a healthier and more beautiful city, he noted with surprise, and perhaps even a bit of irritation, the good nature with which his fellow Parisians daily coped with less than ideal conditions. He reported, "In Paris I often walked through the district bounded by the Place des Vosges and the Stock Exchange— the worst district in the city and the most wretchedly overcrowded. Along the streets, on the skimpy sidewalks, the population moves in single file. By some miracle of group identification and the spirit of the city, *even here* people laugh and manage to get along, *even here* they tell jokes and have a good time, *even here* they make out!"[18]

In Paris today, many of the old slums are gone, having been supplanted by new housing, which is, perhaps, merely a different kind of slum. Freed from the fear of pestilence, provided with ample dwellings, sunlight, fresh air, and views, inhabitants of the new planned environment have not necessarily been removed from the problems of urban living.

Fastidious observers have come to view the uniformity and stupefying scale of new urban complexes as a chamber of horrors, and in retrospect, the old congested slums are nostalgically regarded as humane and vital neighborhoods. And yet, just as Le Corbusier was surprised to find people managing reasonably tolerable lives within the old city fabric, so one may also find evidence that the resilient human spirit has not been totally crushed by the visual regimentation of design formulas. Astonishing as it may seem, *even in Brasilia* people laugh and manage to get along, *even in the grands ensembles* they tell jokes and have a good time, *even in Co-op City* they make out!

There appears no question that in today's critical climate Le Corbusier's urban concepts are widely discredited. Yet it would be a mistake to conclude that the condemnation that he has received in certain circles necessarily heralds the disappearance of his influence and the universal abandonment of his design approach. There is always a time lag in the spread of fashion, and the wave of propaganda inspired by the modern movement continues to be felt in those societies that still view automobiles and glass-walled towers as signs of progress. The power of visual images has always defied logic, and in many parts of the world the old modernist symbolism still works. Like it or not, we may have Le Corbusier to kick around for quite a while.

Notes

1. Le Corbusier, *The City of Tomorrow* (London: The Architectural Press, 1947), p. 301. First published as *Urbanisme* (Paris: Crès, 1925).
2. Le Corbusier, *Oeuvre complète, 1946–1952* (Zurich: Girsberger, 1953), p. 13.
3. Le Corbusier, *Oeuvre complète, 1957–1965* (Zurich: Girsberger, 1965), p. 230.
4. Ibid. Beginning in 1928, the CIAM (Congrès Internationaux d'Architecture Moderne) were organized to provide modern architects with a forum for the discussion of issues relevant to contemporary design. Principles of city planning were defined in the Athens Charter produced by the fourth congress, held in 1933.
5. Ibid., p. 235.
6. Le Corbusier, *The Radiant City* (New York: Grossman, The Orion Press, 1967), p. 230. First published as *La Ville radieuse* (Boulogne/Seine: Editions de l' Architecture d'Aujourd'hui, 1935).
7. Le Corbusier, *The Radiant City*, p. 207.
8. Ibid., p. 177.
9. Atelier Parisien d'Urbanisme (APUR), "Une volonté de remodelage du cadre urbain de Paris: le règlement de 1967," *Paris Projet* 13–14 (1975): 37.
10. Le Corbusier, *The City of Tomorrow*, p. 177.
11. Ibid.
12. Ibid., p. xxi.
13. Quoted by Alex Shoumatoff in "The Capital of Hope," *New Yorker*, Nov. 3, 1980, p. 107.
14. Lewis Mumford, "Architecture as a Home for Man," *Architectural Record* 143 (February 1968): 114.
15. Lewis Mumford, "Yesterday's City of Tomorrow," *Architectural Record* 132 (November 1962): 141.
16. Jane Jacobs, *The Death and Life of Great American Cities* (New York: Random House, 1961), p. 23.
17. Ibid., pp. 372–73.
18. Le Corbusier, *The Radiant City*, p. 12.

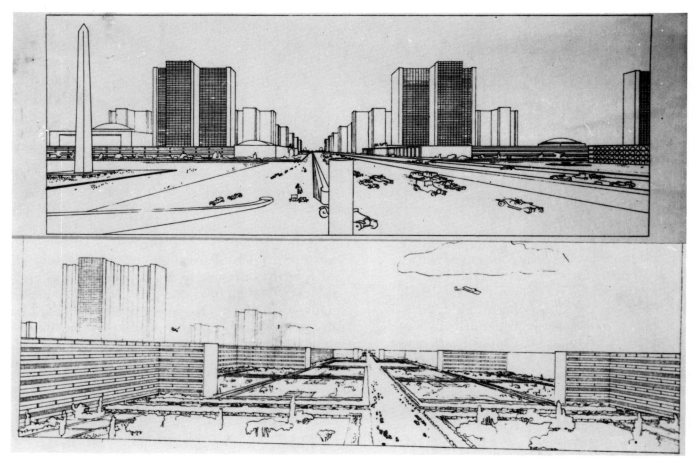

Figure 1 and 2. Fondation #29.712

Figure 3

Figure 4

Figure 5

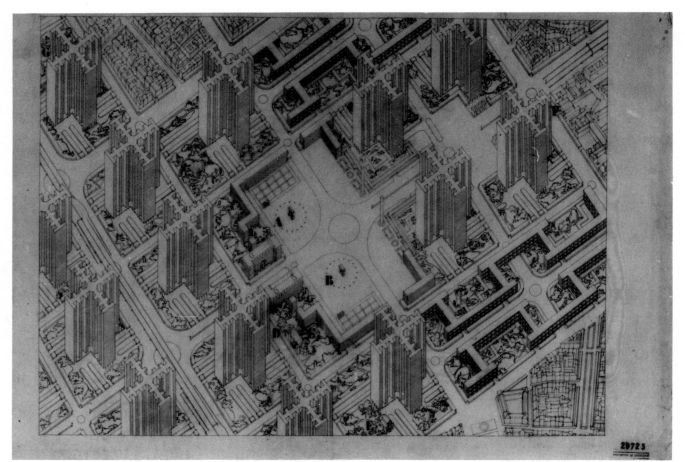

Figure 6. Fondation #29.723

Figure 7

Figure 8

Figure 9

Figure 10

Figure 11

Figure 12

Biographies of Contributors

The Editor

H. Allen Brooks is Professor Emeritus of Fine Arts at the University of Toronto where he had taught since 1958. He is a past president of the Society of Architectural Historians and former Guggenheim Fellow. His book *The Prairie School: Frank Lloyd Wright and His Midwest Contemporaries* received the Alice Davis Hitchcock Book Award in 1973. Other books include *Frank Lloyd Wright and the Prairie School*, *Writings on Wright* (ed.), *Prairie School Architecture* (ed.), and *The Le Corbusier Archive* (32 volumes), for which he served as general editor. He is currently completing a biography/architectural study of Le Corbusier's life and career prior to 1920.

Contributors

Reyner Banham, Professor of History of Art at the University of California at Santa Cruz, has been Advisor to the President's Urban Policy Seminar (1977) and to the Board of International Design Conference in Aspen, Colorado (1968–1978), and has received several international awards. His many publications include *Theory and Design in the First Machine Age* (1980).

Tim Benton is Senior Lecturer in the History of Art at the Open University, England. He has written widely on the history of architecture and design in the twentieth century, as well as the Renaissance in Italy and seventeenth-century architecture in England. For the Open University he has made numerous television programs, two of which have won international awards. He has written several articles on the architecture of Le Corbusier in the 1920s, and his book on Le Corbusier's Parisian villas, published in French and German editions (1984), will shortly appear in English. He contributed four rooms to the Le Corbusier exhibition in Lugano, Switzerland, and organized the major Le Corbusier exhibition in London (1987). Benton is also known for his fine architectural photographs.

Alan Colquhoun practices architecture in partnership with John Miller and R. J. Brearley and is Professor of Architecture at Princeton University. Colquhoun's work with Miller has been examined in *British Buildings* 1960–1964 (1965), and in several articles. Among his collaborative efforts are the Chemistry Building, Royal Holloway College, Surrey (England) and Forest Gate High School, London.

Charles Correa studied in the United States with Buckminster Fuller during the early 1950s and has been a practicing architect in Bombay since 1958. Unlike previous Western-educated architects, Correa has developed a modern architectural style consistent with the Indian climate and topography. His work has been recognized internationally, and he has been the subject of numerous books and articles. In 1984 he was the recipient of the RIBA Gold Medal. He has published articles in periodicals throughout the world.

Norma Evenson is Professor of Architectural History at the University of California at Berkeley. She has worked extensively in Brazil, India, and France. Her publication *Paris: A City of Change, 1878–1978* (1979) received the Alice Davis Hitchcock Award from the Society of Architectural Historians in 1980. Her recent study of the impact of Western architecture and urbanism in India is to be published by the Yale University Press.

Kenneth Frampton studied architecture at the Architectural Association School of Architecture in London. He is currently chairman of the Graduate School of Architecture and Planning, Columbia University. He has examined the history of modern architecture and its proponents in several articles and books. His most recent publications are *Modern Architecture, A Critical History* (1980) and *Pierre Chareau*, with Mark Vellay (1986).

Danièle Pauly teaches the history of architecture at l'Ecole d'Architecture de Strasbourg. She was in charge of cataloguing the drawings at the Fondation Le Corbusier from 1974 to 1977 and 1981–1982. Her many publications include *Ronchamp, lecture d'une architecture* and, with A. Kopp and F. Boucher *l'Architecture de la reconstruction en France*. She was an advisor on the publication of Le Corbusier's *Sketchbooks* and is a member of the comité scientifique of the Fondation Le Corbusier. She has participated in the organization of numerous exhibitions of Le Corbusier's work, including "Le Corbusier and the Patient Quest" (Lugano, 1980), "Le Corbusier, Aspects of the Late Work" (Karlsruhe, 1986), and, as part of the centenary celebrations of Le Corbusier's birthday, "Le Corbusier and the Mediterranean" (Musées de Marseille, 1987), and the retrospective, "Le Corbusier" (Centre Beaubourg, Paris, 1986), for which she was responsible for the section "Plastic Work."

Vincent Scully is the Colonel John Trumbull Professor of Art History at Yale University, where he has been teaching since 1947. His many important books include such titles as *The Shingle Style: Architectural Theory and Design from Richardson to the Origins of Wright, The Earth, the Temple, and the Gods: Greek Sacred Architecture, Frank Lloyd Wright, American Architecture and Urbanism*, and *Pueblo: Mountain, Village, Dance*.

Peter Serenyi is Professor of Architectural History and Chairman of the Department of Art and Architecture at Northeastern University in Boston. He is the editor and contributor to *Le Corbusier in Perspective* (1975). Serenyi has published widely on modern architecture and has organized several traveling exhibitions, including Contemporary Architecture in India (1976) and Le Corbusier in India (1980). He spent the 1984–1985 academic year in India preparing a book on modern Indian architecture.

Jerzy Soltan, Professor Emeritus of Architecture at Harvard University, has worked with Le Corbusier (1945–1949), with Pierre Jeanneret, as well as with Fernand Léger. He holds a degree in architecture from Warsaw University and has worked as a designer and architect in Poland and the United States. He has taught architecture in several countries, chiefly at the Academy of Fine Arts, Warsaw, and Harvard University. He was a member of the ASCORAL (CIAM France) and Team 10. He is also a member of the Akademie der Künste, Berlin.

Manfredo Tafuri is Professor of the History of Architecture and Director of the Dipartimento di Storia dell'Architettura of the Istituto Universitario de Architettura di Venezia. He is a scholar of Renaissance history and of contemporary art and architecture. His most recent books include *Theories and History of Architecture, Modern Architecture, La sfera e il labirinto, Vienna rossa, L'armonia e i conflitti, La chiesa di San Francesco della Vigna nella Venezia del '500* (with A. Foscari), *Raffaello architetto* (with C. L. Frommel and S. Ray), and *Venezia e il Rinascimento*.

Stanislaus von Moos is an art historian and currently Professor of the History of Modern Art and Architecture at the University of Zurich, Switzerland. He has published extensively on Italian Renaissance architecture (his book *Turm und Bollwerk. Studien zur politischen Ikonographie der italienischen renaissancearchitektur* appeared in 1974) and on Le Corbusier (the English version of his monograph appeared in 1979). Between 1970 and 1980 he served as the editor of the Swiss architectural magazine *archithese*.

André Wogenscky worked with Le Corbusier from December 1936 through 1956. He is Architecte en Chef des Bâtiments Civils et Palais Nationaux. He is an Officer of the Legion of Honor and an Officer of Arts and Letters. He has received a medal of honor from the Academy of Architecture and has published a book entitled *Architecture Active*. The 1985–1986 exhibition, André Wogenscky, Five Architectural Projects (Daniel Gervis Gallery, Paris), highlighted his latest projects in Japan, Saudi Arabia, and Lebanon, including Takarazuka Arts University (near Osaka, Japan), the House in the Wind (Faraya, Lebanon), and the Headquarters of the Arab Satellite Communications Organization at Riyadh (Saudi Arabia).

Iannis Xenakis was trained as a mathematician and worked in Le Corbusier's office as an engineer from 1947 to 1959. His work there included the Pavillon Philips at the 1958 World's Fair in Brussels. He is now best known as a music theorist and composer. His book *Formalized Music: Thought and Mathematics in Composition* was published in 1971. He is an Honorary Member of the American Academy and Institute of Arts and Letters (1975) and a member of the French Institute (1983) as well as several other academies.

Index

Admiralty Building (Algiers), 177-178, 194

A.E.G. Elektra Boathouse, AEG Turbine Factory (Behrens), 34, 59

Ahmedabad (India), 16, 163, 164-173; economic growth, 165; effect of Le Corbusier on, 173; history, 164-165; Jain family influence, 165-167; Management Institute (Kahn), 200; Mediterranean tradition and, 24; older houses in, 170; Sabarmati Power Plant cooling towers, 176. *See also* specific buildings, e.g., Millowners Association Building

Air India Company, 180 n.8

Alexandre, A., 230

Algiers: Admiralty Building, 177-178, 194; Casbah in, 210-211, 244; Le Corbusier's monumentalism, 25; Le Corbusier's replanning proposals, 23, 113, 242; Plan Obus, 207, 209, 211, 226-227; urbanism (Le Corbusier's) 23, 209-211

Allgemeine Städtebau exhibition, 33, 219

Alma Rio (Le Corbusier Painting), 36, 227-228, 239

Amigos del Arte, 225-226

Anti-Americanism, 230

Antwerp, Le Corbusier's plans for, 211, 228-229

Anzin (France), 206

Aragon (author), 214

L'Architecture Vivante (journal), 62, 67

Aron, Robert, 230

L'Art décoratif d'aujourd'hui (Le Corbusier), 178

L'Art de demain (Provensal), 30

ASCORAL (Assemblée de Constructeurs pour une Renovation Architecturale), 117, 229

ATBAT (Atelier des Bâtisseurs), 118, 143

L'Atelier de recherche patiente (Le Corbusier), 133

Atelier of Le Corbusier, 1-2, 10-11; *stagiairesat*, 13

Ateliers d'art réunis, 33, 35

Athenian Calf Bearer (Greek sculpture), 51

Athens Charter (*Charte d'Athènes*), 244, 249 n.4, 207

Aujame, Roger, 6, 10, 14, 16

Automobiles: Le Corbusier and, 222-224, 227-228; in *unité d'habitation*, 122

"Aux Cretéts," 219

Badovici, Jean, 14

Baizeau Villa (Tunis), 85-87, 168-169, plan, 97; sketches 100-101,

Baradari gardens (India), 181 n.48

Barcelona, Le Corbusier's plans for, 211, 228-229

Barthes, Roland, 24, 208

Basbevant, André, 224, 236

Basilica of Constantine, 174-175, 190

Bassompièrre de Rutte, 221

Bat'a, Jan, 217 n.35

Bat'a, Tōmas, 217 n.35

Bataille, Georges, 214

Baudelaire, Charles, 32

Bauhaus school, 247

Beaux-Arts Renaissance (American), 178

Beck, Arnold, 35

Behrens, Peter, 15, 219; Le Corbusier and, 33-34, 58-59; urbanism and, 220

Beistegui penthouse, 203-204, 207, 210, 212; roof garden, 51

Bel Geddes, Norman, 247

Benjamin, Walter, 214

Benoit-Lévy, George, 204

Bentham, Jeremy, 205

Berlage, H. P., 57

Bermudez, Guido, 115

Béton Brut, 52, 55; at Chandigarh, 175-177; mass housing, 112-113

Bibliothèque Nationale (Labrouste), 58

Bodianski, Vladimir, 10-12, 118, 143

Bogotá, Le Corbusier's proposals for, 242-243

Borie, Jules, 205

Brancusi, Constantin, 14

Brasilia (Brazil), 245-246, 248-249

Brazilian Pavilion (Paris), 146

Brise-soleils (sun-breakers): brutalism and, 53; at Chandigarh, 198, 213-214; Chandigarh Assembly Building, 176-177; Chandigarh High Court, 174-175; Currutchet house, 6-7, 9; as Le Corbusier signature, 24; Marseille mass housing, 8, 112-114; symbolism of, 169-170

Brooks, H. Allen, 219

Brutalism, 51-53. *See also Béton brut*

Buenos Aires: Le Corbusier's plans for, 211, 228-229; lectures, 83-84, 99; sketches, 99

Buls, Charles, 204

Bunshaft, Gordon, 112

Burnet, John (Sir), 57, 61

Burnham, Daniel, 178, 223; plan for Chicago, 223-224, 235-236

Café Legendre (Paris), 109, 168, 170; photo, 186

Le Cancer américain (Aron and Dandieu), 230

Candilis (associate of Le Corbusier), 11

Caravaggio, 48

Carpenter Center (Cambridge, Mass.), 86

Carrefour à giration (Hénard), 224

Cartesian skyscraper proposal, 228-229

Casbah (Algiers), 210-211, 244

Central Union of Consumer Co-operatives. *See* Centrosoyus

Centrosoyus (Moscow), 21, 61-63; circulation as theme, 63; Palace of Soviets and, 66; sketches, 78-79; urbanism and, 26 n.8

Cerro Grande, (Caracas—Bermudez), 115

Cerro Piloto, (Caracas—Bermudez), 115

Chambless, Edgar, 205, 227

Chandigarh (India): Assembly Building, 27, 39, 176-177, 191; cooling towers, 27; evaluation of, 173-179; failures assessed, 54, 198-200; heroic scale, 113; High Court, 173-175, 189, 198; hyperbolic tower, 176; impact on architecture, 197-202; Indian revisions of, 54-55; Lower House of Assembly Building, 176-177; Mediterranean tradition and, 24, 175; modern assessment, 242-244; monumentalism, 25; political context, 163-164; pool of Reflection, 213; Secretariat, 177-179, 193, 198; seven Vs concept, 212; undulating glass panes, 146; urbanism and, 23-24, 208, 212-214

Chapallaz, René, 29,31-32, 35-36

Charpentier, Théodore, 205

Charte d'Athènes. See Athens Charter

La Cheminée (Le Corbusier painting), 47-48

Chicago School of architecture, 35, 223-224

Chimanbhai, Chinubhai, 165-166

Chimanbhai house, 180 n.13

Chimneys as symbol in Le Corbusier's work, viii, 27, 38

CIAM (Congrès Internationaux d'Architecture Moderne), 244, 249 n.4

Cingria-Vaneyre, A., 34, 37

Circulation motif: Centrosoyus, 63; Villa Savoye, 85

Cité industrielle (Garnier), 220

Cité Napoléon (Paris and Lille), 205

Cité de Refuge, (Salvation Army Hostel—Paris), 21-22, 108, 205-206; communal elements,

113; Seconde Mode format, 110-111; urbanism, 26 n.8, 108, 209, 212

Citroën motors, 222

Citrohan house type, 49-50, 109

Citrohan, Maison, 109, 168; as a design concept, 49-50, double-storied space, 170-171; impact on Sarabhai house, 172

Cittá Nuova (Sant'Elia), 222

Ciudad Lineal (Soria y Mata), 108

Civilisation machiniste, 206

Clarté block (Geneva), 110

Classicism of Le Corbusier, 17-19, 48-50; League of Nations, 57-61; urbanism and, 208, 212

Claudius-Petit, Eugéne, 119

Coates, Wells, 108

Cohen, Jean Louis, 61

Collective organization in mass housing, 120-121

Collectivist ideology, 206

Communalization of services, 8, 108-110, 114; in *unité d'habitation* (Marseille), 121

Considerant, Victor, 60, 242, 237

Considerations sociales sur l'architectonique, 60

"La Construction des villes" (Le Corbusier), 33, 35, 219

La Construction Moderne (magazine), 107-108

Contemporary City for Three Million project, 241, 245-246

Cook Villa, 167, 180 n.19

Le Corbusier *See* Le Corbusier.

Correa, Charles, 173

Costa, Lucio, 111-113, 245

Cottage cooperative concept, 107-109

Couturier (Father), 16, 143

Creation Is a Patient Search (L'Atelier de la recherche patiente) (Le Corbusier), 27-28, 133

Crépin (landscape designer), 96 n.56

Crow metaphor used by Le Corbusier, vii, 70 n.1

Cubism, 8, 17, 20

Currutchet house, 6-7, 9, 16

Curtis, William, 86

Dadaism, 115, 221

Daly, César, 205

Dandieu, Arnaud, 230

de Foville, Alfred, 206

Delacroix, Eugène, 210

Delage motors, 222

Deleuze, Gilles, 49

Delhi embassy (Stone), 197

Delos motif in Le Corbusier's architecture, 143-144

de Mandrot house (Le Pradet), 22, 50, 84

Dermée, Paul, 220

de Souza, Robert, 209

de Stijl architecture, 47, 168, 170, 174

Dioscuri, 58, 70 n.1

Dom-ino concept, 35, 50; mass housing, 108-109; urbanism and, 204, 207, 216 n.16, 219

Doshi, Balkrishna, 173

Drew, Jane, 212, 242

Dubois, Max, 35, 37

Dubreuil, Hyacinthe, 217 n.35

Duchamp, Marcel, 221, 227

Durand development project (Algiers), 211

Ecole d'art (Chaux-de-Fonds), 28, 34-35

Edmond & Wanner, 110

Eiffel Tower, 67

Einaudi, Luigi, 204

Einstein, Albert, 125

Ema, monastery at (Italy), viii, 31, 34, 114; Charterhouse of, 138; Charterhouse of, 138; collectivization at, 121; influence on La Tourette, 144

English common law, impact on Le Corbusier's designs, 174-175

Les Entretiens de la Villa du Rovet (Cingria-Vaneyre), 34

L'Eplattenier, Charles, vii, 24, 28-29, 31-33, 37, 207, 219; hires Le Corbusier for Ecole d'art, 34-35; Monument of the Republic, 34

Errazuriz house, 22, 169

L'Esprit Nouveau (journal), vii, 36; anti-Americanism, 230; illustrations from, 234-235; influence on Le Corbusier's urbanism, 220-221; theory of architecture in, 17-25; urbanism and, 222-223

L'Esthétique des villes (Buls), 204

Étude sur le mouvement d'art decoratif en Allemagne (Le Corbusier), 34, 219

Études sur les transformations de Paris (Hénard), 204

Evenson, Norma, 225

Evreinov, Nikolai, 65-66

Fallet house, 29-30; sketches, 39-40, 233

Familistére, 215 n.7

Family hearth image of Le Corbusier, 49

Family units in mass housing, 120. *See also* Mass housing

Fatehpur-Sikri, 202

Favre-Jacot house, 35; sketch, 43-44

Femmes d'Alger (Delacroix painting), 210

Fenêtre en longueur: League of Nations, 60; Villa Savoye, 60, 84, 88, 90

Ferris, Hugh, 247

FIAT factory (Turin), 227

Fibonacci series, 10, 124

Fiedler, Konrad, 17

Firminy, Le Corbusier at, viii, 3, 16, 119; aesthetics of, 54; Maison des Juenes, 146

First National Bank Building (Detroit), 178, 195

Fischer, Theodor, 33

Fishman, Robert, 110

Five points concept of Le Corbusier, 50-51; Centrosoyus and, 62-63; urbanism and, 207, 216 n.16; Villa Savoye, 85

Flaubert, Gustav, 32

Fondation Le Corbusier archives, ix-x, 127-128

Fort l'Empéreur, drawing for a *redent* at, 113

Fourier, Charles, 107, 205

France, Anatole, 204

Fraternity Temple (Chicago—Sullivan), 223

Frey, Albert, 89

Frugès, Henri, 107-108

Fry, Maxwell, 212, 242

Furness, Frank, 52

Futurists, 208

Gabriel, A.J., 60

Gahura, František, 217 n.35

Gallis, Yvonne, 169

Gandhi, Mahatma, 163, 165, 177, 179

Garches, Villa. *See* Stein-Monzie Villa

Garden City movement, 108, 110, 112

Garnier, Tony, 220

GATEPAC group, 229

Gateway of India (Bombay), 164

Gaudet, Julien, 58

Geddes, Patrick, 202

General Motors exhibit at 1939 World's Fair, 247

Geneva, Le Corbusier's plans for, 228

Gérando, J.-M., 205, 215 n.9

Gestalt psychology, 20-21

Ghyka, Matila, 10

Gillion, Kenneth, 165

Ginzburg, Moisei (Moses Ginsburg), 65, 108, 229

Girardet, Phillipe, 222

Girsberger (Le Corbusier publishers), 9

Glass panes, undulating, in Le Corbusier's work, 144-146

Godin, J. B., 205

Golconda (India), 200, 202

Golden Module. *See* Le Modulor

Gothic Revival, 52

Grammar of Ornament, The (Jones), 29

Les Grands Inities (Schuré), 30

Greek mythology: Le Corbusier's use of, 70 n.1. *See also* Classicism

Gregotti, Vittorio, 134

Gropius, Walter, 21, 47, 110; Palace of Soviets competition, 64

Guattari, Felix, 49

Guebwiller, 206

Gueguen, Pierre, 14

Hadjidakis (associate of Le Corbusier), 11

Hamilton, Hector, 65

Hanning, Gerald, 1-2, 4, 7-8, 10, 12

Harrison, Wallace, 12

Hassenpflug, G., 65

Haussmann, Baron, 221-222, 224

Hegel, Georg, 18

Hegemann, Werner, 219

Heidegger, Martin, 210

Heidi Weber Pavilion, 55

Hellocourt (Bataville), 217 n.35, 229

Hénard, Eugène, 204, 209, 224; boulevard à rédans, 232 n.25

Hilbersheimer, Ludwig, 21

Hirsch pavilion (Neuchâtel observatory), 33

Historicism in Le Corbusier's architecture, 17-18, 134-135

Hitchcock, Henry-Russell, 47

HLM building industry, 114

Hoffmann, Joseph, 31-32, 57

Hood, Godley and Fouilhoux, 229

Horta, Victor, 57

House of the Tragic Poet (Pompeii), 19

Howard, Ebenezer, 108, 206

Howe, George, 229

Human dimensions and architectural design, 10-11, 15-16; *unité d'habitation* (Marseille), 113, 123-125

Hutheesing, Surottam, 165-168

Hutheesing Jain temple, 170, 186

Ideal City (1922), 49

Immeubles-villas concept, 49; Ema monastery and, 31; Marseille mass housing, 107-109, 111, 113-114; recessed terraces, 171

India: impact of Chandigarh on, 199; political history, 163-165; village house, 192

Individualism in mass housing, 119-120

International Style, 15, 47-48, 50, 229

Iofan, Boris, 65

Isokon apartments (London), 108

Jacobs, Jane, 246, 248

Jain culture's influence on Le Corbusier, 165-167, 173

Jain temples (Ahmedabad), 164

Jansen, Hermann, 33

Jantar Mantar observatory, 164

Jaoul, Maisons, 51-52

Jaquemet house, 31-32; sketch, 41

Jeanneret, Charles-Edouard. *See* Le Corbusier

Jeanneret, Pierre, 3, 212; Barcelona study, 229; Centrosoyus, 61; Chandigarh, 242; La Tourette, 145; Palace of Soviets, 66-70; Parc de l'Ariana project, 63-64; Villa Savoye, 87-89

Jeanneret-Perret house, 35; impact on Shodhan house, 163; sketch, 42

Johnson, Philip, 47

Jones, Owen, 29

Kahn, Albert, 54, 178

Kahn, Louis, 200

Kanvinde, Achyut, 173

Katsura Palace, 200

Khrushchev, Nikita, 199

Kline, Franz, 54

Klipstein, Auguste, 34

Klipstein, Felix, 35

Krupp factories, 108

Kunstwollen concept, 18

Labrouste, Henri, 58

La Celle-St.-Cloud weekend house, 172

La Chaux-de-Fonds, Le Corbusier's early housing at, 29-32, 35-36, 41, 43-45, 206, 233

Ladowsky, N., 64-65

Lagardelle, Hubert, 208

Lalbhai, Kasturbhai, 165-166

Lahore (India), 163

Lamour, Philippe, 208

Lance, Adolphe, 204-205

Lannemezan house, 169, 172; photo, 185

La Roche-Jeanneret, Maison, 49, 83, 171; plan, 97

La Rochelle-Pallice, 6, 11, 13, 241

La Sainte-Baume basilica (proposed), 114, 129

La Scala cinema (La Chaux-de-Fonds), 36; photo, 44

La Tourette Monastery, 3; acoustics, 147; aesthetics of, 54; architectural theory and, 25; assessment of, 143-147; atrium, 144; electronic bells, 147; "light guns", 146; Mediterranean tradition and, 24; organ at, 147; overview, 152; photos of, 148, 152, 156-159; as satire, 114-115; sketches, 149-155, 157, 159-162; undulating glass panes, 144-146

Laugier, Abbé, 19, 208-209, 220

League of Nations, 12, 21-22, 51, 57-61, 177; Centrosoyus and, 61-62; *fenêtre en longeuer*, 60; influence on Chandigarh, 177; modern technique in, 59-60; Palace of Soviets and, 69; Parc de l'Ariana site, 63-64; *passerelle bicyclette*, 60; sketches, 71-77

Le Coeur, François, 168

Le Corbusier (Charles-Edouard Jeanneret): Ahmedabad and, 173-175; *les angoisses de la création*, 4; apartment at Porte Molitor, 51, 110; apprenticeship with Perret, 32-33; atelier in Paris described, 1, 10-11; and Behrens, 33-34, 58-59; birth and early life, 28-29; on Bolshevism, 65; on Brasilia, 245; Buenos Aires lectures, 83-84, 99; central European trip, 34; Chandigarh. *See* Chandigarh; classicism of. *See* classicism of Le Corbusier; *conception paysagiste*, 61; correspondence with M. Savoye, 93-94, 95 nn.26-28; creative process analyzed, 127-135; on Cubism, 17; design parameters, 19; double-storied space, 109, 170; drawing as memory, 133-134; dualism (practical vs. ideal), 57, 70 n.1, 89; early work, 29-30, 35; at Ecole d'art, 34-35; L'Eplattenier and, 24, 28-29, 31-35, 37, 207, 219; on feminine-masculine characteristics in architecture, 172; German trip (1910-1911), 33-34; house-palace transposition, 60; Icarus complex, 214; Indian architecture assessed, 163-179; indifference to building costs, 88-89; Italian trip, 34; leaves La Chaux-de-Fonds for Paris, 35-37; literary influences on, 30, 32-33, 204; on mass housing, 107-116; medievalism of, 32-34; modern architecture and, 241-249; New York trips, 178-179, 230; *objets`a réaction poétique*, 128-129; painting and sculpture, 20, 211-212; personality traits, 3-4, 27; photos, 42; Picasso and, 14-15; political views and architecture, 3, 110-111; porportions grid, 124; postwar work, 22-25; post World War II aesthetics, 51-52; pseudonym adopted, vii, 70 n.1; public building designs, 21-22; regionalism in early work, 28-29; rejection of industrial aspects of architecture, 22-23; research strategy, 9; retina separation, 47-48; roof gardens, 166; Second Mode format, 111-112; sketchbooks of India, 164; sketches and notes on Ronchamp, 127-130; sketches of Chandigarh High Court, 173-174; South American trip, 225-228; texts and drawings as research tools, 127-135; theories on architecture, 17-25; Third Mode, 112-113; *tracés régulateurs*, 34; United Nations building proposal, 11-12; urbanism, 21, 47-55, 203-214; work habits, 1-2, 4-7, 12-14, 117-119, Wright and, vii-viii

Le Creusot (France), 206

Lefèvre, Jacques, 118

Léger, Fernand, 3, 14

Lemaresquier, Charles, 57

Lenin, Nikolai, 208

Le Play, Frédéric, 206

Les Halles market site (Paris), 244

Lescaze, William, 229

Le Thoronet, monastery at, 54

Lever House (Bunshaft), 112

Libera, Adalberto, 68

Loucheur legislation, 110

Loucheur, Maisons, 91-92

Lucas, Charles, 204

Lunacharsky, Anatole, 61, 69

Lurcat, André, 113

Luytens, Edwin (Sir), 25, 164, 202; Viceroy's garden, 164

Lyon, Gustave, 68

McGraw-Hill Building (New York), 229

Machine à habiter, 49, 204-205

Machine aesthetic in Le Corbusier, 17-20, 50-51, 55 n.3; in League of Nations, 59-60; Palace of Soviets, 69

McLuhan, Marshall, 225

Maillard, Elisa, 10, 124

La Maison des hommes, (Le Corbusier), 112-116

Maison Minimum, 91-92

Les maisons en série, 107

Malraux, André, 51

Management Institute (Ahmedabad—Kahn), 200

Mandu (India), 202

Mao Tse-tung, 201

Marseille: forebuildings, 113; housing, 11; *unité d'habitation* 52-53, 69. *See also Unité d'habitation*

Marty (Dr.— acoustical specialist), 68

Mass housing, Le Corbusier on, 107-116; cross-over duplex, 116 n.3; family units in, 120; individualism in, 119-120; pavillionaire approach, 110. *See also Unité d'habitation*

Mathes house, 22

Les Matins à Florence (Ruskin), 30

Mattè-Trucco, Giacomo, 227

May, Ernst, 21, 23, 229

Mayer, Albert, 163, 212, 242-243

Mayer, Whittlesey and Glass, 242

Meaux redevelopment plan (France), 241

Mediterranean tradition in Le Corbusier's architecture, 24, 170, 175, 181 n.42

Meinecke, Friedrich, 18

Melnikov, Konstantin, 64

Mendelsohn, Erich, 64, 229

Metastasis (musical composition by Xenakis), 145

Meyer, Hannes, 22, 229

Meyer Villa, 86

Meyer-Wittwer League of Nations Design, 66

Meyerhold, V., 65

Michelin and Le Corbusier, 222-224; advertisement, 234 231 n.20

Mies van der Rohe, 47-48, 55 n.4, 163

Miljutin, N., 229

Millowners Association Building (Ahmedabad), 164, 166-167, 180 n.18, 197; photo, 183

Minimalwohnungen blocks, 110

Misére des villes, 114-116

Model building, Le Corbusier's use of, 6-7

Le Modulor, 10, 145-146; human dimensions and, 10-11, 15-16, 113; Soltan recalls, 10-12; *unité d'habitation* (Marseille), 117, 123-125

Le Modulor (Le Corbusier), 10, 114

Modulor 2, (Le Corbusier), 145-146

Mogul Empire in India, 164-165; impact on Chandigarh designs, 174

Mohanlal Chunilal house, 187

Moholy-Nagy, Sibyl, 198

Molotov, V. M., 64

Monastic tradition in Le Corbusier's architecture, 114-116. *See also* Ema

Mondrian, Piet, 168

Monocular vision, Le Corbusier and, 48, 55 n.2

Monol, Maison, 168, 172

Monument to the Martyrs of the Indian Partition (Chandigarh), 181 n.46, 213

Monumentalism in Le Corbusier architecture, 24-25, 107-109

Monuments érigés en France`a la gloire de Louis XV (Patte), 220

Monzie Villa. *See* Stein-Monzie Villa

Morin (acoustical scientist), 68

Morris, William, 29

Moser, Karl, 57

Mulhouse (France), 206

Mumford, Lewis, 246

Mundaneum's World Museum (Geneva), 166

Museum of Knowledge (Chandigarh), 181 n.46

Museum of Modern Art (New York), 229

Museum of Unlimited Growth (Ahmedabad), 166, 183

Musical analogies, 143-145; in Le Corbusier's work, 19, 21. *See also* Le Modulor

Mussolini, Benito, 110, 208

Muthesius, Hermann, 33, 220

M'zab valley (Algiers): Le Corbusier influenced by, 132-135; mosque at, 140

National Institute of Design (Ahmedabad), 166

Nehru, Jawaharlal, 163-164, 177, 179, 197, 213

Nenot (competing architect, *Société des Nation*), 63

Neoplatonism, 24

New York City, Le Corbusier and, 178-179, 239

New York Times, article on Le Corbusier, 229, 240

Niemeyer, Oscar, 12, 111-113, 245

Nietzsche, Friedrich, Le Corbusier influenced by, 30, 32, 207, 214

Objets à reaction poètique, Beistegui penthouse, 204

Ocampo Villa, 86

Oeuvre complète 1910-1929 (Le Corbusier) viii, 27, 62, 83-85, 87, 129, 219

Olbrich, Joseph Maria, 31

Open Hand (Chandigarh), 214, 217 n.37

Otlet, Paul, 64

Owatonna (Iowa), bank (Sullivan), 36

Ozenfant, Amédée, yii, 17, 27, 168, 220

Ozenfant house, 48-49, 180 n.19

Palace of the Soviets (Moscow), 21-22, 51, 64-70; acoustical shells, 68; air conditioning system, 69; Centrosoyus and, 63; hyperbolic arch, 67-68; influence on Chandigarh, 177; Palace Construction Council, 64-65; *plans inclinés*, 65-67; sketches, 80-81; urbanism, 209

Palladio, Andrea, influence on Le Corbusier, 36, 85

Panopticon, 205

Parc de l'Ariana project, 63-64

Paris: Le Corbusier's reform proposals, 244-245; Plan de Paris (1937), 229; urban reform plans of Le Corbusier, 221-222

Park Hill housing units (Sheffield, England), 115

Parker, Barry, 219

Passanti, Francesco, 55 n.1

Patiala gardens (India), 181 n.48

Patte, Pierre, 220

Paul, Bruno, 33

Pavillon de L'Esprit Nouveau, 31, 49, 171, 221; urbanism and, 203

Pavillon Suisse (Paris), 21, 53, 113; Centrosoyus and, 62; communal elements, 113; Second Mode format, 110-111

Le Paysan de Paris (Aragon), 214

Periscope device used by Le Corbusier, 203

Perret, Auguste, 32, 57-58, 223, 247; Palace of Soviets competition, 64

Perriand, Charlotte, 53

Perrin, Léon, 29-32, 35

Pétain regime, Le Corbusier's reaction to, 3

Picabia, Francis, 221, 233

Picasso, Pablo, 3, 14-15

Piero della Francesca, 15

Pierrefeu, François de, 112, 208

Pilotis: brutalism and, 53; urbanism and, 49-50; in Villa Savoye, 83, 86, 90, 93

Pinjore gardens (India), 164, 174, 181 n.48, 190

Piranesi, Le Corbusier on, 215 n.5

Plan Obus, 207, 209, 211, 226-227; sketches, 238-239

Plan Voisin, 221-222, 224-225, 241, 244-246

Plans magazine, 230

Poelzig, Hans, 64

Le Poème de l'angle droit (Le Corbusier), 173

Pont Butin (Geneva), 35

Pont du Gard (Provence), 175

Ponthieu garage (Perret), 32

Pool of Reflection (Chandigarh), 213-214, 217 n.37

Porta, Giacomo della, 36

Prairie School of architecture, 29

Précisions sur un état présent de l'architecture et de l'urbanisme (Le Corbusier), 60, 83, 226

Prelude group, 210, 217 n. 30

Prince's Gate Apartments, 116 n.3

Promenade architecturale, 92

Propos d'urbanisme (Le Corbusier), 131

Provelenghios (associate of Le Corbusier), 11

Provensal, Henry, 17, 30, 207

PSFS Tower (Philadelphia), 229

Public building design theory (Le Corbusier), 21-22

Puccini, Giacomo, 31

Pullman, George, 108

Purism, 48, 56, 67

Py, Marcel, 118

Quand les cathédrales étaient blanches (Le Corbusier), 219, 230-231

Radiant City of 1930, 241

Rasmussen, Steen Eiler, 198

Raymond, Antonin, 50

Raynaud, Léonce, 204

Red Fort (Delhi), 173, 175; photo, 188, 192

Redressement français movement, 208, 216 n.24

Regionalism in Le Corbusier's work, vii=viii, 28-29

Reliance Building (Chicago), 223; photo, 235

Renan, Ernest, 30, 32

Rentenanstalt office building (Zurich), 21

Rietveld, Gerrit, 48, 168

Rio de Janeiro, 226-228, 242; Ministry of Health building, 111-113; monumentalism in, 25; sketches by Le Corbusier, 238

Rockefeller Center (New York), 229

Roman Catholic Church, Le Corbusier and, 3

Roman law, influence on Le Corbusier, 174-175

Ronchamp, chapel at, viii=ix, 3, 7, 16, 127-135; aesthetics of, 53-54; architectural theory and, 25; crab shell imagery, 127-128, 131; dam as device in, 131, 139; early plan, 137; eastern elevation and tower calotte, 137; Le Corbusier's creative process described, 127-135; lighting serapeum, 138; Mediterranean tradition and, 24; M'zab valley (Algiers) as influence, 132-135; roof sketches, 138; southeastern elevation and plan, 139; southwestern elevation and plan, 138

Ronéo file cabinet system, 178-179, 196

Roof gardens, Le Corbusier's fondness for, 181 n.41

Roq et Rob structural scheme, 55

Rotanda Villa (Palladio), 85

Rousseau, Jean-Jacques, 32, 209

Roux-Spitz, Michel, 110

Rowe, Colin, 36, 61

Ruskin, John, ix, 29-30, 207

Russian Constructivists, 182 n.53

Saarinen, Eero, 68

Sabarmati Power Plant (Ahmedabad), 176-177

Sachlich architecture, 2, 20; Le Corbusier rejects, 23

St. Dié (France): Duval factory in, 11; town center, 5-6; plan for, 241

Saint-Exupéry, Antione de, 203, 228

Saint-Gaudens redevelopment plan (France), 241

Saint Ignatius Church (Paris), 1

St. Petersburg Embassy (Behrens), 58

"Saint-Simonian" colonies, 205, 208

Salon d'Automne, 221

Salt March (Gandhi), 163

Salvation Army Hostel. *See* Cité de Refuge

Sanctuaires d'orient (Schuré), 30

Sant'Elia, 109, 201, 222

Sapin image in architecture, viii, 29-30

Sarabhai, Gautham, 16, 165-166

Sarabhai, Manorama, 171-172

Sarabhai house, 164-166, 171-173, 197; photo, 188

Sauvage, Henri, 109

Savina, Joseph, 211

Savoye, Villa, 50-51, 83-94; color indications, 105; cost overruns, 87-89, 92-93, 95 n. 39; painting scheme, 92; *pan de verre*, 90-91; plan, 97; revisions to design, 88-91, 95 nn.; roof, 111; sketches, 97-99; spiral staircase and ramp, 104; technical failins, 93-94; urbanism in, 207; views of, 103; window sketches, 98

Schmidt, Hans, 229

Schuré, Edouard, 30-31, 207

Schwob, Anatole, 36.

Schwob, Villa, 36; double-storied space in, 109, 171; impact on Shodhan house, 168; sketch, 44-45

Second Mode format, 111-112, 114

Siedlungen block, 110

Sekler, Mary Patricia May, 207

Serenyi, Peter, 113-114

Sert, José Luis, 229

Services, communalization of, 8, 108-110, 114, 121

Servin (French city planner), 221-222

Seven Vs concept, 241-243; Chandigarh, 212

Shapiro, Meyer, 20

Shodhan house, 164, 167-171 *brise-soleil*, 169-170; double-storied space, 171; photos, 184-185, 187; triple-storied terrace, 171

Singh, Maharahah Jai, 164

Sitte, Camillo, 33, 110, 219-220, 222

Slutzky, Robert, 61

Société des Mines de Carmaux, 176, 193

Société des Nations. *See* League of Nations

Society of Civil Engineers (Soviet Union), 61

Soria y Mata, Arturo, 108, 227

Soviet Union, Le Corbusier in, 229. *See also* specific buildings

Speer, Albert, 58

Der Städtebau (Sitte), 33, 204

Stagiaires, 13

Stalin, Josef, 3

Stam, Mart, 229

Steffens, Lincoln, 200-201

Stein-Monzie Villa, at Garches, 50, 60, 89, 171; plan, 97

Steles (Jewish funeral) motif, 133

Stemolak, Karl, 31

Stil magazine, 225

Stockholm, Le Corbusier's plans for, 211, 228

Stone, Edward, 197

Stotzer house, 31-32; sketch, 40

Stübben (author), 204

Style roman (Corroyer), 32

Sullivan, Louis, 36, 223

Summerson, John (Sir), 115

Sun-breakers. *See* Brise-soleils

Surrealism, 115, 203, 208

Swiss Pavilion. *See* Pavillon Suisse

Syndicalism, 23

Tacoma Building (Chicago), 223

Taine, H., 30

Tata, Bhabha, 164

Taut, Bruno, 229

Taut, Max, 61

Taylor, Brian Brace, 205

Technology, architecture and, 17-20; urbanism and, 207-208, 210, 220-222

Teige, Karel, 23

Temporal, Marcel, 221

Tengbom, Ivar, 57

Terner (Zurich engineer), 59

Le Territoire de l'architecture, (Gregotti), 134

Tessenow, Heinrich, 219

Textes et dessins pour Ronchamp (Le Corbusier), 128

Teyssot, Georges, 205-206

Thapar, P. N., 163

Théâtre des Champs Elysees (Perret), 58

Thiersch, August, 34

Third Mode formation, 112-113

Ton-Kalk-Cement exhibition, 33

Towards a New Architecture (Vers une architecture)

(Le Corbusier), 123, 164; architectural theory in, 19

Tractorstoy, 229

Trois Etablissements humains, 117, 122-123, 207

Trotsky, Leon, 3

Turner, Paul V., 30

Une Maison—un palais (Le Corbusier) 60, 85-86, 167

Unité de grandeur conforme, 7, 121

Unité d'habitation (Marseille), 69, 109, 117-125; architectural concepts in, 113-114; background, 117; beauty and poetry, 123; biology, 122; collective organization, 120-121; conflicts with government, 118-119; development of, 24-25; downtown areas, 122; dwelling extensions, 121; family protection, 120; guiding principles (idees forces), 8, 119-123; human establishments, 122-123; individual life concept, 119-120; influence on La Tourette, 144; integration, 121-122; Le Corbusier's work habits, 117-119; modern assessment, 241; monastic tradition, 114; natural conditions, 122; pedestrians and automobiles, 122; services space, 8; team members listed, 125 n.1; teamwork problems, 118; unit size, 7; urbanism of, 212

United Nations building, 11-12, 112

Unités d'habitations other than Marseille, 114

Unwin, Raymond (Sir), 204, 206, 219

Urbanism of Le Corbusier, 23-24, 33, 35, 47-55, 115-116, 203-214; African influences of, 225-226; American influences, 223-224; automobile and airplane, 227-228; Cartesian skyscraper, 228-229; "La Construction des Villes," 33, 35, 219-220; *L'Esprit Nouveau*, 220; housing *à rédents*, 224; Michelin episode, 222-224; modern assessment, 241-249; New York influence, 229-231; origins, 219; Plan Voisin, 221-222; *rue à rédents*, 107-108, 114; social and economic aspects, 224-225; South American influences on, 225-226; Soviet influence on, 229; technology and cultural ready-mades, 220-222

Urbanisme (Le Corbusier), 33, 36, 178, 219-220; modern assessment of, 241; Paris reconstruction proposed, 221-222

van Doesburg, Theo, 48-170; sketches, 185
Vandervelde, Émile, 204
Varma, P. L., 163
Vaucresson, house at, 27, 49
Velikovsky, B. M., 61
Vesnin, Alexander, 61
Vesnin brothers, 229
Vie de Jésus (Renan), 30, 32
Vienna: Le Corbusier's travels in, 31-32; Social-
    Democratic housing, 53
Villa Adriana at Tivoli, viii, 129, 131
Villa Aldobrandini (della Porta), 36
Ville contemporaine, 221-225
La Ville Radieuse (Le Corbusier), 219, 229, 244;
    illustrations, 237; *unité d'habitation* and,
    117, 120, 122-125
Ville Radieuse concept, 59, 206-209, 212, 214,
    241
Viollet-le-Duc, Eugène-Emmanuel, viii, 32
Vionov, V. M., 61
Vitruvian man, 85
La Voie royale (Malraux), 51
Voisin motors, 222
Voisin Plan. *See* Plan Voisin
von Moos, Stanislaus, 210
VOPRA (Soviet political group), 65
Voroshilov (Marshall), 65
Voyage d'Orient (Le Corbusier), 34, 210
Voyage en Italie (Taine), 30

Werkbund Congress, 33, 220
Werkbund Exhibition (1914), 58
White, John, 55
Winter, Pierre, 208
Wogenscky, André, 10-12, 14-15, 143
Wright, Frank Lloyd, vii-viii, 36, 51, 163

Xenakis, Iannis, 11

Zholtovsky, Ivan, 65
Zola, Emile, 204
Züblin (French architect), 176